Covenant House

Covenant House

Journey of a Faith-Based Charity

Peter J. Wosh

PENN

University of Pennsylvania Press
Philadelphia

10 9 8 7 6 5 4 3 2 1

Published by
University of Pennsylvania Press
Philadelphia, Pennsylvania 19104–4011

Library of Congress Cataloging-in-Publication Data

Wosh, Peter J.
    Covenant House : journey of a faith-based charity / Peter J. Wosh.
        p. cm.
    Includes bibliographical references and index.
    ISBN 0-8122-3831-1 (cloth alk. paper)
    1. Covenant House (New York, N.Y.) 2. Ritter, Bruce, 1927– 3. Abandoned children—Services
for—New York (State)—New York—History. 4. Runaway children—Services for—New York
(State)—New York—History. 5. Social work with youth—New York (State)—New York—
History. 6. Church work with youth—New York (State)—New York—History. 7. Church
charities—New York (State)—New York—History. I. Title.

HV885.N49N49 2005
362.74′575′097471—dc22
                                                                                    2004052012

The epigraphs at the beginning of chapters 1, 2, and 3 are from Covenant House by
Bruce Ritter, copyright © 1987 by Bruce Ritter. Used by permission of Doubleday, a division of
Random House, Inc.

Contents

Introduction

The Rev. Bruce Ritter generated little attention in 1968 when he decided to resign a tenured professorship at Manhattan College and move into a dilapidated tenement apartment in New York City's East Village in order to begin a new ministry. A few Franciscan colleagues, some devoted former students, and an assortment of old friends and neighborhood residents joined with him in an idealistic and loosely structured crusade to serve the poor. By the late 1970s, however, "Father Bruce" had achieved considerable fame within the New York metropolitan area. Newspapers and television networks carried adulatory stories concerning this remarkably energetic friar who now lived near Times Square and seemed to be single-handedly confronting smut peddlers, pornography purveyors, and corrupt politicians. Ritter, according to glowing media reports, had personally taken on the task of rescuing lost, abandoned, homeless, and hopeless teenagers in the great metropolis. He had incorporated an organization known as Covenant House to carry on his good works, with a large crisis shelter located near the Port Authority Bus Terminal and a series of group homes scattered throughout the Greenwich Village area. Volunteers flocked to the ministry, inspired by Ritter's sermons, lectures, and monthly newsletters. He preached a gospel of unconditional love, equality before God, and selfless service. The Franciscan spoke with moral clarity, certitude, and passion about the problems of homeless children, and he attracted a large and influential audience.

Growth occurred at a dizzying pace over the course of the 1980s. By the end of that decade, Covenant House's annual budget stood at nearly $90 million. The organization operated twelve programs for homeless youths throughout Canada, the United States, and Latin America. Its expenditures exceeded federal appropriations for runaway children, with over 90 percent of its contributions emanating from private sources. Wealthy Catholic philanthropists allied themselves with the agency, major corporations contributed money and in-kind services, and the organization's direct mail program became a model for nonprofits everywhere. A professional staff coalesced, more sophisticated programs expanded the agency's offerings beyond mere crisis care, and the ministry appeared to be an unqualified success story. Covenant House embodied the pragmatic entrepreneurship, private initiative, and voluntary spirit that politicians praised during the 1980s as the federal government retreated from supporting social programs in the inner cities. Ritter was at the center of it all. He remained the charismatic leader of the organization, attracted universal praise, and personified Covenant House for its supporters and advocates. The Franciscan seemed completely focused on, and perhaps even obsessed with, his mission. His calls to shelter the needy, feed the hungry, and provide troubled teens with a second chance struck a responsive chord and appeared beyond reproach. Ritter had carried his religious commitments out of the pulpit and onto the streets in the best tradition of Catholic social reformers. People supported his efforts with enthusiasm. But matters soon took a surprising turn.

The ministry suddenly appeared on the verge of collapse in 1990. A young male prostitute who resided at Covenant House charged that Bruce Ritter had provided him with money and support in exchange for sexual favors. Additional accusations surfaced. Investigative reporters turned their attention to the agency, leveling charges of sexual abuse, financial improprieties, and official misconduct against the founder. The sensational revelations dominated New York City tabloids and local news broadcasts. Within a few short months, Ritter resigned and Covenant House struggled to survive. Contributions declined by $22 million in one year, the debt skyrocketed, and public confidence dissipated. Now journalists charged that the organization embodied the worst personal and financial excesses that they associated with the 1980s. The fact that Covenant House's troubles occurred on the heels of a series of other religious scandals involving sex and greed further damaged the agency and permanently disillusioned many supporters. Neutral observers questioned whether the organization had lost its moral compass. Covenant House did manage to overcome the scandal, though the process proved to be a long and painful one. The board of directors thoroughly reformed its own operations during the 1990s and also selected Sr. Mary Rose McGeady, D.C., as the new president to replace Ritter. She played a major role in restoring institutional credibility, rebuilding the donor base, and eventually moving the organization in new directions. The agency recovered financially and programmatically from the crisis, though the scars remained visible for some time.

As this thumbnail historical sketch suggests, Covenant House has traveled an extraordinary institutional distance in a relatively short period of time. Its mission, successes, travails, and high public profile make the ministry a worthwhile object for closer scrutiny. Scholars will also find other compelling reasons to examine the history of this nonprofit philanthropy. Faith-based institutions have received considerable attention in recent years. In 2001, for example, George W. Bush created a White House Office for Faith-based and Community Initiatives as part of his effort to increase federal assistance to religious ministries that deliver basic social services. His announcement immediately produced a firestorm of criticism from civil libertarians and generated considerable debate within religious circles.[1] The entire discussion, however, largely lacked historical perspective. Few scholars have studied the origins, development, and growth of specific faith-based social ministries in adequate detail. These nonprofit entities have long exerted a major influence over the course of American history, but their internal operations remain obscure and mysterious to many academics.[2] Their distinctive histories, diverse missions, varied governance structures, administrative peculiarities, and complex relationships with other organizations make broad generalizations difficult. Some question whether they even compose a coherent institutional sector. By examining individual ministries in greater detail, scholars and policymakers may begin to discover whether these organizations really possess common characteristics. Covenant House offers an instructive start.[3] Several themes that profoundly inform the organization's history offer useful points of comparison with other faith-based social ministries.

First, an ongoing tension between charismatic authority and bureaucratic institutionalization remains at the heart of the Covenant House story.[4] Ritter established the enterprise as a highly personalized endeavor. He founded the organization, shaped its mission during the early years, and recruited a loyal band of personal friends and close associates to support his efforts. Ritter left no doubt that divine inspiration guided him and formed the basis of his authority. A complete disdain for institutional forms and bureaucratic routine characterized his rhetoric, and he relentlessly promoted the voluntary aspects of the ministry at every opportunity. The founder emphasized his nearly mystical bond with "the kids" who sought shelter at Covenant House. At various times, he even considered establishing a lay religious community of faithful disciples in order to carry on his work. The Franciscan's followers and supporters appeared dazzled by his personal charisma and spellbinding oratory. Ritter inspired unquestioned loyalty from many subordinates, who imbued even his routine programmatic pronouncements with nearly sacred significance.

But charisma constitutes only part of the Covenant House story. Ritter also functioned as a master institutionalizer. He carefully built a formidable bureaucracy, promulgated a variety of tightly structured rules and regulations for staff, and hired a talented cadre of professionals to administer his agency. Ritter legally incorporated his ministry, established a hierarchical managerial structure complete with flow charts and chains-of-command, and legitimized his group homes and shelters by obtaining licensing with appropriate state agencies. He successfully translated his initial prophetic vision into concrete institutional form, ultimately ensuring that the organization would survive his own departure from the scene. Covenant House in many ways functioned as a routine and stable operation under the founder's direction, with a clearly defined program and a highly structured approach to serving homeless children. Ritter understood the contradictions and often struggled with the implications. Charismatic enthusiasm and institutional routine may coexist effectively within the same organization. They can also serve as divisive oppositional forces, creating confusion and harvesting bitterness among various institutional constituencies. Faith-based organizations typically owe their energy to zealous commitment and a transcendent sense of mission. They face particular problems integrating standard rules and regulations into their operations. Covenant House experienced difficulty reconciling charisma and institutionalization throughout its history, forever attempting to achieve the appropriate balance.

Second, Covenant House struggled with its prophetic and culturally accommodationist qualities.[5] The ministry initially seemed to assume an oppositional and countercultural stance toward secular society. Ritter and his small band of followers chose to live with the poor in a troubled and dangerous New York City neighborhood. They rejected all outward trappings of the seductively alluring consumer capitalist culture that many middle-class Americans found irresistible during the late 1960s. Covenant House's founders mutually pledged to confront oppressive structures, work to end poverty, and expose the blatant inequalities that characterized late twentieth-century American society. Ritter himself aggressively criticized politicians, child care institutions, and governmental bureaucracies for their structural failure to address the problems of homeless youths. Covenant House claimed to operate on radical principles that differentiated its programs from those of conventional child care agencies. During its formative years, the ministry kept both church and state at arm's length. The founder chose not to formally affiliate with Catholic Charities and occasionally pursued policies that placed him at odds with archdiocesan authorities as well as municipal officials. Ritter also operated on the fringes of the social work profession, maintaining an outsider stance and forgoing cooperative ventures with other similarly situated agencies. He seemed determined to preserve the purity and uniqueness of his ministry. Covenant House even maintained a financial independence from both public funding agencies and official Roman Catholic sources by relying heavily on private individual donations. The organization vigilantly guarded its freedom to assume a profoundly critical perspective toward other established institutions.

Countertendencies soon developed. Covenant House's broadly prophetic purposes appeared more difficult to maintain as the organization grew in stature during the 1970s. Ritter became increasingly tied to influential supporters who found his ministry appealing precisely because of its privatistic orientation. Catholic philanthropists, powerful corporate entities, and conservative politicians found it convenient to affiliate with the agency during the early 1980s. They celebrated Covenant House's socially ameliorative qualities and lauded its entrepreneurial spirit. Ritter, who deeply believed in his own program and who knew that a need existed to expand the number of shelters and group homes, gladly accepted their support in the interest of serving "my kids." Such alliances, however, necessarily muted the organization's prophetic voice. Covenant House continued to witness for the oppressed, but by the 1980s it targeted villains who most often appeared to be marginal figures and social outcasts in their own right: child pornographers, peep show proprietors, and pimps. It became increasingly problematic to constructively challenge more respectable political and corporate interests when those very forces composed the financial backbone of the ministry. Covenant House's history thus reflects the difficulties facing all religious institutions that seek to speak with an authoritative moral voice yet also hope to operate effectively within larger secular cultures. Compromises and internal conflicts result as ministries make uncomfortable choices, weighing the benefits of overtly confrontational tactics against the need for practical political alliances.

The struggles of faith-based organizations to define appropriate relationships with secular cultures hints at a third theme that runs throughout Covenant House's history: the interdependence of social sectors. Nonprofit religious organizations do not exist as isolated entities. Their governing boards, administrative practices, financial supporters, and staff overlap with, and remain inextricably linked to, public and corporate institutions. Rhetoric sometimes obscures this fundamental reality. Ritter, for example, always trumpeted his independence from state control and aggressively sought out private sources of funding in order to free his agency from public regulation. Yet the ministry owed its early existence primarily to public/private partnerships. Ritter depended on municipal and state grants to support his programs. Public funding provided him with the legitimacy and stability necessary to approach private donors. State regulations also forced the founder to upgrade his group home operations, thereby providing children with a cleaner and safer environment. Ritter relied on municipal judges, public social welfare administrators, and city policemen, all of whom referred children to his agency and publicized his efforts among other potential supporters. Covenant House even secured its substantial shelter at Tenth Avenue and Forty-first Street in 1979 from the State of New York for a nominal rental sum, owing to the goodwill and support of friendly elected officials. The agency thus never existed as a purely private entity despite the founder's rhetoric. It actually enjoyed a long and often mutually beneficial relationship with the public sector.

Corporate connections proved equally critical for Covenant House. Chase Manhattan Bank, Young & Rubicam, Ziff-Davis, and IBM were just a few of the major corporations that provided the agency with board members, direct monetary support, and consultative advice over the years. Cravath, Swaine & Moore offered pro bono services that helped the organization survive its crisis in 1990, and this leading New York City law firm has represented the agency ever since. Private foundations, financial institutions, direct mail experts, telecommunications agencies, investment bankers, and high technology firms all contributed professional assistance at various historical moments. Covenant House's administrators developed their internal policies and procedures by borrowing from comparable corporate practices. Board members invariably drew upon their experiences in the private sector when advising the philanthropy. Nonprofit entities exist within a complex institutional universe. It remains essential to dissect the personal and professional links between organizations in order to better understand their internal operations and unique administrative styles.

Interinstitutional connections often point historians in unanticipated and surprising directions as seemingly peripheral issues assume center stage. It becomes impossible to understand the founding of Covenant House, for example, without engaging such topics as working-class life in an industrial New Jersey city during the Great Depression, 1960s student culture at a traditional Catholic college in the Bronx, changing theological stances and social commitments within religious orders in the wake of Vatican II, and the tumultuous character of an ethnically divided and socially troubled New York City neighborhood. Covenant House further owed its creation to increased middle-class anxieties over a new breed of runaway teenagers who seemed to be flocking to hippie enclaves in metropolitan areas. Grisly murders, personal quirks, and chance encounters also played important roles. All of these apparently random and disconnected developments coalesced in the late 1960s and early 1970s in order to give birth to Covenant House. Historical coherence only materializes after carefully stringing together these disparate strands of the story.

Covenant House thus appears more comprehensible when viewed against the backdrop of these larger issues involving bureaucratic and charismatic authority, prophetic criticism and cultural accommodation, and the connections that bind seemingly independent and unrelated institutional sectors. The agency's history, however, also touches on some additional themes that deserve consideration. Social attitudes toward youth homelessness underwent a significant transformation as Covenant House matured. During the late 1960s, mainstream media outlets and youth advocates first focused attention on runaways as a serious and widespread social problem. They often depicted homeless teenagers as white children who hailed from comfortable middle-class families in privileged suburban environments. These youths supposedly sought thrills and meaning in America's thriving countercultural venues, forsaking family and friends in order to pursue a more dangerous and inherently unstable existence. This stereotype took hold even as social workers discovered a far different reality. Covenant House's founders recognized that homeless youths in New York City principally constituted abused and neglected children, who typically had been shuffled through a variety of child care institutions. They described these overwhelmingly African American and Hispanic youngsters more accurately as urban nomads, or "throwaway kids." Most had grown up in poverty and lived outside of stable familial and social networks.

As Ritter gained fame and achieved expert status for his work with troubled teenagers, however, he contributed to the creation of a new social stereotype. Covenant House's size and stature ensured that the organization could affect broader cultural debates concerning youth homelessness during the 1980s. Ritter chose to channel his political influence in a peculiar direction. He increasingly identified juvenile prostitution, child pornography, and sexual promiscuity as the critical problems facing transient youths. The founder helped to initiate a national discussion concerning these issues, but his narrow focus on the sex industry obscured other urban problems. Familial breakdown, parental abuse, neighborhood deterioration, substance addiction, joblessness, poverty, and federal welfare policies largely disappeared from the institutional rhetoric even as they reflected the overwhelming daily realities faced by most homeless teenagers. Only in the 1990s, when new leadership emerged within Covenant House, did a more complex consideration of the factors that contributed to youth homelessness once again characterize the institution's advocacy efforts.

Covenant House's history also sheds light on the powerful role of mass media in defining public discourse. Bruce Ritter emerged as an American religious celebrity during the late 1970s owing largely to his communications skills and his ability to craft an appealing public image. His plainspoken, forthright, and direct prose captivated reporters and listeners. He knew how to explain complex issues in easily understandable language. His appeal letters conveyed a reassuring warmth and intimacy that attracted personal and emotional responses. Ritter cultivated contacts among the press corps, and he always appeared ready with the perfect quip for every occasion. He understood the significance of symbolism, and his dual identities as a pious friar and a streetwise New Yorker served him nicely. Journalists found that his story played well with diverse audiences. They never dug too deeply beneath the surface, and their laudatory articles initially reinforced the founder's reputation. These positive press relations did not last forever, however, and Ritter eventually learned a hard lesson concerning the precarious nature of fame.

Sensationalist news stories, salacious headlines, lurid reports, and prurient exposés had become institutionalized practice within many media outlets by the time Covenant House confronted its crisis in 1990. Ritter's high profile and righteous rhetoric made him the perfect target for derision and ridicule as scandalous allegations surfaced. Illicit sex, hidden trust funds, secret identities, and priestly intrigue offered irresistible fodder for the tabloids. The scandal seemed ideally suited for memorable headlines and snappy double entendres: "Broken Covenant," "Sins of the Father," "Fall from Grace." Tainted heroes made excellent copy, and the story appeared a perfect morality play. Ritter initially had embraced media coverage as an effective means of building a broader audience for his ministry. He discovered during the scandal that his message now reached supporters primarily through media filters. It became impossible for him to regain control of the story. Covenant House had creatively used press coverage in order to gain its initial credibility, unsuccessfully attempted to combat negative publicity during the scandal, and struggled to rebuild its image during the 1990s. Mass media outlets now played an extraordinarily powerful role in either conferring legitimacy or destroying institutional credibility.

Covenant House's development additionally coincided with profound transformations that altered American Catholicism over the last half of the twentieth century. The agency's founding clearly reflected the experimental social ministries, innovative spirit, and strong lay involvement that characterized post–Vatican II reforms within the Church. Covenant House remained Catholic in orientation throughout its corporate history, though it never officially existed under the formal aegis of any archdiocesan agency or religious community. This independent status provided the ministry with some flexibility in defining its connection to the institutional church. Generally, however, the ties grew closer over time. The agency relied heavily on Catholic donors, needed to maintain good relationships with archdiocesan officials and social service providers, and carefully developed its policies toward clients in accord with official Church teachings. This alienated some early supporters who viewed the ministry as a countercultural force, but it attracted wealthy and influential backers who felt comfortable within a more conservative Catholic context. At times, Covenant House found itself enmeshed in uncomfortable and touchy public controversies as a result of its political proximity to ecclesiastical officials. In other instances, notably during the crisis in 1990, archdiocesan intervention proved instrumental in saving the ministry from possible ruin.

Covenant House's history most obviously intersected with American Catholic history as a result of the events of 1990. The accusations against Ritter opened a second wave in the ongoing series of clergy sexual abuse scandals that first surfaced in Lafayette, Louisiana, during the mid-1980s and continued into the twenty-first century.[6] The Covenant House scandal contained some similarities with events elsewhere. Press reports revealed the problem. Disbelief and defensiveness initially greeted the accusations. Inadequate internal mechanisms existed for investigating the charges. An unhealthy subculture of secrecy and deference within the organization required reform. Various outside observers attributed broader political and social significance to the controversy in accordance with their own political stances toward the ministry. The accusations shattered public confidence in the institution, and it took considerable time and effort to restore credibility.

But the differences between this scandal and the sexual abuse charges leveled against other Roman Catholic clergymen appear even more compelling. Covenant House's troubles occurred within the context of one specific organization rather than over a broader institutional network. They were largely confined to one individual. The entire duration lasted less than three months from the appearance of the initial newspaper stories through the resignation of the founder. Key individuals came to understand fairly quickly that saving the ministry itself proved more important than protecting the reputation of any particular person. Immediate and substantive reforms ensued. In the long run, the Ritter scandal exerted a significant impact on American Catholicism. The incredible accusations and the abrupt resignation of the founder convinced many lay observers that a broader problem existed within church circles. Ritter was a powerful, respected, and very visible churchman whose reputation and work inspired accolades and who operated on the national stage.[7] Subsequent scandals involving less prominent individuals now seemed more believable and less shocking. The events of 1990 deeply disillusioned many faithful Catholics. Neither Covenant House nor American Catholicism ever appeared quite the same again.

Finally, a few words concerning institutional history seem appropriate. Two other studies of Covenant House exist. Ritter himself penned the first history of the organization in 1987.[8] *Covenant House: Lifeline to the Street* consists of appeal letters that the founder had written to donors between 1972 and 1987 interspersed with some chatty reminiscences concerning the origin and development of the ministry. Ritter fully understood the power of the past. He used his book to construct an authoritative account of the agency's founding, early struggles, and subsequent triumphs. In the process, he enshrined his own personal stories and anecdotes as official history. The founder's interpretation appeared beyond challenge at the time, but within a few short years another voice entered the conversation. Charles M. Sennott, the *New York Post* reporter who first broke the Covenant House scandal story in 1990, wrote *Broken Covenant* in 1992 in order to chronicle his own investigative exploits.[9] The book jacket's synopsis accurately conveys the overriding tone: "*Broken Covenant* is a searing portrait of power at work in Reagan/Bush-era America, in the Catholic Church, and in the sophisticated, ruthless world of big-time philanthropy. It rips away the veil of sanctity shrouding this religious charity to reveal an unholy truth of excess, corruption, and cover-up." Sennott's contribution contains some rich detail and invaluable firsthand interviews, but its relentlessly condemnatory stance undermines its analytical strengths.

Covenant House: Journey of a Faith-Based Charity seeks to serve a different purpose from either of its predecessors. The agency commissioned this book in 1997, in conjunction with the twenty-fifth anniversary of its incorporation. The organization hoped that the project might produce a constructively critical administrative history of the agency based on solid scholarship, extant archival documentation, and oral history interviews. Covenant House has enjoyed a remarkably rich, often dramatic, and occasionally controversial past. This book seeks to place that past in a larger perspective. It especially emphasizes the broader social context that influenced and intersected with specific institutional events. Leadership styles, internal power dynamics, programmatic decisions, fund-raising strategies, and public relations ventures receive considerable attention. Historians necessarily make thematic selections, and this study unfortunately slights several important and interesting topics. Some Covenant House sites and programs receive only brief mention or cursory treatment. Social workers and counselors appear less visible than major administrators and board members. No systematic attempt has been made to recover the perspectives of individual children and clients. These topics all offer extremely worthwhile objects for further investigation, but this history simply has a different focus.

The book itself proceeds in a relatively straightforward chronological fashion. Two narrative elements, however, require some explanation. First, Covenant House as an institution does not actually enter the story until Chapter 3. Earlier chapters consider the prehistory of the agency in detail primarily by examining the life and career of Bruce Ritter. The founder exerted a tremendous influence over Covenant House. His personal background and extensive social networks proved critical in determining the founding and direction of the organization. Biography and institutional history thoroughly complement each other in this instance. Ritter, however, did not operate alone. Other individuals also played an important role in shaping the ministry, though many eventually dropped out of the story. These early chapters seek to recover their stories and recognize their contributions as well. In any case, Covenant House's establishment in 1972 makes little sense without thoroughly considering a range of factors that predated the agency's formal incorporation.

Second, each chapter begins with a substantial excerpt from a primary source. Early chapters reproduce some of the founder's favorite and most frequently repeated stories. Ritter carefully defined the official history of Covenant House during its formative years through his sermons and newsletters. Donors, volunteers, employees, supporters, and colleagues received their impressions of the ministry by listening to his stories and reflections. Ritter's voice dominated the discourse, and it seems appropriate to present his thoughts and analyze his words in considerable detail. By the late 1970s, however, the dynamics had changed. Journalists, politicians, philanthropists, board members, and major administrators now significantly influenced Covenant House, and their opinions carried considerable weight. Accordingly, introductions to the latter chapters contain more diffuse commentary from a broader range of individuals. No single authoritative voice could any longer set the tone for such a diverse and multifaceted agency. In the beginning, however, things functioned quite differently. Covenant House's complex history actually started with a deceptively simple story.

Chapter 1

Creation

"How long will it be before you guys sell out? To money, power,
ambition. . . ? Will you sell out by the time you're twenty-five?"
I finished my sermon on that note and turned back to the altar to
continue the celebration of Mass. I was proud that almost four
hundred students had come to church that brilliant Saturday
afternoon in October 1966. It was a good sermon. I liked that sermon.
I had worked hard on it. It was all about zeal and commitment and
how the students at Manhattan College in New York City should be
more involved in the life and work of the Church. One of the
students, Hughie O'Neill, stood up in church and said, "Wait a
minute, Bruce." He happened to be the president of the student body
and captain of the track team. "Bruce," he said, "you're making two
mistakes. The first mistake you're making is that we are not going to
sell out by the time we're twenty-five; we'll undoubtedly do so by the
time we're twenty-one. Your second mistake, and your bigger one, is
that you're standing up there telling us this and not leading us by
your example and life-style not to. We all think you're a pretty good
teacher, Bruce, but we don't like your sermons. We think you should
practice what you preach." That's a pretty heavy shot to take from
your students on a Saturday afternoon. (There was a general murmur
of agreement from the other kids in church.) I thought about it a lot
over the next few days and realized, of course, that Hughie O'Neill
was correct. The next Sunday, at all the Masses on campus, I
apologized to the student body—for not edifying them—and asked
my superiors and the archbishop for a new assignment: to live and
work among the poor on the Lower East Side of Manhattan.

—*Rev. Bruce Ritter*[1]

Bruce Ritter always understood the power of a good story. From
the beginning, Covenant House's charismatic founder explained his ministry through a series of meticulously crafted and often repeated parables
that emotionally engaged audiences and masterfully articulated his own
religious vision. He began telling this particular tale in the early 1970s,
and it soon became standard fare in his weekend sermons, fund-raising
speeches, staff training videos, and published material. Hugh O'Neill, the
feisty student who emerged as the story's principal protagonist, also recalled
the incident years later, although it possessed less personal significance and

Figure 1. Manhattan College campus, looking out from the administration building, across the quadrangle, toward the De La Salle Chapel. Catholic culture and student life during the late 1960s at this all-male institution in the Riverdale section of the Bronx played a critical role in the founding and early years of Covenant House. Photograph courtesy of the Manhattan College Archives.

dramatic breadth in the young man's remembrance. Within the context of his popular Saturday afternoon dialogue Masses at Manhattan College's student center, Ritter frequently invited commentary on his homilies. Students willingly obliged. O'Neill subsequently regretted the remark, believing that his personal jab probably delivered "more of a zinger" than Ritter typically received or deserved. The incident itself provoked little immediate reaction. O'Neill dutifully attended Mass the following week and remained close to the popular campus minister. Ritter, for his part, continued to teach theology and to direct the Christian Life Council at Manhattan College until 1968. Yet this student challenge clearly touched the thirty-nine-year-old Franciscan in some important ways. After his ministry coalesced in New York City's East Village in the early 1970s, colleagues, journalists, and patrons regularly called upon the founder to explain its origins. Ritter always hearkened back to Manhattan College in 1966 and to this particular dialogue sermon. It offers the perfect starting place for attempting to understand the broader meaning and ultimate significance of his life and works.[2]

Ritter chose to frame this key sermon around the concept of the "sell out." In one sense, this rhetorical device merely attempted to challenge baby-boom Catholic collegians through the use of a commonly understood and increasingly timely theme. By the mid-1960s, social theorists and popular pundits had grown ever more conscious of the power and potential of a newly emerging post–World War II generation. Young people, to an unprecedented degree, seemed both to shape and to reflect the tempo and turbulence of midcentury American culture. Within three months of Ritter's homily, *Time* magazine decided to bestow its Man of the Year Award for 1966 on an entire generation: "today's youth." Americans under twenty-five, this classic middlebrow barometer of mainstream culture observed, would soon outnumber their elders. Characterizing, classifying, and decoding the behavior of this puzzlingly unpredictable new generation preoccupied many journalists. Middle-aged Americans convinced themselves that they faced a "generation gap" of unprecedented proportions. *Time* could resort only to a confused and contradictory imagery in attempting to provide a coherent vision of American youth: "they are well-educated, affluent, rebellious, responsible, pragmatic, idealistic, brave, 'alienated,' and hopeful." Financially secure yet disenchanted with the limitations of American life, the predominantly white and well-bred men and women whom *Time* chose to highlight seemingly possessed the potential to alter fundamental American institutions and values. Ritter's Manhattan College sermon offered a more skeptical generational appraisal. He worried that his students might ultimately forsake their youthful "zeal and commitment" in favor of narrow familial and economic concerns. He agonized over the possibility that their social and intellectual ideals could retreat before the seductive material allure of American prosperity. He expressed concern that they would, in the common parlance of the day, "sell out."[3]

Ritter viewed the issues of money, power, ambition, and selling out through a uniquely personal lens. Born during the economic boom times of the late 1920s to an upwardly mobile second-generation family, Ritter learned early the lessons of depression, hardship, and the fleeting nature of security. His father, Louis, had grown up in the industrial city of Trenton, New Jersey. Louis's parents immigrated to the United States from the Rhineland in 1880 and became naturalized citizens in 1888, the year of Louis's birth. Like many immigrants, the Ritters found their way to the rapidly growing Chambersburg section of Trenton. Louis matured there amid a densely concentrated working-class neighborhood composed of Germans, Hungarians, Slovaks, and Poles who found work primarily in the city's booming shipyards, rubber works, and potteries. "Trenton Makes, the World Takes" became the city's unofficial slogan, proudly proclaiming its industrial heritage and prominently displayed on a bridge that connected the urban metropolis with Morrisville, Pennsylvania. Manufacturing indeed produced considerable local prosperity from 1880 through 1920. Trenton's population, fueled especially by eastern and southern European immigration, grew by 400 percent during this period. The community found itself transformed in the early twentieth century from a relatively sleepy state capitol into a complex industrial city with the attendant labor problems, structural inequalities, geographical dispersion, and strained social services common to many early twentieth-century urban enclaves.[4]

Louis Ritter briefly attended Brown University, but by 1910 he was back in New Jersey working at Trenton Potteries, one of the largest and most prestigious firms in the city. He enlisted in the United States Army during World War I and served overseas before once again returning to his hometown and resuming work as a potter. Louis's career followed a familiar second-generation trajectory. He labored alongside his older brother and other family members in the company, gradually worked his way up to the position of foreman at the plant, and remained active in ethnic organizations despite the intense anti-German feelings stimulated by World War I. He married a local girl, Julia Morrissey, in 1921, and had fathered five children by 1931. Louis Ritter also participated in another movement typical of his generation by relocating the family out of Trenton and into the burgeoning

suburb of Hamilton Township in the early 1920s. Trenton's population leveled off considerably after 1920 as the local industrial boom subsided, and
its white working-class base began building small single-family homes in
new developments that skirted the metropolis. Hamilton's population doubled to over twenty-eight thousand between 1920 and 1930, as Trentonians
sought shelter in an area somewhat removed from the gritty industrial
streets of Chambersburg. Louis chose a tract of land on Lynwood Avenue in
the fashionable Bromley section of Hamilton, which had previously housed
the Fashion Stud Farm of a prominent Wall Street broker and multimil-
lionaire. By February 1931, as young Bruce Ritter celebrated his fourth birth-
day, the family appeared to be thriving and moving into the growing ranks
of central New Jersey's solid middle-class suburbanites.[5]

Tragedy unexpectedly struck. Louis developed a brain tumor and died
at a New Jersey veteran's hospital on Mother's Day in 1931. His wife, Julia,
suddenly found herself an unemployed forty-one-year-old single mother of
five children, ranging in age from six years to nine months, during the worst
years of the Great Depression. Security and middle-class aspirations van-
ished. Julia could no longer handle the mortgage on the Lynwood Avenue
property. She sold the house and moved to a much less fashionable Wesley
Avenue address, which had been vacant for some time and where a family
of chickens had recently taken up residence. She subsisted and raised her
family on a small widow's pension, along with a series of odd jobs and
positions that involved work as a seamstress, a domestic, and an organist at
Saint Anthony's Roman Catholic Church in northeast Trenton. Her hard-
scrabble existence took an emotional toll. The Ritter children and her
neighbors in Hamilton Township remembered Julia as a tough woman, serious about life, distraught over her situation, prone to angry outbursts, and
a strict disciplinarian.[6]

Bruce Ritter rarely dwelled on his childhood and early life in his public statements, but he did remember the 1930s as a period of poverty, financial marginality, and family difficulty. His siblings shared these memories.
Bruce's youngest sister recalled that, even amid the general unemployment,
plant closings, and hunger that paralyzed Trenton's industrial workforce
during the Depression, "we realized we were poorer. It seemed like we had
nothing." The children recalled carrying home bags of rice and flour from
the welfare office, receiving hand-me-down Christmas trees from sympathetic public school teachers during the holidays, and lacking suitable clothing for most social situations. From an early age, they scrubbed floors, sold
flowers at the cemetery, babysat, and scrambled to contribute extra cash to

the family's marginal economy.[7] The children shared a sense of insecurity, embarrassment, and shame with other Americans of their generation. The world was a harsh and cruel place, bereft of possibilities. Money remained an insurmountable problem, powerlessness appeared inseparable from the human condition, and ambition seemed utterly futile in a severely limited universe. When Ritter introduced these concepts to his Manhattan College students in the October 1966 sermon, he did so from the peculiar perspective of a Depression child who knew poverty firsthand and inherently understood the nature of compromise. He took a pragmatic, hard-nosed, and unsentimental view of the relationship between youthful idealism and social reality.

Most historians agree that World War II effectively ended the Depression and marked an important watershed in twentieth-century American life. It clearly fulfilled this function for Ritter. After graduating from Hamilton High School in 1945, and working briefly as a freight car loader in a local industry, the eighteen-year-old Trentonian joined the United States Navy during the waning days of the war. He spent the next twenty months on a variety of office assignments and was stationed eventually at a base in Mississippi. For Ritter, as for many Americans, military service proved to be a broadening and enlightening experience. It removed him from the parochial and intensely matriarchal world of Wesley Avenue, provided a new exposure to people and ideas beyond the sometimes stifling confines of industrial New Jersey, and offered a form of financial stability as well. Ritter subsequently credited his naval experience with sharpening his spiritual searches. An avid reader with wide-ranging interests, he consumed both Zane Gray westerns and biographical treatises on Saint Francis of Assisi from the base library. Increasingly, and for reasons that he never fully articulated in public, Ritter turned to prayer, religious literature, and the Roman Catholic Church in his effort to make sense of his own life and chart his direction for the future. The naval veteran did return briefly to Hamilton Township and his old job on the loading dock following his discharge. In 1947, however, Ritter applied for admission to the Order of Friars Minor Conventual, popularly known as the Franciscans, and his life took a radical turn.[8]

Entry into religious life offered a popular career option and a respected outlet for the spiritual impulses that gripped many second- and third-generation Catholics who came of age in the mid-twentieth century. Seminary rolls expanded, religious orders thrived, and priestly vocations attracted a steady stream of applicants during the late 1940s and early 1950s. The historian Mark Massa has observed that the decade following World War

II proved to be "the high-water mark of American Catholic self-confidence, cultural influence, and optimism."[9] All indications pointed toward unprecedented demographic growth, denominational affluence, and institutional expansion. A brick-and-mortar building boom radically altered the Catholic landscape as suburban churches and regional high schools proliferated. Catholics even entered popular media consciousness to an unprecedented degree. Catholic-oriented movies, ranging from *Song of Bernadette* to *Going My Way* earned thirty-four Oscar nominations between 1943 and 1945, with the Hollywood priest emerging as a stock media figure. From Bing Crosby's studied portrayals of clergymen as regular guys with hearts of gold to Karl Malden's uncompromisingly tough labor priest in *On the Waterfront*, Catholicism became identified with a hip and urbane streetwise sensibility. Such influential social scientists as Will Herberg began viewing Catholicism in the 1950s as simply another assimilated tradition within the broad family of American religious pluralism. As the historian Jay Dolan has noted, Catholics "seemed to sit on top of the world" in mid-century America, with considerable evidence suggesting "that they had embraced the American way of life and still remained staunchly Catholic."[10]

The broad compatibility between American and Catholic institutions that some social scientists associate with the 1950s appeared quite new. For much of its American history, Roman Catholicism had existed as a fundamentally foreign and immigrant-based church, viewed with suspicion and distrust by native-born Protestants. Heavily concentrated in dense urban industrial enclaves throughout the Northeast and the upper Midwest, white ethnic Catholics had crafted and nurtured distinctive insular cultures built around neighborhood, church, and school. These Catholics often literally inhabited a "separate universe" from their Protestant neighbors, living out their lives within well-defined ethnic boundaries. Educational, fraternal, religious, and philanthropic organizations formed tightly structured institutional networks that coalesced around individual parishes. Neighborhood identities often became merged with particular churches. Parishioners described themselves as being "from St. Ann's" or living "in St. Bridget's," and realtors often listed available homes and apartments by parish name rather than street location. Territorial and nationality-based churches anchored urban neighborhoods, fostering a rich liturgical life that cemented religio-ethnic cohesion. Processions, street feste, advent displays, expositions of the Blessed Sacrament, and May Crowning ceremonies publicly defined Catholic turf and enhanced ethnic solidarity. Catholic schools, Catholic clubs, Catholic professional associations, Catholic sports leagues, and Catholic youth organizations proliferated throughout the nation's urban industrial core. The Church successfully created, in the words of historian John T. McGreevy, "a Catholic world in America."[11]

Ritter moved mostly on the periphery of these traditional Catholic boundaries. He attended public schools, grew up in a religiously diverse suburban development outside the confines of the ethnic ghetto, and came to his spiritual awakening as a young adult through purposeful reading and intellectual discussion. His childhood and adolescence featured little of the immersion within Catholic institutional networks that typified the immigrant church experience. Rather, Ritter's military service, movement between secular and religious institutions, and restless mobility reflected newer social tendencies that altered American Catholic subcultures during the 1940s and 1950s. World War II and its aftermath generated dramatic opportunities for many second- and third-generation white ethnic Catholics. The GI Bill stimulated a tremendous expansion in higher education, as returning Catholic veterans entered college to an unprecedented extent. Substantial numbers of Catholics benefited from the economic boom of the late 1940s, rapidly achieving middle-class status and sometimes moving into white-collar occupations. Affordable suburban housing, often guaranteed through low-cost federal loans, integrated Catholics into diverse residential communities. Interethnic marriages proved increasingly common, further blurring traditional cultural divisions within the communion. It seemed anachronistic to view Catholicism as somehow foreign and less than American by 1960. John F. Kennedy's election as president that year proved especially symbolic for many upwardly mobile coreligionists, who shared his secular spirit and drew inspiration from the "insider" status that his political success seemed to provide.[12]

Not all Catholics, however, embraced the easygoing religious sensibility that offered an effortless rapprochement between Roman Catholicism and American capitalist culture. Many intellectuals agonized over whether Catholics, in their postwar rush toward the comforts and conveniences of middle-class respectability, had sacrificed their cultural distinctiveness and spiritual commitments along the way. In many ways, this entire generation grappled with the implications evident in Bruce Ritter's 1966 Manhattan College sermon. To what extent did the promise of upward mobility encourage Catholics to sell out? Could critical cultural perspectives remain intact as these perpetual American outsiders increasingly moved into corporate boardrooms, exclusive residential enclaves, and 1600 Pennsylvania Avenue itself? American Catholic leaders first faced such issues from an institutional perspective in the late 1940s. Some, such as Francis Cardinal Spellman and Fulton J. Sheen, seemingly negotiated the compromise with little personal or professional discomfort. Others found the issues more troublesome and pursued a different course.

Ritter's 1947 decision to enter the Franciscans suggests that he possessed both a spiritual restlessness and an ambiguous perspective concerning secular society. Both themes colored his subsequent ministry. Young men entered religious life and selected specific religious communities for a broad range of individual, familial, and idiosyncratic reasons. They often received their initial exposure to particular orders through childhood experiences at church and school, where personal contacts stimulated interest in the community's broader mission. Ritter attended public school, thus remaining somewhat outside the immediate influence of any particular order. The Franciscans did maintain a strong presence in Trenton, however, and they administered Saint Anthony's Church, where his mother found employment as an organist. The Franciscan commitment to simplicity, poverty, and a structured spiritual life apparently appealed to this young man, who had been reared during the worst years of the Depression and who remained empathetic to the economic struggles and deprivations of others. Like many returning servicemen after World War II, he entered civilian life with few personal attachments, significant questions concerning his future, and heightened spiritual sensibilities. The order certainly provided both an intensely communal culture and a fair amount of ministerial flexibility. Franciscans labored in a variety of educational, health care, and overseas mission ventures. Each Franciscan maintained a commitment to living in community and observing the Rule of St. Francis, but individual ministries might occur in a diverse array of religious venues. Ritter's personal motivations remain obscure, but the implications of his decision to enter St. Francis Seminary on Staten Island were clear. The young Trentonian agreed to live his life as a "stranger and pilgrim of the world," in the tradition of St. Francis, reaffirming the virtues of poverty and simplicity in an American Catholic world grown increasingly consumerist and less certain of its own cultural boundaries.[13]

Ritter's personal journey soon pointed him toward an even more contemplative direction. Thomas Merton's *The Seven Storey Mountain*, which finished 1948 as number three on the best-seller list, deeply moved and influenced the young seminarian.[14] In 1949, Ritter decided to leave the Franciscans. He relocated to the Trappists' Monastery of Our Lady of Gethsemani in Kentucky, experimenting with monastic life at the site where Merton himself resided. This experience lasted only a few short months, after which time Ritter decided to abandon his priestly aspirations completely and instead pursue secular employment in Washington, D.C. Within one year, however, he desired to return to Staten Island once again and resume his seminary studies with the Franciscans. In one sense, his temporary flirtation with monasticism at Gethsemani illustrated the constant seeking, searching, and discontent that defined Ritter's work throughout his life. It also testified to the extraordinarily influential attraction that Thomas Merton's vision exerted over young Catholics during this period of ferment and change within Church and society.[15]

Many postwar religious intellectuals identified strongly with Merton's early immersion in secular pursuits and sensual living, his search for a deeper meaning and spiritual fulfillment, and the series of mental and personal transformations that carried him from leftist politics at Columbia University to the strict regimen of Trappist life in the Kentucky countryside. Merton offered a searing critique of modern capitalism that resonated strongly with a generation seeking to find its place in the dynamic consumer culture that began to emerge fully in the late 1940s. Greed, lust, and self-love became the timeless vices that Merton attacked throughout his book. He firmly believed that "the barren wilderness of our own abominable selfishness" had achieved unprecedented hegemony in twentieth-century Western societies. Only pagan Rome, in his view, produced "such a flowering of cheap and petty and disgusting lusts and vanities as in the world of capitalism, where there is no evil that is not fostered and encouraged for the sake of making money." Merton chronicled the ways in which businessmen artificially generated a demand for useless luxury items and lamented the frightening work pace of factories that manufactured only trivial products. He chastised Western culture for its wasteful preoccupation with meaningless leisure and particularly skewered the consumerist fantasies propagated by the motion picture industry. A profound emptiness, in his view, remained at the core of modernity. Only contemplative life, interior peace, and spiritual perfectionism offered a respite from the disquieting noise that characterized mid-twentieth-century existence. Many Catholics, confused about their new cultural relationships and nervous about the extent to which their embrace of postimmigrant possibilities comprised a "sellout," found his message simultaneously appealing and admonishing.[16]

Ritter quickly rejected the strict regimen of the Trappists, as did the vast majority of sightseers and spiritual seekers who flocked to Gethsemani following the publication of Merton's best-seller. A purely contemplative life seemed an unlikely fit for his urbane instincts, social sensibilities, and wide-ranging interests. He applied for readmission to the Franciscans but remained somewhat pessimistic concerning his chances for acceptance after his brief foray into monasticism. Religious communities viewed uncertainty and hesitation among potential recruits with considerable suspicion during this period of steady vocational growth. Indeed, Franciscan administrators expressed some concern about Ritter's commitment to religious life, but the order ultimately did accept his application for readmission in 1950. A relieved Ritter joined a good-sized class of twenty-one, sixteen of whom eventually received ordination, at the Queen of Peace novitiate in Middleburgh, New York, to begin his training. For the next several years, Ritter and his classmates progressed through the standard Franciscan educational route. One year at Middleburgh was followed by two years studying philosophy at Assumption Seminary in Chaska, Minnesota, where the young men received their Bachelor of Arts degrees. Ritter and his cohorts then returned east for another year of theology at St. Anthony's-on-Hudson in Rensselaer, New York.[17]

Classmates, instructors, and superiors within the Franciscan order quickly realized that Ritter exhibited great potential. Juniper Alwell, a fellow seminarian who first met Ritter in 1948, remembered him as enigmatic and cryptic but also as someone who "struck other students in the novitiate as older, more experienced" and widely read. His term in the military, participation in secular cultures, and willingness to experiment with religious life outside of the Franciscan context made him "seem much more worldly-wise to the other students." Fellow seminarians marveled at his nimble wit, quick intelligence, superior writing ability, capacity for digesting complex philosophical and theological treatises, and skill at reading people. Ritter threw himself into the life of the community, editing the school newspaper and emerging as a student leader. In 1954, the Provincial selected Ritter and several other students to go to Rome and enroll in the Conventual Seminary's five-year doctoral program. This honor placed the young man firmly on a teaching and scholarly track within the order, as the leadership clearly hoped that these students would return from Rome and carry out their ministries within Franciscan educational institutions.[18]

Ritter adhered to his usual pattern by confounding his superiors' expectations. He was ordained in 1956 and completed his thesis on "The Primacy and the Council of Florence" in 1959 but never revised or published it in an academic journal in accordance with seminary regulations. Ritter's failure to publish the thesis meant that he never officially received his doctorate from the institution. He maintained only a tenuous connection with academia and formal scholarship thereafter, similar to many of his American classmates in Rome. For the next three years, Ritter taught at a variety of Franciscan institutions: St. Hyacinth's in Granby, Massachusetts; Canevin High School in Pittsburgh; and St. Anthony's Seminary in Rensselaer. He always appeared somewhat restless and impatient with formal structures within the order, forever attempting to locate his own unique intellectual and social niche. In many ways, Ritter's life history during the late 1950s and early 1960s seemed a prolonged period of searching, seeking, and remaining betwixt and between various institutional cultures. He had alternated between secular and religious employments, left the Franciscans to pursue monastic life in Kentucky, studied in Rome but eschewed taking the final step that would have earned him a formal doctorate, and drifted between various educational institutions within the order.

In some respects, his journey reflected and typified the generational anxieties that confronted many young seminarians during the late 1950s. Consider, for example, the case of James Fitzgibbon (born 1931), a fellow Trentonian, classmate, and colleague who subsequently began the Covenant House ministry with Ritter. Fitzgibbon flirted with a career in missiology, attended the seminary in Rome with some reluctance, and eventually found life as a parish priest unfulfilling. Other options within the order also failed to satisfy him. Fitzgibbon considered himself poorly prepared to teach theology in a rapidly changing educational environment, felt frustrated as a teacher and administrator in upstate New York, attempted to find more socially rewarding ministerial outlets, and eventually left the priesthood to marry. Juniper Alwell, another fellow seminarian who accompanied Ritter to Rome, exhibited some similar tendencies but also illustrated other career possibilities. Alwell never published his dissertation and thus, like Ritter, never received his doctorate. Unlike Fitzgibbon, Alwell remained within the order, though his work within the community carried him far afield from purely educational and scholarly endeavors. Alwell carved out a diversified ministry that included working in vocations, administering the seminary, pastoring diverse churches in Hoboken, New Jersey, and Burlington, North Carolina, serving as superior of the friary, gaining membership on the Covenant House board of directors, and assuming the directorship of the National Shrine of Blessed Kateri Tekakwitha in Fonda, New York. For some Franciscans, like Fitzgibbon, the path to personal fulfillment led away from purely religious life and toward a secular career in social work or psychological counseling. Others, like Alwell, remained within the order but helped to reshape its ministerial commitments and invent new kinds of roles for themselves in the process. Ritter, as always, retained a more liminal status. He moved subtly between worlds and carefully negotiated the permeable boundaries that separated depression and prosperity, Catholicism and Americanism, commitment and sellout.[19]

Ritter's next career move reflected many of these themes, marked an important change in his own life, and proved to be a key moment in the prehistory of Covenant House. In March of 1963, Brother Luke Salm, C.S.C., who chaired the theology department at Manhattan College, contacted the provincial of the Franciscans in Syracuse concerning "the possibility of having one of your fathers assigned to teach theology here." Brother Luke, who played an instrumental role in transforming Manhattan's theology department into a highly respected program that embraced contemporary scholarship, hoped to "attract to the college theologians who are creative enough to adapt theoretical theology to the intellectual needs of the layman in the collegiate situation." A demanding and visionary department chair, Salm noted in his letter to the Franciscans that "we have had to drop some priests who insist on sticking too close to the seminary manuals and [to the] rather dry conceptualized type of seminary course lecture." Ritter already had grown moderately bored with his responsibilities at Canevin High School in Pittsburgh, where he taught religion, served as assistant dean of discipline, counseled "juvenile delinquents and disturbed adolescents," and moderated various student groups. Within two weeks of Salm's request, he applied for the position at Manhattan College and cleared all arrangements with his Franciscan superiors. Colleagues within the order enthusiastically recommended him to Brother Luke. The chair of the philosophy department at St. Hyacinth's Seminary, where Ritter previously had taught, did offer a cautionary observation that proved prescient: "You may have to moderate his zeal a little in that he will expect a great deal from his students in the way of response and performance."[20]

The new assignment once again found Ritter in a characteristically ambiguous situation, as it placed him some distance from the central administration of the Franciscans. Manhattan College, which had been established by the Brothers of the Christian Schools in 1853, remained under the sponsorship of that order. A cordial relationship existed between the Franciscans and the Christian Brothers, with friars occasionally working as chaplains and educators at the brothers' institutions. This arrangement, however, also allowed Ritter considerable autonomy and freedom from his own religious community. He operated primarily within the structure of academic life at Manhattan College, progressing through its tenure ranks and carrying out his primary responsibilities within that institution. Further, his living situation differed both from conventional Franciscan practices and from typical faculty housing arrangements. Manhattan College recently had acquired a small group of private cottages that previously served as a psychiatric recovery facility for wealthy outpatients, and the Christian Brothers provided Ritter with the sole use of one of these units. Surrounded by trees and located in a sylvan setting, his apartment became an informal hub of collegiate life. Ritter transformed it into a makeshift counseling center, a student meeting place, and a convivial gathering spot. Luke Salm recalled that "when the kids would be thrown out of their own home by their parents because their hair was too long or they weren't going to church on Sunday or something like that, he'd welcome them. And then they'd be crawling in the windows at all hours of the night and everything and sometimes he'd have five or six bodies sleeping around on the floor as best that he could."[21]

Ritter became known as a popular and accessible professor, and he developed a very loyal following among the undergraduates. One former student's recollections proved typical: "He had a good stereo. That was one of the big attractions as it turned out. Bruce had a much better stereo than you had in your dorm rooms. And he also kept his refrigerator well stocked with beer and soda and things." These informal arrangements did not always please his Franciscan superiors, who expected members of the order to live in community and to adhere to a stricter spiritual regimen. The theology department's annual report for 1965 noted that "the matter of a single residence for the Conventual OFM's should be reexamined. Father Bruce tells me that their provincial is again raising questions about their lack of community and religious life. We should hate to lose men on that score." But, as always, Ritter managed to maintain his own flexibility and live on the edges of both bureaucratic regulation and community rules. And he also played a significant role in helping to transform the culture of Manhattan College at a critical juncture in its history.[22]

Ritter's movement into Catholic academic life coincided with the liturgical, social, and intellectual transformations within the Church usually associated with the Second Vatican Council (1962–65). Academics continue to debate the extent to which Vatican II introduced revolutionary change or ratified evolutionary developments. Roman Catholics who lived through the period perhaps most vividly recall the expanding choices and possibilities that permeated every aspect of religious life. Sunday churchgoers found vernacular masses, dialogue homilies, guitar music, traditional Protestant hymnody, new styles of ecclesiastical architecture, a greater emphasis on Scripture readings, and a host of other innovations. Members of religious communities exercised a mandate to reexamine their missions and ministries, redefine their relationship with secular society, reconfigure their constitutions, and alter their lifestyles. Ecumenical endeavors, social ministries, sophisticated theological scholarship, and active lay involvement can all trace much of their energy and initiative to the decrees emanating from Vatican II. For many well-established Catholic institutions, the council contributed to an atmosphere where debate, dialogue, and sometimes confusion flourished. Manhattan College proved no exception.[23]

When Ritter arrived at the all-male campus in the Bronx in the summer of 1963, he found a very conservative college that operated within a traditional and orderly Catholic framework. Brother Gabriel Costello, who served as dean of the college in the late 1950s, described the prevailing atmosphere in these terms: "On any day the campus stood still as the noontime *Angelus* rang out from the bells of Chapel; there were outdoor devotions usually before the Grotto of Our Lady; there was an interruption of the scholastic activity for the holding of an annual three-day retreat." Students at Manhattan College possessed limited flexibility in choosing electives, and sixteen credits in religion remained a nonnegotiable requirement. Undergraduate organizations existed for such classically Catholic purposes as revering the Blessed Sacrament, missionizing Latin America, and coordinating charitable work through local St. Vincent de Paul societies. The class of 1966 noted in the school's yearbook that, upon their arrival in 1962, freshmen found that "jackets and ties were the rule, retreats were unquestioned. Thomism was the philosophy and the most the Quad became excited about was food in the Blue and Red Rooms." Even the track team carefully noted that a primary purpose of its largely convivial fraternal organization, the Spiked Shoe Club, involved developing "a spiritual unity among its members." In addition to attending social functions and organizing parties, Spiked Shoe members agreed to "participate in the offering of the Mass" on the first Friday of each month.[24]

Manhattan College, with an enrollment of approximately 3,400 undergraduates, typified many smaller single-sex Catholic liberal arts institutions that participated fully in postwar America's educational expansion. Located in Riverdale, on high rocky ground in the northeastern Bronx and overlooking the Hudson River, the college carefully maintained its significant intellectual and physical distance from the borough of Manhattan. Riverdale remained a beautifully landscaped neighborhood of fine homes and pleasantly winding byways, closer in tone and feel to suburban Westchester County than to the Bronx itself. Significant growth occurred on campus during the 1950s, as facilities multiplied and the college purchased surrounding land in order to keep pace with student demand. Still, the carefully manicured campus remained tightly knit and culturally homogeneous. Manhattan College especially catered to first-generation white ethnic students from working-class and middle-class backgrounds. Undergraduates were most likely the sons of printers, accountants, insurance agents, waiters, bookkeepers, manual laborers, and clerical workers who spent their working lives at such places as the Consolidated Edison power plant and the Mutual Life Insurance Company. They grew up in Brooklyn, Queens, suburban New Jersey, western Long Island, and the more urbanized areas of Westchester County, usually progressing through the parochial school network and often attending Christian Brothers high schools. Manhattan College offered them practical career training, couched within a solid liberal arts tradition and securely ensconced within a Catholic subculture. Engineering, business, and education remained the most popular courses of study, and most students viewed college as a key first step in securing a comfortable middle-class existence and reaping the benefits of the nation's economic boom. The student body was virtually all white, largely Irish Catholic with a growing Italian presence. Over 80 percent of the undergraduate population commuted, typically as straphangers and gate hoppers on the Number One subway line.[25]

Ritter related well to these students. They grappled with some of the same issues concerning faith and affluence, social mobility, transition to adult life, and the shifting boundaries separating immigrant Catholicism from American culture that had complicated his own spiritual journey. As noted previously, Ritter transformed his private residence into a drop-in center where Friday night bull sessions proved common, as a wide variety of students, faculty, priests, and personal acquaintances floated through his cottage. Most students, who had been raised largely in pre–Vatican II households and parishes, considered this easy mingling between clergy and laity a revolutionary innovation. Ritter personified elements of the new liturgical style that Vatican II encouraged, inviting questions and comments on his homilies, celebrating Mass in the student lounge as well as in his house, and breaking down boundaries between the sacred and the secular. He especially attracted a group of students that one former colleague aptly described as "sharp jocks." Track and basketball proved pivotal in defining

Manhattan College's student culture, with athletes often emerging as class leaders. Ritter, an inveterate jogger who made good physical use of the college's hilly terrain, proved especially popular with the cross-country and indoor track teams. Many of these student-athletes, including Hugh O'Neill, who challenged Ritter during his 1966 sermon, subsequently played important roles in the founding and early years of Covenant House. Indeed, the early student and faculty networks that Ritter developed at Manhattan College influenced and advanced his subsequent ministry. He cultivated and refined these networks in several ways.[26]

Ritter always pushed his students socially and intellectually to think through their reigning assumptions and to cultivate a broader social consciousness. Manhattan College remained a relatively conservative campus, culturally and ideologically, during Ritter's tenure. A 1965 mock mayoral election poll among the students, for example, revealed that over 70 percent supported William F. Buckley, the Conservative candidate with strong Roman Catholic roots. Similarly, as antiwar sentiment heated up at other campuses throughout the New York area, Manhattan undergraduates sponsored a 1965 rally supporting Lyndon Johnson's policies and provoked a physical confrontation with a small body of pacifist protestors. The college's administration quickly cracked down on dissent on the rare occasions when it did appear, placing a premium on orderliness and authority. When the student newspaper published an article mildly critical of Francis Cardinal Spellman for banning fraternities and opposing folk masses in 1965, Pres. Gregory Nugent, C.S.C., and his administration rapidly confiscated all issues and suspended publication for the following week. Student periodicals and college records contain few signs of the massive civil disobedience and protest culture that many academics associate with campus politics during the period.[27]

Historians have spent considerable time chronicling dissent at large public universities and elite private institutions during the mid-1960s but have often neglected the more subtle and significant changes that affected such seemingly quiescent places as Manhattan College. Attitudinal shifts did occur on the Riverdale campus between 1963 and 1968, with Ritter frequently serving as a focal point. Colleagues and students certainly did not view him as a theological or political radical, but he helped to broaden the terms of collegiate discussion and debate. By 1966, for example, Ritter pioneered in introducing a new type of student retreat to the campus, transforming and revitalizing this well-worn feature of Catholic college life. His Novocor retreats attracted both Manhattan College students and coeds from such nearby institutions as Mercy College, Mount Saint Vincent's College, and St. Joseph's College in Brooklyn. They featured off-campus weekend experiences where "students live together as a Christian family," discussing problems, listening to speakers from such alternative ministries as the Catholic Worker movement, engaging in innovative liturgical celebrations including folk masses, and participating in a range of recreational activities. Novocors offered a radical departure at the conservative all-male institution, helping to broaden student experiences and enrich campus spiritual life. They also brought together several individuals who would play key roles in the founding and early years of Covenant House, including numerous future board members. Through such activities, Ritter developed a committed cadre of bright and articulate students who sought to explore and live out their Catholic faith in new ways.[28]

Ritter also expanded the religious programming at Manhattan College, linking institutional Catholicism with social action ministries. Beginning in 1967, he directed the newly established Christian Life Council (CLC), a faculty-student committee that coordinated religious activities at the college and offered venues within which members of the campus community might "develop their personal religious commitment and experience liturgical worship." Through his leadership of this organization, Ritter sought to circumvent the influence of Manhattan College's official chaplain, whom he viewed as "well intentioned" but also as someone who "consistently blocks the path to the more intelligent and far-reaching conception and development of the College's response to the worsening religious situation on campus." Both Ritter and his successor on the Christian Life Council found the chaplain "strongly symbolic of so much that our student body and faculty are rejecting in the institutional church." Once again, Ritter appeared to be expanding his boundaries, working outside of purely institutional constructs, and using traditional structures in order to promote moderately reformist, if not radical, ends.[29]

The Christian Life Council's public programs included a potpourri of lectures, student-faculty discussions, folk festivals, and such evening events as Meet a Nun and Meet a Bishop, which were designed to break down clergy-lay boundaries and to encourage greater dialogue. Ritter engaged speakers who had been involved with a variety of alternative ministries, social programs, and intellectual endeavors. Programming for 1967 proved typical. William Stringfellow, of the Congress on Racial Equality, delivered an address titled "Black Power and White Christianity" at one forum. Ned O'Gorman, a Catholic poet, educational reformer, and antiwar associate of the Berrigan brothers, gave a lecture titled the "Anatomy of a Revolution" on another occasion. Fr. Bernard Häring, an internationally respected German moral theologian, visited Manhattan College for a groundbreaking communal penitential service. Msgr. Robert Fox of the Archdiocese of New York spoke to students on the Church and poverty, explaining his ministry in Spanish Harlem and describing the ways in which Catholic perspectives fueled social action programs. The CLC even sponsored an innovative liturgical performance, based on the play "Marat-Sade," in the student center. Such events drew both Ritter and Manhattan College into the wider and more expansive intellectual orbit of late 1960s Catholic activism.[30]

Ritter also operated on the periphery of the Catholic peace movement during this period. He never became known for taking an aggressively activist antiwar stance, and many former colleagues felt that his military service made him less sympathetic to more radical elements within the movement. Still, he built links with the relatively small contingent of Manhattan College students and faculty who questioned American foreign policy in Vietnam. In 1967, Ritter sponsored an Enemies and Brothers Film Festival, which juxtaposed a series of military training films from official American and North Vietnamese sources. This effort to illustrate the similar ways in which opposing governments used propaganda in order to demonize their adversaries proved quite controversial within the conservative context of the college. Alumni remembered it as a cornerstone event of the late 1960s. Those collegians who gravitated toward Ritter frequently took alternative positions on the war. Hugh O'Neill, for example, remained one of the handful of students who participated in a counterdemonstration protesting the 1965 undergraduate rally in support of Lyndon Johnson's policies. He subsequently refused to answer his draft notice in 1969, was arrested and indicted as a draft resister in 1971, and began working at Covenant House thereafter partially in order to fulfill a community service requirement as part of his suspended sentence. Paul Frazier, a 1967 graduate of Manhattan College, received conscientious objector status, eventually published a draft counseling manual, and always remained ideologically close to the Berrigans and the Catholic Worker movement. He subsequently became a member of Ritter's original covenant community, but continued his involvement in pacifist circles. Ritter also maintained antiwar clergy contacts at the Merton-Buber House in New York City, which counseled draft resisters. He clearly enjoyed cultivating the company of this interesting mix of countercultural Catholic intellectuals who began emerging in the late 1960s.[31]

Considerable ideological distance may have separated Ritter from the antiwar clergymen, but he enthusiastically and unhesitatingly drifted into the orbit of priests who had begun to carve out alternative ministries among the urban poor during the late 1960s. Msgr. Robert Fox, who served as director of the Office of Spanish American Catholic Action for the Archdiocese of New York between 1963 and 1969, proved an especially influential contact in this regard. Fox had been a protégé of Ivan Illich in the late 1950s and, as part of his archdiocesan responsibilities, the monsignor had crafted a series of programs designed to lessen the distance between institutional Catholicism and street-level religion. Fox encouraged priests and nuns to move into inner city neighborhoods, "just be with the people," and respond to the needs of their local environments. By 1965, his program had a formal name, Summer in the City, and a substantial budget that drew heavily on federal grants from the Office of Economic Opportunity. Fox built his ministry around such concepts as the use of streets as public forums for ministry, the importance of artistic creativity as a vital tool for self-expression and human liberation, and the need to bring people of diverse backgrounds together as a critical element in advancing human understanding. Summer in the City achieved considerable prominence during the East Harlem riots in 1967, when Fox successfully encouraged Puerto Rican lay activists to engage in street processions as a means to counteract violence and looting. For many socially committed religious workers at the time, his residential programs proved an important arena for self-actualization and a way to carve out new career patterns beyond the sometimes stifling confines of parishes, schools, and diocesan administrative posts.[32]

Fox's inner city ministry proved attractive to Ritter, who cultivated a formal relationship between Summer in the City and his Manhattan College programs. By the summer of 1967, Ritter's Christian Life Council had provided approximately one hundred college students with the opportunity to work in various inner city neighborhoods under Summer in the City's sponsorship. These eager young Catholics developed art programs, interned at community action projects, helped to establish day care centers, tutored in storefront educational programs, and often spent their days simply participating in street life throughout Manhattan and the Bronx. In the fall of 1967, as Fox secured more stable governmental and archdiocesan funding in order to expand his program, some Manhattan College students took up residence in Harlem, the East Village, and other predominantly Spanish-speaking neighborhoods. Many Summer in the City participants subsequently provided the core leadership for Covenant House during its formative years, and most recalled their experiences in 1967 as critical in shaping their own faith life and in sharpening their social commitments. Hugh O'Neill's participation in the program proved to be the first step in his lifetime of public service. Patricia Kennedy, who previously had attended several Novocor retreats under Ritter's direction at Manhattan College and who earlier had considered entering religious life, initially became connected with Ritter's ministry by accepting a Summer in the City position. Gil Ortiz, a navy veteran who had grown up in Washington Heights and spent his adolescence living in the Lillian Wald housing projects on the Lower East Side, first volunteered for the Summer in the City program during a military leave. He recalled a hectic regimen of organizing athletic teams, inventing street games for children, planning block parties, and developing other recreational endeavors. He also became part of Ritter's circle, started attending Manhattan College, and eventually took in a homeless youth who had found his way to Covenant House. All of these anecdotal personal stories suggest a broader point. For many Catholics, both lay and religious, such alternative ministries as Summer in the City brought a new sense of vitality, engagement, and relationship with contemporary urban concerns. Robert Fox's program demonstrated how socially conscious communicants might translate their faith into action. A generation of young, educated, upwardly mobile, white ethnic Catholics found such programs especially meaningful. Alternative ministries offered them a way to maintain their basic social commitments. They also allowed this rapidly suburbanizing generation to remain close to city streets that were becoming increasingly African American and Spanish-speaking and much less structured around traditional Catholic institutions.[33]

Ritter understood the sources and dissatisfactions that drove this generational shift, which subsequent historians have too often ascribed to vague forces like Vatican II. He attempted to articulate the change on the Christian Life Council in 1967 by developing a student survey that charted undergraduate attitudes toward various religious, political, and moral questions. The survey results, which might strike contemporary observers as unexceptional, created an enormous stir on the normally tranquil campus and even prompted rare coverage of college affairs in the *New York Times*. Ritter's survey revealed that students proved much more liberal than the Catholic hierarchy on sexual and social matters: just 7 percent rejected the use of contraception under all circumstances, a mere 26 percent opposed abortion, and only 21 percent proclaimed that premarital sexual intercourse should be considered wrong in every instance. Although the majority of

Manhattan College students claimed that they regularly attended Mass and adhered to most conventional Catholic teachings, a significant minority dissented. Many respondents expressed skepticism concerning formal religious structures, viewed some standard doctrinal points with disbelief, and remained apathetic about participation in local parish activities. Students proved particularly cynical concerning the concept of papal infallibility. Generally, the survey revealed the fascinating combination of social stresses and strains that educated American Catholic youths experienced during a period of extraordinary institutional change within their denomination. It provided an important barometer of social and religious attitudes on the eve of Pope Paul VI's 1968 promulgation of *Humanae Vitae*, the birth control encyclical that served as a defining cultural moment for liberals and conservatives in the twentieth-century Church.[34]

Many administrators, alumni, and trustees interpreted the results as signs of spiritual declension on campus during the late 1960s. Brother Gabriel Costello, Manhattan College's official historian, certainly agreed with this perspective. He decried the loosening of bonds with the Archdiocese of New York, lamented the hiring of a more religiously diverse faculty, scored administrative apathy concerning ecclesiastical affairs, and worried over the changing financial base of the college, which placed greater reliance on state funding and less on support from Catholic institutional sources. All of these factors, in Costello's view, produced a "chilling in the religious atmosphere of the campus" where "the Angelus bell tolled no more." Dress codes disappeared, the student newspaper regularly pilloried most scheduled religious activities, and the theology department eventually transformed itself into a broader and more ecumenical "religious studies" department. Perhaps most symbolically and disturbingly, "the Grotto of Our Lady, that is set in rock near the steps between the Library and the main campus, was desecrated. Now it is behind an iron grating to protect it from destruction."[35]

Not surprisingly, Ritter interpreted the results much differently. Some colleagues attacked him for even conducting the poll, others questioned his methodology, and administrators feared a donor backlash. The Franciscan answered his detractors in an alumni magazine article that thoughtfully critiqued institutional Catholicism in the late 1960s. Ritter focused his analysis on the emerging generational divides that had mushroomed into credibility gaps, on student impatience with dry bureaucratic formalism, on the youthful longing for more social action ministries, and on the Church's unwillingness "to read aright the signs of the times." For Ritter, "this generation longs for prophets," and he claimed not to hear any prophetic voice emerging from within official Church structures: "It is surely not that of Pope Paul; it is quite clearly not that of the American hierarchy." Perhaps reflecting his own long-standing ambivalence and skepticism, Ritter emphasized that the students carried on a "love-hate relationship with the institutional church." He characterized Manhattan College undergraduates as "almost religiously schizoid in their inability to cope with the split between their doctrinal convictions and their moral uncertainties." He sadly concluded that parishes themselves had proven incapable of developing authentic and meaningful ministries for the rising Catholic generation. New structures, new approaches, and a new willingness to engage with youthful concerns might be the only way to bridge the credibility gap between priests and people and to restore the connection between faith and morals that Ritter found lacking in Manhattan College's student responses. Above all, Ritter viewed his survey as an endorsement for institutional experimentation and as a call for the clergy to craft more relevant and meaningful social ministries.[36]

Some of these same views appeared as driving forces in Ritter's life from his earliest days with the Franciscans. He certainly found himself moving away from traditional ministerial roles during his years at Manhattan College. Ritter's informal contacts with students, his broader connections among dissident New York City priests who had begun building new kinds of Catholic institutions in the inner city, and his own innovative programs on campus all contributed to a growing personal dissatisfaction with academic life. As early as January of 1965, after being informed of his promotion to the rank of assistant professor, Ritter observed that "personally, I'm too happy here—which worries me a little." Wryly commenting that "it's not at all good form, I would think, to admit such a thing," he noted that "I don't think I would want to be much happier."[37] By 1968, he had decided to try and find happiness elsewhere. In January of that year, Ritter prevailed on David Schulze, the minister provincial of the Immaculate Conception Province of the Conventual Franciscans, to support his transfer out of Manhattan College. Schulze, in a letter to the apostolic administrator of the Archdiocese of New York, noted that Ritter "has long been desirous of working in inner-city projects" and had "found a suitable venue at St. Brigid's Church" on the Lower East Side of Manhattan. The initial plan called for Ritter to "live in an apartment, hopefully with another priest of our Province or a priest of the Archdiocese, and involve himself in non-parochial ministry in close harmony with the priests of St. Brigid's Parish." Schulze praised Ritter's enthusiasm, his qualifications, and his ability to instill "true concern for their fellowman among his students" at Manhattan College. Within three months, the archdiocese granted its approval, and Ritter began a new experiment with far-reaching implications.[38]

Bruce Ritter's own creation story of Covenant House had presented its origin as a moment of epiphany. He preached a sermon in 1966, a student challenged him, and a ministry emerged. In fact, Covenant House can trace its beginnings to the complex religious, generational, and intellectual forces that came together in the 1960s to permanently alter the nature of American Catholicism. Location did prove important. Covenant House's founding owed much to the constellation of people, events, and currents that swirled around Manhattan College in the mid-1960s. The founder's own difficult early life, the social commitments of Franciscans and other religious figures, the emergence of a new Catholic student culture, and the broader socioeconomic transformations that affected Americans in the decades following World War II all played their parts. Ritter chose, in telling his story, to focus on one catalytic event that prompted an immediate response. Like all of his stories, this one proved highly personal and dramatic, evoking a fundamental discontinuity between past and present. It betrayed his characteristic unwillingness to consider historical and long-range issues, but it made for good theater. By placing his story within other histories, however, it becomes apparent that Covenant House's very ordinary and routine birth made it fundamentally unique and fascinating.

Chapter 2
East Villagers

I became involved with the kids of the neighborhood quite by
accident—and, quite frankly, against my will. One night, at two in
the morning of a bitter day in February 1969, six kids knocked on my
door. It was very cold and snowing very hard, and the four boys and
two girls looked half frozen. They were quite young—all sixteen and
under—and asked if they could sleep on the floor of my apartment.
What could I do? It was snowing outside and cold. What would you
have done? I invited them inside, gave them some food and blankets,
and the kids bedded down on my living-room floor. One of the boys
looked at me. "We know you're a priest," he said, "and you don't have
to worry. We'll be good and stay away from the girls." I thanked him
for that courtesy! . . . One boy went outside for just a few minutes
and brought back four more kids. . . . These ten kids had been living
down the block in one of the abandoned buildings with a bunch of
junkies who were pimping them. The junkies had just forced the
kids to make a porn film before they would give them some food.
The kids hated that. They really hated that. In disgust and a kind of
horror at the direction their lives were taking, they fled the junkies
and came down the street to my place. . . . I wish I could tell you that
my motives were honorable. I wish I could say that I acted out of
zeal, compassion, kindness. My motives were not that noble–they
were much closer to anger, stubbornness, pride, vanity. I am a very
competitive person. I hate to lose. I had just been driven off campus
by my students; my assignment was to be useful to the poor, and I
didn't want to lose another encounter with a bunch of kids. So I
kept them.

—*Rev. Bruce Ritter*[1]

Bruce Ritter's account of the shift in his inner-city apostolate
from general neighborhood advocacy to sheltering homeless youths reveals
several fundamental truths. It illustrates first and foremost the haphazard,
unstructured, idiosyncratic, and vaguely defined nature of his initial mission. Covenant House did not emerge full-blown as part of any master plan
but rather grew out of random encounters between well-meaning Franciscans and the mean streets of New York City's Lower East Side. The story also
reveals Ritter's penchant for compelling narrative. He personalizes the history of Covenant House, claiming to recall the precise moment when his

Figure 2. Bruce Ritter, rapping with an East Village neighbor, ca. 1970. The Covenant House ministry took shape during the early 1970s amid both the countercultural vibrancy and the routine violence that characterized tenement life on the Lower East Side. Photograph courtesy of the Covenant House Archives.

intentions shifted and a new ministry took shape. His personal motivations and foibles—"anger, stubbornness, pride, vanity"—become character strengths, and deadly sins transform themselves into individual virtues. He acts alone and decisively, ignoring bureaucratic niceties and seizing the moment. He simultaneously challenges his readership to do likewise: "What would you have done?" Ritter also cleverly frames his story within the context of a natural disaster that all New Yorkers might instantly recognize: the blizzard of 9 February 1969. This fifteen-inch snowstorm caused forty-two deaths and nearly three hundred injuries, paralyzed the outer boroughs, closed schools for several days, and permanently scarred the once promising mayoral administration of John Vliet Lindsay. It became an important part of twentieth-century city lore, and Ritter took full advantage. His story even anticipates the later direction that Covenant House took after its uptown move to Times Square by referencing pimps, pornographic films, and the sex industry's exploitation of innocent youths.[2]

The historical reality concerning these early years in the East Village proves more complex than Ritter's neat narrative might suggest. The founder never worked alone but rather operated within a larger community framework that included other Franciscans, former students, neighborhood activists, and comparable religious ministries. He claimed that the Franciscans and the Archdiocese of New York "agreed, reluctantly" to allow him to move to the East Village "on the conditions that I not represent anything I did as sponsored by the Church or my Order and that I not ask for financial assistance from either." In fact, Ritter received considerable support and assistance from his superiors, and his mission fit in well with other archdiocesan efforts in the immediate neighborhood. The founder often criticized other child welfare agencies and especially municipal officials for their legalistic and bureaucratic approaches to youth homelessness. Yet he aggressively pursued public funding and eventually incorporated his ministry primarily in order to administer a city grant project. Covenant House's early years thus appear characterized by a messy maze of false starts, seemingly contradictory directions, and rhetoric that frequently fails to square with reality. In order to begin making sense of it all, the best place to start is in the neighborhood itself, on the eve of Ritter's 1968 arrival.[3]

The term *East Village* conjures up a rich countercultural imagery. Bordered by Fourteenth Street on the north, Avenue D on the east, Houston Street on the south, and the Bowery and Third Avenue on the west, the neighborhood began to take shape as a distinct geographical entity in the mid-1960s. The district's cheap and often dilapidated housing stock attracted artists, musicians, and intellectuals who had been displaced and priced out of the Greenwich Village real estate market. They joined a diverse and often volatile ethnic mix of Ukrainians, Poles, Italians, African Americans, and Puerto Ricans who previously had settled in the area and often resented the newcomers. Tompkins Square Park constituted the neighborhood's emotional public centerpiece, as various ethnic, class, and political factions sometimes fought pitched and violent battles over park use and occupation. The new urban intellectual residents created and patronized a series of community institutions that fundamentally redefined the East Village and attracted scores of tourists and out-of-towners. Coffee houses, jazz clubs, funky boutiques, psychedelic art shops, rock bars, avant-garde theaters, antique stores, and trendy bookshops conveyed a bohemian quality to the surroundings, providing the neighborhood with a chic and hip veneer. For older residents, however, kosher groceries, Puerto Rican bodegas, Roman Catholic churches, storefront Pentecostal revival meetings, Ukrainian fraternal organizations, and Polish luncheonettes more likely composed the essential community institutions. It remained a confusing and intensely territorial world, defined by block and occupied by people who existed in parallel universes. When worlds collided, trouble often ensued.[4]

The year 1967 proved to be particularly problematic. Tompkins Square Park erupted in conflict throughout the summer as hippies battled police, ethnic groups squared off against each other, and street crime permeated the area to an unprecedented degree. One especially violent incident in the fall of that year dominated the tabloids, exposed the seamier side of East Village life, illustrated the pervasive neighborhood tensions, and resulted in a Pulitzer Prize in journalism for J. Anthony Lukas of the *New York Times*.[5] On 8 October, police discovered the naked and brutally beaten bodies of two village youths, eighteen-year-old Linda Rae Fitzpatrick and twenty-four-year-old James "Groovy" Hutchinson, in the garbage-strewn boiler room of a slum tenement on Avenue B and East Eleventh Street, around the corner from Tompkins Square. Hutchinson had been a neighborhood fixture and legendary local character for some time. A harmonica-playing drifter from New England, this genial and jovial hipster also boasted a growing police record and a reputation for providing local drug users with cheap marijuana, barbiturates, and various hallucinogenics. Linda Fitzpatrick's story, however, offered a tidier and more intriguing morality play for the local media. As the daughter of a wealthy spice importer, she had grown up amid the trappings of gentility and style in fashionable Greenwich, Connecticut. Fitzpatrick moved easily in the world of fancy prep schools,

Bermuda vacations, indulgent parents, wholesome recreational activities, and a thirty-room mansion on a four-acre estate. Lukas's investigative reporting indicated that she also lived a double life in the East Village, unbeknownst to her mother and father. In New York City, she drifted through a hippie underground that centered around fleabag hotels, shady street characters, "crash pads, acid trips, freaking out, psychedelic art, witches and warlocks." Her death, at the hands of an African American ex-convict and following an all-night LSD party, focused unprecedented attention on the East Village underground, on the mixture of radical and racial politics that threatened many middle-class New Yorkers, and on the pervasiveness of a newly popular drug known as "speed" on city streets.[6] "Some crimes seem to apotheosize an age," observed Richard Goldstein of the *Village Voice*, and this double murder clearly cast a long shadow over the troubled neighborhood. "The fear is all over the East Village today. . . . It is a slum: Groovy's death seems to have awakened that realization. . . . The mindblower is not that love is dead in the East Village, but that it has taken this long to kick the bucket."[7]

By the late 1960s, New York newspapers began viewing the neighborhood as dangerous, crime infested, drug ridden, and in deep decline. The *New York Times* presented the area as a "scene of bad vibrations," where minorities hassled hippies, a drug-oriented youth culture created friction with longtime residents, and even peace activists spoke openly about carrying knives and guns for protection. "The scene is getting increasingly violent," one informant told a *Times* reporter in 1967. "The love thing is dead. The flower thing is dead."[8] The *Village Voice* concurred, noting that bolted doors, insecurity, nervous cabbies, garbage-strewn backyards, and urine-soaked hallways gave "the Lower East Side the bleak air of postwar Europe or industrial Manchester. . . . Night is when you lock the door and hold the fort. If you want to go anywhere you'll have a hard time."[9] Even the *East Village Other* shared this declensionist perspective. This popular underground newspaper, which began its press run in 1965 by celebrating the alternative lifestyles, sexual freedom, drug use and "sometimes squalid, often quaint and authentic old New York streets" that defined the area, offered a somewhat jaded perspective by 1969. "The scene was different" three years ago, argued the editors, as "the runaways lived with the hippies and the hippies lived with their working friends. . . . The vibes were better. It was the winter and spring of love and everyone was trying to help." Gradually, as youths began pouring into the area, lured by the promise of a new bohemia, "the times had changed and the vibes with it . . . the kids poorer and poorer, treated worse, speed freaked or bikered and having to be tougher, I suspect, than most of them want to be . . . suddenly not acceptable to the rest of the neighborhood—a rabble."[10]

For many middle-class Americans, the Fitzpatrick-Hutchinson murders and the general media disenchantment with hippie neighborhoods confirmed widespread fears about a new class of rootless teenagers who appeared to be roaming the American countryside in the late 1960s. By 1967, mainstream media outlets increasingly focused attention on the problem of "runaways." Children appeared to be leaving their families in increasing numbers, often heading for such countercultural venues as West Hollywood, Miami Beach, the Haight-Ashbury section of San Francisco, and the East Village. Perhaps most menacingly, observed Rabbi Samuel Schrage of the New York City Youth Board in August of 1967, "while the ghetto runaway had always been with us, today's runaway was increasingly a middle-class concern." Youth counselors and sociologists stressed that missing children often fit the Linda Fitzpatrick profile, with privileged upbringings, educated parents, and seemingly stable domestic situations. Statistics, though generally unreliable and usually inflated, appeared to confirm the problem. Major metropolitan police forces reported thousands of missing children from affluent communities, law enforcement officials arrested over ninety thousand juvenile runaways in 1966, and youth advocates claimed that perhaps five hundred thousand teenagers had taken to the road.[11]

As young runaways increasingly became viewed as white, middle-class, and middle-western, mainstream concerns mounted. Parents became alarmed to find that their children might end up in such places as Galahad's Pad on New York's Lower East Side. This "haven for homeless hippies," according to Time magazine, offered an oasis where "boys and girls who have left their families are welcomed into the 'community'" and "bed down on mattresses spread over floors of several mean apartments." Even worse, Time cautioned, "for teen-agers who do run away to the hippies, it is increasingly becoming a bad trip that is not only degrading but also dangerous." Runaways occupied abandoned buildings, slept in parks, panhandled in order to support themselves, found drugs and sex easy to come by in big cities, and often ended up as crime statistics. Gradually, an infrastructure of private social welfare organizations grew in response to this newly discovered social malady. Huckleberry House in San Francisco, for example, opened in July of 1967 as a residential facility to support young people in crisis. Located in the heart of Haight-Ashbury and named in honor of Huckleberry Finn, the shelter served over six hundred youths during its first year of operation and received its support primarily from local religious groups. Huckleberry House developed the first such program in the country, and it coexisted uneasily with municipal officials and law enforcement authorities during its first year of operation. In New York's Greenwich Village area, such socially active churches as Judson Memorial and St. Mark's-in-the-Bowery opened free health clinics, operated makeshift shelters, and administered counseling centers to serve transient youths. Still, organization remained rudimentary, efforts appeared scattered and uncoordinated, and nothing approaching a national effort to address the problem existed. For many, the issue of youth homelessness still seemed best left in the hands of local police forces.[12]

Ritter, as he freely acknowledged in his own recollections, certainly did not anticipate ministering to the needs of homeless youths or displaced middle-class children when he began his East Village sojourn in 1968. All accounts agree that his initial goals appeared ill-defined, nebulous, and amorphous. Fr. James Fitzgibbon, who was teaching at the Conventual Franciscan seminary in Rensselaer, New York, in 1968 and reevaluating his own role within the order, conveyed the prevailing tone in a 1998 oral history interview. Ritter approached Fitzgibbon rather suddenly and informally: "He said, 'Hey, you know, I got this idea—talked to the Provincial and he said that I can start a project, you know, down on the Lower East Side or down in the East Village area and there are a lot of problems and drugs, and it's going to be an experimental thing and I need somebody to go with me and would you be interested?' I said, 'Sure.'" Even after Ritter and Fitzgibbon moved to New York City, a general vagueness prevailed. The friars' newsletter noted in August of 1968 that the two Franciscans' "purpose for being in the East Village is simple—they're trying to witness for Christ. They help others where, when and how the situation demands. Drug addiction, alcoholism, run-aways and massive poverty are but a few of the area's major problems." Ritter typically referred to the endeavor as a "ministry of availability," observing that "I had no specific ministry—my assignment was simply to be useful to the poor." The friars sought to demonstrate their usefulness in the East Village by discerning community needs and responding to neighborhood demands. David Schulze, the Franciscan provincial who approved Ritter's initial proposal, insisted that at least two priests participate in the project so that they could continue to live in community and thus adhere to the order's precepts. Generally, however, Ritter and Fitzgibbon received broad latitude to define their own project. Shawn Nolan, who replaced Schulze as provincial in 1969, supported this flexibility and felt that

the conventuals needed to encourage more creative and imaginative ministerial approaches. Not one to "bog things down in legalisms," Nolan allowed
the experiment to define itself and to operate independently with minimal
ecclesiastical oversight.[13]

The Franciscan leadership invested considerable hope in this "inner
city apostolate," as it became known. The East Village ministry matured
amid a critical period of change, reflection, and reassessment for this religious community. By the late 1960s, the Franciscans found themselves grap-
pling with serious demographic issues, generational change, and the full
implications of the Second Vatican Council's *Perfectae Caritatis* decree concerning the renewal of religious life. Declining manpower remained central
to the story. The vocations boom that had renewed and rejuvenated community life in the 1950s appeared a distant memory as ordinations slowed
to a trickle in the late 1960s. Shawn Nolan faced the grim administrative
reality of fewer candidates for the priesthood, a growing number of separa-
tions and defections to secular life, and an aging community that seemed to
be thinly spread over a broad range of parishes, educational institutions,
chaplaincies, retreat houses, foreign mission fields, and social service agencies. The number of priests and brothers within the Immaculate Conception
Province declined from 307 in 1967 to 281 in 1969. Experts projected a 60
percent decrease in the number of priests ordained annually from the hal-
cyon days of the 1950s, and the average age of the friars had risen from forty
years in 1950 to forty-eight years in 1969. Further, an extensive management
study commissioned by Nolan in 1969 revealed that the majority of friars
now evaluated their sense of community as "poor." Franciscans increasingly
questioned the order's institutional priorities, expressed support for greater
social involvement in inner city programs, felt disconnected from provincial
leadership, and desired more opportunities for individual development
within the context of community life.[14]

Many of the seminarians who sought dispensation from their vows and
the friars who decided to leave the order were among the most innovative,
intellectually engaged, and socially committed individuals within the community. Steven Torkelson, who played an instrumental role in the early years
of Covenant House, offers a good example. Torkelson had grown up in a
working-class household in New Dorp, Staten Island, where he attended
parochial schools. He first learned about Franciscanism from the friars who
helped out at his parish on weekends, and he found their mission especially
affecting. Torkelson took to heart the image of St. Francis kissing the leper
and recognized this symbolic act as part of a broader theological stance that

imbued every creature with intrinsic worth. After making a commitment to religious life, the young Staten Islander progressed through the standard Franciscan institutions, entering the minor seminary in 1957, attending the novitiate in 1961, and eventually graduating from St. Hyacinth's College in 1966. By the time he began his graduate training at St. Anthony's-on-Hudson the following fall, Torkelson had met Bruce Ritter, participated in several Novocor retreats, and grown interested in the inner city ministry that seemed to be taking shape. Increasingly, the thoughtful seminarian found himself asking the question "Where would Saint Francis be?" Torkelson's answer always seemed to carry him farther away from the stately mansions and carefully manicured seminary grounds in Rensselaer, New York. He formed a folk singing group with several fellow classmates, thus expanding his network beyond the seminary walls. The young seminarians performed their Bob Dylan–inspired repertoire at area colleges, high schools, and neighborhood centers throughout the greater Albany area. Torkelson began openly questioning the theological basis of such concepts as transubstantiation and the real presence of Christ in the Eucharist, and sought to carry out a more practical social ministry among the urban poor.

Torkelson's desire to work with community-based groups in the rough-and-tumble south end of Albany encountered a bit of institutional resistance within the order. By January of 1969, he decided to leave the Franciscans. Several of his seminarian friends reached similar conclusions around the same time, and they all became part of the troubling exodus from religious life in the late 1960s. After a brief foray into Manhattan College's highly regarded graduate program in theology, Torkelson moved to a Greenwich Village apartment and started studying educational psychology at New York University. For the next two years, he worked a variety of factory, construction, and bartending jobs while pursuing his graduate degree, moving briefly to Utah before earning his M.Ed. from NYU in 1971. Throughout this period, he remained in contact with Ritter, visiting his apartment on East Seventh Street, periodically volunteering to help out with the inner city apostolate, and eventually joining the Covenant House staff in 1971 as a counselor. Torkelson left the order, but certain aspects of the Franciscan mission remained with him throughout his life and career. He never lost the desire to be with the poor. He played a key role in institutionalizing and professionalizing the Covenant House ministry and subsequently helped to organize a series of group homes for babies with AIDS in Newark and Jersey City during the mid-1980s. Torkelson represented the energy, vitality, and commitment that provincial administrators wished to

retain within the Franciscan fold. Yet the institutional church simultaneously found it difficult to accept and confront the very real intellectual and
social challenges that such younger seminarians posed.[15]

Shawn Nolan hoped that Ritter's inner city apostolate, along with similar innovative programs, might mobilize committed recruits, revitalize the
community, and serve as a focal point for future growth. The ministry also
seemed perfectly to reflect the spirit of the Second Vatican Council, which
encouraged religious communities to confront life in the modern world, re-
connect with the spirit and aims of their founders, and appropriately engage
the cultural needs of the larger society. Not all Franciscans, however, viewed
the East Village project in such positive terms. Some seriously questioned
whether priests should be allowed to live in apartments and outside of community. Others feared that the ministry might merely attract fringe elements within the order and would simply serve as a first step for those
who sought to join the secular exodus. Still others observed that the community already appeared overcommitted to a broad range of ministries that
received inadequate support. They wondered whether inner city concerns
really deserved priority over missionary programs in Costa Rica and other
more time-honored endeavors.

And Ritter himself generated some controversy, provoking a range of
reactions among his colleagues. Though clearly not viewed as a prophetic
radical or a disaffected priest, he did operate on the edges of Franciscan
authority structures. Where some saw brilliance, others detected arrogance.
One friar noted that "he did not suffer fools gladly," and his lack of diplomatic skills cost him some support. But most Franciscans apparently viewed
the mission as a positive development and supported his efforts. Further, the
order's leadership did exert some control over the experiment. They directed
Ritter and Fitzgibbon to live in community with each other, minimized
direct financial contributions, and instructed the two friars to support
themselves by obtaining some outside employment. Perhaps most tellingly,
the Franciscans and the Archdiocese of New York formally attached the
inner city ministry to Saint Brigid's Church on Tompkins Square.[16]

Saint Brigid's had been established on Avenue B and Eighth Street in
1848, primarily to serve the spiritual needs of postfamine Irish immigrants
whose arrival in New York City had strained the Catholic Church's meager
institutional resources. In September of 1967, however, faced with declining
attendance and cognizant of changing neighborhood needs, Francis Cardinal
Spellman approved its transformation into a bold new experimental parish.
Cardinal Spellman, who was now in the twilight of his long episcopate, had

earned his reputation as the embodiment of a conservative Irish Catholic ecclesiastical style that tolerated little pastoral dissent and largely side-stepped social justice issues in the pulpit. Saint Brigid's represented a radical innovation and a somewhat startling break with tradition for the Spellman administration. The church would be governed by a team ministry of three coequal priests who would operate collectively and collegially rather than according to traditional hierarchical managerial principles. The archdiocese hoped to revitalize the parish by encouraging extensive lay participation, developing innovative liturgies, and crafting dynamic social ministries. A mandate existed for the priests to reach out beyond the aging Polish communicants at Saint Brigid's and to begin attracting the African Americans, Puerto Ricans, and hippies who now composed significant populations within the neighborhood. Archdiocesan administrators anticipated considerable synergy between the church and Msgr. Robert Fox's ministries, which already maintained an important community presence near Tompkins Square. Cardinal Spellman appointed three young, socially active, and reform-minded clergymen—Matthew Thompson, John Calhoun, and Dermod McDermott—to spearhead the radically reconstituted parish. Both Franciscan and archdiocesan officials hoped and believed that Ritter and Fitzgibbon might thrive within this creative and experimental environment.[17]

Saint Brigid's subsequent history perfectly captured the idealistic, messy, confused, occasionally incoherent, and invariably intense religious atmosphere that pervaded urban street Catholicism in the late 1960s and early 1970s. Liturgical changes proceeded at a whirlwind pace. McDermott subsequently recalled that, as one of the team's initial acts, "we tore out the old altar with all its curlique distraction and hovering saints and replaced it with a simple altar." Saints' statues became relegated to the basement, and a "People's Mass" focused on free-form dialogue between priests and communicants. Easter Vigils featured contemporary Stations of the Cross, with such socially relevant symbolism as Christ being crowned by the thorns of poor education and inadequate social services. Parish council meetings carefully discussed and debated every innovation in extraordinary detail, reflecting the passion with which parishioners greeted change. Church leaders hoped to initiate a laundry list of community-based programs, ranging from day care centers to drug prevention clinics to draft counseling. If focus and specificity appeared lacking at times, the sheer breadth of projects and proposals conveyed an impressive social vision. Perhaps Matt Thompson best articulated the underlying philosophy when he envisioned "the church of the future" as "not a big church building as we have it now" but rather a more amorphous entity located "in buildings on the different streets in the neighborhood."[18]

The church opened its doors to all. The Young Lords, an activist and leftist Puerto Rican organization, used the school to conduct its training classes. Rallies and prayer services to support the Black Panther fugitive Angela Davis, workers' dinners in the rectory, the opening of a youth discotheque, and cooperative liturgies with area Protestant churches all took place within the walls of Saint Brigid's. At any given moment, the rectory provided sleeping quarters for neighborhood activists, local transients, and Christians who sought a communal living experience. This free flow of people and ideas occasionally bordered on the bizarre. Thompson recalled that a white drug addict named Tex, invariably dressed in a diaper and well known throughout the neighborhood, would frequently attend the People's Mass, wander down the aisle, drink some communion wine, and occasionally steal something. A Three Kings procession in January of 1971 featured teen skits structured around the theme "Death of Santa Claus." A boy dressed as a television set shot Santa Claus in one tableaux, while another youth costumed as a "capitalist pig" poisoned the jolly old elf in a second performance. Eventually, Saint Brigid's proved too administratively unwieldy, bureaucratically problematic, and overtly controversial for diocesan authorities. Chancery officials finally terminated the experiment in 1972 after McDermott made front-page news by publicly discussing his close personal, and implied romantic, relationship with a young female social worker. Thompson, McDermott, and Calhoun all eventually left the priesthood and married.[19]

Critics might easily caricature the experimental parish's apparent excesses and criticize its flaws. Certainly, the ministry generated considerable controversy within the local community during its brief lifetime. Polish parishioners resented the new liturgies, argued that their own traditions had been devalued, and felt marginalized within a structure that appeared responsive only to minority and East Village intellectual sentiments. Older and more religiously conservative Puerto Rican communicants agreed. Several felt that the young priests sacrificed spirituality in the interest of appearing socially relevant and pursuing a leftist political agenda. They longed for the rich liturgical life, traditional music, and elaborate statuary that characterized Catholicism on their native island. Some felt that the priests needed to place more emphasis on parochial schooling and less on political consciousness raising. Generational and ideological divides became institutionalized. Three separate Sunday Masses catered to three distinct constituencies: one Mass attracted the "old-time" Polish parishioners, a Spanish language Mass proved popular with Puerto Ricans, and the dialogue Mass catered to those who wished to participate in an alternative worship experience. Rarely did the three groups mix. Even Holy Week observances gradually grew segregated by generation as traditional ceremonies attracted adults and more contemporary offerings were geared toward teens.[20]

But an exclusive focus on controversy obscures some very real accomplishments. All three priests played a constructive role in calming tensions in a very tough and troubled neighborhood. Thompson and McDermott especially maintained a high-profile presence on the streets, working closely with Summer in the City's Brigade in Action community center. They orchestrated block parties that successfully brought together warring ethnic factions within the area, walked a fine line between encouraging legitimate protest and curbing violent outbreaks during disturbances in Tompkins Square Park, and maintained an open dialogue with Puerto Rican youths who often found themselves trapped between contending cultural forces. The ministry itself also made Roman Catholicism spiritually meaningful and inspirational for many lapsed Catholics. Marguerite Colonnese, for example, was working as a nurse in Bellevue Hospital's pediatric ward when she discovered Saint Brigid's. She had grown up in a Catholic neighborhood in the Bronx during the 1950s and attended Catholic schools but gradually found herself turned off by traditionalist clergymen, routine liturgies, and an excessive pastoral emphasis on personal discipline and social sins. Like many contemporaries, she drifted away from formal religious observances. Saint Brigid's opened her eyes to an exciting new postconciliar Catholic world. She discovered "a real hodgepodge of people" at the parish and recalls "I found it fascinating and just interesting that all these different people, you know, were there at church and talking about their faith and dialoguing and everything. That attracted me . . . during the Mass somebody would walk in off the street, a homeless person or an alcoholic, and they weren't turned out or anything. And it just seemed very accepting to me." The racial diversity, intellectually stimulating dialogue, and spiritual enrichment appealed to her. Colonnese decided to quit her nursing job in 1969, moved to East Seventh Street, and volunteered for one year with the Covenant House ministry in order to translate her newfound religious enthusiasm into practice. Her commitment, which involved considerable financial hardship for a young single woman in New York City, illustrated the sense of mission and excitement that motivated many young Catholics to embrace street ministries and renew their faith in the process. At such times, Saint Brigid's seemed to embody the best impulses and highest ideals expressed at the Second Vatican Council.[21]

Ritter and Fitzgibbon maintained a very loose and largely informal relationship with the parish. They occasionally attended meetings, conducted a few retreats, and received some volunteer recruits from the ranks of such parishioners as Marguerite Colonnese. Generally, however, the Franciscans kept both a physical and an ideological distance from the controversial team ministry. Ritter defined his mission as living in the neighborhood rather than maintaining any close association with the institutional church, even one with the edgy reputation of Saint Brigid's. He quickly found a fifth-floor apartment in a dilapidated tenement at 274 East Seventh Street, near Avenue D, and the two friars set up housekeeping in this building during the late spring of 1968. "Most of my neighbors were junkies, dealers, and speed freaks," the founder subsequently recalled, but the building offered the dual virtues of cheap rent and complete immersion in the daily reality of urban street life. Heroin addicts used the tenement roof as a shooting gallery, petty thieves regularly visited and robbed the Franciscans' apartment, and "war zone" remained the most common contemporary characterization of the immediate neighborhood. In accordance with the stipulation governing their assignment, both priests soon found part-time jobs in order to support themselves. Ritter began teaching a few theology courses at Saint John's University in Queens and also accepted several weekend preaching assignments. Fitzgibbon secured a position working with drug addicts at a rehabilitation facility known as Liberty Village in New York City, and traveled to nearby Secaucus, New Jersey, on Sundays to celebrate Mass. Both friars recalled driving taxis and accepting various other temporary jobs in order to make ends meet.[22]

For the first year especially, the project lacked direction and focus. Ritter observed, "I became involved in all the problems you'd expect to find if you lived and worked in a slum: the poverty, the violence, the drug scene, the unemployment, the police corruption that was rampant," but he also acknowledged that "my ministry to the poor didn't seem to be getting anywhere." In some ways, the lack of specificity proved to be a virtue. Both Franciscans spent considerable time learning the intricacies of the neighborhood, talking with people, and connecting with other groups in the area. Fitzgibbon remembered a steady stream of late-night visitors who would arrive at the apartment to "check us out" as well as endless rap sessions concerning poverty, politics, and potential programs. One particularly knowledgeable and sympathetic African American community activist approached the Franciscans with an offer to "break you guys in. . . . You could run with me for a few days and see what I do." He introduced them to a barely visible, yet extraordinarily influential, community network of local bars, pawn shops, semilegal establishments, and uptown gun dealers. Ritter purchased a handgun, using it on several occasions to frighten off potential thieves and car jackers. He appeared increasingly attracted to his new role as savvy and streetwise cleric, using muscle as well as priestly persuasion to confront the junkies, slumlords, street drunks, and drug dealers who populated his corrupt urban underworld.[23]

All accounts confirm that the notion of sheltering homeless youths emerged almost accidentally and developed to satisfy real neighborhood needs rather than in accordance with any grand preconceived strategy. Although Ritter always insisted that the February 1969 snowstorm provided the critical turning point, others remembered this shift in ministry as much more gradual, ongoing, and coincident with various complementary activities. Fitzgibbon recollected that "there were guys who, you know, were drunk and causing trouble on the streets and we'd invite them to come up. They'd sleep there for a couple of days and sleep off the drunk. And it was very non-structured and open-ended." Eventually "a few kids came up and needed a place to crash so we said, 'Alright, you could stay here for the night.'" As word spread throughout the neighborhood that 274 East Seventh Street offered safe and hospitable lodging for needy youngsters, "we were starting to get uptight because we didn't know what to do with these kids." The tiny railroad-style tenement apartments consisted of a living room, a kitchen containing both sink and bathtub, two very small bedrooms that really blended into one room, and common hallway toilets. Ritter and Fitzgibbon soon recognized that the need for shelter by the adolescents and young adults who always seemed to be hanging out on the street far outstripped their available facilities. They began looking for additional apartments within the seventy-two-unit brownstone, taking advantage of the vacancies, transiency, and squatting that proved endemic to the neighborhood.[24]

Gradually, throughout 1969 and 1970, Ritter and Fitzgibbon accumulated additional units in their own tenement and in similar buildings on East Seventh Street. They physically renovated apartments, created makeshift sleeping spaces, and began taking in increasing numbers of homeless youths for temporary lodging. Ritter claimed that he eventually appropriated twenty-six apartments in the immediate vicinity, ranging from basement garrets to fifth-floor walk-ups, by a combination of renting, squatting, and physically evicting criminal occupants. The priest also began relying on a growing network of relatives, fellow priests, friends, and acquaintances who contributed time and money to the endeavor. Help materialized from several sources. Fitzgibbon's sister, Theresa, became attracted to the project and spent some time living in the East Village. Several Franciscans decided to affiliate with their colleagues, as positive publicity concerning the project filtered through the community. Fr. Laurent Ceremsak, formerly a missionary to Costa Rica, became the first Franciscan who requested a transfer to the inner city ministry in 1970. Approximately fourteen friars went to work as house parents for Covenant House over the course of the next several years. Shawn Nolan recalled that most assignments proved temporary and relatively brief. Many sympathizers burned out within a few months, and few could maintain Ritter's exhaustive pace for extended periods of time. Still, the experiment attracted attention within Catholic circles, and other priests who sought alternative ministries gravitated to East Seventh Street. David Gregorio, a Vincentian father who recently had arrived in New York City and been assigned by his order to a teaching position at Saint John's Preparatory School, found a network of sympathetic antiwar and reformist priests who pointed him in Ritter's direction. For Gregorio, who felt that seminary training and teaching had narrowed his horizons and removed him from real world issues, volunteer work in the East Village "was like I was being born again and not in a religious sense but in total exposure to the city and people and everything. And Covenant House was right at the heart of that." Gregorio eventually left the priesthood, married Ritter's niece, and spent much of his subsequent career working in Covenant House on child care issues.[25]

Catholic college students, aspiring social workers, and former acquaintances at Manhattan College proved especially loyal and dedicated volunteers. A few examples illustrate the larger patterns. Adrian Gately had graduated from Manhattan College in 1962 and returned there to teach electrical engineering in 1966, when a mutual friend introduced him to Ritter. Gately found the Franciscan "a refreshing person to see" on campus, and the two became fast friends and occasional jogging partners. By 1969, Gately had grown dissatisfied and bored with his academic career and sought a more meaningful and dynamic lifestyle that better squared with his social concerns and sensibilities. He had visited with Ritter several times on the Lower East Side and decided to move into one of the East Seventh Street apartments that the Franciscans had renovated, across the street from the original tenement, in order to help out with the growing number of homeless youths. Patricia Kennedy had been working at a Summer in the City site in the East Village during the summer of 1969. The notion of neighborhood ministry appealed to Kennedy, and she decided to move into one of Ritter's tenement apartments along with Theresa Fitzgibbon and a third woman, Pat Coonerty, who had attended Novocors while studying at St. Joseph's College in Brooklyn. Kennedy remembered that "Bruce had just a raft of these former Manhattan College students who just flocked to him for help, for money, to cry on his shoulder, to tell their problems to. He was sort of a therapist to this huge group of guys and some women who[m] he had met when the Novocors began." Many of these former students became the early backbone of his ministry, and Ritter aggressively recruited several to serve as house parents and neighborhood settlers.[26]

Paul Frazier took perhaps the most circuitous and unique route to East Seventh Street. The Manhattan College graduate returned to New York City in 1969 after earning a master's degree in social work from the University of Michigan and participating vigorously in the vibrant antiwar movement in Ann Arbor. Deciding that he wished to devote his time to war resistance work and draft counseling, Frazier affiliated with the Catholic Worker and the Catholic Peace Fellowship movements, both of which maintained offices on the Lower East Side. He also needed a convenient place to live. One of Frazier's former classmates at Manhattan, who had been somewhat friendly with Ritter, suggested that they both join the growing group of young Catholic activists who had gravitated to East Seventh Street: "It's cheap, it's exciting, we're down there doing draft resistance work anyway . . . live and work with the poor. It was still a thrill, excitement. It was like, holy cow, what's this life all about?" Frazier and his friend moved into a tenement apartment down the street from Ritter and Fitzgibbon, split his time between the peace movement and work with neighborhood youths, and even convinced Manhattan College to hire him in its student affairs office as a draft counselor. He illustrates the fascinating mixture of idealistic motives, personal contacts, and idiosyncratic happenstance that fueled the early Covenant movement.[27]

Volunteer expansion, along with the tighter focus on homeless youths, occasionally produced tension and disagreement. The relationship between Ritter and Fitzgibbon began to fray early on. Personality issues accounted for some of the conflict. Ritter's aggressive, intense, frenetic, and confrontational style contrasted sharply with Fitzgibbon's much more serene, placid, and measured approach to problems. Seemingly petty disagreements concerning the use of the Franciscans' car and the organization of a local block party mushroomed into disputes over authority, control, and commitment.

Ultimately, these immediate causes of strain masked a differing approach toward the inner city apostolate itself. Fitzgibbon supported the original notion of simply maintaining a presence in the neighborhood. He was attracted to such nearby ministries as Dorothy Day's Catholic Worker and Charles De Foucauld's Little Brothers, both of which operated on the Lower East Side. Humility, service, building community solidarity, and meeting the immediate physical and spiritual needs of local inhabitants remained central to such efforts. Ritter, by contrast, kept other East Village religious institutions at a distance and never cultivated intellectual or social connections with these seemingly related endeavors. He preferred to operate alone and seemed intent on carving out his own ministerial niche. He steadily moved toward developing a more organized, structured, and specialized operation that concentrated primarily on caring for homeless youths and runaways.

By 1970, Fitzgibbon decided that the two Franciscans had reached an impasse, and he moved out of the East Seventh Street apartment. He found nearby lodging on East Fifth Street, devoted more time to drug counseling and working in nursing homes, and befriended some ex-priests and ex-seminarians who shared his vision. Fitzgibbon maintained some occasional contact with Ritter, but their team ministry effectively had ended. In 1971, Fitzgibbon left the priesthood and married Marguerite Colonnese, precipitating a further break with his former colleague. Contemporaries recalled that Ritter did not handle this news well. He felt personally betrayed, believed that the defection placed his project in a questionable light within the order, and feared that for others it would confirm the dangers of departing from traditional Franciscan notions of mission and community. Communication between Ritter and Fitzgibbon ceased.[28]

Other supporters also questioned the direction of the movement. Patricia Kennedy recalled considerable ambivalence concerning the youth ministry: "We weren't interested in these kids at all, I must confess to you. They were about six or seven years younger than we were." Kennedy and her cohort viewed their work in the East Village as part of a larger mission to live out the principles of the Second Vatican Council and embrace more radical reforms. Tutoring children and providing a structured environment for street kids "was not our sort of thing, our idea. But that more and more became the thing Bruce became interested in." Paul Frazier also viewed the increased focus on runaway children as too narrow, given his broader interest in social justice and peace issues. He remembered transforming his tenement apartment into "kind of like this peace center, and several peace activists moved in for days or weeks or months at a time." Frazier's politically committed colleagues now spent time "negotiating space with runaway kids" often to the detriment of both their antiwar activities and the children's immediate needs. Frazier believed that the homeless youth problem really reflected larger structural discontinuities within American society. Affordable housing, neighborhood revitalization, and antipoverty programs remained more significant reform causes, in his estimation. Frazier affiliated with Ritter's program, but he never abandoned his other social commitments and never narrowed his critical stance toward American capitalist culture.[29]

Ritter struggled with many of these same issues as his ministry took shape. Throughout the summer and fall of 1969, he participated in an ongoing dialogue with key volunteers and neighborhood residents that aimed at better defining their purpose and providing some structural coherence to their efforts. Ritter, Kennedy, Frazier, and Gately carefully debated their differences and considered their mutual concerns. They crafted a document that articulated their communitarian impulses, charted some concrete ministerial directions, and mapped out a global vision for the future. Their ruminations resulted in the creation of a new organization: Covenant I. This constituted the first recorded use of the term *covenant* in connection with Ritter's efforts, and as such it deserves extensive consideration. It provides a snapshot of preinstitutional thought during the 1969–70 period and illustrates themes that would emerge again and again as Covenant House developed and matured. Covenant I also hints at the possibilities of an alternative ministerial vision that never fully coalesced. It remains a road not taken, revealing the political and practical pressures that caused Covenant House to move eventually in a somewhat different direction.[30]

Covenant I, in the words of its creators, presented a blueprint for "a viable self-perpetuating structure within which a group motivated by Christian principle may express and realize its commitment to this ideal." Ritter, Kennedy, Gately, and Frazier proposed to create a cooperative, "independently of existing ecclesiastical or civil structures," where they would live in community for a variety of purposes. They pledged first to commit themselves to each other, nurturing the personal growth and fulfilling the human needs of each member of the covenant. They also agreed "to meet the immediate physical and psychological needs of the East 7th Street community, e.g. to provide shelter and food and human support for the many homeless persons in the area, to provide legal and other professional assistance, etc." The group further inserted a prophetic clause into their covenant, calling for a "programmatic effort to effect systemic social change," seeking to provoke "constructive confrontation when useful and necessary," and agreeing "to involve and cooperate with other power structures and value-producing institutions, e.g. universities, churches, etc."

Structurally, the Covenant I founders envisioned a democratic and communal movement. The full membership would elect a leader each year, whose authority "will be derived from the consent of the cooperative." Food became an essential component of Covenant operations. Members agreed to break bread together and to share meals on a weekly basis. These dinner meetings served important business and communal purposes. The founders conceived them as informational sessions where members presented reports, sought advice, and engaged in mutual constructive criticism. Guests and local residents might also attend these weekly gatherings, offering input and building relationships. Extensive self-scrutiny would occur during monthly all-day seminars and annual week-long retreats, where programs might be refined and missions examined. Covenant I provided a variety of membership and residential options, depending upon the amount of tithing and the extent of commitment that each individual wished to make. All members, however, agreed to live in the cooperative apartments on East Seventh Street, to support themselves financially, to donate a substantial portion of their income to the ministry, and to receive approval from 75 percent of the existing cooperative prior to joining the group. Significantly, all Covenant I members committed themselves "to stand in opposition to and confront those elements in the body politic which are not responsible to the needs of our disadvantaged citizens." The founders also envisioned extensive external relationships with churches of all faiths, sympathetic corporations, and academic institutions.[31]

Several striking themes emerge from the document. Consider the covenant itself. The founders envisioned this as a solemn agreement to bind the members in community rather than as a means of dealing with client populations. They couched their cooperative in the language and symbols of contemporary liberal religious traditions, drawing upon such rituals as breaking bread and such organizational principles as consensual politics. A classical and Christian-based communitarianism clearly informed their efforts. Covenant I also embraced a remarkably radical and confrontational approach toward social structures and institutions. The founders called for dramatic social changes, envisioned a broad-based political strategy in order to accomplish their ends, and outlined a wide-ranging series of specific projects. The latter included "housing, narcotics addiction, welfare problems, sanitation, runaway youths, feeding and sheltering the hungry and homeless, legal assistance, bail bonds for the indigent, day care centers for working mothers, etc." If Ritter's ministry increasingly focused on youth homelessness by 1969, Covenant I sought to recapture the broad mission that informed his initial efforts. The Covenant I document offered a blueprint for measured expansion. The signatories anticipated various partnerships with local universities, including student internships, participation in the federal work-study program, and synergistic intellectual relationships with sympathetic academics. They hoped to obtain grants of clothing, food, furniture, and cash from national fraternal and corporate institutions. Community members themselves pledged to contribute professional legal advice, systems analysis, public relations assistance, and other services based on their own skills. They also requested a five-thousand-dollar commitment from the Franciscans, along with the guarantee of release time for one friar to work with the group.

Ritter attempted to secure this last contribution at a Franciscan definitory meeting that was held at Rensselaer in February of 1970. He presented the Covenant I document to his superiors within the order, but his efforts met with a decidedly cool response. The friars raised a number of questions concerning the potential community. Some felt that the document reflected an excessively humanist orientation, leaving little room for the gospel and for religious proselytization. Others worried about the extent to which the province should commit itself to this mission when religious needs elsewhere appeared so great. The concept of communal living raised some concerns, given the minimal participation of the Franciscans in the project and the fact that one of the four signatories was a woman. Further, Fitzgibbon had already moved out of East Seventh Street and played no role in drafting the document, which undoubtedly disturbed some friars. Ultimately, the definitory decided to refer Ritter's document to the consulting firm that had been conducting an ongoing review of all Franciscan missions. The consultants recommended against supporting Covenant I, much to Ritter's disappointment.[32]

Covenant I never fully functioned exactly as its founders envisioned, but some elements of the document influenced the ministry on East Seventh Street throughout the early 1970s. Adrian Gately, the only participant with a reasonably regular though modest income, did contribute a significant portion of his paycheck to the cause. Patricia Kennedy and Paul Frazier also donated money as circumstances allowed. The group met regularly for food and fellowship, some individuals engaged in political activism and supported various social causes, and the expanding band of volunteers built strong personal relationships that often endured for decades. Individuals dropped in and out of the core group, as volunteers drifted through: Paul Frazier assumed a somewhat less prominent role, while Adrian Gately and Patricia Kennedy continued their intense involvement. A few small corporate and institutional contributions also supported the work. David Orlow, for example, an East Seventh Street resident and Covenant I supporter who worked for the Ziff-Davis public relations firm, secured some financial donations from his employer. The intensely communal and overtly prophetic elements of Covenant I, however, receded into the background though they never completely disappeared. Organized political activism and constructive confrontation largely fell by the wayside, and the multifaceted ministries envisioned in the Covenant I document never really materialized.

Homeless youths became the almost exclusive focus of Ritter's efforts in the early 1970s and dominated the work thereafter. Stereotypical white runaways from the suburbs composed a significant percentage of this group at first, but East Seventh Street volunteers soon noticed another growing population of street children who they would subsequently characterize as "urban nomads." These older teenagers usually had been shuffled through New York's foster care system and frequently ended up in the East Village without skills or education. Some came from abusive homes, many were African American and Spanish speaking, and more than a few suffered from serious addictions. No existing public or private agencies appeared to address their specific problems. One of the first youths who found his way to East Seventh Street subsequently described himself as follows: "I am a throw away baby orphan. I stayed in an orphanage until five years old. After five, I was placed in a Foster Home and later kicked out at 15 years old and slept under Manhattan bridge for several months. Homeless, no family, a 4 x 4 box of clothes, and a semi-secluded park bench was my only property." His story appeared far from unique. Paul Frazier recalled that, after "the word got out in the institutional world" about the homeless shelters on East Seventh Street, "literally kids were dumped. . . . I mean the song was, 'Congratulations, You're Sixteen, Goodbye.' And here's the address to Covenant House." Ritter and the other volunteers sought to protect these youths from East Village street life by providing basic food and shelter at night in a safe and supervised environment. That became their overriding purpose, their primary mission, and their full-time occupation.[33]

By the early 1970s, the inner city apostolate appeared on the cusp of a great transformation. A vaguely defined ministry, staffed initially by two Franciscans who sought merely to maintain a spiritual presence in a troubled neighborhood, had taken an unanticipated turn. Focus, structure, and purpose gradually emerged from the bubbling cauldron of East Village street culture. But chaos, disorganization, and randomness also played an important role. Covenant House's founders struggled over competing and sometimes incompatible notions of Christian belief, communitarian commitment, social activism, and ministerial direction. Franciscan support proved critical, but the institutional church remained at arm's length. Youthful volunteers, animated by diverse motives that often blended religious zeal with social action, provided the energy and the passion. Bruce Ritter, when spinning his foundational stories, often ignored this supply side of the ministerial equation. His 1969 snowstorm parable also neglected larger environmental factors and presented institutional transformation as a highly personalized encounter between the founder and the kids. Despite the inherently problematic nature of this narrative device, Ritter correctly placed issues relating to runaways and homeless youths on center stage. Accordingly, it seems appropriate to conclude this chapter in Covenant House prehistory with another story. Paul Frazier vividly recalled the informal meetings, dinner table debates, and carefully constructed dialogue that surrounded the creation of Covenant I. "We were having those discussions, and we get our documents, and then the kids started showing up. And one night Eric says, 'Where are you going?' I said, 'We're going next door. We're having a meeting—a Covenant I meeting.' And he said, 'Well what are you talking about?' And he says, 'Well, if you got that, we've got our own meetings here.' And I said, 'Well what are you talking about?' And he says, 'Well you got that, then we're—Covenant HOUSE.' And he named it. I mean, that's the name. 'If you're that, we're Covenant HOUSE.' This is a fifteen-year-old black kid. I don't know where he was from. And a great kid, just a smile on his face, you know." Unbeknownst to both Eric and Paul Frazier, changes appeared on the immediate horizon. In 1972, the newly named Covenant House would acquire its own corporate charter, bylaws, board of directors, and annual budget. Institutionalization and structure would introduce some fundamentally new dynamics into the organizational life. And the inner city apostolate would never remain the same.[34]

Figure 3. West Eleventh Street Group Home, between Fifth and Sixth Avenues, fourth entrance from right. By the middle 1970s, Covenant House had evolved into an increasingly reputable and fully incorporated institution that administered licensed group homes in some very fashionable Greenwich Village neighborhoods. Photograph courtesy of the New York University Archives.

Chapter 3
Corporate

Ever since the incorporation of our agency in 1972, a certain inevitable
process of assimilation into the child-welfare system began to occur.
It seemed to me that little by little the mission of Covenant House to
street kids was gradually being absorbed and colored and finally
shaped by the system. Our easy, no-questions-asked openness to any
kid who came to our doors was being replaced by the intake criteria
imposed by the city and state. We were told which kids we should
take, how long we should keep them, and what we could do for them.
Despite the encroachment upon our flexibility and openness, between
1972 and 1975 Covenant House flourished and grew quickly into a
classy little group-home program with ten residences for about 120
kids. And I was getting bored—and frustrated. What started out as a
model of openness and availability to any kid on the street was
quickly becoming like any other agency, dependent on government
funds, subject to government priorities. Covenant House in 1975 was
crisply professional, carefully compassionate—and rapidly becoming
indistinguishable from any other group-home program in New
York State. It was time for me to leave, I thought. Covenant House
certainly no longer needed me. Since I loathe sitting behind a desk,
I couldn't imagine that God would want me to spend the next ten
years administering a child-care agency.

—*Rev. Bruce Ritter*[1]

Covenant House struggled to refine its purpose and to carve out
its unique institutional niche during the early 1970s. Diverse perspectives
existed within the movement, and Ritter's account nicely captured some
of the inherent ambiguities. Supporters agonized over the proper balance
between public accountability and private initiative. Questions arose concerning
the optimal size of the ministry, debates occurred over political
action and cooperative projects with similar institutions, and nervous discussion
took place about the extent of bureaucratization within Covenant
House. Some board members and staffers emphasized the religious aspect
of the ministry, holding firm to the organization's Catholic and communal
origins. Others carried a more secular orientation to the work, informed by
their graduate degrees in social work and by their immersion in the helping
professions. Although these perspectives need not clash, and indeed often

achieved satisfactory resolution within the same individual, they reflected the tensions between mission and structure that typically create conflict within religious and nonprofit institutions.

Ritter's public statements appeared to leave little doubt concerning his own sentiments. His description of Covenant House in the early 1970s underscored a personal disdain for bureaucratic form, a deep impatience with governmental regulation, and an undisguised contempt for "the system." Ritter portrayed himself as a charismatic maverick, willing to walk away from Covenant House in a heartbeat should it lose its vitality. He refused to spend his life "sitting behind a desk," had no interest in "administering a child-care agency," and always appeared ready for the next personal challenge. Most significantly, like all charismatic leaders, he recognized no external human authority: "The only thing that really makes sense for me is to do what God wants, what pleases him. Nothing else really matters to me. I do what I do because of God." With one sweeping statement, Ritter thereby placed himself above temporal accountability. Legal restraints, professional norms, and bureaucratic procedures all receded to the background. He claimed to internalize the ministry's charisma and appropriated the liberty to shape it through his own sense of personal calling. Mere earthly contrivances and regularized routines held no sway.[2]

Ritter's rhetoric seemed intended to resonate with a broad audience. The early 1970s constituted a period of widespread cynicism concerning governmental authority and bureaucratic structures within the United States. From the publication of the *Pentagon Papers* in 1971 through the resignation of Richard Nixon in 1974, Americans found their faith in large institutions shaken and battered beyond repair. Feelings of personal impotence against a seemingly all-powerful and interconnected system generated a diverse range of responses. Conspiracy theorists achieved surprising credibility in all forms of popular media. Advocacy journalism, usually directed against exposing institutional abuses, flourished on the national and local levels. Community action groups proliferated, and local control became a key political concept that inspired reformers in venues ranging from parks and playgrounds to public education. Once again, Ritter had demonstrated his remarkable talent for crafting an appealing rhetorical flourish that perfectly suited the particular historical moment.

Covenant House's real history during this period, however, moved in more diverse directions than the founder's comments might suggest. Ritter himself actually played a major role in institutionalizing the ministry and in initiating the changes that he subsequently criticized. He aggressively sought public support, drew up articles of incorporation, hired an administrative staff of full-time professionals to manage day-to-day affairs, and began taking steps to place Covenant House on a sound business basis. The founder would prove adept at such solid administrative tasks as raising funds, negotiating real estate deals, and working behind the scenes in order to strengthen the ministry's financial infrastructure. His public rhetoric, however, steered clear of such topics and crafted a very different image. Ritter found it advantageous to position himself as an action-oriented pragmatist, impatient with regulation and unrelenting in his contempt for bureaucracy. In fact, as future events would demonstrate, Ritter proved to be a master institutionalizer. He brilliantly combined the rhetoric and persona of the charismatic leader with the institutional sensibility and keen eye for detail of the careful bureaucrat. This creative tension, exemplified by the founder's own complex personality, defined much of the ministry during the early 1970s.

On one level, Covenant House's history between 1972 and 1975 seemed to be a straightforward story of corporate maturation and steady programmatic growth. Signs of formalization appeared everywhere. The agency filed a certificate of incorporation with the State of New York in November of 1972, received tax exempt status from the Internal Revenue Service in March of 1973, opened a corporate savings account in order to hold grant money in April of 1973, began executing contracts with city and state agencies as a child care provider shortly thereafter, and started hiring full-time professional staff. Ritter even incorporated a separate institutional entity, known as Testamentum, in April of 1973 in order to obtain and hold real estate, which would then be leased on favorable terms to Covenant House.[3] Property acquisition proved instrumental in allowing the agency to rapidly expand its services throughout Greenwich Village and the Lower East Side. In addition to the original tenement apartments at 274 East Seventh Street, Covenant House opened an intake center at 504 LaGuardia Place in 1972 and secured office space nearby on West Twelfth Street the following year. Ritter leased two fashionable townhouses with an option to purchase on West Eleventh Street and West Fifteenth Street in 1973, in order to accommodate homeless girls. He acquired additional tenements for boys on East Sixth Street in 1973 and East Seventh Street in 1974.[4] Ritter also expanded his geographical scope beyond Manhattan and expressed some interest in placing inner city children in more suburban locales. He opened a group home on Wheeler Avenue in Staten Island in 1973, carefully designed "to give our most stable boys, for the first time, community-based care in a family-style

setting, in a fine residential neighborhood." The founder even briefly conducted an unsuccessful experiment at a Franciscan retreat house in Middleburgh, New York, between the fall of 1972 and the winter of 1973, hoping to
remove children from disruptive urban influences and introduce them to
country living.[5]

Despite this impressive flurry of activity, growth did not occur in a
purely linear manner, and structural change produced considerable debate
and disagreement among supporters and staff members. Covenant House's
initial annual report, issued in September of 1973 in order to acknowledge
"the first year of our *formal* corporate existence," illustrated well the conflicted nature of the organization. Surprisingly, considering the founder's
anti-institutional rhetoric, the annual report concluded that Covenant House's
"transition from a small, highly personal effort of friends to, in the best
sense, a bureaucracy, is absolutely crucial." The first annual report remains
a very ambiguous document, celebrating the informal nature of the ministry yet calling for more rules and increased structure. The tension appears
more understandable upon considering the life and career of its principal
author. Hugh O'Neill, the former Manhattan College student whose verbal
challenge during Ritter's 1966 dialogue sermon supposedly prompted the
founder to establish his inner city apostolate, wrote the annual report.
O'Neill's very presence within Covenant House testified both to its communitarian roots and to its growing sense of bureaucratic professionalism.
He provided an important symbolic link to the original vision and to the
socially committed Catholic college students throughout New York City
who had attended Novocor retreats and who sought to live out their faith
commitments by participating in urban ministries. After graduating from
Manhattan College in 1968, O'Neill entered a doctoral program in political
science at Columbia University in the hopes of pursuing an academic
career. As noted previously, his initial involvement with Covenant House
fulfilled a community service requirement, occasioned by his refusal to reg-
ister for the military draft during the Vietnam War. He appeared representative of the alternative and countercultural forces that contributed to the
organization's establishment.[6]

O' Neill's personal history, however, also pointed toward some important transformative influences within the agency. As a married graduate
student living in the Bronx, he elected not to move into one of the renovated tenement apartments on East Seventh Street, where he would live in
community with other members. O'Neill instead maintained his uptown
residence, thereby drawing some boundaries between his personal life and

his Covenant House commitments. He also joined the organization during a period of administrative expansion. Between June of 1973 and October of 1973, when the board of directors formally appointed O'Neill to the newly created position of assistant director for operations, Covenant House added the following staff positions: one accountant, one education specialist, a second full-time counselor, a second full-time social worker, one physician, one nurse, four practicum students from New York University's counseling department, and one legal intern from the New York University Law School. The organization sought to hire people with solid academic credentials and specific skills that related to child care work. The board of directors hinted at the implications in December of 1973, observing that the boys' group home on East Sixth Street had experienced a rapid personnel turnover: "The hiring of staff members to fill these vacancies marks a new stage in Covenant House personnel policies, in that it is now hiring people through newspaper advertisements, and checking references." As the organization grew larger and more complex, older and less formal mechanisms gave way to newer methods of doing business.[7]

Ritter relied heavily on O'Neill to coordinate Covenant House's transition from informal ministry to structured institution. The founder clearly valued this personal connection with a trusted former student, but he also exhibited great confidence in the young man's administrative abilities and professional accomplishments. Ritter understood that the agency needed an individual who could prepare effective grant proposals and negotiate his way through New York's labyrinthine system of group home regulations and certification requirements. O'Neill filled that requirement. Ritter also hoped that the Columbia graduate student might shepherd the organization through its early institutional phase. O'Neill, for his part, viewed Covenant House as a temporary stop on a career path that might include either a professorial position or some form of public service. Indeed, he left Covenant House somewhat abruptly in 1974 to work as a political organizer for Hugh Carey's successful New York gubernatorial campaign. O'Neill continued to maintain occasional contact with Ritter, and actually helped Covenant House to finalize an important real estate transaction with the State of New York in 1979, but his direct involvement with the ministry ended when he accepted the position with the Carey campaign. He personified the new breed of administrator that Ritter needed to attract and retain if the founder hoped to expand his program.[8]

O'Neill's annual report, written of course with the complete approval of Ritter, reflected this broader administrative perspective and emphasized

several themes that captured the culture of Covenant House during this
fluid period in its early history. Most critically, the report identified "the
increased professionalization of our efforts" as the key component necessary
to ensure "the betterment of our existing fine program." O'Neill presented
the professionalization process as an inevitable, though admittedly controversial, companion of programmatic expansion. A defining moment for the
agency occurred in July of 1972, when Ritter and four key staff members
traveled to bucolic Raquette Lake in Hamilton County, New York, for a
combination vacation, retreat, and planning exercise. O'Neill forthrightly
reported that a "stormy, conflict-filled meeting" resulted. Covenant House's
leadership team carefully considered the extraordinary increase in homeless
youths whom they had served during the first six months of 1972, the
special services that these troubled adolescents required, and the inadequate
financial base that had heretofore hindered institutional operations. The
Raquette Lake attendees concluded that only two realistic options existed:
"to close down Covenant House—or to expand and professionalize our
efforts." They selected the latter course, but this produced considerable
grumbling and dissent. Some ministry supporters remained committed to a
more wide-ranging and less formal approach to neighborhood problems.
After the July meeting, however, debate largely ended and the basic philosophical decision appeared in place. Covenant House would work toward
becoming a more specialized organization that focused on youth homelessness and would recruit a trained staff with particular expertise in child care.
Ritter and his close associates clearly viewed this tighter focus as a positive
accomplishment.[9]

Staffing remained the key problem in advancing the professionalization process. The 1973 annual report recalled that Covenant House had
begun as "a small group of friends, rarely more than six, informally caring
for homeless kids because this was important and needed doing." By the fall
of 1972, it had evolved into a full-fledged "institution, a child-care agency
with a staff of fifty . . . a much larger, more professionally organized group."
The nature of the ministry did change with this infusion of new staff and
new ideas, though not quite as radically as the annual report implied. Ritter
actually relied heavily on his own social network of ex-Franciscans, former
students, and personal acquaintances in his efforts to professionalize the
agency. Steven Torkelson, for example, had known Ritter as a colleague
since the mid-1960s, when the two Franciscans summered at St. Anthony's-
on-Hudson in Rensselaer, New York. By 1971, Torkelson had left the order,
earned an M.A. in educational psychology from New York University, and

was living in an apartment in Greenwich Village. Ritter could not convince Torkelson to join the Covenant I community, but he did hire the ex-Franciscan as the organization's first paid counselor. Paul Frazier proved instrumental in recruiting another key staff member, David Cullen, based on his Manhattan College connections. Cullen had been a student of Ritter at Manhattan in the mid-1960s. After graduating from the college, he served a tour of duty in Vietnam and learned the basics of financial management by working in the banking industry. Cullen had enrolled in a few theology courses at Manhattan College in 1971, where he met Frazier, who had been living in one of the tenements on East Seventh Street. Cullen visited Frazier, and Ritter quickly talked his former student into joining the community. Once Cullen moved to the East Village, and it became evident that he possessed a thorough understanding of financial matters, the board of directors appointed him assistant director for finance and treasurer of Covenant House. Often, the process of professionalization occurred in just such a personal and seemingly idiosyncratic fashion.[10]

Similarly, Ritter carefully selected old friends and close associates to serve on Covenant House's first board of directors. He cemented his connection with the institutional church by including the provincial of the Conventual Franciscans, the superior general of the Franciscan Sisters of Syracuse, and a representative from Catholic Charities of the Archdiocese of New York on this thirteen-member governing body. Former colleagues and acquaintances from the founder's days in academia, many of whom had now gravitated toward professional careers in the child care and social work professions, played equally important roles on the original board. Adrian Gately had by this time resigned his position as a professor of electrical engineering at Manhattan College and was serving an internship in pediatrics. He had married Patricia Kennedy, who still lived on East Seventh Street and had begun working on her graduate degree in psychology from Fordham University. Mary Hanrahan, who first encountered Ritter through her participation in Novocor retreats while she earned her B.A. at St. Joseph's College in Brooklyn, had just begun a distinguished career in social work by securing a position at the Riker's Island correctional facility. Ritter appointed Gately, Kennedy, and Hanrahan as directors, thus blending personal contacts with professional expertise.[11]

Ritter also began expanding his network during the early 1970s in an effort to satisfy various institutional needs. Some seemingly temporary contacts turned into long-standing relationships. Edmund J. Burns, a young New York attorney, prepared Covenant House's incorporation papers in

1972 as one of several pro bono projects that he volunteered to undertake for various nonprofit and philanthropic organizations around this time. Burns found Ritter's enthusiasm infectious, grew increasingly enamored of the ministry, and served as corporation counsel from 1972 until 1990. Other influential supporters emerged from the neighborhood itself. David Z. Orlow resided on East Seventh Street while also working for the Ziff-Davis communications conglomerate. Associates viewed Orlow and his wife, Nancy, as memorable examples of the alternative countercultural types who gave the agency much of its experimental quality: "real, real hippie wild people," in the words of one Covenant House board member. Orlow's solid corporate connections, however, also propelled the organization in more conventional directions. He introduced Ritter to such colleagues and acquaintances as Selwyn I. (Si) Taubman, the chief financial officer at Ziff-Davis. Taubman became a Covenant House director in 1972, serving as one of its only non-Catholic members, and he remained a major presence on the board until the late 1980s. Orlow further placed Ritter in contact with the accountant who conducted the agency's first outside audit as well as several donors who became known to community members as "the money people" because of their financial generosity toward the ministry. Gradually, and somewhat more intentionally during the early 1970s, the institutional orbit widened to encompass a range of interests and personalities far beyond the original corps of committed volunteers.[12]

These board additions and staffing shifts redefined Ritter's role within the ministry. Once again, O'Neill's 1973 report shrewdly articulated the change: "The Executive Director will be able to devote a significant and increased portion of his time and attention to an organized fund-raising effort—a task he has up to now, performed at best in a desultory way." Ritter found himself constantly scrambling for financial resources during Covenant House's formative years, but his efforts often seemed haphazard. The early ministry really survived because of the dedication and monetary contributions of community members as well as the resourcefulness of Covenant House administrators. Staff members assumed a variety of part-time jobs that ranged from selling speed-reading programs to Catholic schools to driving taxis during their off hours in order to make ends meet. The Franciscans provided institutional support in the form of volunteers, apartment furnishings, used automobiles, and occasional emergency appropriations. In October of 1971, for example, when Ritter experienced some difficulty in meeting his immediate obligations, the provincial governing board voted unanimously to assist him "in the payment of rent and utilities for the next six months at a rate of $600 per month." Generally, however, the Franciscans maintained a bit of distance from Ritter's operations. Insurance considerations, legal liability issues, the substandard quality of Covenant House's tenement apartments on East Seventh Street, and the controversial nature of the experimental ministry within the order all dictated a cautious approach by Franciscan authorities.[13]

Covenant House's financial practices remained fluid in the early 1970s, and early administrators still marvel at the informality, chaos, and hand-to-mouth quality of the operation. David Cullen, whose formal title of assistant director and treasurer suggested more authority and structure than he actually possessed, accurately captured the random nature of the operation in 1972: "I started keeping books and, I don't know, it seems like it was probably a waste of time 'cause nobody really cared. But maybe we needed some figures in there to start with something." The "corporate office" at 504 LaGuardia Place really existed in a cramped and renovated rental storefront next door to a Greenwich Village Italian bakery. It served multiple functions as administrative office space for four staffers, an intake center for homeless youths, and an occasional sleeping quarters for Covenant House administrators. David Gregorio recalled the character of early staff meetings at LaGuardia Place: "I was outside running a crash pad from the other side of these walls that we built. So they [Ritter, Torkelson, and Dave Cullen] would be in there trying to conduct business. I'd be outside screaming at the kids, you know. And they used to say, 'Oh could you keep it down in there.'" Roles remained flexible, structures appeared malleable, and budgetary constraints carried little weight in formulating programs or considering expansion.[14]

Still, it seems possible to overstate the informality and the unplanned aspects of the ministry. By 1972, as Ritter focused more exclusively on homeless youths and discerned the breadth of this particular social problem, he also began to appreciate the need for more reliable sources of income in order to fuel programmatic expansion. Initially, he blended several traditional fund-raising mechanisms with a few innovative strategies. Ritter relied on voluntary contributions and personal sacrifices among community members, but he also kept his eyes open for new opportunities and more diversified revenue streams. Intuitively, the founder understood that the very nature of philanthropic fund-raising appeared to be moving in new directions during the early 1970s. Convinced that his organization carried out a worthy mission and addressed a unique problem, he sought out new public and private partnerships that might allow him to better serve an expanding client population. Aggressive fund-raising practices often introduce troublesome issues into modest-sized ministries. Available revenues can easily dictate programmatic shifts, causing an institution to veer in unanticipated directions. New constituencies emerge within an organization as donors, foundation officials, and public administrators begin to feel some ownership over a grant recipient's internal affairs. Power relationships change, internal dynamics grow more complex, and committed supporters may feel marginalized. Perhaps Ritter did not foresee these difficulties as he considered the future of his venture in the early 1970s. He certainly insisted in future years that all of his thoughts and energies centered on "my kids." Undeniably, though, the founder began to build an independent financial base in the early 1970s that both placed new demands on his ministry and created new opportunities for innovative programming. Several related fund-raising strategies helped him to accomplish this, and all appeared in evidence by 1972: preaching on weekends, developing a direct mail program, cultivating wealthy donors and private foundations, and aggressively pursuing public funding.

Weekend preaching assignments offered Ritter very reliable and conventional, yet extremely important, fund-raising opportunities. Franciscan colleagues throughout New Jersey and upstate New York began inviting Ritter to their parishes to discuss his inner city ministry during the early 1970s. Many friars supported his experimental efforts generally, and they also knew that his dynamic personal style would energize their Sunday services. Ritter seized upon such chances to expand Covenant House's limited financial base and to present the runaway issue to a much broader audience while simultaneously reaffirming the ministry's Catholic roots. He spoke often at between six and eight Masses on weekends, always distributing and collecting contribution envelopes. Ritter's piercing blue eyes, his spellbinding oratory, and his talent for turning ordinary stories into meaningful parables generated great enthusiasm among his comfortable middle-class audiences. The Franciscan network also included several well-placed churches that proved instrumental in supporting the ministry. Ritter found especially large crowds and receptive summer audiences at St. Peter's in Point Pleasant and St. Catherine of Siena in Seaside Park, both located along the New Jersey shore. Summer vacationers from throughout Delaware, Pennsylvania, and upstate New York, as well as daytrippers from northern New Jersey, frequented these seaside communities. They heard Ritter speak and returned to their hometowns and local parishes with stories of a dynamic, working-class priest who labored among runaway youths in New York City. Covenant House's story thus spread informally throughout the middle-Atlantic states, and the ministry achieved great visibility and recognition within suburban Catholic circles.[15]

Parish envelopes might net between five hundred dollars and four thousand dollars on a prime summer weekend, but Ritter shrewdly used his preaching assignments to map out a broader fund-raising strategy as well. He carefully accumulated the names and addresses of church contributors from his weekend assignments, arranging them alphabetically and storing them in shoeboxes at his LaGuardia Place office. Kathy Wallace, Ritter's niece and a community member who had also worked as an administrator at the Ford Foundation, purchased an IBM Mag Card machine and initiated the first attempts at automating the Covenant House operation. This IBM machine essentially served as an early form of a memory typewriter, based on a system of punch cards. It allowed Covenant House to create form letter appeals as well as to customize donor acknowledgments. Each contributor rapidly received a personally signed response from Ritter, thereby cementing a connection with the ministry and creating the comforting illusion of intimacy with the founder. The organization thus created a virtual community of supporters and interested observers that slowly extended across an expanding geographical area. During 1971 and 1972, Ritter contacted these donors only infrequently and somewhat irregularly. As the ministry evolved, however, his approach changed.[16]

Ritter wrote his first appeal letter to donors in May of 1972, and direct mail soon became an important component of Covenant House's administrative program. By the 1973–74 fiscal year, the organization had developed a mailing list of 3,400 prospects and projected an annual income of sixty thousand dollars from these primarily small donors. Mail contributions composed roughly 15 percent of the agency's annual revenues, providing its largest single source of private funding.[17] And the value of these systematic solicitations far exceeded the immediate financial returns. Monthly mailings served as Covenant House's principal point of contact with the general public during a period when the organization remained virtually invisible to mass media outlets. Direct mail allowed Ritter to reach beyond his immediate East Village surroundings and cultivate a completely new constituency for his efforts. It also provided an opportunity for the founder to shape and codify the Covenant House story, construct an orthodox institutional history, and coherently articulate his ministry's purpose in a straightforward manner. The appeal letters apparently satisfied an important personal impulse as well. Writing in the late 1980s, Ritter observed that "if you think it at all important for you to know who I am, read these newsletters. Who and what I am, for better or worse, is smeared all over these pages." A closer look at their content during the early 1970s provides some insight into what the founder chose to reveal concerning his philanthropic efforts.[18]

A thematic consistency unites the appeals written between 1972 and 1975. These early solicitations typically portrayed Covenant House's clients in stark and unsparing terms: "My kids are afflicted by unclean spirits, my kids have dirty hearts. Many are cruel and vengeful, selfish and carnal. Some of my kids lie and cheat and steal at times, and there is little truth in them at times. They exploit and are cynical, lazy, and dishonorable at times. They don't bathe often enough either, and their feet stink." Individual adolescents emerge as morally flawed, psychologically unstable, physically unattractive, and deeply disturbed. Hector "was sixteen, gone on bad trips, a jumper-out-of-windows, illiterate, and a moron, maybe." Ralphie "lived here, betrayed and robbed us, is dying of glue and aloneness, has no morals." Paul "stole everything and anything—a turnip the cook was going to serve for dinner, wallets and radios and money, your socks and keys." These children tested the limits of Christian love, responded to kindness with suspicion and cynicism, and lived in a dark and tawdry netherworld that appeared virtually incomprehensible to stable, churchgoing families.[19]

Ritter purposefully contrasted the life stories of the homeless urban youths served by his agency with the comfortable, orderly, and sentimental vision of childhood that predominated among his suburban Catholic donor base. He recalled preaching on a summer Sunday in Seaside Park, giving out Communion "to all the beautiful children with their sunburned noses and freckles and their clear eyes and squeaky-clean faces." Covenant House's troubled adolescents appeared so disconnected from this happy, contented, and family-oriented seashore culture that they required a special vocabulary in order to describe them. Ritter rejected the term runaway since "they're not the young, poignant, attractive, sympathy-inducing, nice runaway children that everybody likes to help." Rather, he preferred to view them as "urban nomads," reflecting their more diffuse origins, complex life experiences, and mixed motivations. Most had fled from abusive, broken, and poverty-stricken family situations. They drifted aimlessly through a depressing institutional culture of child care agencies, foster homes, and municipal shelters. Eventually, they turned to the street, "left stranded, high and dry, on the concrete reefs of the city when their shipwrecked families founder and go under." Covenant House offered these children unconditional love, food, a place to stay, and an opportunity to salvage their situation. It remained a simple, clear-cut, and noncontroversial ministry that met primary needs, serving a population that seemed almost invisible and completely alien to most middle-class Americans.[20]

Ritter's appeal letters generally avoided happy endings, highlighted only modest successes, often acknowledged fundamental failure, and stressed the need for Christians to contribute to the cause out of pure love rather than "guilty gratitude." The story of "Dave," modeled after an actual occurrence on East Seventh Street, illustrates the typical pattern. Covenant House personnel found him "wandering aimlessly, dazed, in a drenching rain" in the East Village during the fall of 1972. Ritter described him as "eighteen, very sick, and very, very, very sad." Dave stayed in the East Seventh Street tenement for a few days, "silent, totally alone," before wandering away again. He drifted in and out of Covenant House over a period of several weeks, occasionally grabbing a free meal or a night's lodging. Dave remained enigmatic, resisted suggestions to take up regular residence, and pursued a lonely existence. His movements appeared impulsive, irrational, and unpredictable. Ultimately, he shocked the staff and the residents by leaping out of a window on the fifth floor of the tenement. A parked car broke his fall, he managed to survive with relatively minor injuries, and he was recuperating at the Bellevue psychiatric hospital as Ritter concluded his appeal: "He should have died, but he didn't. We don't know yet if Dave will return to us after his release from the hospital. I rather suppose he will. We hope he does." No guarantees. No closure. No heartwarming accounts of modified behavior. Ritter introduced readers to a world of perpetual instability, daily struggle, modest accomplishment, and incremental change at best. Transformed lives remained the exception rather than the norm. Success meant one hot meal, one night off the streets, and perhaps a brief moment of eye contact. This message connected well with a Catholic cultural sensibility that viewed instantaneous conversions with suspicion, freely acknowledged the harsh realities of daily existence, and accepted the ongoing struggle with sin as an inevitable element of the human condition. Only a gospel of unconditional love, a concept inherent in the Franciscan tradition and central to Ritter's spiritual vision for Covenant House, applied in such seemingly hopeless situations.[21]

Ritter also carefully used these appeal letters to place his unique stamp on the ministry and to craft his own complex public personality in the process. Although the early newsletters often used the plural "we" when discussing Covenant House, only one clearly defined and recognizable figure emerged from the myriad anecdotes and stories: that of Bruce Ritter. The founder presented himself as involved with every aspect of Covenant

House: he grilled burgers and stirred vegetables on the stove at the La-Guardia Place "crash pad," he found part-time jobs for unruly kids at a Nathan's hot dog stand, he argued with troublemakers and never backed down from a fight. Ritter screened new arrivals, familiarized himself with their life stories, established a personal rapport, conducted weekly house meetings, broke through formidable psychological barriers, and participated in all significant diagnostic discussions. He dominated staff meetings, established institutional policies, and argued with professional social workers, always trusting his own instincts and his sense of Scripture. The man and the ministry completely merged. Donors would find it impossible to imagine one without the other.

An appealing and formidable image of the founder emerged through these early newsletters that would shape public perceptions of Covenant House for many years thereafter: that of the streetwise friar. Hip to the ways of the world and following the way of the cross, Ritter projected an earthy and reality-based spirituality that eschewed pious absolutes and embraced direct action. His readers entered an intensely masculine universe, which the founder communicated in short sentences, staccato prose, and street slang. When a fifteen-year-old threw "a nicotine fit on my floor," Ritter decided to "preserve his sanity and mine by staking him to a pack of Kools." He carefully articulated the covenant philosophy to another "gaggle of blighted, tough-as-nails kids" and "scowled menacingly as I said it." Ritter recounted physical confrontations with several youths, bragged about his 140-pound snarling German shepherd, and frequently characterized his religious philosophy as "muscular Christianity." Newsletter recipients learned about daily life in the East Village underworld: the street scams, the drug scene, the social climate, the seasonal rhythms, and the petty crime. For many Catholics who had participated in the massive postwar movement to middle-class life in suburbia, Ritter's literature offered a vicarious glimpse into once-familiar back streets, alleys, and dead ends that they now encountered only through the media. Many readers responded generously with their checkbooks, and direct mail thus became an important and reliable source of institutional revenue.[22]

Ritter's cultivation of small donors through his monthly mailings did not preclude other fund-raising initiatives. Rapid expansion often meant intense pressure to raise large sums of money in short periods of time. Buildings required extensive renovations in order to meet state group home standards, balloon payments came due on mortgages, and a professional team of nurses, psychologists, and social workers could not survive on

Covenant House's traditional fifty-dollar-per-week stipend. By late 1973, the ministry's financial report showed a fifteen-thousand-dollar operating deficit, and administrators recalled many instances of deferred payments and unhappy creditors.[23] Increasingly and intentionally, Ritter broadened his social network in the early 1970s to include wealthy individual philanthropists and foundation board members. Financial connections often occurred accidentally or, as Ritter might explain them, through the mysterious workings of divine providence. Justine Wise Polier, for example, served as an appointed judge in the New York State Family Court of the City of New York and remained one of the nation's foremost authorities concerning child welfare in the early 1970s. She expressed great admiration for Covenant House's open intake policy and for its willingness to address the needs of older adolescents who fell outside of the child welfare system. Polier often referred youths to Covenant House's care in her judicial capacity. She also served on the board of directors of the Field Foundation in New York, and she shepherded an important five-thousand-dollar grant through this philanthropic agency to Covenant House at a particularly critical moment in the fledgling ministry's history.[24]

Other chance acquaintances produced even longer-lasting dividends. David Gregorio, who served as Covenant House's director of intake during the early 1970s, recalled one such incident that occurred in January of 1974. The agency appeared on the verge of losing its lease on the West Eleventh Street girls' group home, owing to a fifty-thousand-dollar revenue shortfall. A fellow Vincentian priest had casually introduced Gregorio over dinner to Mary B. Mahoney, a vice president of Chase Manhattan Bank who had graduated from Marymount College in Manhattan and who appeared charitably inclined toward Catholic social causes. Gregorio arranged a meeting between Mahoney and Ritter, and the founder aggressively pursued the connection. Within days, Mahoney secured a fifty-thousand-dollar loan from Chase Manhattan Bank that allowed Covenant House to exercise its option to purchase the group home and even place a healthy down payment on the West Eleventh Street property. Mahoney also presented the issue of youth homelessness to "a group of concerned graduates of Marymount College" who proved to be loyal long-term supporters. And she placed Ritter in contact with other influential colleagues at Chase. These senior administrators agreed to refinance Testamentum's property in a manner advantageous to Covenant House, explored the feasibility of linking the agency with the United Fund, and worked on coordinating a major capital campaign for the organization. Not all of the bankers' plans achieved fruition, but the connection introduced a new complexity and sophistication to Covenant House's financial planning. Chase executives continued to play a prominent advisory role to the agency, occupying seats on the board of directors through the 1990s.[25]

The prestigious Madison Avenue advertising agency of Young and Rubicam also emerged as an important corporate supporter during the early 1970s. Ritter initially approached this firm through the influence of his Ziff-Davis connections, and the advertising executives proved particularly receptive to his appeals. Edward Ney, the president of Young and Rubicam, took a deep personal interest in the ministry. He guaranteed a fifty-thousand-dollar line of credit for the agency through Citicorp Venture Capital, publicized Ritter's ministry through his corporate communications network, and agreed to work with Chase Manhattan Bank on the proposed capital campaign. Covenant House was one of only three nonprofit philanthropies that received a major grant from Young and Rubicam's community service branch in 1973, and the connection grew even closer thereafter. The firm provided considerable assistance to Covenant House over the course of the next two decades in developing media strategies, preparing public service announcements, and orchestrating advertising campaigns. Beginning in 1978, a Young and Rubicam vice president occupied a seat on the Covenant House board of directors. Informal corporate contacts quickly solidified into long-term partnerships that helped to transform the scale and scope of the agency.[26]

Corporate philanthropy and wealthy donors offered great potential to fuel future growth and guarantee long-range structural stability. Public funding, however, largely shaped the agency's initial programs. During the 1972–73 fiscal year, Covenant House relied on city and state grants for fully 73 percent of its $431,000 in revenues. Despite Ritter's subsequent antistatist rhetoric, the organization owed much of its early viability to a public-private partnership and to the founder's entrepreneurial aggressiveness in obtaining municipal money. Public funding, more than any other single variable, forced Covenant House to formalize its structure, to hire professional staff, and to upgrade its physical facilities. Bureaucratic regulation surely imposed some inconvenient rules and regulations on the agency, yet by all accounts Covenant House still managed to maintain its autonomy, creativity, and experimental nature. Government money provided the organization with a new legitimacy, increased its visibility within child welfare circles, and pushed the administrative staff to create a permanent institutional infrastructure. Eventually, Covenant House would shift its revenue base toward the private sector, and Ritter would emerge as an important national spokesperson for private philanthropic enterprise. In the beginning, however, Covenant House owed its very existence to public financing.[27]

Ritter's initial partnership with the public sector appeared to be a questionable fit. During 1972, he contacted the Addiction Services Agency (ASA), a municipal body that had been established in 1967 with a mayoral mandate to oversee all antidrug efforts in New York City. During the late 1960s, the ASA operated several methadone clinics, youth centers, and drug prevention and treatment programs, including the well-known Phoenix House. The ASA had moved gradually away from administering its own programs by the early 1970s, however, and had become primarily a grant-giving agency that funded a variety of nonprofit ventures very loosely grouped around the themes of drug prevention and substance abuse rehabilitation. Ritter convinced ASA administrators that his program met their eligibility criteria for funding, owing primarily to the fact that Covenant House dealt with "at-risk" adolescents and young adults who fell into regular patterns of drug dependency. The ASA, which favored experimental programs and interpreted its mandate very broadly, awarded Covenant House two hundred thousand dollars in 1972 in order to expand its efforts and continue its work, thereby immediately increasing the fledgling ministry's revenues by over 500 percent.[28]

Ritter possessed neither the wherewithal nor the support structure necessary to administer this money, so he quickly moved to create both an organization and a program. He incorporated the agency in November of 1972 and held his first formal board meeting on 7 December with his enthusiastic assemblage of old friends and more recent acquaintances. The founder's introductory remarks to the board on this occasion reflected some of the tensions inherent in the organization's more formal stature. During this initial meeting, Ritter expressed his desire to remain "on the frontier of the problem areas in child care where legal and social perimeters are not clearly defined," and he dedicated the agency "to the needs of the totally abandoned and rejected children of society." Though he recognized the need for institutional development, Ritter drew a distinction between "the needs of the children who seek Covenant House's care" and the "nebulous administrative and legal considerations that underlie and govern that care." He acknowledged the necessity for rules, regulations, and standards but insisted that the "basic human commitment become paramount." The notion of "covenant," which previously had been used by the founder in order to explain the community members' commitments to each other, now came to describe "the relationship of Covenant House to its children . . . one that involves a formal and articulated recognition of their needs, the promise of loyalty and trust on Covenant House's part to them and on their part to Covenant House." Public funding had produced a new corporate structure and prompted a redefinition of institutional purpose.[29]

Covenant House walked a fine line between fulfilling its original mission and satisfying the needs of its various funding agencies. In April of 1973, after the organization had been licensed by the New York State Department of Social Services, and after its properties on Staten Island and West Eleventh Street had been certified as group homes, Covenant House began to receive significant financial support from the New York City Bureau of Child Welfare (BCW). This money, which amounted to $120,000 between April and September of 1973, allowed the agency to hire additional professional staff and made possible the opening of two more group homes on West Fifteenth Street and East Sixth Street.[30] The new infusion of cash did not arrive without cost, however. Ritter had established the principle of open intake, whereby every child who walked into a Covenant House facility would receive shelter and a full range of services with no questions asked, as a nonnegotiable institutional policy. BCW funding threatened to alter this mandate. David Gregorio recalled some of the implications: "Right away what that meant was we couldn't take anybody that walked in the door. It had to be a referral from the Bureau of Child Welfare . . . so we kept apartments where we could send these kids [who had not been referred by the BCW]. . . . We got more and more group homes and it became more and more difficult to maintain open intake. We still did it in principle, but . . . the question always came up, is this kid eligible for BCW? And that became, started to become, a criterion for whether or not we could accept the kid." Covenant House quickly learned that contributions rarely arrived without altering the program in some manner.[31]

Distinctions developed between Covenant House's various group homes, based largely on funding considerations. The tenement apartments at 274 East Seventh Street, for example, could never receive state licensing owing to their inherent structural deficiencies and to the landlord's ongoing refusal to undertake renovations that would place the property in conformance with building codes. Ritter thus could not house any BCW referrals at this location. He could, however, apply money from the Addiction Services Agency grant to 274 East Seventh Street since this stipend carried fewer restrictions and allowed greater experimentation. The tenement soon took on a unique character. Ritter alternately characterized it as a "tiger's cage" or a "lion's den," appropriate for "severely damaged boys who need an environment in which greater acting out can be tolerated." He considered this facility "the heart of the program both spiritually and in terms of how Covenant House operates" since it catered to the toughest children, reached an older population of troubled adolescents who remained outside of the child care agency network, and adhered most rigorously to his open intake philosophy. As time passed and the importance of BCW funding increased, however, 274 East Seventh Street functioned as something of an anomaly within Covenant House. The agency concentrated its resources primarily on developing stronger programs at the more stable and state-approved group homes. By September of 1974, Ritter accepted the inevitable and closed 274 East Seventh Street, placing all eligible residents in the licensed facilities.[32]

Programs remained rudimentary at all group homes during the first few years. Residences housed between eight and fifteen children at any given time, with most routinely exceeding their stated capacities. Covenant House staffers devoted most of their efforts simply to stabilizing the children, many of whom had spent time previously in various state institutions. Residents could stay in the apartments as long as they agreed to abide by the basic house rules: no violence, no drugs, and mutual respect. Violations meant immediate ejection. Counselors occasionally reconnected runaways with their families, but this rarely proved viable owing to case histories involving parental abuse and mutual estrangement. Group home administrators primarily addressed immediate problems and crises. They referred children to free medical clinics and cooperative local hospitals, which treated the youths for problems ranging from head lice to substance addictions to sexually transmitted diseases. Staff made every effort to place youngsters back in school, and some remedial tutoring took place within the homes. Counselors helped children to accomplish such seemingly mundane yet formidable bureaucratic tasks as obtaining working papers. Daily structure and routine took on enormous importance. House parents expected their charges to maintain regular schedules, make their beds, clean their rooms, prepare occasional meals, and assist with household chores. All residents observed daily curfews, and staff sought to rigorously monitor any contact with former friends, street acquaintances, and local gang members. Children received careful attention and tight supervision, as each group home operated with five full-time employees and one cook. The close quarters often produced conflict and disagreement between counselors and clients. Arguments and negotiations occurred on a daily basis at all homes, but some operations proved particularly volatile. Physical confrontations and fistfights often erupted in the more rough-and-tumble tenements on East Sixth

Street and East Seventh Street. Other programs gradually assumed different characteristics, based on their unique geographical locations, staffing patterns, and resident personalities.[33]

The West Eleventh Street girls' group home offered a case in point. In this instance, the founder initially appeared reluctant to proceed. Patricia Kennedy recalled that she and fellow board member Mary Hanrahan had lobbied Ritter heavily for years "that really, to be a full-service [agency] you would have to have a house for girls. And he didn't want to do it in the worst way. He did not want to deal with the birth control, abortion issue. He did not want to deal with it." Ritter's public rhetoric and fund-raising appeals focused almost exclusively on male runaways during the early 1970s, and he rarely addressed issues relating to homeless girls. Eventually, however, the founder acknowledged the force of Kennedy's arguments and bowed to the wishes of the board. He recognized that group homes for girls would enhance Covenant House's stature and credibility as well as meet a real social need. Still, he moved cautiously, and his approach attracted some internal criticism. Ritter elected to forge a partnership with the Sisters of the Third Franciscan Order Minor Conventuals in Syracuse. Mother Viola Kiernan, who served as the superior general of the Franciscan Sisters from 1965 through 1977, had first encountered Ritter in 1972 following one of his weekend preaching engagements in Syracuse. The founder had discovered Mother Viola's misplaced wallet in a church pew, returned it to her personally, and took the opportunity to promote the Covenant House cause. She found the project intriguing and offered him the chance to address an upcoming sisters' chapter meeting concerning his work.[34]

Covenant House seemed a surprising ministerial departure for the Franciscan Sisters of Syracuse. The community traditionally focused on educational and health care ministries, with most of the order's institutions concentrated in upstate New York, New Jersey, and Hawaii. Further, Mother Viola had adopted a very conservative stance toward the reforms associated with Vatican II, often finding herself in opposition to her more liberal local bishop, David Cunningham of Syracuse. She attended the initial meeting of the Consortium Perfectae Caritatis, which had been supported by some religious communities as a conservative alternative to the National Assembly of Women Religious, and she resisted the calls for renewal that emanated from more progressive Catholic circles. The Franciscan Sisters, during Mother Viola's administration, did not embrace the movements toward more individualized social apostolates, secular dress, and procedural reform that characterized other religious communities during the period.

Considerable internal discord resulted, and several sisters left the Franciscans in the late 1960s, apparently in response to the order's conservatism.[35] Mother Viola may have viewed participation in the Covenant House ministry as a belated effort to address the social implications of Vatican II and to offer the sisters an opportunity to participate in a meaningful yet reasonably mainstream social apostolate. In any event, Mother Viola's own observations at the time, which she articulated in a letter to Ritter, probably provide the best insight into her thinking: "Our Communities [Franciscan men and Franciscan women] have a long and beautiful history of cooperation and we feel that the type of work that you are doing is the answer to our prayer as to how we can become involved in the problem of the needy in a true Franciscan way."[36]

Ritter presented a moving and eloquent appeal concerning the need for girls' group homes in New York City to the Franciscan Sisters' chapter meeting in August of 1972. Several sisters volunteered to join the Covenant House apostolate, and the order worked closely with Ritter during the fall and winter of 1972 in order to transform these plans into reality. The founder located an attractive building at 40 West Eleventh Street, between Fifth and Sixth Avenues, to house the new facility. This stately nineteenth-century Greenwich Village townhouse contrasted markedly with the graffiti-scarred tenements that lined East Seventh Street, and Ritter considered it a more appropriate location for his reform efforts. Support from the Franciscan Sisters took several forms. Individual convents and order-affiliated hospitals throughout the Syracuse area donated furnishings and equipment. Mother Viola used her connections among upstate contractors and truck drivers to arrange for physical renovations to the structure and to coordinate equipment deliveries. A parish priest at St. Anthony's of Padua in Utica brought a group of middle school children from his local Franciscan parish to New York City in order to clean the townhouse and assist with the moving chores. Sisters cooked, cleaned, and even shopped for appliances at a Sears Roebuck department store in Union City, New Jersey, in order to avoid paying New York City's steeper sales taxes. In all of these ways, the opening of West Eleventh Street reflected the appealing blend of chance connections, entrepreneurial enthusiasm, community cooperation, and earthy pragmatism that characterized Covenant House's early years.[37]

The order also provided longer-term personnel and financial commitments. Sisters Kathryn Rush and Gretchen Gilroy arrived in New York in March of 1973 to staff the group home. Sister Gretchen eventually assumed a series of progressively more responsible administrative posts within

Covenant House until she left the organization in 1985. At least eighteen Franciscan Sisters carried out mission work at Covenant House between 1973 and 1985, and a much larger number than that volunteered their services for brief periods of time during the summer months and vacations. Some staffed West Eleventh Street, while others played key roles in administering the girls' group homes that Covenant House opened on West Fifteenth Street in 1973 and East Tenth Street in 1975. Several sisters worked at the agency's uptown location, when Covenant House inaugurated a facility near Times Square in 1977. The order also provided direct financial support for the ministry. Mother Viola committed $17,200 to Covenant House in 1973, thus making the Sisters of St. Francis of Syracuse the largest single private donor to the agency during that year. She introduced Ritter to Richard J. Schmeelk, a friend of the community and a general partner of Salomon Brothers. Schmeelk immediately contributed one thousand dollars to the cause and soon secured a larger donation from his investment banking firm. He remained close to the ministry in subsequent years, serving on Covenant House's board of directors from 1984 until 1991, and remaining as an honorary director thereafter. Ritter's connection with Mother Viola and her order had paid a variety of unanticipated and long-term dividends.[38]

Covenant House's supporters and staff members, however, did not unanimously welcome the Franciscan Sisters with enthusiasm. Both philosophical and practical considerations created some discord. Ritter had, after all, declared at his first board meeting that "Covenant House in its origin was and should remain non-sectarian," and he ostensibly rejected any formal affiliation with Catholic Charities of the Archdiocese of New York for that reason. His agreement with the Sisters of St. Francis sent a different message. Patricia Kennedy, who vigorously supported the need for girls' group homes, remembered that Ritter had provoked "the infuriation of Mary Hanrahan and [myself] by getting a group home for girls and making nuns run it. . . . We were saying 'My God, these boys have all these regular people but the girls have to have nuns.'" Kennedy, who participated in case consultations at the girls' homes, recalled that stressful situations often developed "because the girls rightly felt that the story in the boys' houses was very different. And they were being kept, you know, under lock and key with the nuns. And I couldn't deny that." Other lay staff expressed similar misgivings, and even some of the clergy members questioned Ritter's decision to place group homes under the supervision of the sisters. David Gregorio, who was still a member of the Vincentians at the time, recalled that "I used to argue with Bruce about [one of the sisters] all the time because they were not inner city nuns and they came down to New York City and they were thrown into the fray." Few Franciscan Sisters of Syracuse had formal training or practical experience in social work: most had labored as nurses or elementary school teachers. They typically hailed from small towns and had limited cultural contact with the largely minority population served by Covenant House. The sisters remained bound to support and advocate the Catholic Church's official teachings on abortion and birth control, maintained a chapel in the West Eleventh Street group home, and continued to wear modified habits in accordance with the order's conservative dress policies. Lay staff and administrators, many of whom maintained a critical distance from the institutional church during the early 1970s, felt a certain unease. Although most eventually reached some accommodation and grew to express considerable admiration for the Franciscan Sisters' work, many continued to struggle with Covenant House's relationship to formal Catholic Church structures.[39]

The arrival of the sisters coincided with a physical expansion throughout Greenwich Village, which produced other problems for Covenant House. By 1974, the girls' group homes had been established in the attractive townhouse on West Eleventh Street as well as in a stately structure on West Fifteenth Street that had been occupied most recently by the television personality Orson Bean. Covenant House's corporate offices and clinical services had moved from the storefront location on LaGuardia Place to the much more expensive and fashionable surroundings on West Twelfth Street. When Ritter occupied his ramshackle tenements in the East Village, he encountered little community opposition. Local residents generally viewed his efforts as a positive development that might serve to reclaim rundown apartments from drug dealers and squatters. Greenwich Villagers proved far less enthusiastic about the presence of group homes in their more upscale neighborhoods. Ritter typically concluded his real estate arrangements without fanfare, and local residents received no advance warning concerning their new neighbors. Block associations strenuously objected, and the Sisters of St. Francis spent considerable time and energy soothing residents' feelings. They attended local meetings, finessed myriad daily incidents involving clients and residents, and tirelessly participated in neighborhood cleanups and similar civic endeavors. Still, tensions persisted.[40]

Carol Greitzer, a Greenwich Village councilwoman, proved particularly perturbed at Covenant House's expansion. She objected especially to the location of administrative and clinical offices on West Twelfth Street, arguing that "too many institutions are moving into the West Village, thus spoiling its historical and residential value." Greitzer also possessed the requisite political muscle to make life uncomfortable for the young agency. She convinced the New York City controller's office to conduct a special audit of Covenant House's books, requested that the Board of Estimate lay over Covenant House's ASA contract in 1974 and thereby prevent the agency from receiving any increase in funding, and encouraged municipal authorities to investigate the Testamentum real estate holding company. Ritter and his board recognized that continued dependence on city funding would regularly subject their organization to these types of administrative pressures. The founder elected to cancel the Addiction Services Agency grant for the 1974–75 year, thereby effectively phasing out the residential program at 274 East Seventh Street. This decision did not mean that Covenant House eschewed all public funding. State money remained an integral component of Covenant House revenues, with the BCW reimbursements continuing to influence local programs. The agency even successfully pursued some federal grants, receiving seventy thousand dollars from the National Institute of Mental Health in 1974 in order to establish a program for urban nomads that contained a substantial aftercare component. Covenant House had learned a valuable new lesson, however, concerning municipal politics and the obligations that accompanied public funding. Ritter began to perceive that the financial well-being of his ministry might well lie in another direction.[41]

In some respects, Covenant House appeared solidly institutionalized by 1974. Growth in the early 1970s had provided a clear shape and direction for the ministry, which now concentrated on providing immediate shelter and care for homeless youths between the ages of thirteen and eighteen. Community organizations, city agencies, judges, police officers, and transit officials all regularly referred street children to Covenant House, which had begun to earn a solid local reputation for admitting troubled youths into its facilities immediately and with minimal bureaucratic hassle. The ministry appeared to have stabilized its finances, relying on a creative combination of public funding, foundation support, donations from wealthy individuals, and direct mail solicitations. A growing professional staff coalesced and administered day-to-day operations. Committed volunteers still played important roles. Ritter remained the key figure in the organization. His own responsibilities had altered appreciably, however, as he concentrated much more on fund-raising and general administration and had less daily contact with clients and community residents.

This seeming stability proved illusory. Major questions concerning the ultimate shape of the ministry remained to be answered. Covenant House had not yet defined a clear relationship with the institutional church, and conflicting visions within the movement persisted. Professional administrators did not always blend well with community members who felt that they had imbibed the essential charisma of the organization. Available funding clearly propelled the program in some directions, but the agency also retained a certain flexibility and an experimental edge. Ritter himself remained vague and a bit remote concerning his personal vision for the ministry. David Gregorio best captured the situation that prevailed in 1975: "The more we needed to become professionalized, the more we needed to start looking at guidelines and regulations and providing clinical services and stuff like that, the more the original group of people became disenchanted . . . a lot of people who felt [that] we operated well by flying it from the seat of our pants, when they started facing . . . paper work, and regulations, and all that, [they] just really got turned off by it. And—as frequently happens in charismatic movements—they left in anger." Gregorio himself left both Covenant House and the Vincentians in 1976, moving to Massachusetts in order to pursue a career in carpentry and construction. He returned to Covenant House in 1988, but by that time things had changed appreciably. The ideology of open intake remained in place, and a basic philosophical continuity did link past and present. Structurally, however, the agency in 1988 seemed barely recognizable to anyone familiar with its operations in the early 1970s. Beginning in the mid-1970s, Covenant House veered in several unanticipated directions, dwarfing the innovations and changes that defined its early history. The resulting ferment left a fundamentally different organization in its wake.[42]

Figure 4. Bruce Ritter, maintaining a presence amid the burlesque shows, X-rated movies, and sex shops on Eighth Avenue, ca. 1979. Ritter reinvented the agency in the late 1970s by opening a large shelter for homeless youths near the Port Authority Bus Terminal and aggressively confronting pimps and pornographers, prompting one reporter to label him "the Mother Teresa of Times Square." Photograph courtesy of the Covenant House Archives.

Chapter 4
Street Life

The Times Square sex industry chews up and spits out thousands
of children a year. Some find their way to Under 21. The founder and
head of Under 21 is a Franciscan priest, Father Bruce Ritter. He is to
Times Square what Mother Teresa is to Calcutta. "When I walk along
Eighth Ave., I feel as though I'm wading in sewage," Father Ritter said
the other day. He sat on a red pillow on the floor of Under 21. The
bright, homey haven occupies a six-story building on Eighth Ave.
above 43d St. "People have no idea how unspeakable this area is,"
Father Ritter went on. "Times Square has become Dodge City.
Civilization has broken down here. Walk along 42d St. late at night.
Drifters, hustlers, junkies, pushers, midnight cowboys, gangs of
marauding youths, pimps by the hundreds, Johns by the thousands."
Under 21 gets the runaway and the throwaway kids who are sucked
into this sinkhole. Typical of them is a recent arrival at the haven, a
scrawny 15-year-old with long hair and delicate features. He is what
the Village Voice would call a pretty boy. But this poor, preyed-upon
child knows nothing about gay rights. He is an expert on gay wrongs,
though. A real Times Square victim. . . . Under 21 is more than a
haven, it is a religious community. The volunteer workers, who come
from Texas, Minnesota and Ohio among other places, pray together
daily in the cellar chapel. A score of volunteers are coming during
summer vacation from college. "This work has to be done out of
Christian commitment," Father Ritter said. "The rewards, such as
they are, are purely spiritual." . . . And so Under 21, a lonely offering
to God in the midst of the $1.5 billion-a-year Times Square lust
empire, needs contributions from you and me. I just sent a check for
$20 to Under 21, 692 Eighth Ave., New York, N.Y. 10036. I pledge $20
a month for as long as Father Ritter needs it. I can afford it. I quit
cigarets a while ago. I'll bet many of you could send Father Ritter a
few bucks a month, too. The thought of those children being evicted
into the arms of the pimps is enough to make you go right to your
checkbook.

—*Bill Reel*[1]

Bruce Ritter began to lose control of the Covenant House story
in the late 1970s. This may appear to be a strange statement at first glance
since, by virtually every objective measure, the ministry enjoyed unprecedented
prosperity and public acclaim. Balance sheets and revenue statements reveal

an important part of the story. Financial support for Covenant House, which included both cash contributions and donated services, increased from approximately $112,000 in 1975 to over $6,000,000 by 1980. Revenue from grants and contracts more than doubled from less than $700,000 to more than $1,600,000 during the same period. Property, physical plant, and equipment assets, valued at less than $13,000 in 1975, exceeded $1,500,000 a mere five years later. A small 1975 operating deficit had been eradicated, and Covenant House had accumulated sufficient cash to begin a modest investment program in money market accounts and certificates of deposit in 1979.[2] Remarkably, this solid record of expansion occurred during a protracted downturn in the national economy characterized by sluggish growth, persistent inflation and high unemployment. New York City itself teetered on the edge of bankruptcy during the mid- and late 1970s, suffering massive public employee layoffs, crippling cuts in municipal services, and severe budgetary shortfalls. Covenant House, however, appeared to be thriving.[3]

Further, Ritter successfully consolidated his own power within the organization during the late 1970s. Longtime colleagues, many of whom had supported the ministry since its formative years in the East Village, began to resign from the board of directors. The founder reconfigured Covenant House's governance structure in order to achieve tighter personal control over the organization's operating philosophy and ongoing activities. He assembled a new managerial team and created a community of volunteers that drew inspiration from his charismatic personality. A series of aggressive private fund-raising initiatives decreased reliance on public money, thereby allowing greater institutional autonomy and programmatic flexibility. Ritter more intentionally cultivated power brokers within the Roman Catholic hierarchy and developed important personal relationships with moneyed and nationally prominent laypersons. He emerged as a recognizable media figure. National press outlets and state legislative bodies sought out Ritter's "expert" opinion on topics ranging from Times Square redevelopment to youth homelessness. Local columnists and beat reporters, such as Bill Reel of the *New York Daily News*, provided valuable publicity and promoted the Covenant House cause to broader audiences. Ritter appeared to have built a formidable organization that served a very real social need, achieving considerable power and influence in the process.

Ritter's actual control over both events and institutional life, however, proved quite illusory. New individuals, with less loyalty to Covenant House's communal and Franciscan origins, began exerting more influence within the ministry during the late 1970s. They often pushed the organization in unanticipated directions, exhibiting minimal regard for its complex historical traditions and carrying Ritter along with them in the process. Widespread media coverage also placed very different demands on the founder. When he relied exclusively on sermons and newsletters to promote Covenant House in the early 1970s, Ritter completely and effectively controlled the institutional discourse. Now, his words and deeds often reached the public only after being filtered through the perceptions of journalists, editors, and television newscasters. Initially, this attention proved unremittingly positive and intoxicatingly seductive. Ritter soon discovered, however, that journalistic scrutiny contained a significant downside. The highly competitive, glitzy, tabloid-driven world of New York City news valued novelty, celebrity, controversy, and neatly packaged morality tales above all else. The rise of a popular folk hero from obscurity to fame always proved to be a good media story; the disgraceful fall of a flawed institutional icon appeared even better.

Bruce Ritter surely continued to spin appealingly attractive stories during the late 1970s. Increasingly, however, those stories became defined by broader socioeconomic currents and events beyond the founder's control. Covenant House's core mission to serve homeless youths remained relatively intact, but that mission became articulated in very different ways as a response to changing new constituencies and altered external circumstances. Perhaps the most significant story from this period, and the one that best illuminates Covenant House's institutional transformation, appeared completely disconnected from Bruce Ritter and New York City. In order to fully understand the changing nature of Covenant House's institutional story during the late 1970s, it remains instructive to consider first a grisly series of events that occurred in a seedy industrial suburb of Houston, Texas, during the summer of 1973.

Elmer Wayne Henley, a seventeen-year-old ninth-grade dropout who had been estranged from his abusive and alcoholic father, decided to spend the night of 7 August 1973 as he had so frequently over the previous three years: partying with his thirty-three-year-old friend, Dean Allen Corll, an unmarried electrician who worked for the Houston Power & Light Company. Cruising the streets of his working-class neighborhood early in the evening, Henley made fast friends with a twenty-year-old male drifter and a fifteen-year-old girl who had decided to run away from her family. He invited both over to Corll's single-story gray slate cottage in Pasadena, Texas, for a night of glue sniffing, paint inhaling, and general fun. Trouble began shortly thereafter. Henley recalled that Corll "was mad because I brought the chick over there. . . . I thought it was safe. I didn't know no better." The three youths soon passed out after sniffing vapors from a spray can of acrylic lacquer, and when they awoke things had taken a turn for the worse. Corll had stripped his companions naked, handcuffed them, strapped Henley's friends spread-eagle to a five-foot torture board that he had rigged up in his bedroom, and stood over all three with a .25-caliber revolver. Henley thought fast: he had known Corll nearly all of his life. He frequented the electrician's neighborhood candy store as a five-year-old and shared innumerable holiday meals, festive occasions, and joyrides with the person whom neighbors and coworkers invariably described as "a nice polite man who loved to be around kids." Henley knew how to handle the older man and figured he could talk his way out of the situation. He quickly convinced Corll that he would be happy to help him sexually molest, torture, and kill his two recent acquaintances. Corll thereupon agreed to remove Henley's handcuffs and a struggle ensued. Henley wrested the revolver from Corll, pumping five bullets into his lifelong friend and killing him instantly. The shaken seventeen-year-old then freed the other two youths and, recognizing the hopelessness of the situation, called the police. Soon an even more bizarre tale began to unfold.[4]

Houston detectives discovered that Corll, Henley, and an eighteen-year-old friend named David Owen Brooks had carried out one of the worst mass murder sprees in American history between 1970 and 1973. Corll used Henley and Brooks to lure at least twenty-six young boys to a series of apartments that he rented throughout the Houston area for all-night parties during those years. Corll's accomplices picked up hitchhikers, preyed on runaways, and convinced casual acquaintances that the older man would provide them with food, drugs, and other "goodies." Corll promised to pay his young accomplices two hundred dollars for every boy they produced, though he usually only gave them five or ten dollars in pocket change. During the all-night parties, Corll would routinely rape, sodomize, sexually abuse, torture, and ultimately shoot or strangle his victims. The three men would then wrap the bodies in plastic, place them in specially constructed wooden boxes, drive them to isolated burial spots, and liberally cover them with limestone in order to disguise the stench. Brooks and Henley led police to three massive grave sites at a boat storage shed in Houston, a deserted woodland area near Lake Sam Rayburn, and a windswept peninsula beach on the Gulf of Mexico. Henley's confession, conviction, and sentencing to six consecutive ninety-nine-year prison terms for the murders brought quick closure to the case's legal proceedings. Its cultural implications proved more far-reaching.

The Houston murders proved pivotal in highlighting the nation's "runaway problem." Several public policy initiatives resulted directly from the events of August 1973. A Runaway Youth Bill sponsored by Sen. Birch Bayh of Indiana, which had languished in committees since 1971, quickly passed the U.S. Senate in 1973 and the House of Representatives in 1974. This program allocated thirty million dollars over three years to support runaway shelters, counseling services, and neighborhood centers throughout the United States.[5] Caspar Weinberger, serving in 1973 as secretary of health, education, and welfare for the Nixon administration, publicly advocated a broader governmental role in addressing youth issues, created a juvenile delinquent prevention agency within his department, and began systematically collecting statistical information in order to maintain a national runaway registry. The federal government established a nationwide toll-free telephone line for runaways in 1974 in the hopes that they might send messages to their parents. Operators reportedly handled two thousand calls per month. Municipalities, private coalitions, and religious organizations sponsored increased numbers of local shelters, but many occupied makeshift facilities and viewed governmental responses as inadequate. The Parent Community Center in Houston, for example, was established in 1974 as a runaway shelter in the Heights neighborhood that provided Corll with many of his youthful victims. Rocky Mayhew, a burly navy veteran and former truck driver who served as the center's executive director, colorfully summarized the attitude of many social workers toward the new public programs: "I got a lot of plaques that's hangin' out there on the wall, but I still ain't got no goddam money. Every stick of furniture in this place I done bummed. That's the kind of sumbitch I am."[6]

Perhaps even more significant than the new public programs, the events in Houston also contributed to a cultural redefinition of youth homelessness during the mid-1970s. Commentators and national news weeklies increasingly focused on broken homes, dysfunctional families, and abusive domestic situations in their efforts to explain the runaway problem. Leaving home appeared to be a rational choice in many instances, as children confronted impossible living situations beyond their control. *U.S. News & World Report* summarized the issue as follows: running away "for more and more children, is becoming an escape from home conditions they find intolerable—not a quest for adventure, pleasure or socio-political protest as happened during the 'hippie-yippie' era of the 1960s." Celeste MacLeod, writing from a much more liberal perspective in the *Nation*, concurred. She documented the way in which unwanted teenage girls often found themselves shuffled back and forth between parents, friends, grandparents, foster homes, and juvenile halls until they chose streets as a preferable alternative to being "locked away in state institutions." Other observers blamed factors ranging from the national recession to parental alcoholism and drug abuse, but a general consensus emerged that youth homelessness reflected a more general "crisis" or deterioration of stable familial structures in late twentieth-century America.[7]

Popular literature following the Houston murders also began to link runaway culture much more closely with sexual deviance, exploitation, pornography, and prostitution. *Time* magazine characterized the Houston story as "an incredible tale of horror, homosexual sadism, and mass murder," and similar accounts focused on Dean Corll as a "sexual psychopath" who found easy and often willing prey among the nation's runaways. Virtually all examinations of homeless youths during this period focused on their encounters with the sex trade. *U.S. News & World Report* argued that runaways easily "fall into the company of procurers, sex criminals, drug addicts, thieves, and murderers." Celeste MacLeod confirmed that West Coast runaway girls survive "by the only means open to them—panhandling, subsistence, prostitution and sometimes petty theft." A New York City police spokesman hypothesized that 10 percent of the city's estimated twenty thousand runaways "become involved with male and female prostitution or other crimes, often because they were cajoled by smooth operators." *Time* claimed to uncover "a new and alarming wave of prostitution by teen-agers and young children" in 1977, with some suburban youngsters actually managing to "live at home and turn tricks for pocket money," though most appeared to be more traditional "runaways."[8] The Houston tragedy seemed to crystallize fears among a broad coalition of concerned parents, mainstream politicians, social critics, academic analysts, and crusading journalists that the nation's children and young adults appeared both dangerously naive and sexually out of control. Inflated statistics, alarmist predictions, and a heavily sexual emphasis pervaded this mainstream literature. Indeed, the runaway discussion seemed to reflect a broader cultural ambivalence concerning the sexual revolution and the changing nature of adolescence that many commentators associated with the late 1960s and early 1970s.

Bruce Ritter, interestingly, initially resisted this temptation to link runaways with prostitution, promiscuity, and sexual permissiveness. His commentary concerning the Houston murders, contained in his August 1973 newsletter, offered a thoughtful and measured reflection on the root causes and depressing consequences of youth homelessness. Though decrying the "sad, sick, and murderous events" in Houston and acknowledging that "the homicidal insanity" in Texas "has aroused great revulsion and great anxiety in us all," Ritter chose to place his emphasis elsewhere. He urged his readership to look beyond the sensational stories of runaways and to consider instead "the walkaway, throwaway kids" from broken homes who wandered the streets of urban America without hope and without a future. Ritter argued that "the individual act of abuse or exploitation, however criminal and ugly" paled in comparison to the spiritual death and cynicism that defined the lives and thoughts of homeless teenagers: "Time telescopes on and collapses upon children of the streets, their dying prolonged beyond those of Houston." Ritter ended his August 1973 appeal by calling for "a concerted community/government approach on a nationwide scale" to address the rootless lifestyles and disconnected realities faced by homeless teenagers who operated outside of any familial or institutional structure.[9] Ritter here resisted the opportunity to engage in sensationalist rhetoric and made no effort to tie his organization to the issues of prostitution, pornography, and adolescent sexuality that preoccupied the popular media. Within a few short years, however, this would change. By the late 1970s, Covenant House's name became closely linked with protests against teenage prostitution and crusades against New York City's commercial sex industry. Ritter himself aggressively promoted this connection. It constituted a defining moment in the ministry and produced a fundamental reorientation for the organization. The transformation itself began at Times Square and in the neighborhood that bordered the corner of Eighth Avenue and Forty-second Street.

Times Square had long enjoyed a well-earned reputation for disreputable entertainment, commercialized sex, and sleazy underground pleasures. Most observers agree, however, that its problems appeared more visible and threatening both to tourists and to native New Yorkers during the late 1960s and early 1970s. Massage parlors, peep shows, adult book stores, pornographic movie theaters, topless bars, liquor stores, pinball arcades, fleabag hotels, and cheap boardinghouses dominated the area by the early 1970s. The *New York Times*, whose corporate offices sometimes appeared to its editors to be too close for comfort on nearby West Forty-third Street, opined in 1975 that Times Square had grown "distinctly pathological: sick, criminal, aberrant and offensive to even the most tolerant sensibility." Irregular sanitation pickups, massive potholes perpetually in need of repair, a soaring violent crime rate, aggressive pimps and prostitutes, floating three card monte games, street corner drug use, and vacant storefronts testified both to New York City's fiscal crisis and to the general neglect of municipal services in the Times Square neighborhood.[10]

City politicians recognized the severity of the problem and initiated a series of measures during the early 1970s designed to strengthen law enforcement in this very visible and highly symbolic area. Mayor John Lindsay established two new police precincts named Midtown North and Midtown South in 1972, thereby dramatically increasing the number of patrolmen assigned to the district. The police department also established a special runaway unit that same year. By 1976, Abraham Beame's mayoral administration had announced the creation of a Midtown Enforcement Project. Municipal officials promised to close down brothels, massage parlors, and other sex-oriented businesses by coordinating efforts among various city agencies, rigorously enforcing building codes, and drafting new legislation. A series of highly publicized raids on topless bars ensued. Periodic sweeps and roundups, designed to remove prostitutes from the streets, also occurred. Generally, however, these measures proved ineffective. Bars typically reopened within hours of raids, while nuisance abatement acts and zoning restrictions proved vulnerable to successful legal challenges. Some reformers leveled charges of organized crime infiltration, corruption, and payoffs against the city's vice squad. New York City's fiscal problems also played a major role. The police department's runaway unit had been established with six men and a sergeant supervisor in 1972. Layoffs reduced the operation to two overworked officers by July 1975. Many questioned whether City Hall possessed either the political will or the administrative ability to combat the thriving and highly profitable commercial sex industry.[11]

Several additional factors increased public concerns over the perceived deterioration of Times Square during the mid-1970s: heightened anxieties over teenage prostitution, the discovery of a thriving trade in child pornography, and community reactions to proposed development projects on the city's west side. Following the Houston murders, law enforcement officials and media observers increasingly linked teen runaways with the proliferation of prostitution in midtown Manhattan. One influential *New York Times* article in November of 1975 accurately summarized the new perception, arguing that contemporary runaways did not fit the image of "the Norman Rockwell Saturday Evening Post cover of the lovably defiant and appealingly freckled 14-year-old boy with his clothes in a bandana tied to the end of the stick." Rather, a composite sketch of New York City runaways in 1975 would depict "a 14-year-old girl in platform shoes and hot pants on a street corner on Eighth Avenue, asking passers-by whether they want a good time."[12] Police in the early 1970s began referring to a stretch of Eighth Avenue near Times Square as the Minnesota Strip, claiming that pimps had created a national pipeline to recruit thousands of young blond-haired and blue-eyed midwestern prostitutes to New York City, where they might ply their trade in a more open and lucrative climate. This nickname and image quickly captured the popular imagination and remained an enduring cliché that defined the neighborhood for years thereafter. A well-publicized visit to New York City in 1977 by two Minneapolis policemen further cemented the connection in the public mind. Lt. Gary McGaughey and officer Al Palmquist boldly declared their intention to walk the strip, return hundreds of teenagers to their heartland homesteads, and smash the pimp pipeline. The fact that they failed to turn up a single Minnesotan had little impact on popular perceptions. Serious social workers might accurately view youth homelessness as a more complex urban phenomenon that had been romanticized and simplified by an exclusive focus on the Minnesota Strip. For most middle-class Americans in the mid-1970s, however, urban runaways became virtually synonymous with the haunting image of Jodi Foster portraying a vulnerable adolescent streetwalker in *Taxi Driver* (1976) or the angelic-faced young male prostitutes who plied the "chicken hawk trade" in the pinball arcades that lined Forty-second Street.[13]

Child pornography also became intimately intertwined with the issues of runaways and Times Square improvements during this period. Dr. Judianne Densen-Gerber, who in 1966 had founded a therapeutic community for alcoholics and drug addicts in New York City known as Odyssey House, called a press conference at One Times Square on 14 January 1977 in order to focus attention on child pornography. Densen-Gerber dramatically produced a series of magazines, which she had purchased at adult bookstores on Forty-second Street, that featured sexually explicit photographs of children aged three to eighteen. She also revealed the existence of "chicken movies," which captured children performing sexual acts on film. An outraged Densen-Gerber accused Manhattan District Attorney Robert Morgenthau of ignoring the problem and failing to take the issue seriously. Representative Edward I. Koch, in the midst of his successful 1977 mayoral campaign, attended the press conference, vowing to enlist the federal government and support new legislation in the fight against what rapidly became known as kiddie porn. Densen-Gerber's revelations, and her denunciation of these magazines and films as a form of child abuse, provoked national outrage. *U.S. News & World Report* described Americans as being "up in arms from coast to coast," while *Parents' Magazine* characterized the problem as "a hideous aspect of modern life which has spread across the nation." Most commentators echoed the words of *Time* magazine in claiming that the perceived surge in child pornography resulted at least in part from "the steady stream of bewildered broke runaways" who served as "a ready pool of 'acting talent' for photographers." Federal legislators soon moved to combat the problem by applying existing postal regulations and interstate commerce acts to child pornography. Several states attempted to strengthen their obscenity statutes. In the short run, the kiddie porn issue contributed to public perceptions of the Times Square sex industry as, in the words of *Daily News* columnist Bill Reel, "a sewer of greed and lust" that "symbolizes the evil of New York."[14]

The final issue that actually proved most directly instrumental in bringing Covenant House to Times Square, however, involved community concerns over real estate development and the quality of life in the surrounding neighborhood. Politicians and media commentators often discussed Times Square as an abstraction, as an entertainment emporium that existed purely for consumption and one that catered to a rootless population of tourists and transients. The largely blue-collar New Yorkers who occupied the tenements and railroad flats west of Eighth Avenue between Thirtieth and Fifty-ninth Streets, however, considered Times Square an unfortunate part of their everyday reality. By the 1970s, this neighborhood, which had been known historically as Hell's Kitchen, appeared particularly troubled and facing an uncertain future. The area's working-class housing, small businesses, and relatively stable white ethnic population had been gutted through much of the mid-twentieth century by several massive transportation projects: the Lincoln Tunnel (1937–57), the Port Authority Bus Terminal (1947–50), and an elevated expressway known as the West Side Highway (1931–48). A severe local economic downturn occurred during the 1960s: the area's once-bustling railroad yards lay dormant, rotting and abandoned piers lined the Hudson River shoreline, and housing conditions further deteriorated. Hell's Kitchen, in fact, became widely known in law enforcement circles as a haven for racketeers, gamblers, loan sharks, and strong-arm men. This criminal element lived side by side with a tough, determined, and hard-core blue-collar community that either refused to relocate or possessed insufficient means to find alternative housing in the city.[15]

Rampant real estate speculation, based on the proposed construction of a New York City Convention and Exposition Center in the West Forties, created another community crisis in the 1970s. Local boosters now referred to the neighborhood as Clinton in an effort to remove the stigma of the Hell's Kitchen designation. Investors and developers began buying up substantial quantities of property, in anticipation of quick profits. They raised rents from 50 percent to 100 percent in order to evict longtime tenants, drove out the small businessmen who ran Greek pastry stores and Italian ravioli shops in the interest of attracting more upscale establishments, and leveled working-class housing in order to create parking lots for the anticipated influx of conventioneers. The city's fiscal crisis, however, soon doomed the proposed convention center and the anticipated boom fizzled. Clinton was left with seedy gin mills, glass-littered vacant lots, ramshackle tenements, and empty warehouses. Heroin and street-level narcotics appeared on Ninth and Tenth Avenues in the 1970s, and a ruthless local Irish gang known as The Westies increased the area's notoriety. Further, the Times Square blight continued to move west. Block associations complained by 1976 that drug addicts and transvestites occupied the front stoops of many tenements, while prostitutes routinely flagged down cars from the West Side Highway and transacted their business in vacant parking lots. Street-level crime, ranging from muggings to break-ins to assaults, increased. Mothers complained publicly that their children could not walk home from Holy Cross School on West Forty-second Street without being accosted by a sleazy array of peep show patrons and adult bookstore customers. For embittered residents and community leaders in Clinton, commercial sex did not constitute a victimless crime.[16]

Clinton did contain a creative, cohesive, and vocal network of grassroots organizations that lobbied their state representatives to confront the prostitution problem. Manfred Ohrenstein, a state senator from the area, managed to shepherd a bill through the New York State Legislature in 1976 that criminalized loitering for the purposes of prostitution. Richard Gottfried, another state senator from Manhattan's west side, found it somewhat difficult to support Ohrenstein's initiative owing to the more liberal elements within his own legislative constituency. Still, he understood the need to respond to Clinton's neighborhood concerns and also felt intense pressure from local groups. Accordingly, Gottfried managed to obtain an eighty-nine thousand dollar grant for the Clinton Planning Board from the New York State Division for Youth in order to support any innovative social programs that might combat youth prostitution. Rev. John P. Duffell, a young community activist and associate pastor at Sacred Heart Church on

West Fiftieth Street in the heart of Hell's Kitchen, chaired the Clinton Planning Board's Public Safety Committee. He thus accepted the responsibility for receiving proposals and for awarding the grant.[17]

Duffell shared neighborhood concerns about the expansion of the commercial sex industry, but he also recognized the futility of simply channeling adolescent prostitutes into the judicial system. Criminal prosecution too often merely initiated young adults into a seemingly endless cycle of jail time followed by renewed streetwalking. When serving as a deacon at Saint Peter's Church on the Lower East Side in the late 1960s, Duffell had become acquainted with Bruce Ritter's ministry among transient youths. He now wondered whether this type of group home approach might make sense for Clinton in the mid-1970s. Ritter and Steven Torkelson met with Duffell's committee in the spring of 1976, presented an impressive proposal to open a residence for runaway girls and urban nomads, and expressed their willingness to tailor their program toward young prostitutes. The committee, which Duffell humorously described as "one lawyer, myself, a couple of old Irish ladies—and the old ladies were in my pocket," enthusiastically approved the Covenant House proposal and also received support for the idea from both the Port Authority Police and the New York City Police Department's Runaway Squad. A vacant brownstone on West Forty-seventh Street near Tenth Avenue, which had served as an Irish funeral home, was acquired shortly thereafter. Covenant House opened a small residential program, designed to accommodate between six and nine girls at West Forty-seventh Street, in November of 1976.[18]

This initial foray into midtown soon produced an even more significant programmatic shift for Covenant House. When Duffell visited Ritter's office in May of 1976 in order to finalize the agreement for the Forty-seventh Street group home, the young priest took the opportunity to raise some broader community concerns. Duffell had long felt the need for a more visible church presence near the Port Authority Bus Terminal, which served as a principal point of entry for many runaways and a fertile recruiting ground for area pimps. Ritter initially appeared somewhat reluctant to undertake any project near the transit facility, raising significant practical objections. He questioned whether an adequate building existed to house a youth shelter in Times Square and wondered whether Roman Catholic churches in the immediate neighborhood would appreciate such outside interference. Ritter also expressed skepticism about whether Terence Cardinal Cooke would support the endeavor. Duffell managed to meet each of these objections. He alerted Ritter to the existence of a vacant property on

Eighth Avenue between Forty-third and Forty-fourth Streets owned by the Christian and Missionary Alliance. He assured the founder that the politically powerful Catholic pastors at Saint Malachy's Church and Holy Cross Church shared his concerns and would welcome the Covenant House ministry. Duffel even offered to brief the cardinal concerning the project at a meeting that he had scheduled for the following day and report the results to Ritter. Events moved rapidly thereafter. Terence Cardinal Cooke enthusiastically affirmed his support for the undertaking, Ritter made some preliminary overtures to the Christian and Missionary Alliance, and Covenant House's board of directors first learned of this groundbreaking project at its meeting of 2 June 1976.[19]

Ritter characterized the initiative to the board as an "outreach center" that "would serve both children new to the neighborhood, and children who had been living in the area for some time." He proposed naming the facility Under 21 and emphasized that his program "would not be able to service real 'hard-core' kids." It would, however, dramatically expand the scope of services and programs available to Covenant House's clients. Under 21 would function, in the founder's words, as "a multi-service center for children and young adults, providing information, non-psychiatric counseling and referral services, food, non-residential shelter, medical, educational and vocational services, and related programs for those who are in need." Ritter also underscored the Christian nature of the operation, describing it as "the physical manifestation of a religious principle," and using language that hearkened back to the foundation of the Covenant I community on East Seventh Street. He hoped to attract a committed cadre of unpaid volunteers who would transform the Times Square area by maintaining a very visible religious presence on the streets. Indeed, Ritter even considered designing a special religious uniform to distinguish this "faith community."[20]

Many board members and administrative staffers appeared understandably stunned by the scope and scale of the project. Si Taubman, the Ziff-Davis executive who chaired the board, expressed safety concerns, especially since Ritter anticipated aggressive efforts by Covenant House personnel "to lure potential prostitutes away from this profession." Taubman also worried about organized violence against the agency, fretted over "the adverse effect of negative publicity on potential contributors, should Covenant House become involved in a fiasco" and questioned the financial impact of Under 21 on other programs. Ritter routinely had kept the institution on the edge of financial insolvency during the early 1970s, accumulating real estate and opening new group homes when fiscal prudence dictated a more conservative consolidation of existing resources. Under 21, however, considerably upped the ante. Acquiring individual brownstones for $100,000 or $200,000 with minimal down payments involved one level of risk; the proposed Christian and Missionary Alliance deal, on the other hand, meant a commitment to *rent* the building for two years at $50,000 per year with an option to buy for $1,000,000 at the end of the first year and $1,300,000 at the end of the second. And this did not include the inevitable professional staff increases and structural renovations necessary to maintain a twenty-four-hours-per-day facility that would serve dozens of children and young adults at any given time. Sr. Gretchen Gilroy, who served as Ritter's assistant director and often argued for a more conservative growth strategy, also expressed reservations. She focused especially on the founder's plan to relocate his residence and administrative offices from West Twelfth Street to Forty-fourth Street. Symbolically, this shift signaled that the really significant institutional action would now move to Midtown. The group home staff, scattered in small facilities throughout Greenwich Village and the Lower East Side, would remain more isolated within, and peripheral to, the central organization. The establishment of Under 21, board and staff members recognized, would alter every aspect of organizational life ranging from Covenant House's charter to the daily operations of its clinical workers.[21]

Ritter ultimately carried the day as board members reaffirmed their faith in the founder. Frenetic activity characterized the ten-month period between Ritter's decision to move forward and the formal dedication of Under 21 on 1 April 1977. An aggressive fund-raising campaign produced impressive results: Cardinal Cooke approved a $50,000 contribution from the Archdiocese of New York, the Franciscan Friars committed to donations totaling $75,000, and the Culpeper Foundation, which had provided some small grants to Covenant House in the past, added an additional $25,000 for this project.[22] Ritter masterfully cultivated the local media in order to generate publicity and secure smaller gifts. When Judianne Densen-Gerber called her January 1977 press conference to highlight the issue of child pornography in Times Square, for example, Ritter made sure to appear on the scene, and he used the occasion to trumpet the imminent opening of his new shelter. He enthralled reporters with the story of his work in the East Village, claiming that "the first ten kids" who arrived at his doorstep on East Seventh Street "had been given money to appear in pornographic films." Favorable stories concerning Under 21 appeared in the *New York Times*, *New York Post*, *New York Daily News*, and *Newsday* throughout the spring of 1977, boasting such titles as "A Haven for the Sexually Exploited" and "An Oasis for Runaway Teen-Agers Appears in a Pornographic Desert." Ritter found an especially enthusiastic advocate in Bill Reel, a *Daily News* reporter whose "Reel People" column especially resonated with its intended working-class Catholic audience. Reel became captivated by Ritter's personality and good works: within a few weeks of their initial encounter the young reporter admiringly referred to Covenant House's founder as "the Mother Teresa of Times Square, the uptown Dorothy Day, the spirit of St. Francis personified." He occasionally even used his column to solicit funds for Covenant House. Two particular journalistic appeals in May 1977, including the one quoted at the outset of this chapter, generated forty thousand dollars in small donations as readers jammed ten-dollar and twenty-dollar bills in envelopes and designated them for the use of "Father Bruce." Ritter shrewdly added these new donors to his mailing list, thus expanding his growing corps of grass-roots financial supporters. By the summer of 1977, Covenant House appeared on an extraordinary upward trajectory, and the ministry had achieved unprecedented public visibility.[23]

Under 21 changed everything in several ways. First and foremost, it clearly energized the founder. Prior to assuming the Times Square project, Ritter appeared characteristically restless. He surprised board members in February 1975 by announcing his intention to resign from Covenant House "sometime during the 1976 calendar year" and urging the directors to make new provisions for future governance. He vaguely discussed personal plans to pursue missionary work in Africa or Asia, decided to take up flying lessons and actually earned his pilot's license, and generally appeared bored by the myriad details of administering, in what increasingly became a derisive term for the founder, "a child care agency." Contemporaries differed over whether Ritter seriously considered resigning. Shawn Nolan, who initially authorized Ritter's experimental ministry on East Seventh Street, observed that his fellow Franciscan could be "a little Sarah Bernhardtish." Others felt that he may have used the threat of resignation in order to reorganize the board, which he successfully accomplished in 1975 by establishing himself as the sole member of the corporation. Whatever his motives, Under 21 clearly ended any talk of resignation. Ritter moved uptown and threw himself back into the ministry with a renewed vigor.[24]

Under 21 also stimulated a fundamental institutional restructuring. Staff now routinely spoke of Covenant House's "two divisions": Under 21 and Group Homes. Ritter redefined his responsibilities so that he might focus primarily on fund-raising, public relations, and youth advocacy. By December of 1978, he began referring to himself as "the public symbol of the agency" and discussed the need to shed more mundane administrative obligations. Ritter delegated day-to-day supervisory responsibilities, administrative chores, and child care program oversight to Sr. Gretchen Gilroy. Her close eye for detail complemented the founder's visionary perspective, and her considerable experience with the group home operation allowed Ritter to ease his personal involvement with the child care arm of the agency. Ritter also began assembling a professional management team in the late 1970s that included institutional outsiders with extensive experience in other organizational cultures. Keith Brown, formerly an executive at Citibank, became an executive vice president concerned with business management under Ritter. Robert Cardany, formerly the director of finance at St. Agatha's Home for Children, assumed a comparable position at Covenant House. Patricia Connors, formerly the executive director of the Kennedy Home, began her association with the agency as assistant director in charge of the group home division. All three emerged as major administrators with significant programmatic responsibilities. The founder now appeared willing to cede some control over administrative functions to reliable staff members, though he retained a tight grip over institutional philosophy and possessed a meddlesome managerial style that often irritated senior staff.[25]

The Under 21 initiative further allowed Ritter to embrace more directly the institutional church and to reaffirm the overtly religious nature of Covenant House's core mission. Ritter aggressively persevered throughout the late 1970s in his efforts to affiliate Covenant House formally with the Franciscans. Still, both Shawn Nolan and his successor as minister provincial, Aubert J. Clark, preferred to maintain some distance. Indeed, as Clark noted, individual friars proved even less willing to commit time to Covenant House after Ritter "made residence in his 'religious community' a non-negotiable condition of working at Under 21. . . . It is just not our life style!" Sensing his inability to persuade the Franciscans, Ritter briefly negotiated with the Jesuits in the hopes that they might assume responsibility for the agency. He also cultivated a much closer relationship with the Archdiocese of New York. Cardinal Cooke blessed Under 21 both personally and financially at its 1977 dedication ceremony, and Ritter took special care to maintain deeper programmatic ties with Associated Catholic Charities. The founder articulated these commitments at a board meeting held in January of 1977, arguing that "the agency's relationship with the institutional church should be deepened and made clearer" and announcing that he now sought "individuals with religious motivation to work in Under 21" so that "the religious dimension of Covenant House" might "become more apparent at this point in time."[26]

Ritter continually refined his vision of Covenant House as a religious community and placed increasing emphasis on the need for Christian commitment among staff and volunteer workers. His August 1976 newsletter, which actually predated the opening of Under 21, extended "a serious invitation to anyone who would like to give a year of his life to the Lord and to work with us and the kids on Eighth Avenue." He offered volunteers room and board, pocket money, and insurance in exchange for "a chance to practice the corporal and spiritual works of mercy." Ritter expected volunteers to "live a strict ascetic life in union with the worshipping Church," receive the Eucharist daily, and practice the virtues of chaste love. He also went to great lengths to emphasize "the religious dimension of the Under 21 Project" in staff manuals, arguing that Covenant House needed to move beyond simply administering a first-class social welfare program. For Ritter, "it is almost, but not quite, enough to feed the hungry, clothe the naked, shelter the homeless, comfort the afflicted." He expected more. Employees and volunteers must "express clearly the transcendent saving mission of the Church" and engage in the work of religious renewal by exercising "a commitment to poverty and a life of prayer in union with the Church." Such appeals proved powerful and produced impressive results. By 1980, the founder counted two hundred volunteers committed to his community, with one-fifth of those working at Covenant House full time.[27]

This new proliferation of "God talk" and the increasingly cozy relationship with institutional Catholicism, however, also alienated many of Ritter's longtime supporters and produced significant turnover on the board. Patricia Kennedy proved especially vocal in her opposition to the proposed affiliation with the Franciscans. She reminded Ritter at a board meeting that he "had promised that it would never be a religious organization," and she voted against the resolution that allowed the executive director to establish himself as the sole member of the corporation. Kennedy and her husband, Adrian Gately, both resigned as directors in November of 1975. William Juska, a young attorney who had committed himself to working on the Lower East Side and whom Ritter had invited to join the board in 1973, resigned in January of 1976 after observing that he "felt quite impotent in the position" and that his service "had placed a strain on any number of my personal friendships, including that with Bruce." Mary Hanrahan stopped attending board meetings following Ritter's description of his religious vision for Covenant House in January of 1977. Shawn Nolan, a plainspoken and direct individual who proved perfectly willing to challenge Ritter as appropriate, also left the board in 1976 when his term as minister provincial of the Franciscans expired. Many of the founder's closest associates and most constructive critics, including the core of the original Covenant I community, had moved on by the late 1970s. Ritter now possessed an even greater opportunity to reshape the organization and to create a new institutional image.[28]

And this new image itself became the final, and perhaps the most significant, transformation that accompanied Covenant House's move to midtown and the establishment of Under 21. Readers who examined the organization's promotional literature in the late 1970s might well assume that Covenant House's core clientele consisted almost exclusively of prostitutes, street hustlers, and refugees from sex emporiums. Prior to 1976, Ritter virtually never mentioned prostitution or pornography in his monthly appeal letters. Rather, he tended to highlight the systemic factors that fostered youth homelessness among the urban underclass: abusive domestic situations, widespread poverty, rampant adolescent drug use, poor medical care, and inadequate educational opportunities. Covenant House's rhetoric changed dramatically with the move to Times Square. Donors now received a steady diet of stories that probed the life histories of Covenant House children who sought refuge from New York's seamy sexual underworld. A frightened eighteen-year-old southern girl had found herself in the clutches of a ruthless pimp who repeatedly raped her, beat her, and "shot her full of heroin" before attempting to recruit her to service his clients. A fourteen-year-old runaway named Mark had been befriended by a seemingly affectionate older man who quickly marketed the youngster as a "pretty boy" transvestite and ultimately involved him in a classy male prostitution ring that catered to Fortune 500 companies. A suicidal bisexual named Peter walked the midtown streets daily in "muscle-tight brief cut-offs and a body shirt unbuttoned to the waist" and spent his nights stripping for tips as a go-go boy on Second Avenue. These remarkable stories clearly struck a chord with Ritter's audience, and direct mail income skyrocketed during the late 1970s. They also contributed to the social redefinition of youth homelessness in the popular consciousness, tying it inextricably to prostitution and pornography. Covenant House's supporters now heard very little about the Greenwich Village group homes or the problems that plagued the vast majority of the agency's young clients. The new focus on sex sensationalized the organization's work and brought it unprecedented media attention. It also meant that Covenant House would now need to perform a delicate balancing act. A very real danger existed that the exclusive concentration on Times Square could trivialize the broader issues that gave birth to the agency and simultaneously skew outsiders' perceptions concerning the ministry.[29]

A good example of this tension occurred in March 1979, when the top-rated television news weekly *60 Minutes* aired a special report on teenage prostitution, titled "Runaways, Throwaways." The program began with a fifteen-minute segment that focused almost exclusively on Covenant House, thus providing the organization with its first really significant national exposure. Bruce Ritter dominated the broadcast. Confident, self-assured, and gregarious, he led the journalist Dan Rather on a whirlwind walking tour of Forty-second Street, boldly striding past pornographic theaters with neon marquees that advertised XXX-rated movies. Ritter wore a street uniform appropriate for the dreary and cold winter day, complete with down jacket, turtleneck sweater, jeans, and sneakers. He expertly demonstrated his insider's knowledge of New York City prostitution, detailing its economic structure, working conditions, and social geography to the neophyte reporter. A solemn Rather intoned: "Who is this man who knows so much about the hustlers in Times Square? Is he a pimp? A cop? A social worker? No, he's a Franciscan Friar, Father Bruce Ritter, who, with some assistance from federal, state, and local agencies, is trying to stave off the bankruptcy that threatens his child-care center, the only one in New York's worst red-light district." The broadcast provided compelling television. A hard-edged realism dominated the segment, as *60 Minutes* staffers interviewed an array of teenage prostitutes, runaways, and social workers. But Ritter remained front and center throughout, rapping with kids, cajoling staff members, and leading the camera crew through every nook and cranny of Under 21. The agency appeared as a warm and friendly beehive of frenetic activity. The program very effectively reinforced Ritter's carefully crafted self-image as a streetwise priest, made him synonymous with the ministry, highlighted the agency's precarious financial situation, and focused primarily on teenage prostitution. The *60 Minutes* segment truly constituted a defining moment for the organization, but it also publicly defined the organization in ways that would have significant long-term implications. Sunday night viewers might well carry away an enduring image of Covenant House as a highly personalized and charismatic operation that worked almost exclusively with children and young adults in the sex industry. This message clearly sold, but it also simplified.[30]

The *60 Minutes* broadcast pointed toward another shift in the agency's image that occurred during the late 1970s as well: its emergence as an advocacy organization for youth and one that increasingly proved willing to practice confrontational politics. The cameras followed Ritter, now formally attired in his clerical collar and priestly garb, to a speaking engagement before an all-white audience of earnest high school students in the affluent suburban community of Darien, Connecticut. Responding to a question from one adolescent, Ritter observed that "there hasn't been a single pimp put in jail in four years in New York City for pimping a child." He noted that "our political leaders, our police commissioner, our district attorney, our mayor" needed "to get off their duffs and do something about this problem," but he expressed extreme pessimism that this would happen "unless they are embarrassed politically, unless they are threatened politically." Ritter also informed Dan Rather that well-connected organized crime interests controlled the juvenile prostitution and child pornography trades, and that an entrenched system of payoffs to government officials in exchange for protection precluded rigorous prosecution.[31]

Ritter aggressively used his newfound celebrity status in the late 1970s as leverage in prodding municipal officials. He regularly chided Robert Morgenthau, the Manhattan district attorney, for failing to control vice in the Times Square area. At various times, Ritter could be found in the New York press attacking Mayor Edward Koch, the New York City Police Department, lenient judges, and apathetic prosecutors. He organized a highly public campaign against Democratic congressman Fred Richmond of Brooklyn, who had admitted to soliciting sex from a sixteen-year-old boy in 1978. Ritter received considerable attention for protesting a celebrity-studded fund-raising dinner held in Representative Richmond's honor at the posh Rainbow Room in Manhattan that year. Covenant House's growing list of journalistic advocates knew that they could always count on the tough-talking and seemingly straight-shooting Franciscan for a controversial quote and a juicy sound bite. Still, Ritter craved more than mere media attention. He firmly believed that Covenant House should spearhead "a massive effort to stop the destruction and abuse of children, most notably by the sex industry of Times Square," and he continually articulated this vision to the board of directors during the late 1970s. He began to move toward institutionalizing an advocacy function within the agency, even arguing that the board should establish a new organization called Covenant II for that purpose. Ritter took the position, again reminiscent of his early days in the East Village, that "it might be the Church's role to confront the state" concerning children's issues. And he appeared perfectly willing to do precisely that.[32]

Ritter's ability to blend confrontational public politics with shrewd back-room wheeling and dealing produced perhaps his most astounding institutional triumph in 1979. The Under 21 shelter had already exceeded all projections and expectations. Covenant House estimated that approximately three thousand youngsters entered the facility during its first ten months of operation. On any given night, dozens of children received temporary housing, hot meals, clean clothing, showers, counseling, and emergency medical attention. An outreach staff aggressively patrolled the streets, seeking out potential clients and inviting youngsters into the agency's programs. A growing number of residents chose to stay for longer periods in exchange for observing the basic principles of the covenant: avoiding drugs, eschewing violence, dealing with staff in an atmosphere of mutual love and respect, and following a set daily schedule. Under 21 had been planned with the intention of serving approximately twenty clients per night; staff reported in 1978 that daily intakes sometimes approached one hundred youths. This high demand for services strained institutional resources and produced an almost immediate pressure to expand the Eighth Avenue facility.[33]

Medical care proved to be the most difficult challenge that confronted Covenant House staffers. Counselors referred clients to various local hospitals and clinics, but bureaucratic problems inevitably surfaced. Intolerably long waits at emergency rooms, billing difficulties that emerged when young people proved unable to pay, and questions surrounding the appropriateness of treating minors without parental consent sometimes placed Covenant House workers at odds with hospital staff. By July of 1978, Ritter had managed to negotiate an arrangement with St. Vincent's Hospital in Greenwich Village. Administrators and physicians at St. Vincent's agreed to help Covenant House establish a medical clinic, provide back-up services that would include inpatient care, and start serving Under 21 youngsters in the hospital's outpatient facilities. Ultimately, however, the board and key administrators believed that Covenant House should move toward establishing its own quality health services center. Ritter aggressively pursued public and foundation funding to achieve this goal throughout 1978, but the plan hinged on Covenant House's ability to renovate and expand its physical plant.[34]

Controversy greeted the proposal and Covenant House soon received its first dose of negative publicity. Gerald Schoenfeld, the chairman of the Schubert Organization and a major spokesman for theater and restaurant interests in midtown, complained that the scale and scope of Covenant House's operation damaged the city's proposed Times Square revitalization efforts. In Schoenfeld's view, which echoed the concerns of many local merchants, the homeless shelter had evolved quickly into a "crash pad" that attracted roving bands of dangerous youths. Homeless kids loitered outside the agency, threatening passersby and theatergoers by their very presence, and contributing to the area's disreputable character. Further, Ritter's plan to expand Under 21 meant that several tenants would be evicted from the ground floor of 692 Eighth Avenue, including a delicatessen, a barber shop, a ticket agency, and a record store. Municipal officials, who hoped to attract more commercial businesses to the area, vigorously opposed the evictions and pressured Covenant House to work more closely with community groups. The city's Board of Estimate even voted in January of 1979 to hold over an $183,000-per-year state appropriation for Covenant House's youth home on Eighth Avenue, contingent upon the agency's willingness to resolve its outstanding issues with other neighborhood interests.[35]

Publicly, Ritter reacted vigorously and self-righteously to the criticism. He excoriated community groups and elected officials for engaging in "extortion" and "blackmail." He derisively observed that "a barber is not in danger of being killed, raped, taken over by a pimp." Couching the debate in stark moral absolutes, Ritter proclaimed that "if I had to match the life of one kid against the convenience of one merchant, I would take the kid." He reveled in his role as spokesman for the disinherited and portrayed himself as the lone defender of the powerless. Privately, the founder exhibited a cool ability to tone down his rhetoric, negotiate with power brokers, and work his growing network of political connections. He agreed with the board that "all possible efforts short of compromising Covenant House goals and objectives should be made to maintain favorable relations with the neighboring business community and in particular the Community Planning Boards." By December of 1978, the agency committed itself to working with community groups to find alternative locations for the health services center. Attention soon focused on the Manhattan Rehabilitation Center, a vacant three-building complex that occupied an entire city block on Tenth Avenue between Fortieth and Forty-first Street.[36]

The Tenth Avenue center had served as a substance abuse rehabilitation center for the State of New York and thus contained ample facilities for a medical clinic, classrooms, dormitories, and other Covenant House needs. Ritter spent the first few months of 1979 massaging community planning boards, corresponding with state officials, attempting to satisfy local business groups, and negotiating favorable lease arrangements. The deal appeared to fall apart in late March when the state's director of operations informed Ritter that "other State agencies have already requested that this facility be made available to them for state purposes and activities."

Governmental policy dictated that these requests "be given priority," and the state official regretfully notified the friar that "your request for leasing the Manhattan Rehabilitation Center cannot be met at this time." Ritter persevered, using his archdiocesan and governmental contacts to bring the matter directly to the attention of Governor Hugh Carey. Kevin M. Cahill, a well-connected and influential Manhattan doctor who served as personal physician to both the governor and Cardinal Cooke, pitched the project to Carey and brokered a meeting between him and Ritter. Governor Carey appeared moved by the Covenant House project and quickly ordered his commissioner of general services to get "the keys to the building on Father Ritter's desk within a week." Since the state could not legally grant the facility to Covenant House outright, officials negotiated an arrangement whereby the agency would lease the facility for ten years at the nominal rate of one dollar per year.[37]

Figure 5. Under 21, formerly the Manhattan Rehabilitation Center, Tenth Avenue and Forty-first Street, New York City. Photograph courtesy of the Covenant House Archives.

Covenant House opened the new complex on Tenth Avenue and Forty-first Street in December of 1979 to widespread acclaim and general approbation. The facility contained 115 single rooms, a library, a gymnasium, a fully staffed health services unit, a large institutional kitchen, an alternative school affiliated with the New York City Board of Education, a vocational training center, and administrative offices. Under 21 continued to operate a crisis center on Eighth Avenue, but the major component of the operation had moved westward. Public officials praised the program, Schoenfeld and other Times Square business leaders appeared satisfied, and peace momentarily reigned. The move from Eighth Avenue to Tenth Avenue crystallized several themes that characterized Covenant House's history in the late 1970s: Ritter's commitment to programmatic expansion and real estate acquisition, the agency's increasing visibility and masterful use of positive public relations, the creative use of public financing and governmental seed money in order to finance a private social welfare program, a willingness to play political hardball in public yet quietly negotiate in private, and an increasing reliance on influential friends and contacts in order to advance institutional interests.[38]

Perhaps most of all, the move to Tenth Avenue captured the dynamic sense of energy and urgency that permeated Covenant House during the late 1970s. Robert Cardany, who joined the organization as director of finance in 1977, vividly recalls those initial years as "exciting, heady times." His previous experience in nonprofits occurred in lower key environments where "everybody just kind of went to work, took care of the kids, and went home again." At Covenant House, however, frenetic activity and relentless advocacy prevailed. The founder often appeared on the nightly news, testified before city and state investigative committees, publicly challenged his adversaries, and always appeared on the move. As Cardany observed from his perspective as a key administrator, "You kind of lived vicariously through that. And it was wonderful." Others sensed the energy as well. Justine Wise Polier, the retired family court judge who had supported Ritter's efforts throughout the 1970s, toured Under 21 with her secretary in 1978. She was impressed by the physical surroundings: "The rooms were bright and cheerful, and the use of color and space created an open, airy atmosphere. . . . There has been no graffiti on any walls." She shared a meal with Ritter in the dining hall, "served in cafeteria style and there was a choice of soup, spaghetti and meat sauce, kidney beans, salad, bread, a cold or hot drink." Polier especially enjoyed a "delicious cake" that had been donated by Bloomingdale's department store. Throughout her visit, this experienced observer of the child care system noted the friendliness of the staff, the spirit of hopefulness that prevailed, and the very real commitment to the work. Her secretary's final remarks concerning the tour offer an appropriate testimony to Covenant House's programmatic expansion in the late 1970s: "The warmth of feeling and real contact of the staff with the children dominated my impressions of the program. It was difficult to separate the spirit of the program from the spirit of energy, creativity, hopefulness, and determination of Father Ritter. I felt that something exciting was happening there, and could not help wanting to be part of it."[39]

Figure 6. Bruce Ritter, Attorney General Edwin Meese, and J. Peter Grace at a black-tie affair. As Covenant House's prestige grew, the organization became a favorite philanthropy for many conservative activists who celebrated its entrepreneurial spirit, faith-based values, and heavy reliance on private funding. Photograph courtesy of the Covenant House Archives.

Chapter 5
Ideas, Men, Money

Dear Father Bruce,

It was an honor and a joy to have had you with us on Sunday for our flight to Florida. Ever since we arrived I have been thinking about your problems and I have become even more convinced that planning and organizational changes will provide the solutions that you seek. You are now involved in the typical situation that a small business, founder-owned, encounters as it grows dramatically just as Covenant House has. . . . Now you face new challenges—the spread of your work to other parts of the United States and, indeed, to other countries. This means a whole new set of problems and opportunities. . . . In reviewing the expansion situation as you described it, there appears to be a need here for a proper coordination of three basic elements: a) ideas b) men c) money. If ideas outgrow the money and the manpower, then a project will founder. If the ideas are adequate but there is no implementation or the money is not forthcoming, a project will founder. In your situation, your ideas are still terrific. What you need are men with business experience both in the United States and abroad as well as national and international contacts to help you overcome the new kinds of problems you will be facing as you establish Covenant Houses outside of New York. . . . Your ideas will always be well-received around the world but you must balance the other two ingredients—men and money—in order to implement your remarkable scheme. If you decide to follow my suggestion about forming this small group of advisors, we should talk about it when you return from Florida and begin to put it into being as a sort of super structure for your Covenant House activities outside of New York. This group would make it possible for all of your ideas, problems and opportunities to be run through a screen of very intelligent people who have worldwide knowledge and contacts both in America and abroad. . . . It was great, as always, to be with you again and your presence honored our airplane which I should have asked you to Bless before you departed with Bob [Macauley].

—*J. Peter Grace*[1]

It seemed as though just about everyone wanted to be part of Covenant House during the early 1980s. Wealthy Catholic philanthropists, such as J. Peter Grace and William Simon, lent their international prestige and considerable connections to the ministry. Hundreds of volunteers from throughout the United States swelled the ranks of the Faith Community, working in the program in exchange for room and board and a twelve dollar weekly stipend. Many diocesan authorities and civic leaders urged the organization to open programs within their jurisdictions and Covenant House often obliged. The agency successfully established operations in Guatemala (1981), Toronto (1982), and Houston (1983) during this period. Plans called for even more dramatic expansion in the future. World leaders, politicians, and entertainment celebrities regularly toured the New York center as the ministry's fame spread: Mother Teresa of Calcutta visited in 1981, Liv Ullman participated in an agency-sponsored international symposium concerning street kids in 1984, and Nancy Reagan received a Covenant House T-shirt and proclaimed Under 21 "a great program" that "deserves the support of everybody" during her 1985 trip to the Tenth Avenue and Forty-first Street facility. The organization proudly basked in the bright glow of positive publicity, unprecedented donor support, and international visibility.[2]

Rapid growth during the early 1980s, however, contained both obvious and hidden costs. The founder's wealthy acquaintances and influential friends now both expected and received a much greater voice in defining institutional policies and procedures. The highly committed corps of youthful volunteers in the Faith Community did not always mix easily with a growing paid staff that valued its professional identity and sought to bring a new programmatic sophistication to the operation. Geographical expansion occasionally embroiled the agency in both complex international political situations and contentious local controversies. Some observers began to identify the organization with the conservative political theories and approaches to social reform that held sway within the federal government during the 1980s. Still, it remained relatively easy for board members, administrators, and staff to ignore the critics and exhibit a relentless optimism throughout this period of expanding resources, exciting new programs, and rapid change. Ideas, men, and money appeared in abundant supply. It seemed certain that Covenant House would thrive and grow throughout the foreseeable future.

As the agency charted new directions in the early 1980s, it appeared an opportune moment to discontinue some services and sever some historical ties. Covenant House's group home program proved the earliest and most controversial casualty. Bruce Ritter first formally proposed closing the group homes at a board of trustees meeting in March of 1980. In fact, the program had occupied an increasingly marginal status within the organization for several years. Since 1977, the founder had concentrated virtually all of his attention, fund-raising appeals, and energy on developing the Under 21 facility, largely delegating the responsibility for group home management to Sr. Gretchen Gilroy and other trusted administrators. By March of 1980, Ritter described the eight group homes as "a major bureaucratic irritant." He especially expressed his desire to terminate Covenant House's financial dependency on New York City's department of social services, which largely financed the group home program. Ritter characterized his relationship with that municipal agency as "punitive" and "essentially adversarial," as he grew increasingly disdainful of bureaucratic regulation and oversight. Covenant House, in the founder's mind, now needed to "consolidate and concentrate its resources" on the Under 21 program in Times Square. After all, this operation served more children, attracted overwhelmingly favorable publicity, provided a unique edge to the ministry, and received unprecedented support from private donors and corporate sponsors.[3]

Covenant House's changing financial circumstances clearly influenced Ritter's thinking. During the 1976 fiscal year, which constituted the last budgetary period prior to the opening of Under 21, fully 82 percent of Covenant House's $1,292,000 total income resulted from government grants. This money primarily reimbursed the agency for child care expenses connected with the group homes. Ritter's preaching engagements, monthly newsletter, and personal solicitations netted only $127,000, or approximately 8 percent of the total revenue. Corporate contributions and foundation grants barely exceeded $100,000. That financial mix had already changed dramatically by 1980, the last fiscal year in which Covenant House administered its eight group homes. Overall income had increased approximately sixfold between 1976 and 1980, to $7,732,000, but government grants now provided less than 22 percent of this total, accounting for $1,625,000. The agency's direct mail efforts and speaker's bureau generated over $2.9 million in 1980, or nearly 38 percent of the institution's income. Covenant House estimated that in-kind contributions from volunteers and members of religious communities amounted to over $1.6 million in 1980, and corporate-foundation philanthropy now exceeded $800,000.[4]

Ritter's successful efforts at raising private funds for Under 21 provided him with an extraordinary opportunity. As he bluntly informed the board, "Whoever controls your funding, your intake policy, and your discharge policies, controls the destiny of your agency, or at least the destiny of those programs so funded." Eliminating the group home program offered the promise of virtually removing Covenant House from public control and oversight. The agency would no longer be required to provide long-term care for seriously disturbed, aggressive, or abusive children who had been referred by municipal and state authorities but who had failed to respond to the Under 21 program. Open intake would remain Covenant House's philosophical cornerstone, but the organization would now gain the flexibility of referring chronically violent or drug-addicted clients to more appropriate facilities. The New York City Board of Estimate could no longer scrutinize Covenant House expenses and threaten to withhold grants in response to external pressures or community relations problems. Further, the department of social services recently had inaugurated new programs to more rigorously monitor and review child care agencies. Covenant House recognized that it would need to alter its internal bureaucratic mechanisms substantially if it hoped to comply with these new procedures, a move that the founder wished to avoid. Perhaps most significantly, Ritter claimed that the group home program itself ran a deficit that would approach $400,000 for the 1979–80 fiscal year. Municipal funding did not adequately cover the daily child care costs. Ritter feared that continued contractual arrangements with New York City would force Covenant House to maintain a small but expensive program during lean economic times, limit the agency's flexibility, and ultimately compel the organization to subsidize the group homes "at the expense of its more important free-funded Under 21 programs." The founder gambled that he could virtually eliminate the governmental subsidies for group homes yet still continue to expand his pet programmatic projects by aggressively tapping his private funding sources.[5]

Ritter rarely lost a bet during the early 1980s, and this proved no exception. The 1981 budget summarizes the bottom line: despite eliminating six group homes, Covenant House's income soared to $11 million, a 30 percent increase over the previous year. Direct mail and related solicitations exceeded $5.8 million and accounted for approximately 52 percent of the agency's revenues; government grants declined to less than $750,000 and now composed a relatively insignificant 6.8 percent of organizational income. This private-public funding mix, which appeared remarkable for any social service agency, placed Covenant House on solid financial footing and effectively removed its operations from close governmental scrutiny. Ritter's plan to close the group homes also contained some tangential benefits. The founder's real estate speculations had proven particularly shrewd in two specific instances. By 1980, the group homes on West Eleventh Street and West Fifteenth Street constituted valuable properties in increasingly desirable residential neighborhoods. Covenant House, through its Testamentum holding company, could now sell these brownstones at a substantial gain, thereby guaranteeing that the agency could meet its upcoming obligation on an $800,000 balloon mortgage on the Eighth Avenue facility. Other less marketable properties, such as the East Seventh Street tenement and the two group homes on Staten Island, faced substantial repair and renovation costs in the immediate future that might potentially drain agency resources. Ritter quickly disposed of the Staten Island homes to the Mission of the Immaculate Virgin at Mount Loretto, a child care institution administered by the Archdiocese of New York. He planned to offer the somewhat dilapidated East Seventh Street property to various social service agencies as well. All in all, his proposals made excellent business sense.[6]

Some colleagues and supporters questioned the programmatic implications. A few board members worried about the closing's impact on children currently receiving care. Others openly wondered whether Catholic Charities and secular agencies could easily absorb the resulting loss of forty-seven beds. The directors appeared especially nervous about damaging the agency's relationship with the city, since other cooperative programs between the two entities existed. Ritter downplayed the impact of his proposal on both individual children and the region's child care system. He argued that "other organizations in New York City and State operate group homes—and do it well," thereby rendering Covenant House's programs for "hard to place" children duplicative and superfluous. He agreed to continue operating two group homes on East Tenth Street and West Forty-seventh Street. These might serve as alternative residences for appropriately stable older adolescents who required longer-term shelter than Under 21 could provide. And he pledged to phase out the other group homes gradually, cutting down intake and thereby reducing the program largely through attrition. Ultimately the board supported Ritter. The directors accepted his description of the financial realities, reluctantly admitting that smaller residential facilities no longer served as the heart and soul of the Covenant House program. They voted to phase out the group homes by July of 1980.[7]

This decision generated some disappointment, disagreement, and hard feelings among staff. Group home workers felt that their clientele responded well to the smaller, highly personalized, and more structured environments in their facilities. They had built solid relationships with individual children and expressed considerable reluctance about discharging them into the city's child care system. Some grumbled that the much larger Times Square operation reflected a "warehousing" approach to youth homelessness that failed to prepare youngsters for more permanent and stable living situations.

Sr. Patricia Larkin's reaction reflected the ambiguity felt by many workers. A Franciscan Sister of Syracuse, Larkin had begun her ministry at Covenant House in 1978. She was living at the group home for girls on West Eleventh Street when Ritter announced his intention to phase out the program. She recalled being "very, very upset over the whole thing because I just knew how much the kids were invested in living there and I really felt we did a good job with the kids." Larkin recognized the reality of the situation but still questioned the outcome in a 1999 interview: "Intellectually I heard it, intellectually understood it, but emotionally I was still really angry because I still know, sure we can turn those kids over to the City, but in all my years even after that I knew that the City does not take care [of its] kids." She remained with Covenant House until 1992, working at the West Forty-seventh Street group home and eventually at Under 21, yet her fondest and most vivid memories date to her earliest years in the smaller and more manageable facilities on Staten Island and West Eleventh Street.[8]

But the group home program and the small-scale community activism that it represented reflected Covenant House's past rather than its future. The ideas that held sway at the uppermost organizational levels in 1980 envisioned a very different type of agency: broader in scope, more influential politically, aggressively expansive, and closely tied to institutional Catholicism. The founder had already created the necessary financial infrastructure to implement such plans. He also carefully began the process of recruiting adequate personnel to realize his objectives. Ritter created and filled three important administrative positions in 1980, hiring individuals who would play critical roles in the organization over the course of the next decade: Dr. James Kennedy became director of medical services, Patrick Kennedy was engaged as director of development, and Sandra Hagan accepted a position as director of program development. The number of full-time paid staff employed by Covenant House expanded dramatically from 81 in 1976 to 250 by the end of 1980. A growing corps of clinical psychologists, social workers, caseworkers, licensed teachers, counselors, accountants, and information specialists now worked at the agency. The organization lost a certain degree of intimacy, as Ritter could no longer rely primarily upon trusted former students and personal contacts to staff professional positions. Institutional roles grew clearer, departmental structures appeared more complex, line and staff relationships developed, and personnel procedures became more formalized. The founder appeared well on his way to assembling the combination of ideas, men, and money that would permit Covenant House to achieve new levels of service and visibility.[9]

The emergence of formal administrative structures clearly played an important transformative role within the agency. Ritter's informal network of associates, confidantes, and connections, however, perhaps proved even more influential. By the early 1980s, the founder operated within a social and institutional milieu that bore scant resemblance to the alternative East Villagers, idealistic college students, and aspiring activists who composed the original Covenant I community. His visibility and success carried him away from the margins and closer to the centers of social power within the Church and the nation. Ritter's celebrity status generated high-profile connections, which meant unprecedented support for his social programs. He began traveling in elite international circles that included high-powered philanthropists, conservative politicians, and globe-trotting capitalists. The founder believed that his "throwaway kids" would benefit most from these efforts to cultivate and nurture important contacts. During the early 1980s, several influential friends did prove particularly helpful in supporting the ministry and in charting Covenant House's future. In the beginning, everything appeared quite positive.

Robert Macauley, an enigmatic and somewhat mysterious businessman, emerged as one of Ritter's principal supporters and closest friends. Macauley always claimed that he first learned of Covenant House while sipping a cup of coffee in his New Canaan, Connecticut, home on a May morning in 1977. A *New York Daily News* column by Bill Reel caught the fifty-three-year-old philanthropist's eye, and he decided to telephone the Franciscan friar in order to learn more about his Times Square ministry. Macauley possessed several personal qualities that might well have endeared him to Ritter. One positive public relations article described Macauley as someone who "speaks quickly in sonorous cadences" with "the casual yet alert affability of a veteran salesman—the big hello, the hearty handshake, the solicitous manner, the winning way with a story." He enjoyed shocking his more pious acquaintances with tales about "playing the piano in a French cathouse" in order to support himself following his military service in World War II and proved as resourceful as Ritter in embedding his life history in myths, stories, and appealing morality tales. Within a short time of their initial meeting, Macauley effortlessly charmed his way into Ritter's inner circle.[10]

Macauley encountered Ritter at a pivotal moment in the businessman's own life. He had grown up as an Episcopalian in wealthy Fairfield County, Connecticut, where he forged a childhood friendship with George H. Bush, progressed through fashionable prep schools and Yale University, and eventually followed in his father's footsteps by entering the paper industry. In 1973, he established the Virginia Fibre Corporation in central Virginia, a corrugated container manufacturing company that earned him a considerable fortune. Conservative politics and international philanthropic endeavors proved his true passions, however, and they began to consume increasing amounts of his time and energy by the mid-1970s. In 1975, Macauley became interested in the plight of Vietnamese war orphans and organized a charity known as the Shoeshine Boys Foundation, which enabled homeless children in Saigon to earn money by working as bootblacks. He also mortgaged his house that same year so that he could personally charter a Pan American plane in order to airlift orphans out of Saigon following the Communist takeover. Covenant House's program fit well with Macauley's growing interest in homeless children, and its religious base appealed to his spiritual impulses as well. After meeting Ritter in 1977, Macauley became convinced that he could provide the corporate expertise, philanthropic know-how, and risk-taking mentality that would transform the agency into a significant global enterprise.[11]

Macauley formally joined Covenant House's board of directors in 1978 and rapidly became a major force within the organization. He committed substantial personal funds and contributions from Virginia Fibre to the charity, successfully promoted the Covenant House cause to wealthy business associates, spearheaded an endowment campaign, and provided lucrative investment tips that helped to solidify institutional finances. Macauley also involved himself in every aspect of organizational culture. Ritter consulted him concerning all major personnel decisions, senior staff meetings and retreats frequently took place at Macauley's Millbrook Farm estate near Poughkeepsie, and the paper magnate carefully nurtured his own informational sources among key Covenant House administrators. The relationship also grew deeply personal. Ritter typically spent Christmas week at Macauley's vacation home in Delray Beach, Florida, and he became an important spiritual force in the family's faith life as well. But business had brought the two together, and institutional concerns cemented their relationship.[12]

Macauley peppered Ritter with a steady stream of correspondence, invariably labeled "personal and confidential," that contained detailed accounts of conversations with key Covenant House contacts and brutally frank thoughts concerning people and programs. One especially revealing 1984 letter, which purported to discuss "the philosophy of the constitution of our various Boards of Directors, particularly the Covenant House parent board," aptly summarizes the real power relationships within the organization during the early 1980s. Covenant House had been under some pressure during this time to diversify its board of directors, which remained overwhelmingly white, male, and Catholic. Further, the establishment of Covenant House subsidiaries in Guatemala, Toronto, Houston, and Fort Lauderdale required the creation of additional local boards based in those locations. Board expansion, in the minds of Ritter and Macauley, needed to be managed in a careful and meticulous manner. Macauley framed the issue in stark terms. He warned Ritter against recruiting "active, prestigious individuals, on a Board which we may not be able to control." Such a board, which would "operate on facts, figures and pragmatic assumptions," might question or threaten new programmatic directions, dilute Macauley's influence, and create an institutional culture "that would preclude us from 'pushing them around.'" The Virginia Fibre executive preferred staying the course and establishing a "captive" board, which "will operate as in the past, simply on faith." This time-tested model offered the advantage of maintaining the supportive and deferential "constituency that has permitted you and me to do practically everything we ever wanted." Ritter and Macauley had successfully created a highly centralized and conveniently informal managerial structure during the early 1980s. They devised institutional policies with minimal board oversight, and they carefully controlled initiatives by administrative staff. Since the results appeared so positive, few questioned the procedures.[13]

Macauley also found his Covenant House affiliation advantageous in promoting his other charitable causes. In 1979, he incorporated the Americares Foundation, which soon emerged as a leading disaster relief organization and earned a reputation for being the first private humanitarian agency to arrive at the scene of any major global calamity. This philanthropy relied heavily on Macauley's Covenant House contacts for support. Ritter was soon named a vice president of the foundation, and prominent board members during the 1980s included J. Peter Grace and William Simon. Americares took full advantage of Roman Catholic contacts and charitable networks throughout the world. Ritter and Grace arranged a meeting between Macauley and Pope John Paul II in 1981 that resulted in a massive program to airlift medical and pharmaceutical supplies to Poland in March of 1982. Macauley frequently funneled aid through the Knights of Malta, an international Catholic lay organization that enjoyed full diplomatic rights in many countries and counted J. Peter Grace as one of its principal power brokers in North America. The Knights connection allowed Americares to bypass traditional diplomatic routes, as well as customs inspections, in many

Catholic countries. Macauley's agency seemingly appeared on the scene with aid in every global conflagration that the Reagan administration deemed strategically significant in the 1980s: Afghanistan, Ethiopia, Nicaragua, the Philippines, and Armenia. This prompted several leftist journalists to charge that Macauley's good works operated as a philanthropic arm of right-wing American foreign policy interests. Some connected him with covert Central Intelligence Agency operations. Macauley vigorously denied those allegations, but his political sympathies remained closely tied to conservative forces throughout the globe.[14]

J. Peter Grace, another influential colleague of Ritter and Macauley, certainly made no secret of his political stances.[15] Opinionated, outspoken, and notoriously gruff with his subordinates, Grace once described his principal hobbies as "economics and anti-Communism." As the third generation of his family to serve as president of W. R. Grace & Company, he inherited a corporation with far-flung Latin American business interests. He retained a lifelong commitment to building a strong capitalist economy with a favorable investment climate for American entrepreneurs throughout that region. He made his mark within his own corporation by dramatically diversifying the family business. W. R. Grace was transformed under Peter's leadership from a shipping and trading company into a vast industrial complex that manufactured chemicals, engaged in banking and insurance operations, retained a serious interest in air and ocean transportation, operated a chain of kidney dialysis service centers, and owned subsidiaries ranging from Herman's Sporting Goods to the El Torito restaurant chain.

Grace never actually served on the Covenant House board, but he convened an informal group of advisors to the agency, which included Macauley and other corporate associates. Grace offered Ritter easy access to such wealthy individuals as Charles Keating and William Simon, international connections ranging from Mother Teresa to Pope John Paul II owing to his leadership role within the Knights of Malta, and a new legitimacy within church and state. By embracing Peter Grace, Covenant House gained the support of perhaps the nation's most prominent and socially connected Catholic philanthropist. Ritter clearly enjoyed his association with this larger-than-life layman who invariably carried a pistol in his belt, usually appeared in public flanked by a bevy of bodyguards, and regularly ferried the Franciscan around the globe on his private corporate jet. Grace's involvement undoubtedly benefited Covenant House in many tangible ways. His corporation provided important in-kind contributions to the ministry, such as office supplies, medical equipment, maintenance services, and food product donations. Grace also recruited new board members, raised some capital that allowed the organization to initiate ventures outside of New York City, and freely lent his prestige to institutional endeavors.[16]

Ritter easily justified his friendship with some of the wealthiest and more conservative figures in American Catholic culture by citing the undeniable financial advantages for his program. The founder remained supremely confident that he could accept their support without corrupting his own core values and principles. As the 1980s wore on, however, neutral observers might question his certitude. Ritter's personal lifestyle remained relatively modest, but his social commitments appeared more difficult to discern.[17] His focus narrowed, his cultural critiques seemed less systemic, and he embraced only the most conventional political crusades. For sure, Ritter publicly spoke out against child pornography, vigorously attacked the sexual advice dispensed by popular radio talk show host Dr. Ruth Westheimer, and excoriated middle-class Americans for attending *Oh Calcutta*, the long-running nude musical on Broadway. Yet public pronouncements that appeared fresh and insightful during the late 1970s seemed somewhat timeworn and predictable by the early 1980s. Ritter now targeted safe and popular causes, intended more to coalesce than to challenge his increasingly conservative constituency. The founder had discovered, perhaps unconsciously, that the cost of doing business with his new colleagues meant muting his sharply critical perspective concerning mainstream American culture. In subtle ways, Covenant House seemed in danger of losing its prophetic character.[18]

A small example illustrates this larger point. In 1982, Ronald Reagan named Peter Grace to chair the President's Private Sector Survey on Cost Control in the Federal Government in order to root out alleged waste and inefficiency in the public domain. Grace quickly embroiled himself in a public controversy during an address to the American Food and Grain Manufacturers Association on 27 May. He departed from his prepared text and declared the federal food stamp program "basically a subsidy for Puerto Ricans." As he explained to the somewhat stunned audience, "Nine hundred thousand [Puerto Ricans] live in New York, and they're all on food stamps, so this food stamp program is basically a Puerto Rican program." Political and community leaders called for his resignation from Reagan's commission. Protesters demonstrated outside of the W. R. Grace headquarters on Forty-second Street in New York City. Grace offered a half-hearted apology that characterized the speech as an "oratorical mistake." Bruce Ritter's reaction proved telling. The Franciscan had begun his "ministry of availability"

in the late 1960s by occupying a tenement in a largely Puerto Rican neighborhood on the Lower East Side, hoping to somehow be of service to the
poor. In June of 1982, he quickly dashed off a note to Peter Grace "to let you
know that my thoughts and prayers are with you at this time." Grace's social
commentary inspired Ritter to quote the following passage from the Twenty-
sixth Psalm in the hopes of bolstering the wounded executive's spirits:

> I never take my place with liars
> and with hypocrites I shall not go
> I hate the evil-doer's company
> I will not take my place with the wicked.

As Ritter concluded in his missive, "I admire your courage and integrity,
Peter. And if I never told you that before, I should have." There would be
numerous opportunities in the future for Ritter to reinforce his admiration,
as he continued on his journey into respectable conservatism.[19]

Evidence indicates, however, that Ritter still sought to retain some of
the countercultural vitality that had attracted so many talented young
people to his movement. He hoped to accomplish this largely through the
volunteer program and the Faith Community. By 1980, thanks in large part
to the favorable publicity provided by mass media outlets, both endeavors
appeared to be thriving. Covenant House estimated that forty full-time
community members and two hundred part-time volunteers participated in
the ministry. Part-timers typically worked at the Under 21 shelter for a few
weeks or an entire summer. Faith Community members committed themselves to nine- or twelve-month terms. During this period they agreed to
live simply and avoid ostentation, maintain a lifestyle that would never
exceed the resources available to the lower middle class, practice chastity,
maintain the integrity of the Eucharist, and stand firmly within the guidelines and teachings of the Roman Catholic Church. They engaged in three
hours of communal prayer and one hour of private prayer daily, worked at
tasks that ranged from cleaning bathrooms to counseling teenagers, and
viewed themselves as the visible manifestation of Christ's presence in the
ministry. By encouraging such volunteerism, Ritter thought that he might
nurture the selfless and deeply spiritual impulses that initially drove the
covenant project while simultaneously smoothing its rougher and more
radical edges.[20]

Volunteers could prove surprisingly diverse and bring unanticipated
skills to the organization. Marvin Liebman, who came to Covenant House
through a very circuitous route, provides a perfect example. An accomplished

public relations executive, Liebman had earned an industry-wide reputation for his expertise with direct mail marketing. He owned a firm that specialized in coordinating publicity and postal campaigns for right-wing political causes, and he became identified both socially and ideologically with William F. Buckley and his *National Review* circle throughout the 1960s and 1970s. Liebman's autobiography, however, also described a "private gay life" that he secretly concealed from his conservative friends and colleagues. His dual existence left him emotionally and spiritually spent. He became a restless seeker, hoping to reconcile his conflicted conscience by pursuing an authentically satisfying religious experience. Liebman eventually found solace within the Roman Catholic communion, converting from Judaism in 1979 and faithfully attending weekly mass at the Church of Saint John the Evangelist on Fifty-fifth Street in Manhattan thereafter.[21]

Shortly following his conversion, Liebman heard Bruce Ritter deliver a guest sermon at Saint John's. The founder's appeal for volunteers intrigued the fifty-five-year-old conservative, who had often "cruised the streets of Times Square searching, looking" for brief liaisons. Liebman "had a bad image of myself for doing this, for being gay at all" and now hoped that "I might atone for my guilt by serving these young boys and girls." The public relations executive met privately with Ritter, offering to serve food and scrub floors at the Under 21 facility. The founder suggested that his skills might more appropriately benefit Covenant House's direct mail operation instead. Liebman promptly drafted a fund-raising appeal, purchased thirty-five thousand names from the Catholic List Company, and received a 30 percent response rate on his first endeavor. He soon entered into a more formal business relationship with the organization that produced excellent dividends. During the first three months of 1980, Covenant House expanded its mailing list to nearly sixty thousand names and generated over $150 thousand in revenue from its postal solicitations. Thanks in large measure to this solid foundation, the agency's direct mail program now operated on a much more systematic basis. Liebman ended his affiliation with the ministry in 1980 and eventually created a cause célèbre within both conservative and gay circles by publicly revealing his secret life. At Covenant House, the direct mail operation became integrated into ongoing administrative functions, continued to thrive and mature under the leadership of Keith Brown, and remained perhaps the most important element of fund-raising activities throughout the 1980s.[22]

Liebman's background and story proved atypical from that of most Covenant House volunteers and Faith Community members. Overall demographic information appears lacking, but a statistical sampling of thirty-two individuals who joined the community between September 1983 and April 1984 provides some general clues to the broader patterns. Nearly 70 percent of these volunteers were women, over 80 percent possessed at least a bachelor's degree, over 80 percent were unmarried, and 50 percent were under thirty years of age. Students accounted for nearly 25 percent of the community members, while educators and medical professionals composed over 30 percent. Not surprisingly, and very much in keeping with Ritter's vision, the Faith Community attracted young, educated, impressionable, and highly committed individuals who believed intensely in both the founder and his ministry. Ritter recruited many community members through his speaking engagements at local parishes. Others sought to join after reading about the ministry in their hometown newspapers. By November of 1980, Covenant House had compiled a waiting list of two hundred applicants for entrance into the Faith Community, and its potential appeared limitless.[23]

Ritter used the community as a source for filling important staff positions throughout the 1980s, and many young male volunteers moved rapidly up the administrative hierarchy. Gregory A. Loken, a Faith Community member who had earned his J.D. from Harvard University in 1977, found himself directing the agency's youth advocacy program and contributing to briefs that would be argued before the United States Supreme Court by the early 1980s. Patrick Atkinson, who had completed bachelor's degrees in criminal justice and social work from Moorhead State University in Minnesota in 1981, was named by Ritter to administer the Casa Alianza program in Guatemala City in 1983 at the age of twenty-four after serving a stint with the community. John Spanier, who had just turned thirty when he completed his tenure in the community, emerged as an important leader within the institution and an assistant to Ritter. Jim Kelly, though never a member of the Faith Community, was still in his twenties when he received the primary responsibility for starting a Covenant House program in New Orleans. Kelly even came under serious consideration for the position of chief operating officer of the entire organization before reaching the age of thirty. The rapid rise of such young men from volunteers to major administrators unsettled some professional staffers, who derisively referred to them as the "true believers" and the "golden boys." Many possessed direct access to Ritter, most exhibited more youthful enthusiasm than solid administrative experience, all appeared unswervingly committed to the founder, and their influence blurred conventional line-and-staff relationships. They satisfied Ritter's desire to mold a loyal cadre of mission-driven followers who would check institutional tendencies toward routine and bureaucratization. Their prominence, however, also contributed to an unhealthy division within Covenant House by privileging personal loyalty and volunteerism at the expense of honest dialogue and professional commitments. It remained a difficult balance to maintain.[24]

The Faith Community proved especially instrumental in implementing one particular initiative. Covenant House's decision to open Casa Alianza in Guatemala in 1981 crystallized many of the themes that defined organizational life during the early 1980s. It suggested the forces that now influenced institutional decision making, highlighting power relationships on the board of directors and relying upon a delicate combination of international connections, professional expertise, and communitarian commitment for its success. Casa Alianza illustrated both the perils and the possibilities of aggressive expansionism. The Guatemalan experiment reflected an innovative programmatic impulse, but it also testified to the political limitations that now constrained the organization. Perhaps not surprisingly, considering the direction that the ministry appeared to be taking, Covenant House's Guatemalan venture began with a trip by Bruce Ritter to Rome in April of 1980.

Peter Grace financed and orchestrated this journey to the Eternal City. Impressed with the Under 21 program in Times Square, he believed that Ritter might work toward replicating his remarkable success elsewhere. Accordingly, the philanthropist instructed the Franciscan to "get a team together" and prepare a report that contained "super extensive/detailed step-by-step procedures for opening up programs in any city of the world."[25] Grace believed that the Knights of Malta, which brought together some of the world's wealthiest and most powerful lay Catholics in the interest of funding and encouraging charitable work throughout the globe, constituted the perfect conduit for supporting Covenant House's efforts. He further felt that an American-sanctioned and Catholic-inspired philanthropic endeavor might prove especially useful in Central America and South America. Viable leftist political movements threatened American business interests throughout this region during the late 1970s, and the growth of liberation theology, in Grace's mind, too often placed the Roman Catholic Church in league with rebels and dissidents. The Knights had targeted Latin America as a special outlet for more conservative charitable works, and Covenant House's noncontroversial and essentially apolitical program fit well with this philosophy.[26] Bob Macauley agreed, suggesting that Ritter might serve an even nobler national purpose. He worried over the global proliferation of an "unfortunate and undeserved image of the 'Ugly American' that has become so rampant abroad, especially during the last ten or fifteen years." The Americares founder hypothesized that "envy is one of the most significant factors" in fueling what he believed to be this unfair caricature. He thought that Ritter might play an important role in rehabilitating America's global reputation through his good works. Macauley enthused to Grace: "Did you ever stop to think how great a contribution could be made by Covenant Houses worldwide? The potential effects, all over the world, tend to boggle even my imagination, which is not known for its infertility." Armed with such heady sentiments, Grace sent Ritter to Rome to meet with powerful officials within the Knights of Malta and to pitch his program to potential financiers.[27]

The Roman trip appeared to be an unqualified success on several levels. Ritter met with the grand master of the knights, who clearly "seemed impressed by the work and seemed inclined to sponsor . . . the work of Covenant House in other parts of the world—he made it plain that he was thinking mostly of South America." He also cultivated Baroness Aieleen Schell, a German noblewoman and friend of Peter Grace, who had toured the Under 21 facility in New York and appeared another likely source of international support. He further discussed expansion with the procurator of the Franciscans and presented his program to William Cardinal Baum, the former archbishop of Washington who now directed the Sacred Congregation for Catholic Education. Covenant House's founder also found time to visit his alma mater, attend a general papal audience, tape an interview with Vatican Radio, and characteristically "spend as much time as I could wandering around the streets quite late at night, dressed in secular clothing of course" in order to investigate prostitution, homelessness, and "nomadism" in Rome.[28]

Ritter's actions and conversations suggest that he was moving in several directions. A Covenant House facility based somewhere in Latin America appeared quite feasible and fundable, but his real interests lay elsewhere. Ritter especially hoped to establish a program in Rome itself, and his April 1980 visit reinforced that dream. He sought out laywomen who had been involved with social ministries, learned about modest programs that had been administered by the Sisters of the Good Shepherd and Mother Teresa's religious community, and investigated a small-scale drug rehabilitation program that operated under the jurisdiction of an Italian priest. His late-night wanderings convinced the founder that more systematic and large-scale efforts appeared necessary. Ritter found that "prostitution is very highly organized, all the girls do have pimps . . . and they are just as cruel and vicious as American pimps." A stroll down the Via Veneto convinced him that Italian prostitutes "were much older than those we find working 8th Avenue." During another late-night excursion, he observed "women obviously in their forties, sitting on rocks and stones—apparently they would simply take their customers back in to the bushes or behind one of the ruined arches of the Baths." The founder quickly sized up the situation, made snap judgments, and appeared willing to commit substantial institutional resources to a program in Rome based on his cursory and impressionistic review of social conditions. He informed Franciscan officials that he would provide $250,000, advisory personnel, and technical assistance to the friars if they agreed to establish a Covenant House in the city. They listened politely, exhibited a "tentatively, very tentatively favorable" response but took no further action, and the project never materialized.[29]

Ritter also used the trip to promote his notion of the Faith Community. He found extraordinary interest concerning this volunteer program among all of his contacts, especially within the Franciscan hierarchy: "People here seem genuinely impressed by it, see it as a sign of life in the church and by extension I suppose in the Order itself." The flattering response stimulated Ritter to crystallize his plans concerning the community, which appeared increasingly central to his vision for Covenant House generally. Shortly following his return from Rome, Ritter wrote to Baroness Schell that "I am more and more convinced that the future of the Church will rest firmly and undeniably in the hands of the laity and that new forms and structures will be developed by the Holy Spirit to permit his complete and free action through people such as yourselves and the Knights and the Community." His thoughts appeared to be moving him toward a more radical and decidedly postconciliar conception of the Church as the "people of God," whereas he believed that "most religious orders and the structures of most Dioceses today represent old wineskins." Ritter professed a respect for traditional Roman Catholic structures, but he expressed his growing conviction that "new life in the Church, the life of the Holy Spirit, will be made manifest in the efforts and lives of dedicated laymen and women more than in and through the institutional clergy." He thus articulated a virtually mystical and transcendent notion of lay community. Covenant House's volunteer program now assumed a spiritual significance in the founder's mind that moved it well beyond the more mundane and essentially pragmatic considerations that had prompted its initial establishment.[30]

The short-term results of Ritter's trip to Rome proved more practical than visionary. He returned home with verbal commitments from the Knights, a freshly cultivated global network of supporters and admirers, and a growing recognition that his expansion plans should focus first on Latin America. The founder immediately debriefed an enthusiastic Macauley, who recalled spending a "glorious evening in New Canaan" with Ritter in May of 1980 "when, after becoming sufficiently anesthetized, we agreed on [five] new homes," thereby proving "that the greatest decisions in life are arrived at when the hour before the dawn is darkest!"[31] Ritter still needed to settle on a specific location for his first venture outside of New York City, and his newfound international contacts proved helpful. Covenant House quickly received an invitation to participate in an International Congress for the Family of the Americas, which had scheduled a meeting in Guatemala City in June of 1980. The event had received Pope John Paul II's approval, promised an appearance by Mother Teresa, and hoped to attract approximately one thousand lay and ecclesiastical leaders who endorsed its principal theme of natural family planning. It would afford Ritter an ideal opportunity to introduce his program to potential sponsors in a region that deeply interested Grace, Macauley, and the Knights of Malta. The conference itself, however, already had generated some controversy within liberal church circles.[32]

Catholic activists protested the June 1980 conference less for its emphasis on natural family planning than for its location in Guatemala City. Human rights groups had been attempting to organize an international boycott of tourism to Guatemala, citing the government's role in encouraging violence, torture, repression, semiclandestine death squads and the mysterious "disappearances" of dissidents. The nation had been engulfed in political violence since 1954 when the Central Intelligence Agency organized an invasion to dislodge the left-leaning presidential administration of Jacobo Armens Guzman. Most observers agreed, however, that brutality and repression spiraled out of control during the late 1970s. The Carter administration had suspended military aid to Guatemala in 1977, citing continuous human rights violations. President Romeo Lucas Garcia, who relied heavily on military officials and conservative businessmen for his support, assumed office in 1978 following an election that featured widespread rioting, strikes, and an electoral boycott. Violence increased during his regime. Amnesty International estimated that approximately three thousand individuals labeled "subversive" or "criminal" by government officials had either been assassinated or murdered while in custody between January and

November of 1980.[33] Mayan peasants were the most common victims, but the *New York Times* estimated that sixty-three student leaders, forty-one university professors, four priests, thirteen journalists, thirty-eight opposition party officials, and several dozen labor leaders had also been killed during the first eight months of 1980. Leftist guerillas, operating primarily in Guatemala's poverty-stricken mountainous regions, carried out their own assassinations and terrorist assaults against policemen, army officials, and right-leaning businessmen. This political violence occurred against a regional backdrop of leftist revolutionary fervor in Nicaragua and El Salvador, further inflaming tensions and increasing right-wing resolve to repress protest movements by any means necessary.[34]

Ecclesiastical politics within Guatemala also appeared quite volatile. The *National Catholic Reporter* characterized the Guatemalan hierarchy as "among the most conservative on the continent" in 1980, observing that they "have made no attempt to bring themselves closer to the people, or to the priests and nuns who work with the people." Guatemala's archbishop Mario Casariego, who had spent most of his formative years in Spain and had assumed charge of the see in 1964, maintained an especially cozy relationship with the nation's ruling oligarchy. He warned his diocesan clergy against engaging in political activity, criticized religious orders for their leftist leanings, and advised public officials to exile meddlesome clerics from the country. Escalating tensions between church and state, however, made Cardinal Casariego increasingly uncomfortable. A series of events in 1980 placed governmental officials at odds with Roman Catholic authorities. Several activist priests and missionaries either mysteriously disappeared or were found murdered over the course of the year. Pope John Paul II issued a strong condemnation of violence and church persecution in Guatemala, prompting President Lucas Garcia to refuse to receive a papal envoy. The Guatemalan president also barred Archbishop John Gerardi of the Quiche diocese from reentering the country following his criticism of local authorities. Considering the worsening climate within Guatemala, several prominent clergymen attacked the International Congress for the Family of the Americas for ignoring the human rights boycott. Fr. Alan McCoy, the president of the Conference of Major Superiors of Men, excoriated "organizations so closely associated with the church" for selecting Guatemala as the site for the world meeting. Fr. Simon Smith, director of Jesuit Missions, chastised the conference as "a gross legitimization of the present regime" in Guatemala and argued that it undermined both current papal pronouncements and United States foreign policy interests. Ritter, however, elected to participate in the proceedings and to distance himself from the broader political protests.[35]

His attendance proved fruitful for Covenant House's program. Ritter immediately struck up a friendship with Mercedes Arzu Wilson, one of the conference's principal organizers. Wilson, who hailed from a prominent Guatemalan family, had established the World Organization of Ovulation Method (Billings) for the USA in 1977.[36] Her promotion of the Billings method of natural family planning, which encouraged women to monitor their mucus in order to determine their fertility periods and accordingly modify their sexual behavior, earned her a degree of influence within Vatican circles. She also provided an entrée to Guatemala's economic and political elites. Her brother Alvaro Arzu served as the national tourism director under Lucas Garcia, and her father, Enrique, was a wealthy landowner with far-flung economic investments in various Guatemalan industrial enterprises.[37] Ritter successfully cultivated connections with the Arzu family. Enrique and Alvaro became major patrons and supporters, providing both the financial guarantees and the political clout necessary for Covenant House to establish its operations in Guatemala. Ritter also found ecclesiastical officials friendly and cooperative. Cardinal Casariego viewed Covenant House a safe social welfare agency that met a real need and one that the institutional church could wholeheartedly support. He assigned Eduardo Fuentes, his newly appointed auxiliary bishop, to formally invite the ministry into the country and to serve as the principal diocesan liaison. Ritter also received a financial commitment from the Franciscans to support the first year of the project, thus making the endeavor more palatable to his own board of directors. He returned from the conference energized and optimistic. The Guatemalan initiative offered an opportunity to establish a model program that would have a significant social impact locally and push Covenant House beyond the boundaries of New York City.[38]

Casa Alianza, however, proved problematic on a variety of levels. Ritter relied heavily on the Faith Community to establish and administer this program from the outset, sending five volunteers to Guatemala City in October of 1980 on an exploratory expedition. This decision exemplified Ritter's intensifying commitment to the lay community, but it also introduced several pragmatic difficulties. His Guatemalan team possessed no relevant language skills, a minimal understanding of the nation's legal structures, rudimentary knowledge of the country's political and ecclesiastical peculiarities, and cursory contacts with other social service providers. They truly operated primarily by faith. The group gradually developed some sense of the local situation, but their inexperience generated several missteps. Still, Ritter persisted. He appointed two executive directors at Casa Alianza during the early 1980s: both had been faithful community members, but each struggled with his administrative responsibilities. The executive directors found it difficult to satisfy the occasionally competing and always complex demands of the Arzu family, Ritter, their own support staffs, and the children. Both ultimately resigned under less than satisfactory circumstances. Ritter continued to insist that the Faith Community play an integral role at all Covenant House facilities despite the mixed results evident at Casa Alianza. His transcendent belief in the volunteer program sometimes clouded his administrative judgments.[39]

Guatemala's political situation also proved difficult to negotiate. Military coups, violence, guerilla warfare, massacres, human rights violations, and torture persisted throughout the 1980s. Politicians more aggressively confronted church structures during this period, fearing that religious institutions threatened the ruling establishment. Many social action and relief agencies recalled their personnel and abandoned their Guatemalan operations. Covenant House remained, but it necessarily took a very low political profile and scrupulously avoided social criticism. This produced internal conflicts and frustrations for some staff members. Gregory Loken, a member of the initial Faith Community team, suffered some pangs of conscience after reading an Amnesty International report concerning officially sanctioned violence in the nation and discovering that Alvaro Arzu appeared personally connected with President Lucas Garcia. Writing to Covenant House's corporate counsel, he raised a difficult moral issue: "On an ethical level, can we justify our involvement with such people, an involvement which may seem to legitimize them?" Yet he refrained from asking these same questions in his correspondence with Ritter, fearing that the founder "has heard enough pessimism from my corner for the time being."[40] Casa Alianza focused exclusively on caring for homeless children and war orphans during the 1980s, electing to avoid any involvement in broader political causes. Ritter viewed this as a practical compromise that allowed the agency to focus on its primary mission of helping children. Human rights advocates took a less charitable perspective, charging that silence supported a fundamentally corrupt sociopolitical system that religious ministries merely ameliorated.

Casa Alianza further complicated long-standing relationships and procedures within Covenant House. Board members did not uniformly support the initiative. Si Taubman, who had served as a director since 1972, raised "doubts about the involvement of Covenant House personnel and funds in Guatemala" at a January 1981 meeting, in a rare demonstration of dissent. Donna Santarsiero, another board member and early Ritter associate, also expressed her opposition. The new venture required Covenant House to modify some of its established practices. The institution elected not to raise funds in Guatemala, partly in deference to local diocesan officials and partly in order to maintain the agency's purposefully low profile. Casa Alianza shunned publicity from Guatemalan media outlets, avoided endorsements from local politicians, and remained almost exclusively dependent on corporate headquarters in New York and a few wealthy Guatemalan patrons for support. Ritter himself rarely mentioned the project in his own fund-raising appeals, preferring to keep the focus primarily on New York City and maintaining some institutional distance from the initiative. Tensions occasionally surfaced between Casa Alianza administrators and the Arzu family, who desired considerable input into staffing issues and programmatic decisions. All in all, the venture proved more complex and internally divisive than initially envisioned.[41]

Perhaps most problematically, the children themselves posed unique challenges. Violence and poverty had produced a substantial population of orphans and abandoned youths who wandered the streets of Guatemala City, begging, stealing, shining shoes, and watching parked cars in order to obtain money. Many suffered from malnourishment, infectious skin diseases, and parasites. Most arrived at Casa Alianza between the ages of six and twelve, and Covenant House sought to provide long-term residential care that would sustain them until they could live independently at age sixteen to eighteen. This required a substantial commitment to building educational facilities, developing vocational and agricultural training programs, and offering sustained medical care. The shelter itself, an abandoned hotel located on twenty-four acres in Antigua, housed approximately eighty to one hundred boys at any given time. The program thus attempted to deal with large numbers of children in a massive facility yet provide them with the intimacy and attention that characterized smaller group home programs. Ideals sometimes outpaced realities, and good intentions frequently surpassed administrative abilities.[42]

Despite its difficult beginnings, the Guatemalan project evolved over the course of the 1980s into a much more comprehensive program that featured a crisis center for street kids in Guatemala City, transitional residences, group homes in the rural town of Nebaj, health clinics, and expanded services for children with physical disabilities. Casa Alianza focused on immediate and practical care, seeking primarily to make a positive difference in individual lives. Its successes seemingly reinforced the benefits of cooperating with governmental authorities and illustrated the advantages of adopting a nonconfrontational approach toward extant power brokers. Guatemala's broader socioeconomic structures, however, ensured that issues concerning street children would remain an enduring national scandal. The social needs that prompted Ritter to open his shelter in Antigua would not soon disappear.

Covenant House viewed its Guatemalan initiative as a model, and geographic expansion proceeded rapidly during the late 1980s. Central America continued to be an important focus as the organization opened facilities in Guatemala City (1986), Honduras (1987), Mexico City (1988), and Panama (1988). Within North America, Covenant House established operations in Toronto (1982), Houston (1983), Fort Lauderdale (1985), New Orleans (1987), Anchorage (1988), Los Angeles (1988), and Atlantic City (1989). The agency formally institutionalized its procedures for establishing youth centers, and site development typically reflected the methodology employed in Guatemala. Faith Community members conducted initial environmental analyses and retained considerable influence, the organization carefully covered its bases with local leaders and church authorities, crisis intervention proved the cornerstone of the program, and Covenant House acquired large-scale physical facilities in visible and symbolic locations. The organization now possessed the rationale and the resources to replicate its efforts in a variety of diverse locales.[43]

Expansion, however, also exposed limitations in the Guatemalan model. Site openings occurred on a much more random and haphazard basis than the institution's orderly bureaucratic documentation might imply. Chance encounters, serendipitous invitations, and blind entrepreneurial faith all played a role in the decisions to establish new facilities. Each Covenant House venture depended for its success on a unique combination of particularistic circumstances, energetic and committed individuals, and carefully honed relationships with inherently fragile coalitions of supporters. Community opposition retarded and doomed some projects. Others moved along smoothly but contained their own programmatic peculiarities. Successfully exporting the national program into a broad range of idiosyncratic local venues would prove to be one of the principal administrative challenges facing Covenant House throughout the late 1980s. Guatemala provided a framework for future endeavors, but its real significance lay elsewhere.

The Guatemalan experiment testified, above all else, to the unique confluence of factors that drove institutional growth during the early 1980s. Ritter firmly believed that his Under 21 program constituted the one best system for addressing youth homelessness, and he aggressively promoted it as a model. His successful cultivation of influential financiers, politicians, and ecclesiastical authorities provided him with the wherewithal to implement his vision. Decreased dependence on government grants meant that he could operate largely as an independent entity, with limited public scrutiny. But Ritter's model also contained some systemic shortcomings. He relied on a relatively narrow group of similarly situated white male businessmen for advice. The program counted largely on their benevolence and good feelings for its support. He also cultivated loyal followers through the Faith Community who revered his leadership but failed to provide the critical perspective necessary in any healthy institution. Somewhat paradoxically, as his global connections expanded, Ritter's world became more circumscribed. Eventually, this parochialism would exact an institutional price. Freedom from public oversight, if carried too far, could easily produce a lack of public accountability. Such concerns, however, failed to temper the enthusiasm of the early 1980s. Ideas, men, and money ruled the day.

Chapter 6
Boom Years

And then there are unsung heroes: single parents, couples, church and civic volunteers. Their hearts carry without complaint the pains of family and community problems. They soothe our sorrow, heal our wounds, calm our fears, and share our joy. A person like Father Ritter is always there. His Covenant House programs in New York and Houston provide shelter and hope for thousands of frightened and abused children each year.

—*Ronald Reagan*[1]

     Covenant House's remarkable story contained considerable appeal for conservative politicians during the 1980s. The agency's success offered eloquent testimony, in their view, to several core principles that fueled the Reagan revolution. It illustrated the virtues of private philanthropy during a time when federal officials sought to retreat from supporting social services. Covenant House's heavy reliance on private funding and the founder's aggressive entrepreneurship seemingly offered replicable models for similar organizations that faced deep governmental cuts. Ritter's antibureaucratic rhetoric further struck a responsive chord with conservatives seeking to slash regulatory activity and allow nonprofit institutions freer programmatic reign. His ability to navigate around rigid state and local regulations in the interest of delivering services directly to a deeply troubled clientele appeared an excellent tribute to creative pragmatism. Voluntarism also became enshrined as a cardinal American virtue during the 1980s, and here again Covenant House's program seemed exemplary. Admirers praised the activist spirit, selfless sensibility, and individual social commitments that inspired such programs as the Faith Community. Perhaps best of all, the organization operated within a well-defined religious framework that appeared increasingly compatible with other conservative causes. Ronald Reagan successfully courted disaffected Catholic Democrats, who formed an important component of his electoral coalition, and such organizations as Covenant House appeared ideal in cementing that alliance. Religious ministries that preached sexual responsibility, opposed abortion, and emphasized strict personal morality fit comfortably within a Republican strategy that aggressively appropriated the term *family values* as part of its

Figure 7. Adolescents and young adults bed down for the evening at Covenant House in Toronto, ca. 1983. Expansion dominated the 1980s, as Covenant House opened shelters in venues ranging from Anchorage, Alaska, to Tegucigalpa, Honduras, diversifying its programs in the process. Photograph courtesy of the Covenant House Archives.

national political crusade. Ritter's increasingly moralistic rhetoric, highly publicized attacks on the sex industry, and commitment to orthodox Catholic teachings made him an especially attractive figure for right-wing activists, an "unsung hero" in the words of Ronald Reagan.

Covenant House as an organization, however, had evolved into a much more complex entity than the foregoing conservative caricature might suggest. Ritter himself recognized the paradox. In a 1982 report to Peter Grace, he identified his "most pressing" management concern as the need to reconcile the organization's mythical public image with its very real administrative challenges. Ritter understood that supporters viewed the ministry in "unrealistic" and "romantic" terms as "a smallish kind of agency where this noble priest sits, patting nice little lost kids on the head with one hand and fending off pimps with the other, while all the time worrying about paying the bills." Privately, he hoped to emphasize a new "professionalism" within Covenant House. He desired to institute a formal planning process, recruit quality middle managers, offer more competitive compensation packages to employees, and develop an "information management system" that might better monitor ongoing programs. Ritter also hoped to reduce dependence on direct mail fund-raising and to explore "public funds which may be available for research and demonstration projects." In short, he sought to better institutionalize and more appropriately bureaucratize the agency by implementing classic managerial techniques: recruiting professional staff, developing a strategic plan, diversifying his revenue stream, and instituting careful recordkeeping procedures in order to maximize quality control. He still needed to "maintain the romantic perception of Covenant House as a small, struggling agency" based on the virtues of voluntarism in order to solidify public support. Programmatic expansion and growth, however, dictated a private commitment to the more traditional bureaucratic virtues of efficiency, managerial expertise, and carefully considered marketing campaigns.[2]

Covenant House's public strategy proved largely successful throughout the 1980s. Ritter remained front and center, playing an important symbolic role. He continued to hone his image as defender of the dispossessed and vigorous opponent of the sex industry. The founder established an aggressive youth advocacy program that sought to enhance "the perception of Covenant House as a leader in the fight for child rights."[3] A series of expertly executed skirmishes with governmental officials solidified this reputation on the local level. Influential Republican connections heightened his national visibility. Ritter received an invitation to the White House and a flattering mention in Ronald Reagan's 1984 State of the Union speech.

Attorney General Edwin Meese III named the Franciscan as a member of his controversial Commission on Pornography in 1985. George and Barbara Bush visited Covenant House in 1989, partly to promote the president's Points of Light Initiative that sought to resolve social problems through a combination of voluntary effort and a national service program. Americans voted generously with their pocketbooks to affirm Ritter's efforts. Donor contributions and financial support increased throughout the decade at a staggering pace: $20.5 million in 1983, $30.5 million in 1985, $45.2 million in 1987, and $88.1 million in 1989.[4]

Internally, Ritter worked to refine his institutional infrastructure. Robert Macauley became chairman of the board in 1985, and by the late 1980s the directors represented some of the most influential and successful firms within American corporate capitalism.[5] New initiatives flourished. Covenant House moved well beyond its initial emphasis on crisis care in order to provide a broader range of services and longer-term assistance for homeless children and troubled young adults. The agency inaugurated Rights of Passage, a coherent programmatic package that combined residential care, secondary education, vocational training, counseling, and mentoring. Services increased for residents with special needs, disabilities, and chronic medical conditions. A toll-free national hotline offered confidential counseling and crisis intervention for adolescents and runaways. In many ways, the agency appeared to have resolved the perpetual struggle between charismatic and bureaucratic impulses that typically characterized religious and nonprofit institutions. Ritter provided the public persona that attracted donor loyalty and created a special aura around Covenant House. Professional and support staff provided the solid administrative infrastructure that nurtured successful programming and made a difference in the lives of individual children. As long as charisma and bureaucracy remained in proper tension, the organization thrived.

Ritter recognized the need to maintain this delicate balance, and he tinkered constantly with organizational structure during the early 1980s in an effort to achieve an appropriate level of institutionalization. Most significantly, he created the senior staff position of chief operating officer in 1984 and committed himself to recruiting an outsider in order to fill this critical administrative post. Ritter had long understood the need to assemble a more professional managerial team and paid considerable lip service to the importance of designating someone as his second-in-command. Still, he struggled with the notion of delegating responsibilities. By the mid-1980s, the founder's fund-raising obligations and high national profile, coupled with Covenant House's geographic expansion, left him no choice. Ritter worked closely with Macauley to shape this new position and to recruit potential candidates. Both relied heavily on church contacts and board colleagues to solicit résumés, but they retained tight control over the interview process. They needed someone with impeccable administrative credentials and strong leadership skills in order to unite a somewhat contentious and highly competitive staff. A familiarity with the politically complex world of Catholic social welfare organizations also appeared essential, considering the ministry's close ties to the institutional church. And, as Macauley recognized, the chief operating officer needed enough self-assurance and independence to challenge the founder, thereby counterbalancing the unquestioning loyalty exhibited by many staff members. Ritter and Macauley ultimately engaged James Harnett, a candidate who satisfied many of their desirable characteristics.[6]

Harnett had grown up steeped in the thriving middle-class Catholic culture of suburban Long Island during the 1950s and 1960s.[7] He seriously contemplated entering the priesthood but, having been much affected by the social and political turmoil of the late 1960s, left the seminary in 1968. A period of service with the Peace Corps in India followed, and when Harnett returned to the United States, he gravitated toward a professional career in the helping professions. He obtained a position with Catholic Charities in the Diocese of Brooklyn in 1972 and spent the next eleven years enmeshed in social service administration on a grass-roots level. Thomas DeStefano, who served as his mentor at Catholic Charities, recalled that Harnett was part of a dynamic "infusion of new blood" that reinvigorated the agency during the 1970s. He personified the new breed of community-based charities administrator "who would say yes, would work out of a briefcase, work at any time around the clock, and live with ambiguity."[8] Harnett initially labored primarily in the child care division, but he also helped parish teams that assisted families in the economically depressed Bedford-Stuyvesant neighborhood in Brooklyn. He further participated in a variety of community advocacy activities involving senior citizens and the developmentally disabled. Harnett also operated within a broader institutional and professional network that transcended the boundaries of Brooklyn Catholicism. He earned his graduate degree in public administration at New York University, gravitated toward managing government grants at Catholic Charities, became increasingly fascinated with public finance, and eventually left the diocese to assume an administrative position in the pediatrics division of Columbia Presbyterian Hospital in 1982. His career appeared a particularly good fit for Covenant House's needs. Harnett combined deeply felt social commitments with considerable administrative acumen. He retained an excellent reputation within Catholic institutional circles yet also moved easily and effectively in more secular surroundings. Perhaps best of all, Harnett possessed an earthy practical bent and a shrewd political sensibility that nicely complemented Ritter's own approach to social work. Despite some initial reservations, Harnett found the position of chief operating officer attractive, and he began work at Covenant House in June of 1984.[9]

Harnett arrived at a transitional moment. Formidable administrative challenges confronted the ministry in the mid-1980s. Geographical expansion introduced complex planning issues and irrevocably altered the institutional culture. Nine facilities opened throughout the United States and Central America between 1985 and 1989. Each contained its own executive director, governing board, volunteer community, and local support structure. Most administrators at these sites had no previous connection with Covenant House, thus interjecting fresh professional perspectives into the organization. New York exerted considerable programmatic and fiscal control over the subsidiaries, but each facility maintained some autonomy. At times, managers struggled to find the appropriate balance between centralized direction and local discretion. Covenant House's core philosophy guided the local operations, which retained some freedom to adapt and alter the national program in order to fit their own unique circumstances. The organization's federated structure might nurture a dynamic relationship between the corporate headquarters and the field operations, or it could produce a routine conformity. It remained for individual administrators to work out the proper relationships. Harnett mostly recalled the excitement and exhilaration that accompanied expansion, though growth hardly occurred in an orderly fashion. The chief operating officer worried at the time about overextending resources. His pragmatic caution served as a useful counterpoint to Ritter's unbounded optimism, even if the founder's vision inevitably carried the day. Ritter's enthusiastic spontaneity and opportunistic strain meant that strategic planning often took a backseat to impulsive action. The agency expanded somewhat haphazardly, though each new program clearly met a very real and specific social need.[10]

Alaska offers a good example. In this instance, a brief 1987 encounter between Ritter and the archbishop of Anchorage resulted in a significant long-term institutional commitment at a very unlikely venue. Alaska had experienced an economic boom in the late 1970s and early 1980s that completely transformed the state and its largest city. The Iranian revolution produced tremendous pressures to develop domestic energy sources, and North Shore oil became a highly desirable commodity. Anchorage exploded with activity. Between 1978 and 1982, Alaskan employment surged by 9.5 percent, the state poured billions of petroleum-generated dollars into new construction projects, and the city became a bustling urban metropolis with a population that exceeded 200,000. By the mid-1980s, however, the local economy suffered a severe downturn. When the Oil Producing Export Countries (OPEC) agreed to slash petroleum prices in 1982, Alaska's prosperity rapidly crumbled. Signs of distress abounded in Anchorage as foreclosures, depopulation, state layoffs, and property devaluation dominated daily news broadcasts. High rates of alcoholism, homelessness, and suicide overwhelmed the city's social service providers. Rootless teenagers proved a particularly troublesome concern for local civic leaders. A mayor's task force estimated in 1986 that approximately 3,200 homeless youths roamed the city's streets each year, more than three times the number found in comparable-sized cities elsewhere.[11]

Archbishop Francis T. Hurley found these statistics especially disturbing. Since assuming charge of the Anchorage see in 1976, he had made Catholic Social Services an important priority within his geographically dispersed and sparsely populated diocese. Throughout the early 1980s, Hurley responded to Anchorage's social distress by establishing and supporting several homeless programs: the Brother Francis Shelter for adults (1982), the Clare House shelter for men and women with children (1983), and McAuley Manor, a voluntary long-term residence for girls aged twelve to nineteen (1985). Still, as the archbishop recognized, the available number of beds for homeless citizens did not begin to match the growing need. Archbishop Hurley invited Ritter to a speaking engagement in Anchorage in March of 1987, hoping that the Franciscan's national reputation would raise local consciousness concerning the mayor's task force report on youth homelessness and stimulate lay Catholics to react to the issue in a more generous fashion.[12]

Harnett cautioned Ritter against making any commitments in Alaska, but the Franciscan typically charted his own course. Hurley related to the founder on a personal and professional level, allowing Ritter to pilot his private plane and extracting an on-the-spot commitment that Covenant House would open a facility in Anchorage if the archdiocese could secure a suitable building. Everyone appeared stunned by the swiftness of the agreement. The archbishop himself acknowledged to Ritter that "I had not anticipated your openness to founding a house here, or the enthusiasm of the local people." Several Covenant House board members "took exception to the fact that the Anchorage invitation was accepted without first letting the Board Expansion Committee look into the offer," and two voted against the Alaskan venture. Harnett recalled "getting a bad feeling" as soon as he heard that Hurley had taken Ritter aboard his aircraft and observed that "if there was any more plan to it" than the founder's seemingly spontaneous whim, "it was not apparent to me." As usual, immediate opportunity trumped careful planning. Hurley proved as resourceful as Ritter in seizing the moment. He rapidly located a dilapidated and vacant YMCA building in downtown Anchorage, secured a $500,000 grant from the state, received an additional $150,000 from the city, and eventually purchased the facility for $950,000. In October of 1988, less than twenty months after the initial meeting between Ritter and Hurley, Covenant House opened its Alaskan crisis center.[13]

The Anchorage program actually functioned quite well, though it diverged in several respects from other Covenant House endeavors. Alaska's geographic isolation, depressed economic situation, small Catholic population, and rudimentary philanthropic infrastructure meant that the program depended much more heavily on New York than did comparable facilities in the lower forty-eight states. The national office contributed nearly 85 percent of Anchorage's $1.3 million operating budget during the 1988–89 fiscal year. The shelter itself proved considerably smaller than other Covenant House operations, attracting approximately thirty youths per night, with intake statistics peaking during the depressingly dark and cold winter months. The crisis center also catered to a somewhat different clientele than did other Covenant Houses. The children proved much younger and more female, consistent with the population in other Anchorage shelters. Alaskan youths exhibited significantly higher rates of suicide, teen pregnancies, chronic alcoholism, drug abuse, and physical and sexual assaults than the national average. The crisis center population also reflected uniquely local ethnic demographics. For the 1988–89 fiscal year, over 60 percent of the children served by Covenant House identified themselves as Caucasians. Native Alaskans, many of whom had flocked to Anchorage from tiny and remote fishing villages, composed over 20 percent of the agency's clients. This contrasted with Covenant House programs elsewhere, which typically served much higher percentages of African American and Hispanic children.[14]

The Alaskan program progressed smoothly for several reasons. Covenant House hired Fred Ali as executive director, an individual with deep roots in the area and extensive knowledge of the local terrain. Ali had arrived in the state with a history degree from Santa Clara University in 1972 as a member of the Jesuit Volunteer Corps. He had taught high school social studies to Yupik Eskimo students along the Bering Sea coast for several years, held a variety of governmental and academic administrative posts within the state, and most recently served as vice chancellor of student services at the University of Alaska, Anchorage. Ali also made special efforts to attract Native Alaskan staff counselors and recruited a board that both represented prominent corporate interests and included well-known individuals within the social service community. Results proved modest, but progress appeared steady. Planned discharge rates among shelter residents increased from 31 percent to 46 percent over the first three years of operation. A small program in East Anchorage placed seven youths in jobs and stimulated three more to continue their formal education in 1990. A health clinic treated several hundred youths annually while also conducting prenatal and parenting classes. The agency even initiated an aggressive outreach effort designed to attract youths who spent their nights sleeping in transit centers, seeking shelter in recycling bins, and huddling under the Captain Cook Memorial. Covenant House enjoyed excellent relations with Catholic Social Services, established a cordial cooperation with child care agencies throughout the state, and offered expert testimony at governmental hearings concerning youth homelessness. Of course, problems existed. Vandalism, violent incidents, and threats to staff members caused considerable concern. Many chronic street youths repeatedly appeared at the shelter and seemed little affected by aftercare services. Overall, however, Anchorage illustrated the way in which Covenant House's national program could meet real local needs by securing strong leadership and carefully embedding the operation within the community.[15]

Other Covenant House ventures faced stiffer challenges. Community opposition often surfaced, dooming some programs and creating considerable start-up delays in other instances. Fort Lauderdale's experience proved illustrative in this regard. As usual, the program owed its origin to a combination of serendipitous circumstance and some careful calculation. Linda Idaerosa, a young Floridian who worked in the security industry and who also operated supportive crisis counseling services for Christian women, initially approached Ritter in the fall of 1981 concerning a possible facility in the Fort Lauderdale area. She arranged several speaking engagements for the founder and introduced him to such wealthy potential supporters as Joseph Sciortino, the president of Plantation/Sysco foods. Ritter sized up the local situation and concluded that conditions favored Covenant House. Miami's diocesan officials appeared supportive, potential patrons seemed enthusiastic, and the founder became convinced that the Fort Lauderdale environs constituted "a wilderness area as far as the lack of social programs is concerned." Ritter quickly engaged a local realtor, found a strategically situated resort motel named the Sand Castle that was on the market and coincidentally owned by one of Sciortino's partners at Plantation/Sysco, and promptly entered into serious negotiations to purchase the building.[16]

Fort Lauderdale seemed a good location for a variety of reasons. Since the 1950s, the town had served as a favorite destination for college students during spring break. Its unique place in youth culture had been immortalized in a variety of teen-oriented movies and popular magazines. The city's reputation as a party town peaked in the early 1980s, when springtime vacationers exceeded 300,000 annually. *Playboy* magazine, which dubbed Fort Lauderdale "the girl-watching capital of the free world" in a 1983 article, reflected and reinforced the city's hedonistic stereotype. The editors claimed that the town offered an endless series of beer-chugging bouts, wet-T-shirt competitions, and exotic kissing contests every March where "the only restriction [at most bars] is that you keep your pants on." Permanent residents, however, had grown tired of the institutionalized rowdiness and attendant vandalism by the mid-1980s. Municipal officials enacted a series of laws, including open container ordinances and restrictions on lascivious shows at beachfront bars, in an effort to alter the resort's image. Several well-publicized police sweeps and crackdowns eventually took their toll. Florida's springtime youth scene soon shifted north to Daytona Beach, and Fort Lauderdale's boosters hoped mainly to attract families, senior citizens, and conventioneers. But some social dislocation remained.[17]

The area itself was experiencing an unprecedented population boom that had increased the number of year-round residents from 620,000 in 1970 to over 1,000,000 in 1980. Fort Lauderdale's character appeared to be changing, but its wide-open reputation still attracted transient youths, and its social service infrastructure appeared inadequate. Estella Mae Moriarty, a circuit court judge in Broward County who became an important Covenant House supporter, characterized the city as "a haven" for runaway children who "flock to the Fort Lauderdale 'Strip' where they make their living as prostitutes (homosexual and heterosexual) or as subjects of pornographic films. They fall prey to drug pushers. They are the victims of disease and violence. Many of the runaways are throwaways from abusive or neglectful homes." Such characterizations struck an especially responsive chord in Ritter, who heard the echoes of familiar themes that he had been emphasizing for several years. When he learned that Broward County contained only a handful of shelters and foster care facilities to deal with a youth population that, Judge Moriarty believed, was "doomed to a life of sin, crime, violence and despair," the founder stepped up his efforts.[18]

Covenant House soon discovered, however, that the local situation proved more complex than initially had been anticipated. A hotel and motel owners' association formed to fight the shelter project. Opponents claimed that the facility would generate negative publicity, serve as a magnet for troubled teenagers, depress beachfront real estate values, and interfere with efforts to transform the community into a family-oriented resort. Ritter's aggressive style also infuriated some civic boosters. His August 1983 newsletter derided Fort Lauderdale as "the runaway capital of the United States" with "a street scene that is as bad as any in the country." He also described an early morning encounter with a young male hustler, informed his readers that "anything goes on the Strip," and criticized local hoteliers for promoting debauched entertainment.[19] Not surprisingly, Fort Lauderdale officials grew frustrated with the Franciscan, chiding him for failing "to make peace with your proposed neighbors." Public hearings sometimes degenerated into confrontational shouting matches. One prominent politician implored Ritter to compromise with his critics by abandoning the Sand Castle site, opening an intake center on the beach, and locating the shelter "in a slightly less sensitive area that . . . in the long run would probably [have] cost you a good deal less money and would not have daily discharged into a residential area a group of [somewhat aimless] young people." Ritter confidently forged on without heeding such local advice. Covenant House's attorneys successfully battled their opponents' zoning challenges, and the agency eventually opened the refurbished Sand Castle motel to runaways in September of 1985.[20]

The actual program proved less controversial than the contentious prelude. Once again, the choice of an executive director proved fortuitous. Nancy Lee Matthews, who served in that capacity from 1984 through 1997, was a popular and stabilizing influence. She had spent eighteen years in the Franciscan Missionaries of Mary before leaving religious life and had established roots in the Fort Lauderdale area by working as executive director of the Early Childhood Development Association of Broward County prior to joining Covenant House. The organization also earned praise from the local community by spending over two million dollars to renovate and landscape the seedy and rundown Sand Castle motel, neatly blending it into the surrounding architecture. The program itself clearly filled a local need: in 1989, Florida's shelter averaged over 130 children per night and admitted over 6,000 during the year, making it the largest Covenant House operation outside of New York City.[21] Yet the controversial beginnings in Fort Lauderdale revealed some disturbing problems that plagued the agency during its period of rapid expansion. Ritter sometimes failed to exhibit the patience necessary for building effective local coalitions and carefully explaining his program to diverse audiences. He relied heavily on ecclesiastical sanction when considering a new territory but paid less attention to grass-roots groups, other service providers, and community dissenters. Some believed that Covenant House exhibited too much self-confidence, perhaps bordering on self-righteousness, by refusing to compromise or modify its programs even when confronted with realistic alternatives. Others questioned whether the national organization adequately understood the unique local ecologies of individual communities and whether programs designed for Times Square in New York really translated well to other cities. Local leaders also worried that Covenant House might siphon off limited philanthropic resources to New York, thereby diluting successful smaller programs that already competed for scarce financial resources.

Many of these issues surfaced during one notably unsuccessful venture. Following two years of discussion with concerned clergy and laypeople, Ritter had secured an invitation from Humberto Cardinal Medeiros to open an Under 21 facility in Boston in 1982. The archdiocese of Boston offered Ritter some attractive financial incentives in order to encourage his program. Cardinal Medeiros authorized the Franciscan to accept preaching invitations throughout the archdiocese and agreed to dedicate an annual Sunday collection for Covenant House at all of the 450 parishes within his jurisdiction. The cardinal also allowed the founder to solicit funds among Boston Catholics through postal appeals and offered to invite the most prominent laymen in the area to a dinner kicking off a major capital campaign for the shelter. Ritter well understood the significance of maintaining close relationships with church officials. Warm receptions from diocesan administrators had guaranteed his successful programs in Toronto and Houston; tensions with ecclesiastical authorities prevented him from beginning a project in Los Angeles. Given the cardinal's enthusiasm and support, Ritter anticipated smooth sailing. By December of 1982, the founder had purchased the dingy and semiabandoned Avery Hotel in the heart of Boston's notorious "combat zone" and announced plans for a $6 million renovation to the eleven-story structure. The future appeared bright.[22]

Problems soon emerged on several levels. Local property owners had placed their faith in a pending redevelopment project that would transform the Washington Street area from a tawdry red light district into an upscale retail zone. In their view, Covenant House's arrival threatened neighborhood renewal efforts. They feared a new influx of homeless youths into the troubled downtown and pondered the effects on an already depressed business environment. As one restauranteur observed: "Can you imagine the impact of a bunch of kids coming down Avery Street? They should put it in the financial district or in South Boston, West Roxbury or on Beacon Hill."[23] Such comments partly reflected the "not-in-my-backyard" syndrome faced by most social service providers, but they also testified to real frustrations by small-scale and economically marginal entrepreneurs who had remained committed to the area during its decade-long decline. The "combat zone" had deteriorated during the 1970s into a dangerous and crime-infested adult entertainment emporium that featured open prostitution, public intoxication, strip clubs, pornographic bookstores, and peep shows. Municipal officials appeared willing to tolerate this concentrated vice district, but most legitimate businesses had boarded up their stores and departed for safer havens by the early 1980s. For the few remaining holdouts, the sudden and unanticipated announcement of a new crisis center within their midst generated more disillusionment and resignation.[24]

Covenant House worked to soothe these neighborhood anxieties and took some important steps early in 1983 to sell its program to skeptics. The organization assembled a prominent local board, carefully nurtured relationships within Boston's Chamber of Commerce, arranged for positive press coverage from both archdiocesan and secular media outlets, and even expressed a willingness to explore alternative sites. Other critical voices, however, proved more difficult to overcome. Sr. Barbara Whelan, C.S.J., quickly emerged as the most effective adversary. She had founded the Bridge over Troubled Waters ministry in 1970 in order to assist street children and runaways in Boston, rapidly expanding her operation to include youth services, outreach vans, transitional living facilities, and medical assistance. Sister Barbara found several aspects of the Covenant House proposal troublesome. Cardinal Medeiros's generous financial support for Ritter's program clearly generated some resentment. The cardinal had inherited an enormous debt estimated at $50 million when he assumed charge of the archdiocese in 1970, and his troubled episcopate featured service cuts, belt tightening, and lean times for social service providers generally. Medeiros proved unable or unwilling to help the Bridge over Troubled Waters when the agency faced a severe financial crisis in 1978, and budgetary difficulties recently had caused the ministry to lose its facility on fashionable Beacon Street. The cardinal's enthusiasm for allowing a New York agency to raise funds within his episcopal jurisdiction proved very problematic for such struggling Boston-based operations as the Bridge.[25]

Sister Barbara publicly couched her opposition in broader terms, citing several philosophical disagreements with Ritter. Covenant House had described its "combat zone" location as "a conscious choice, based on our desire to be a visible, therapeutic and attractive option" for street youths who already frequented and populated the area. Sister Barbara argued instead that youths needed to be removed from urban areas and immediately placed out with families: "Give a girl of 14 two weeks in the city and you lose her." She feared that Covenant House would become a magnet, providing only a temporary safety net for children who would soon fall prey to the surrounding temptations and manipulate social service agencies in order to support their street-based lifestyles. Covenant House placed great stock in the value of easy access to a temporary, no-questions-asked shelter. The agency argued that its core clientele consisted of hardened street kids with a tough and cynical edge who would not respond to more structured programs. Sister Barbara contrastingly insisted on the primacy of transitional living facilities and the importance of modifying behavior through careful screening and counseling. The size and scale of the operations also dramatically differed. Covenant House believed that the extent of the homeless problem in Boston required a large facility, designed to serve as many youths as possible: the Avery Hotel included 150 guest rooms and the organization anticipated housing at least 75 adolescents per night. The Bridge considered its modest size a virtue: the ministry placed out individual children in 20 foster homes that were available for one- to three-night stays and also operated 7 ninety-day supervised apartments. In fact, the Covenant House and Bridge programs complemented each other in many ways. Each approach potentially formed part of a larger coordinated strategy that might address the many complex facets of youth homelessness.[26]

Unfortunately, archdiocesan politics and the competition for limited resources ensured that the two programs would remain at odds. Sister Barbara believed that Ritter operated in a heavy-handed and imperious manner that precluded real collaboration between the organizations. The founder himself suggested that his staff members "take a low-key approach to Sr. Barbara and the Bridge," preferring to work behind the scenes with diocesan authorities and sympathetic municipal officials. Privately, however, Ritter more than willingly expressed "some opinions about small programs that he preferred would not be public at this time" to his Boston board of directors. No easy resolution to the conflict appeared on the horizon. Only

Cardinal Medeiros's death in September 1983 finally settled the issue. Bernard Law clearly wished to avoid this increasingly contentious public controversy following his appointment to lead the Archdiocese of Boston. The new archbishop also expressed his philosophical preference for supporting longer-term social service programs targeted at young mothers with infants and older adolescents with emotional problems. In 1984, Law formally withdrew the invitation to open an Under 21 facility. Ritter abandoned his Boston plans but continued to focus on expansion programs elsewhere. Covenant House sold the Avery Hotel a year later for $1,500,000, which more than covered the cost of the initial purchase and renovations, owing at least in part to the successful redevelopment efforts that now had begun to transform the "combat zone."[27]

Geographical expansion clearly occupied considerable administrative energy during the late 1980s, but other endeavors proved equally transformative. Covenant House worked especially hard to refine, revise, and perfect its core program in New York City. Professional staff increasingly supported initiatives that transcended crisis intervention and promised to produce more lasting changes within individual lives. A period of experimentation ensued, as the agency subtly expanded its range and scope. Rights of Passage (ROP), a transitional living program that sought to provide shelter residents with the skills necessary to achieve personal independence, exemplified the new focus. ROP rapidly achieved great significance within the organization. It became a focal point for fund-raising appeals, a replicable model adopted by most subsidiaries, and a principal rationale for the organization's acquisition of the National Maritime Union Building in New York City. If Under 21 very much captured Covenant House's crusading spirit during the late 1970s, Rights of Passage embodied the more mature institutional approach of the late 1980s.

Rights of Passage actually emerged from concern over the long-term prospects for shelter residents. Covenant House staff consistently found during the early 1980s that roughly one-third of the children entering the crisis center eventually left with some sort of planned discharge: a few returned to their families, others entered a group home or transitional living arrangement, and a very few managed to secure a job and apartment. For most adolescents, however, Under 21 offered only a temporary respite from a life of episodic violence, substance abuse, forced institutionalization, and aimlessness. Indeed, over one-third of the children eventually drifted back to the crisis center, and nearly three-quarters of these recidivists returned multiple times. One documented example, though extraordinary owing to its duration, indicates some general patterns. A fourteen-year-old African American male named Tim first visited Under 21 in November 1979, covered with scars and bruises as a result of repeated beatings by his mother. He abruptly left the facility after four days but returned to Covenant House twenty-one times over the course of the next six years. A lengthy stay at a residential treatment center in upstate New York and an unsuccessful stint with the United States Marine Corps punctuated his visits, but the young man rarely stayed away from the shelter for longer than two months. Tim typically resided at Under 21 for periods ranging from a few days to three weeks, always picked up some new clothing at the facility, and genuinely considered the institution's staff his "family." His day-to-day behavior, however, remained problematic. Staff continued to discharge him from the facility for a variety of offenses ranging from fighting to inability to follow his work plan. Covenant House's open intake policy ensured that he could always return after a specified time period. Tim worked a variety of transient jobs, engaged in some petty crime, and operated a few minor scams during his interludes on the street. In 1985, at the age of twenty, his future seemed bleak. He could not articulate any personal goals, grew depressed at the prospect of no longer being able to return to the shelter when he turned twenty-one, and lacked any positive support system outside of the institution. In the judgment of his counselors, Tim appeared to be merely killing time and "doing away with himself slowly on the street."[28]

Covenant House had attempted to develop some vocational and educational programs for street kids during the early 1980s, but the efforts proved too short term and piecemeal to have much impact. In 1981, for example, a self-employed businessman named Kenneth Carlson convinced Ritter to establish Dove Messenger Service in order to provide employment opportunities for shelter residents. Results proved mixed at best. The venture turned out to be a financial drain on the agency, the service could not compete in terms of speed and efficiency with comparable commercial concerns, and the jobs themselves typified the dead-end and low-skill positions that offered urban youths little future. Even worse, the messenger service placed adolescents who often possessed a history of drug problems and criminal behavior on the streets, in an unstructured and minimally supervised work environment, during the height of New York City's crack cocaine epidemic. Not surprisingly, a 1986 internal study found that over 70 percent of the forty-two messengers who left the agency during the course of that year failed to complete three months on the job. Nearly half of this group quit or were terminated. Clearly, only more systematic and carefully considered programs could help residents make a successful transition to independent living.[29]

Rights of Passage attempted to fill that void. David Gregorio, who served as residential director of the program, succinctly summarized the goals: "These were eighteen, nineteen, twenty year olds who were at a pretty critical point in their life. . . . It was about giving them the time to change direction, to learn skills, to get jobs, to start thinking of mainstream ways that they could go."[30] Staff envisioned ROP as a selective program, open to older shelter residents who had exhibited the "maturity, self-control, and commitment" that formed the necessary precursors for independent living. A formal application and screening process sought to attract young adults who varied in educational level and vocational skills but who appeared ready to commit themselves to a more structured lifestyle. Applicants agreed to live in a dormitory-style arrangement for a period of six to eighteen months, during which time they would receive individualized job training, access to educational facilities, and instruction in such basic life skills as money management, apartment maintenance, nutrition and meal preparation, and personal health and hygiene. ROP placed considerable emphasis on mentoring. Covenant House engaged corporate executives who served as both role models and counselors for the youths, remaining in weekly contact and offering advice on job-related issues. Ritual and structure also assumed great significance within the program. Retreats, formal dinners, songs and symbols, holiday tournament athletic events, and graduation ceremonies became institutionalized.[31]

Ritter introduced the concept to an enthusiastic board of directors in April of 1984 and quickly moved into full fund-raising mode. ROP proved attractive to foundations, public agencies, and corporations. The Culpeper Foundation, which had supported both the group home program and Under 21 in earlier years, granted Covenant House $300,000 from 1985 through 1987 in order to establish the program. New York State contributed $250,000 in grant funding during 1985, and substantial gifts also materialized from the Charles Hayden Foundation, Chase Manhattan Bank, and the William Randolph Hearst Foundation, among others. Renovations proceeded rapidly, and Rights of Passage welcomed its initial class of five young men to the fourth floor of the Under 21 center in March of 1986. Covenant House soon inaugurated a comparable women's program, complete with child care facilities, at its Fifty-second Street location in October of 1987. Ritter successfully drew upon board members and business contacts to develop the vocational program. Early corporate executives who served as mentors included representatives from Bear Stearns, Merrill Lynch, Salomon Brothers, and Haley Associates. The agency explored other cooperative arrangements as well, such as one innovative program involving St. Michael's College in Winooski, Vermont. ROP sent several residents to the small school in suburban Burlington during the summer of 1987 in order to audit courses, receive tutorial instruction, work at campus jobs, and socialize with their student sponsors. On every level, Rights of Passage sought to connect young adults with real-world situations and to emphasize the ways in which internalizing structure and discipline could lead to positive results for the participants.[32]

Practicality permeated every aspect of the program. Bruce Henry, who served as the first director of ROP, had gained considerable experience previously working with troubled street youths in the Bedford-Stuyvesant neighborhood of Brooklyn. His philosophical orientation always favored "getting programs into direct service to poor people" over the therapeutic interventionism that often held sway among trained social workers. Indeed, his own graduate degree was in public administration, and he found himself especially attracted to Covenant House in 1984 when he heard "that Ritter didn't like M.S.W.'s." Henry remained firmly committed to the primacy of vocational training and the need to encourage personal discipline and responsibility among program participants. He respected Ritter's belief in "concrete things" and believed that the key to ROP's success "is the jobs and the development of that" aspect of the program.[33] David Gregorio agreed and stressed the importance of integrating homeless young people into mainstream American culture. He acknowledged that the "far out or fringe person would say, 'We don't want them to get into the mainstream.' Well that's bullshit. They live in this society. If they're going to have something to eat, if they're going to have a roof over their head, if they're going to have a shot at feeling okay about themselves, then part of what they're going to judge themselves on is: how does society accept them? And this is what they need to do in order for society to accept them."[34] Covenant House's key administrators all subscribed to this pragmatic orientation. Their day-to-day experiences reinforced their ideological preconceptions, and their earthy approach to problem solving gave the organization a very recognizable style. Making an immediate difference in individual lives appeared a more laudable and realizable goal than vaguely seeking to transform deeply entrenched socioeconomic systems. This message obviously pleased Covenant House's corporate sponsors and conservative supporters, and radical critics might easily caricature the tone. But it also reflected a streetwise realism firmly grounded in working-class roots and urban life that ought not to be dismissed in a cavalier manner.

ROP's initial results appeared to justify the agency's practical focus. A survey of the first thirty-five male residents who completed the program between March of 1986 and February of 1987 revealed some interesting trends. The graduates roughly approximated the larger ethnic composition of the Under 21 shelter: African Americans accounted for 65 percent and Hispanics made up another 11 percent. Impressively, nearly 80 percent either remained employed or reported attending school in July 1987. Their jobs ranged from accounting clerk to cable installer to warehouse mover, with all concentrating in blue-collar or lower white-collar occupations. Most occupied these positions within the context of such substantial corporate enterprises as investment banks and advertising agencies, largely mirroring the workplaces of their mentors. Educational advancement occurred for some, though less regularly. Residents occasionally completed high school programs, a few received GEDs, and some even enrolled in college courses. When ROP administrators trumpeted the success of one resident who "graduated from the New York School of Food and Hotel Management and accepted a trainee position with a fine midtown hotel," they testified to the very real difference that the program might make for a young homeless man. ROP seemed to be functioning well as a small and manageable experiment that carefully monitored its graduates, provided good aftercare services, and offered reasonable opportunities for individual accomplishment.[35]

Rights of Passage reflected one major programmatic innovation in the late 1980s, but the organization forged ahead on several other fronts as well. Outreach and advocacy efforts assumed a heightened prominence. Covenant House initiated its Off the Streets program during the fall of 1986, thereby making the agency's silver-blue van a familiar fixture in New York City. Anne Donahue, a thirty-year-old attorney, served as director of Off the Streets and appeared especially committed to the work. She had become inspired by Bruce Ritter in the late 1970s when he delivered a guest presentation at her suburban New Jersey parish. After completing her education at Boston College and Georgetown Law School, Donahue volunteered in the Faith Community, joined the legal department at Covenant House as a paid staff member, and even moved to a neighborhood in the Bronx where several former community members resided and attended the local church. She threw herself completely into the ministry, rapidly rose through the administrative ranks, and eventually became the first director of Covenant House in California in 1989. Off the Streets constituted her first major administrative assignment. Donohue recruited teams of counselors who agreed to cruise the city in the Covenant House van between 10:00 P.M. and 5:00 A.M. They ran a regular route to such areas as the Hudson River piers, the meatpacking district, and "The Loop" on East Fifty-third Street that served as hangouts for juvenile prostitutes, transvestites, and homeless children. The counselors distributed hot chocolate, sandwiches, informational literature, and advice in an effort to build trust with street regulars. They also hoped to make newcomers and recent arrivals aware of available services in the metropolis. Staff transported some youngsters directly to Under 21 for crisis care, bringing 130 children back to the facility during the first three and one-half months of operation. The van proved especially popular with journalists and board members, who took advantage of occasional night rides to get a glimpse of an underground culture that appeared off limits for most respectable New Yorkers. And the program undeniably contained a romantic edge: counselors gained familiarity with some of the meanest streets of Manhattan and fancied themselves as a rescue team that removed potential juvenile prey from the clutches of pimps and drug dealers. Some even formulated plans to place the children in "safe houses" where they might begin a transition to a more stable lifestyle. A few outreach team members actually allowed street children to live in their homes on a temporary basis. Off the Streets clearly increased the ministry's visibility and reputation within New York City, illustrating well its proactive and experimental nature.[36]

Another program, however, generated even greater national attention. John Kells, Covenant House's talented young vice president for public relations, developed the concept for a national toll-free runaway hotline. He introduced it to the board in January of 1987, arguing that the program could pay multiple dividends. It would offer children and parents free and easy access to the organization's services, contain a spiritual dimension for donors who wished to use it as a prayerline, and provide the necessary communications infrastructure for a possible telemarketing system in the future. The directors enthusiastically approved the concept, and Jim Harnett assigned Patricia Connors to direct the undertaking, which became known as the Nineline. The program succeeded on several levels. The catchy number, 1-800-999-9999, became emblazoned on billboards, inscribed in print media, and broadcast in public service announcements throughout the United States. Hundreds of part-time workers and volunteers, trained in crisis intervention and listening skills, staffed the agency's phone bank around the clock. These operators handled approximately four thousand requests per day during Nineline's first few months of operation, and that volume soon increased even more. They maintained a computerized listing of approximately twenty thousand social service providers in order to conduct immediate referrals and coordinate on-the-spot conferences between callers and appropriate agencies.

Nineline also brought Covenant House to the attention of the Advertising Council, which granted the organization campaign status in 1989. This designation resulted in an estimated $25 to $30 million of free advertising for the Nineline program. Covenant House authorized Young & Rubicam, a long-time supporter of the ministry, to prepare promotional materials for the Ad Council campaign that highlighted both the hotline and the agency. Jon Bon Jovi, a popular rock star with an enormous audience among white suburbanites, recorded several public service announcements reminding his fans that "the streets are tougher than you are." Print advertisements depicted troubled teenagers sleeping in alleyways and abandoned buildings. Slogans emphasized the experience of "throwaway" children who had been abandoned by their families, using such lines as "Her parents thought she was old enough to be on her own. She was already 16." The campaign depicted homeless youths as largely white and middle class, a caricature not supported by the crisis center's own history and statistics. Still, it remained effective advertising, especially given the institution's donor base. And Nineline counselors clearly did reach a large audience of desperate teens and nervous parents. As an outreach and advocacy initiative, the hotline broadened the institution's influence, effectively made Covenant House's name synonymous with youth homelessness, and raised general public consciousness concerning the problems of troubled adolescents.[37]

During the 1980s, the agency's advocacy efforts moved beyond outreach vans and personal counseling services to include legal action as well. The immediate impetus here stemmed from a case involving a 1977 New York State statute that prohibited the production and sale of films and photographs depicting sexual performances by children. Paul Ira Ferber, an adult bookstore owner in Manhattan, had sold two such films that featured young boys masturbating. Unfortunately for Ferber, his client turned out to be an undercover police officer, and a speedy conviction ensued. New York's highest court overturned the verdict and invalidated the statute in 1981, however, ruling that the use of children in sexually explicit material could not be prohibited unless the state also proved that the resulting materials met the legal definition of obscenity. By introducing such a standard, the court significantly limited prosecutors' ability to try child pornography cases. Robert Morgenthau, the Manhattan district attorney, decided to appeal the ruling, and the United States Supreme Court agreed to hear his argument.[38]

Ritter eagerly threw himself into the fray after learning of the case. He accepted an invitation from ABC's *Good Morning America* television program to debate Ferber's high-profile criminal attorney, Harold Price Fahringer, whose other clients included several prominent figures in the adult entertainment industry.[39] Ritter, appearing in full Roman collar, derided the dapper civil libertarian as "the top smut lawyer in the country," a man who "wears four-hundred-dollar suits" and "makes a lot of money defending very rotten people." Several appeal letters and press releases also focused on the *Ferber* case, with the founder depicting himself as a humble and commonsense Franciscan who reluctantly accepted the burden of leading the fight against child pornographers: "I felt I really had to do it. I'm no constitutional lawyer, but somebody, I felt, had to speak for the kids and, God knows, we've met scores of these sad and destroyed youngsters at Covenant House." In this instance, however, the organization moved beyond mere public relations. The agency's legal team, directed by Edmund Burns, joined the fight and prepared an amicus curiae brief supporting Morgenthau's position. Much to Covenant House's satisfaction, the United States Supreme Court unanimously overturned the state ruling in 1982 and upheld the statute. *New York v. Ferber* became a landmark decision that placed child pornography outside the protection of the First Amendment's free speech provision. Ritter's triumphal claim that he had scored "a clean, decisive knockout in the final round. . . . No TKO or split decision, no ambiguities" may have overstated both Covenant House's role and the court's clarity, but the experience did move the organization in new directions. The *Ferber* case had energized the legal staff, provided a useful opportunity to cooperate with local politicians, offered good public relations, and illustrated the virtues of legal activism in achieving social change.[40]

Ritter understood the potential and moved to institutionalize the function. He persuaded Gregory Loken, the young attorney and former Faith Community member who had helped to establish Covenant House's Guatemala program, to assume directorship of an Institute for Youth Advocacy (IYA) in 1982. This new entity would carry out a mandate to litigate, lobby, and research issues that touched upon child pornography, homeless adolescents, the foster care system, and similar organizational concerns. Over the next several years, the IYA filed amicus curiae briefs in several prominent cases concerning sexual exploitation. Loken himself offered expert testimony in a variety of public hearings, fostered the passage of such legislation as the federal Child Protection Act of 1984 and the Alaska State Runaway Youth Act of 1988, and produced several reports concerning youth homelessness and child prostitution. The young attorney also played a major role in advising Ritter concerning the founder's work with Attorney General Meese's Commission on Pornography. Indeed, some felt that the institute's emphasis had become skewed, focusing too narrowly on the sex industry and slighting other advocacy efforts that might affect a much broader youth population. Ritter remained firmly convinced, however, that the IYA's work could build on the solid accomplishments, excellent public relations, and cooperative spirit with public officials that had emerged from the *Ferber* experience.[41]

Fostering such collaborative ventures and seeking positive press appeared increasingly desirable during the 1980s, as the ministry sometimes operated at odds with municipal officials and local politicians. Newspapers still presented overwhelmingly positive portrayals of the fighting Franciscan, but several situations emerged that slightly tarnished Ritter's image. Some issues resulted from the close ties that bound the agency with the Archdiocese of New York and its controversial new leader. Archbishop John J. O'Connor's arrival from Scranton in 1984 signaled a dramatic change in style and leadership in New York. The archbishop almost immediately asserted himself as combative, eager to participate in public debate, and highly conscious of media coverage, in direct contrast to his low-key predecessor, Terence Cardinal Cooke. The new archbishop's conservative approach to such issues as abortion, homosexuality, and the ordination of women embroiled him in contentious debates with more liberal New York politicians and community activists. Journalists greatly enjoyed the highly quotable and often unpredictable statements that emanated from the cardinal's weekly press conferences following his 10:15 A.M. Sunday Mass at St. Patrick's Cathedral. Archbishop O'Connor also demonstrated an uncanny ability to tweak his political opponents by selecting symbolic issues, staking out uncompromising stances for media consumption, and exerting his personal charm behind the scenes in order to soothe wounded egos.[42]

The controversy surrounding Executive Order 50, which placed Covenant House in a particularly precarious public position, offers an example. Mayor Edward I. Koch had promulgated this administrative directive in 1980, as part of a broader effort to prohibit job discrimination by municipal contractors. Under the language of the order, all firms conducting business with the City of New York agreed to ensure "equal employment opportunity" in their hiring practices. A key clause barred contractors from discriminating on the basis of "sexual orientation or affectional preference," an attempt by the mayor to guarantee equal treatment for homosexuals and bisexuals in the workplace. The Archdiocese of New York served as a major municipal contractor, receiving over $70 million in the early 1980s to administer a variety of child care and social service agencies. Still, neither Cardinal Cooke nor his episcopal counterpart in Brooklyn had taken much notice of the directive and business proceeded as usual. All of this changed when the new archbishop arrived on the scene. In June of 1984, Cardinal O'Connor joined with the Salvation Army and Agudath Israel, an Orthodox Jewish philanthropy, in commencing a state supreme court action that challenged Koch's authority to promulgate the order. The cardinal also stunned Koch at a City Hall press conference in December of 1984 by proclaiming that "the Mayor doesn't know this: we have been examining how we would provide precisely the same services without any city, state, or Federal support at all" and implying that he stood ready to cancel all municipal contracts if Executive Order 50 remained in force. Cardinal O'Connor especially angered gay rights advocates by emphasizing that the archdiocese stood firm against any regulation or legislation that could be interpreted as "condoning homosexual activity or the teaching of homosexuality," though he also proclaimed his philosophical support for antidiscrimination efforts.[43]

Archdiocesan attorneys identified Under 21 as the lead agency in the litigation against Executive Order 50, thus placing the ministry in an embarrassing situation. Covenant House received four contracts totaling over $800,000 from the New York City Human Resources Administration in order to operate its crisis shelter, as well as other funding from the New York City Youth Bureau. The agency staunchly maintained that it did not discriminate in its hiring or employment practices, and it also appealed to a broad social constituency. The litigation drew Covenant House into a controversial public issue that had the potential to alienate gay supporters. It also threatened to identify the ministry as narrowly Roman Catholic at a time when the organization hoped to broaden its donor base to include Protestant evangelicals. Further, it might raise questions concerning the agency's conservative approach to condom distribution and sexual counseling during the height of the AIDS epidemic. As the *Executive Order 50* case progressed through the courts, Covenant House also found it necessary to address related public relations problems. The New York City Bureau of Labor Services received two complaints from a job applicant and a former employee of the agency. Both alleged that Covenant House required its staff "to adhere to a Christian philosophy as a condition of employment" and that its mission statement "relates the work efforts at Covenant House to a Christian philosophy." Such policies potentially violated other provisions of Koch's executive order, thereby prompting another city investigation and attracting more unwanted media attention.[44]

Privately, Ritter urged archdiocesan attorneys to reach a practical accommodation with the Koch administration and end the controversy, since "the Archdiocese has clearly gotten the worst of it in the public eye." The founder articulated his own political and public relations assessment as follows: "The Cardinal and the archdiocese are seen by many as intransigent, insensitive, politically unsophisticated in the uses of power, preoccupied with the myth of a 'gay menace' and moved by a circle-the-wagons mentality" that relied heavily on a "strategy of saber-rattling, apocalyptic warnings and doomsday pronunciamentos" to achieve success. Cardinal O'Connor elected to pursue the matter through the courts, however, and won a significant legal victory in June of 1985. The state Court of Appeals ruled that Koch had exceeded his authority by promulgating the order and asserted that the sole power to initiate such a policy properly resided with the city council. Financially, the litigation had little lasting effect. Covenant House and the archdiocese continued to execute their annual contracts with the city, personnel policies and mission statements remained in place, and social services operated as usual. Politically, the controversy increased tensions between gay leaders and Catholic social service agencies. Cardinal O'Connor's sixteen-year episcopate would continue to be marked by frayed relationships and testy exchanges with gay activists. Covenant House, though not directly involved in most specific controversies, would receive some peripheral fallout.[45]

Not all of the agency's political problems in the late 1980s stemmed from external sources. Ritter's territorial expansion and real estate acquisitions also generated controversy, as illustrated by his experience with the Times Square Motor Hotel. Covenant House purchased this landmark fourteen-story structure on the corner of Eighth Avenue and Forty-third Street in November of 1984. The hotel had fallen on hard times, with nearly one-third of its 735 rooms vacant and more than half of the 500 residents either indigent or subsisting on fixed incomes. Ritter decided to buy the building for several reasons. It bordered on Covenant House's other Eighth Avenue properties, and its acquisition would allow the agency to control virtually the entire block. The facility seemed appropriate for multiple institutional uses in the short run, including an expanded Rights of Passage program and administrative office space. Over the long term, Ritter hoped that the hotel might pay lucrative dividends as a speculative property, especially considering the city's plans to rehabilitate and develop the Times Square area. Unfortunately, the venture once again placed Covenant House in a tricky relationship with municipal authorities.[46]

New York City faced a severe low-cost housing shortage in the mid-1980s, as well as a homeless situation that had reached crisis proportions. Single-room-occupancy (SRO) dwellings, such as the Times Square Motor Hotel, remained at the heart of the problem. During the 1970s and early 1980s, approximately 35,000 single rooms throughout the city had been demolished or converted into luxury space for upper-income housing, or adapted for commercial use. The Koch administration, acknowledging the severity of the problem and facing a barrage of criticism from housing reformers and homeless advocates, acted to regulate the speculative tide at the precise moment that Ritter launched this real estate venture. New York placed a moratorium on the alteration or demolition of any SRO, effective 9 January 1985, and attempted to prevent property owners from harassing and forcing out low-income tenants. This moratorium effectively scuttled Covenant House's plans to modify the building, severely limited its use options, and diminished the Times Square Motor Hotel's ultimate resale value.[47]

Covenant House now found itself managing a low-rent residential facility at enormous institutional expense, thus straining its resources and expertise. Ritter informed the board that the organization would probably need to invest $12 million in the hotel between 1986 and 1991, a cost almost equal to the purchase price itself, and his estimate proved conservative. Annual operating deficits exceeded $3 million. The ministry had to address myriad problems ranging from peeling lead paint to inoperative elevators to delinquent rent. Over one thousand housing code violations accumulated. Vocal tenants leveled a litany of public complaints against the agency, alleging petty harassment, mismanagement, and unfair evictions. One spokesperson for the city's Coalition for the Homeless even characterized Ritter as "the Simon Legree of non-profit hotel management." The entire venture mushroomed into a financial and public relations fiasco, and the problems only deteriorated over time. Even a seemingly successful sale of the facility in 1988 proved futile, as the new owner promptly declared bankruptcy, the mortgage reverted to the agency, and Covenant House continued to operate the hotel as a debtor in possession of the property. The Times Square Motor Hotel provided Ritter with a sustained dose of negative publicity and also raised some troublesome questions concerning the focus of his ministry in the late 1980s. The founder's impetuousness and speculative bent had committed the organization to managing a deteriorating midtown hotel, a function far removed from its mission and purpose. Some administrators and board members wondered whether Covenant House somehow had veered off track. One final undertaking from the late 1980s underscored those questions and uncertainties, even as it proved that Ritter had not lost his public relations touch.[48]

The founder's difficulties with the Times Square Motor Hotel stiffened his resolve to find an appropriate facility for expanding the Rights of Passage program. He believed that he had stumbled onto a "once-in-a-generation opportunity" to accomplish precisely that in August 1987 when a supporter directed him to the National Maritime Union Building on the corner of Ninth Avenue and Seventeenth Street in Manhattan's Chelsea neighborhood. The complex consisted of two eleven-story structures that had been completed in 1966 in order to provide housing, recreational space, medical facilities, and a training center for seamen employed on the Hudson River docks. It featured several unique architectural elements, such as a sloping front wall that fronted Seventeenth Street, rounded windows that resembled portholes in order to accentuate the nautical feel, and a cooking facility that ran on electricity and steam in conformity with ship kitchens. Ritter enthused to Cardinal O'Connor that "it seems almost to have been built with Rights of Passage in mind," owing to its existing classrooms, trade shops, dormitories, gymnasium, pool, and 950-seat auditorium. He envisioned expanding the ROP program from a handful of participants to 300 children per year and eagerly formulated plans to use every inch of the 282,000 square feet in the facility. Only one problem stood in his way.[49]

New York City had its own agenda for the Maritime building. Municipal authorities had entered into negotiations with the union during the summer of 1987 and offered a purchase price of $30 million. The city planned to convert the building into a residence for eight hundred homeless men from the Bellevue Men's Shelter on First Avenue and use it to house a work-release program for two hundred former prison inmates from the Riker's Island correctional facility. Neighborhood residents and Manhattan politicians expressed outrage over the plan and grew further infuriated at the Koch administration's agreement to sell the Bellevue property to a developer who would then build luxury housing at that site. For many, the entire deal epitomized municipal arrogance. It disregarded the needs of neighborhood families, promised to introduce a questionable criminal element into an area that already suffered from open drug dealing, privileged the desires of developers and wealthy speculators, and failed to provide adequate or permanent housing for the working poor and homeless. During the summer of 1987, the local community board in Chelsea passed resolutions opposing the sale, concerned businessmen hired an attorney to explore legal options, and the neighborhood organized protests outside of the building. David Dinkins, the Manhattan Borough president who harbored mayoral hopes for the upcoming 1989 election, also lent significant political support to the opposition, as did Councilwoman Carol Greitzer.[50]

Ritter moved rapidly to take advantage of the political turmoil. He called a special meeting of his board of directors on 28 August, shortly after making contact with the maritime union. Ritter played every card at his disposal in order to obtain board support. He argued that separating the ROP population from the crisis shelter would remove the youths from "the sordid and seedy Times Square area" and deposit them in "the up and coming neighborhood of Chelsea," where they would soon "be graduated to productive and happy tax-paying careers." He outlined his vision for a

Figure 8. National Maritime Union Building complex, Ninth Avenue and Seventeenth Street, New York City. Photograph courtesy of the Covenant House Archives.

"street kids academy" on the site, where young men would "sleep dorm style," dine in a communal cafeteria, attend classes, learn trades, "enjoy the recreational and social activities of campus life," and function "like other college students . . . enjoying the cultural opportunities which New York City offers." His sales pitch worked wonders with the board, and the directors authorized him to move ahead. Within two weeks, Ritter quietly outbid the city by offering the union $33 million, and Covenant House found itself the owner of another major property in Manhattan.[51]

Mayor Koch did not react well to the news. He threatened to initiate condemnation proceedings and seize the facility for public use, telling local reporters that "I don't believe you should allow someone to go in and steal your building." The founder effectively countered, masterfully manipulating the media and transforming the drama into excellent community theater. Ritter had been diagnosed with Hodgkin's disease earlier in 1987, and newspapers contrasted the images of a bullying and irascible mayor with a gaunt and weary priest who cared only about securing an appropriate facility for his "kids." When Koch held a press conference, Covenant House's public relations staff solemnly informed reporters that Ritter lay in a hospital bed, recovering from chemotherapy and able only to issue written statements. When Ritter held a press conference, he "sat on a stool. . . . He was pale, very thin and tired." He struck precisely the appropriate tone of victimization and Franciscan humility: "I bought the building fair and square. . . . I feel intimidated. I feel pushed around. I feel threatened. . . . I am no David. I have no ability to withstand the steamroller that the mayor has aimed at Covenant House." Tabloid headlines throughout September drew the appropriate contrast and made no secret of their sympathies: "The Mayor Steps on a Helping Hand," "City Vows to Throw Away Key: Tug of War As Koch Covets Ritter Building," "City Raids Priest's Hotel," "Ritter Will Fight On," and "Holy War!"[52]

Most Chelsea residents found any plan for the building preferable to the city's scheme and supported the Covenant House venture as a viable alternative. Community newspapers described Rights of Passage youths as "highly motivated people who cannot live at home, but do want to get on with the rest of their lives" and expressed cautious optimism concerning the program. Covenant House's administrators cultivated neighborhood support by providing tours of the facility, making presentations before the community board, and responding to security concerns. Ritter also effectively lobbied the city's Board of Estimate, which would have to approve any attempt by the mayor to condemn the building, and won support from most members. In the end, Koch grudgingly admitted defeat. By late October, the mayor acknowledged that he could not "compete with a priest who has cancer" and ceased his opposition. Bad feelings lingered, however, as Koch accused Ritter of violating the Golden Rule, charged him with "abusing his position," and continued to describe himself as being "infuriated" over the imbroglio. Eventually, the two reached an uneasy truce. A smiling Koch attended Covenant House's dedication ceremonies at the site in October of 1988, contributed two hundred dollars to the ministry, and made political peace with his formidable Franciscan adversary. Ritter played the gracious victor, joking with reporters that "friends yell at each other. I mean, they always do" and placing Koch's name in the agency's Book of Honor. The entire affair culminated in an unqualified public relations triumph for Ritter, and the opening of the National Maritime Union Building seemingly signaled a high point for Covenant House.[53]

Internally, however, the National Maritime affair raised some corporate eyebrows. Jim Harnett openly disagreed with the decision to purchase the building at the time, considering it a very risky venture that could overextend the ministry and create substantial long-term obligations. Bruce Henry, who directed Rights of Passage, questioned the need for such a large facility, viewed Ritter's notion of a "street kids academy" as impractical, and worried about the effect of multiplying his own program tenfold. Henry recalled that another important program person "was very angry. He wanted to leave because he thought that [ROP] would lose a lot of what its strengths were, the ability to bond with the kids, to tie them in." The board of directors, still reeling from its involvement with the Times Square Motor Hotel, testily instructed Ritter to sell that facility prior to closing his deal on the National Maritime Union site. Both board and staff appeared somewhat shell shocked by the dizzying array of programs, publicity, and problems that had emerged during the late 1980s. Covenant House subsidiaries appeared to be popping up everywhere, new ventures had transformed the operation into a much more complex and multifaceted enterprise, and growth seemed the only constant. Some influential voices on the board believed, as the decade drew to a close, that the time had come to take stock of the ministry and to begin planning in a more systematic and strategic manner. Perhaps, they hoped, 1990 would prove to be a more orderly year.[54]

Chapter 7
The Crisis

I am absolutely confident that the allegations of financial impropriety against Covenant House are simply nonsense. The other and more painful allegations about my personal misconducts are deeply offensive to me. As you might suspect, this has been, without doubt, the most difficult week of my entire life. By innuendo, insinuation, by allegation, and by misstatements and inaccuracies, the impression has been given that I have been guilty of sexual misconduct. I categorically deny those allegations. I categorically deny them.

—*Rev. Bruce Ritter, 14 December 1989*

I am profoundly saddened by the allegations against me and the need to deny them constantly. I have no way of proving my innocence. My accusers cannot establish my guilt. I devoutly hope the inquiries currently underway will bring an end to this incredibly painful chapter in my life. The work of Covenant House is a 24-hour-a-day job requiring my full attention. That is not possible under the present circumstances. Therefore, I have decided to take several weeks off to rest and recuperate to deal with the personal stress caused by this controversy as well as its impact on Covenant House.

—*Rev. Bruce Ritter, 6 February 1990*

The undersigned hereby resigns as President and Chief Executive Officer of Covenant House's subsidiaries and related corporations.
Dated: New York, New York
February 27, 1990

—*Rev. Bruce Ritter, 27 February 1990*[1]

Bruce Ritter's story took an unexpectedly tragic turn in 1990, with seemingly disastrous consequences for Covenant House. Ritter had constructed a compelling narrative over the course of two decades that explained his life and work to a largely admiring audience. He even carefully codified his vision in print. *Covenant House: Lifeline to the Street* appeared in bookstores in 1987, seamlessly weaving the personal and the institutional into an inspirational and triumphant tale. Three short years later, however, the founder's official version of Covenant House's history rapidly crumbled. New voices entered the conversation, competing for public attention and

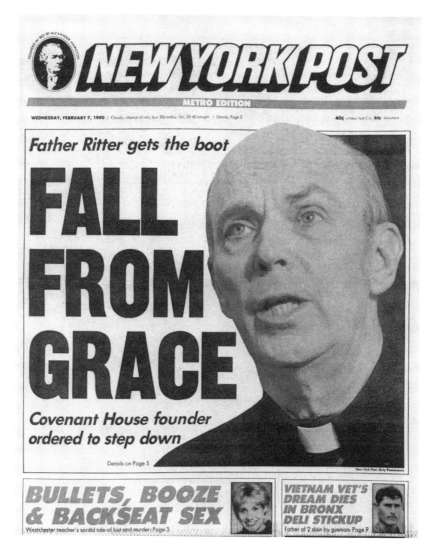

Figure 9. "FALL FROM GRACE," 7 February 1990. Covenant House found itself embroiled in a sexual and financial scandal beginning in December of 1989 that threatened its existence and provided excellent fodder for New York City tabloids. Photograph courtesy of the *New York Post*.

creating a confusing buzz of constant noise. Suddenly, almost without warning, the organization faced a bewildering barrage of charges and accusations from multiple sources. Events spun wildly out of the founder's control. Covenant House's troubles played out daily in the tabloid press and nightly on local news broadcasts. Serious journalists, radio shock jocks, and alternative media outlets skewered the organization and satirized the founder. Public confidence wavered, as donations dropped dramatically and formerly loyal supporters expressed serious misgivings and disillusionment. Some board members resigned in anger, several key administrators received severance packages, and the agency faced an uncertain future. Expansion halted, growth gave way to contraction, crisis management replaced strategic planning, and heady optimism dissipated amid an atmosphere of gloom and malaise.

For Bruce Ritter, the crisis meant an abrupt and humiliating end to his long ministerial journey. The founder's final act played itself out on the public stage between December of 1989 and February of 1990. Many people who cared deeply about Covenant House and its work feared that the organization would never recover from the events that unfolded over those three months, which collectively became known as "the scandal." Others who found themselves caught up in the dizzying round of daily revelations required several years of reflection and distance before developing a balanced perspective concerning the controversies. Some never reconciled the contradictions. The story itself seems deceptively straightforward and linear in the retelling. It breaks down neatly into four distinct phases. Clear turning points emerge, while key decisions and missteps loom large. This retrospective clarity, however, only masks the chaos and confusion that really characterized this brief institutional interlude. The scandal damaged individual reputations, but its ultimate impact proved even more profound. The crisis forced Covenant House to seek new leadership and to rewrite its own institutional history. Neither Ritter nor his narrative survived 1990 intact. The founder became alienated from his institution, and the organization needed to craft a new story that explained this unsettling period of change and uncertainty. Few could have foreseen these implications, however, when the crisis began on a cold and snowy December day in 1989.

"TIMES SQUARE PRIEST PROBED" screamed the front-page banner headline of the *New York Post* on 12 December. Bleary-eyed commuters who bothered to find the actual story on page seven would also learn from a suggestive subhead that a "former male prostitute charges 25G rip-off of Covenant House funds." As the complicated tale started to unfold over the next several weeks, certain generally agreed-upon facts became clear. On 31 January 1989, an articulate and attractive young man found his way to Covenant House's crisis center in New Orleans. The red-haired and hazel-eyed youth claimed that he had drifted into town from Dallas the previous day searching for work, spent the night sleeping in a park, awoke to find his wallet missing, and was referred to the shelter by a local policeman. He stayed at Covenant House for a few days, attended a job seminar, informed his case manager that he had managed to secure a position as a maintenance man in a French Quarter apartment building, and left the facility with a planned discharge on 3 February. Within two weeks, however, the drifter returned to Covenant House and related a much more remarkable and intriguing tale to the institution's ombudsman.[2]

The young man still lacked identification and admitted to using a series of aliases but desperately appealed to the shelter for sanctuary. He now claimed to be on the run from organized crime, having spent the last several years as a call boy in a male prostitution ring that operated around the Dallas area. He vividly described his days as a street hustler, turning tricks and running drugs in metropolitan areas throughout the United States for his crime family. Recently, he had become disenchanted with "the life" and fearful for his safety. He fled from Dallas and hoped to begin anew in the urban anonymity of New Orleans. A chance encounter with a former escort service patron ruined these plans, however, as the young man's background quickly became common knowledge in the Big Easy's back streets and gay bars. His previous employers in Dallas soon tracked him down and began making threatening phone calls. With nowhere to go, the former hustler turned to Covenant House. The crisis center staff found the young man's story credible and further believed that they needed to transport him to another location in order to ensure his safety and remove him from the clutches of organized crime. Fortunately for all concerned, Bruce Ritter had recently arrived in New Orleans for a routine site visit, and local administrators consulted the founder concerning this special case.

Ritter enthusiastically sprang into action. The hustler's tale contained precisely the proper combination of elements that reinforced the Franciscan's basic beliefs and instincts. It offered a rare opportunity to undertake the type of reclamation and rescue project that Ritter had described in so many newsletters and sermons. It thrust the founder squarely into a world of danger, intrigue, and urban vice that he found both repulsive yet oddly compelling. It provided a gritty dose of street-level reality for a friar whose ministry now centered largely on donor cultivation, staff development, and property acquisition. Ritter wanted very much to believe in the young man and his story, which appeared such a perfect fit with the institutional myths that he had crafted over the past two decades. Incredibly, and without conducting any additional background investigation or verification, the founder immediately flew the former hustler back to New York and authorized an extraordinary series of steps. Over the course of the next several months, Ritter instructed his staff to procure a new identity for the young man, provide him with a low-level clerical position and modest stipend at the Institute for Youth Advocacy, and establish him in a private apartment owned by Covenant House on Eighth Avenue and Forty-fourth Street. The Franciscan justified all of these decisions as necessary in order to protect his charge from criminal elements and to begin helping him construct a new life. For a time, things went smoothly.

Tim Warner, as the young man became known throughout the agency, soon emerged as a popular and likable fixture around Covenant House.[3] Ritter continued to take a special interest in the case, serving as the former hustler's primary mentor throughout the spring and summer of 1989. The Franciscan believed that Warner needed strong social support and a new network of friends, and encouraged staff members to establish solid personal relationships with the troubled youth. Various Covenant House employees invited Warner to spend time with them, engaging in such activities as picnics in Prospect Park, rides on the Staten Island Ferry, excursions to the Great Adventure Amusement Park, shopping expeditions in downtown Manhattan, and dinner and drinks at various night spots. Ritter himself spent several weekends with Warner at the Vincent Astor mansion in Rhinebeck, New York, which had been provided for the founder's use by James Maguire, the estate's owner and a Covenant House board member. Warner appeared thoroughly integrated into the agency's social network, even accompanying Ritter overnight when the friar officiated at the wedding of an organizational official in Reading, Pennsylvania. By late summer, Ritter had arranged for Warner to receive a scholarship from Manhattan College, with Covenant House providing room and board expenses. Warner moved into his dormitory room at the Bronx campus on 29 August, and his prospects appeared bright. Here, the stories began to diverge.

Ritter claimed that Warner gradually reverted to his previous lifestyle over the course of his first semester at Manhattan College. He stopped attending classes, kept a very irregular work schedule at the Institute for Youth Advocacy, began frequenting gay bars, and became increasingly petulant with the founder. By November, their strained relationship reached a breaking point when Ritter insisted that Warner must either make an honest academic effort or find employment elsewhere. The young man soon stopped showing up for work, cleaned out his apartment, and disappeared. Warner related a very different account. He claimed that Ritter had initiated a sexual relationship with him shortly following their February plane ride from New Orleans to New York. Contact occurred weekly over the course of the year at a variety of venues ranging from the Astor mansion teahouse to the Eighth Avenue apartment. The young man considered his stipend, clothing allowances, room and board, and miscellaneous expenses to be payment for sexual favors. By the fall of 1989, Warner had become increasingly frustrated with the degree of control that Ritter exerted over his life and concerned over the nature of their relationship. He worried that he could never escape from his situation and grew paranoid about the potential consequences of rejecting the founder. Warner formulated a plan to protect himself and his interests by taking his story to the media, and he contacted the *New York Post* in late October.

Events moved rapidly thereafter. Charles M. Sennott, the young *Post* reporter who had been assigned to the story, met with Warner and harbored some reservations concerning the young man's veracity and credibility. Still, he remained interested and pursued the lead. Warner also apparently repeated his allegations to some friends among the staff at Covenant House in early November, but they remained conflicted about how to handle the situation and never informed anyone within the agency. He next contacted the Crime Victims Unit at St. Luke's Hospital in Manhattan, where counselors urged him to take his story to District Attorney Robert Morgenthau. A month-long series of meetings with Morgenthau's staff followed, and Warner carefully kept his *Post* contacts informed during the entire process. The newspaper engaged in its own brand of surreptitious intrigue throughout November. When the district attorney's office wired Warner with a small microphone on 15 November in order to record his conversations with Ritter during a trip to New Jersey, *Post* employees lurked in the background. They secretly snapped photographs of the founder and the ex-hustler entering the Franciscan's automobile. By early December, prosecutors believed that they had sufficient evidence to move the investigation beyond the preliminary stage, and they placed Warner in a witness assistance program. Sennott and his editors also became convinced that they had adequate cause to run the story.

The reporter contacted Ritter on 6 December, while the founder again was visiting Covenant House's New Orleans operation. Ritter immediately denied the allegations, though he admitted the existence of a "safe house" program that provided shelter and services for Warner. The district attorney's office soon confirmed that its fraud division had launched an investigation into the charity, and the *New York Post* announced its intention to publish Sennott's story on 12 December. Ralph Pfeiffer, the former IBM executive who had replaced Robert Macauley as chairman of Covenant House's board less than a month earlier, called an emergency directors' meeting on 11 December. Board and staff initially exhibited unswerving loyalty to Ritter. His denials proved satisfactory. No one seriously suggested that the founder temporarily step down, and any internal investigation seemed superfluous. The controversy pitted the reputation of a popular and respected Catholic clergyman against a shadowy ex-hustler whose identity itself proved murky and mysterious. For those within the organization, Ritter possessed all of the credibility. Pfeiffer set the tone for the 11 December meeting by characterizing the accusations as "scurrilous" and presenting them as the product of "a very troubled young man." Since everyone presumed Ritter's innocence, the legal strategy appeared clear: cooperate with the district attorney, carefully examine and audit all financial accounts that had been used to reimburse Warner, and engage a special outside counsel to defend the founder and handle criminal charges.[4]

Public relations issues produced more complex challenges. The crisis unfolded during the most critical fund-raising period in Covenant House's calendar year. Christian philanthropies count heavily on strong December donations to balance their annual budgets, and Covenant House proved no exception. The organization anticipated contributions of $15 million in December of 1989 in order to meet its financial projections, and any hint of scandal clearly jeopardized that goal. The *Post* story itself appeared on the eve of a celebrity auction and Christmas benefit for the agency hosted by the artist Peter Max, placing a definite damper on that affair. The more media-conscious members of the board of directors, such as Mark Stroock of Young & Rubicam and Ellen Levine of *Woman's Day* magazine, understood the need to respond quickly and effectively to the charges by taking control of the situation and placing the proper institutional spin on the allegations. Stroock obtained the services of Young & Rubicam's high profile public relations subsidiary, Burston, Marstellar, to advise the agency and to develop a coherent response to the crisis. Over the course of the next few days, several elements of the organization's strategy became clear.[5]

Covenant House shrewdly turned the *New York Post*'s credibility into a major issue. The financially troubled tabloid occupied a peculiar place within the city's media universe. New Yorkers chuckled over its clever headlines, casually enjoyed the celebrity gossip on "Page Six," and avidly devoured the sports pages, but few viewed the paper as a serious journalistic enterprise. The Ritter coverage well illustrated the newspaper's typical modus operandi. The story appeared somewhat tame and anticlimactic in many respects. The district attorney, after all, had confined his investigation to the fraud allegations and the misappropriation of a relatively insignificant sum of $25,000 in a budget that approached $90 million. Consensual sex between Ritter and Warner, however unseemly or improper, did not constitute a criminal offense. The *Post* reported on the finances but highlighted the sexual innuendos. Headlines during the week of 12 December invariably referred to the "male hooker" and the "male prostitute." Front-page photographs depicted the cheap motel in Reading where "Father Ritter stayed with his accuser during an overnight visit" as well as the Franciscan and "former male prostitute Tim Warner" getting into a car together under cover of darkness. When Ritter held a press conference on 14 December to answer the charges, the *Post*'s front-page headline ignored his message and editorialized instead: "Experts Question Ritter's Secret Program."[6]

Other local newspapers took a more measured approach. The *New York Times* confined its initial coverage to a seven-paragraph story on page five of its metropolitan section, relying principally on official statements from Morgenthau's office and Covenant House executives as source materials. The *New York Daily News*, which vied with the *Post* for a tabloid readership, took a much lower key stance than its competitor and provided a favorable account of Ritter's press conference. Columnist Bill Reel, who had been instrumental in bringing Ritter to the attention of the public in 1977, vigorously defended the Franciscan in his *Daily News* column. Covenant House cooperated with all media outlets other than the *Post*, freely granting television interviews and questioning the newspaper's ethics at every opportunity. Jim Harnett especially emerged as a fiery public spokesman for the institution, branding the story the "lowest form of tabloid journalism" and arguing that the accusations appeared "totally groundless . . . an outrage . . . just scurrilous." Considering the *Post*'s tarnished reputation and its desperate financial condition, it appeared quite reasonable to view the entire story as a self-promotional and irresponsible attempt to besmirch a respected ministry through innuendo and unsubstantiated generalization. Morgenthau's own statements, which tersely noted that several news reports contained "numerous inaccuracies," raised further suspicion concerning the story. As the week wore on, and few journalists lined up to defend the *Post*, Covenant House's strategy appeared to bear fruit.[7]

Ritter further suggested that he had been targeted for harassment as part of a broader and more far-reaching conspiracy. Initially, he implied that organized criminal elements, which controlled the sex industry, may have manipulated Warner. By the time of his 14 December press conference, however, the founder had begun referring more obliquely to "certain groups and organizations" that carried a vendetta against him and hoped "not only to embarrass me but to embarrass the Church." Though he refused to specify the perpetrators, few observers could miss the implication. On 10 December, just two days before the *Post* published its initial story, members of the AIDS Coalition to Unleash Power (ACT-UP) aggressively confronted Catholic parishioners at St. Patrick's Cathedral during Cardinal O'Connor's morning mass. Tensions between the Archdiocese of New York and gay activists had approached the breaking point over the previous few months, as the cardinal issued increasingly strident statements that condemned the use of condoms and needle exchanges to combat the AIDS epidemic. Cardinal O'Connor's standard statement that "good morality is good medicine," as well as his assertion that he would change his approach only "over my dead body," especially infuriated his opponents. Over 4,500 demonstrators arrived at St. Patrick's on 10 December, chanting slogans and carrying placards on Fifth Avenue. Several dozen ACT-UP demonstrators decided to storm the cathedral, chaining themselves to the pews, lying in the aisles, heckling the cardinal, and disrupting the well-attended Sunday service. Police eventually arrested over one hundred protestors, and relationships frayed even further. Considering the intensely confrontational climate, and given Ritter's effort to closely associate his ministry with institutional Catholicism, his conspiracy theory appeared credible to some and cast further doubt on the allegations.[8]

Covenant House relied heavily on Ritter's reputation and public relations skills throughout the early days of the crisis. By placing the Franciscan front and center, the organization clearly tied its own credibility to the fate of its founder. Board and staff found it virtually impossible to imagine Covenant House without Bruce Ritter, and the agency implicitly accepted the unity of the individual and the institution. Initially, this seemed to be the prudent course. Ritter's 14 December press conference proved pivotal. It was well received by all media outlets, excepting the *Post*. The founder appeared calm, confident, and completely in control of the facts. He released a meticulously itemized account of the money distributed to Warner by Covenant House over the course of 1989, which amounted to considerably less than the $25,000 claimed by the young man. Ritter noted how his own philanthropic efforts supplemented the agency's work: "I gave him some sweaters I didn't need. I gave him some socks, a warm jacket because it was cold." He struck a note of chastened humility and self-reflection: "If I had to give a reason for my own personal failure, it was probably hubris. I thought I knew more than I did. I misread his agony. I was too busy to listen. I could not reach out to him." Yet Ritter saw no need to apologize for his conduct or his program even as he acknowledged his mistakes: "I think I know more about these kids than anybody in the United States and I know what they need and I know what we have to do in order to help them." He signaled his intention to continue mentoring troubled young adults, striking up close social and personal relationships with them whenever possible regardless of how others might misinterpret his behavior. Significantly, he expressed compassion and forgiveness for his accuser: "If he came back today we would welcome him back to Covenant House. There are many people here who care very deeply about him."[9]

The press conference inspired confidence, suggested that the scandal stemmed more from personal magnanimity than institutional flaws, and presented the agency as an organization deeply grounded in such solid Christian virtues as selfless charity, mutual trust, and unconditional love. Still, one public performance could not end the crisis, since the district attorney continued to conduct his investigation and donors appeared cautious throughout December. Covenant House soon made another strategic decision, however, that seemingly had the potential to restore trust in Ritter and to effectively combat the allegation. It proved controversial in many respects, sacrificing several long-cherished institutional values in the interest of resolving the immediate crisis. Board members and administrators believed that they were locked in a life-and-death struggle for the survival of the agency and that extraordinary steps appeared necessary. They remained completely convinced that Ritter needed to continue in his capacity as president in order for the operation to remain viable. Any strategy that helped to accomplish that goal seemed justifiable. No one appeared willing to risk the consequences should the charismatic founder need to abdicate his institutional role.

The most controversial element in Covenant House's strategy emerged from some clever detective work by Malcolm Host, the executive director of Covenant House's Houston subsidiary. After following through on several leads, Host discovered that nineteen-year-old Tim Warner was really a twenty-six-year-old Texan named Kevin Lee Kite. Host located the boy's father, Alton, in the small town of Gainesville near the Oklahoma border, and the elder Kite appeared horrified by his son's allegations. Alton Kite, a serious and soft-spoken accounting professor with deep evangelical religious convictions, had been estranged from Kevin for some time and had not seen his son in nearly a year. Covenant House administrators believed that they now had the ammunition they needed to finally bury the scandal story. They flew the elder Kite to New York City, videotaped an interview with him, and transmitted copies of the professionally produced recording to all local television networks. Alton Kite projected an image of emotional stability, complete credibility, and deep personal sadness. He detailed his son's long history of forged checks, credit card theft, chronic debt, "pathological" lying, and unsuccessful attempts at therapy. Kite and his wife disapproved of their son's "homosexual lifestyle," and they also found themselves in serious financial difficulties as they sought to make good on his bad debts. Alton bitterly concluded that "we have almost no resources left, financially or emotionally" to deal with the pain caused by their son's behavior. The entire interview, which Covenant House released on 20 December, had a sobering effect on the story. Ritter himself acknowledged that, when he met the boy's father, "I just hugged him. He was in such great pain. He didn't want his son to hurt anyone else." Television newscasters declared that Ritter "may have the evidence he needs to clear his name" and repeatedly ran interview excerpts. The *New York Daily News* featured a photograph of Alton and Kevin on page one with the banner headline "My Son Lies, Says Father in Ritter Case." The elder Kite returned quietly to Gainesville, and his distraught son soon checked himself into a psychiatric clinic. Covenant House effectively had destroyed the young man's credibility, and Ritter himself began referring to the crisis in the past tense. The worst seemed to be over.[10]

In the euphoria of victory, however, it remained easy to overlook some basic core values and standard institutional policies. By revealing Kite's identity to the press, the organization violated its own long-standing commitment to client confidentiality. This ethical breach bothered several board and staff members, some of whom felt that senior administrators and public relations consultants now had too much unchecked influence over agency affairs. Ritter also began exhibiting an inappropriately triumphal tone concerning the controversy. His 21 December newsletter to donors proclaimed that "it's not over till it's over, but I feel a lot better" and also included a newspaper reprint concerning the Alton Kite interview. He conducted a series of upbeat television interviews, casually attired in blue jeans and a black sweatshirt and brandishing a mug of coffee in order to emphasize his relaxed demeanor. He dismissed Kevin Kite's allegations with the observation that "any sick kid can say anything he wants," foregoing the language of Christian forgiveness. Ritter also characteristically interpreted the meaning of the scandal through a highly personal lens, viewing the events as part of his own faith journey and his ongoing conversation with God. He described the tribulation as a time of testing, articulating the scandal's ultimate purpose to a reporter in vaguely cryptic tones: "He got my attention. . . . I think God wants me to be better than I am." Ritter continued to remain at the center of his own universe, and Covenant House as an organization sometimes confused its desire to defend the founder with its responsibility to fulfill its mission and maintain the loftiest professional standards. During the hothouse atmosphere of the crisis, lines often became blurred.[11]

Such philosophical considerations and historical perspectives, however, remained far removed from the minds of most agency executives who found themselves caught up in day-to-day administrative realities throughout January of 1990. As Jim Harnett observed to the board, the agency appeared on a "roller coaster ride" in its fund-raising efforts. Contributions exhibited a significant decline in December of 1989, falling 20 percent below the anticipated target of $15 million, but they rose dramatically following Alton Kite's appearance in New York City. Early January proved to be an exceptionally lucrative period, and revenue for the first month of 1990 amounted to nearly $14 million, approximately doubling the agency's projections. As the Kite scandal gradually faded from the front pages, and the organization anticipated a quick and favorable resolution to the district attorney's investigation, there appeared cause for optimism. Media outlets began running positive stories concerning the work of the agency. The *New York Times* proved particularly supportive. Its 9 January editorial page bemoaned the declining contributions to Covenant House and urged District Attorney Morgenthau to complete his investigation so that the organization might solicit funds with a clean bill of health. Abraham M. Rosenthal, the influential *Times* columnist, contributed another article two days later that praised the organization's work, trivialized the accusations as scurrilous tabloid journalism "based only on the word of a young man whose own father later said he was a habitual liar," and urged New Yorkers to support the ministry. The mood around Covenant House appeared upbeat, but the agency soon confronted even more damaging revelations from another journalistic source.[12]

Philip Nobile, a freelance reporter writing for the weekly *Village Voice*, inaugurated the second phase of the crisis with a cover story that hit the streets of New York on 24 January. Nobile first turned his attention to Ritter in 1985 when the journalist began covering the Meese Commission on Pornography in his capacity as an editor at *Penthouse* magazine. During the course of his investigative work concerning the Meese Commission, Nobile became acquainted with John Melican, a former Covenant House resident who periodically returned to Under 21 between 1972 and 1986. Melican had suffered from substance abuse problems and money troubles over the course of that period, wandering around the country and disappearing for prolonged periods of time. He found himself driving a cab and hustling the streets of New Orleans during the early 1980s, but his health began to deteriorate from years of neglect and abuse. Melican decided to return to New York briefly and resume contact with Ritter in 1986, apparently in search of financial assistance from the founder and the agency. The thirty-year-old drifter grew disenchanted with the Franciscan during this visit, receiving neither the money nor the emotional support that he sought. He wandered into *Penthouse*'s Manhattan offices, "hoping for a big score" in the words of Nobile, and related his story concerning a long-term sexual relationship with Bruce Ritter that began when the troubled youth first arrived at East Seventh Street as a sixteen-year-old runaway. Nobile viewed Melican with some ambivalence: "Reed thin and almost toothless, his best hustling days were long gone. But he was smart, quick-tongued, and engaging." The *Penthouse* editor administered a polygraph test, which Melican passed, but Nobile ultimately decided against printing the story in 1986. Melican "ran up a huge hotel bill" and engaged in a wild "spending spree" over the course of two weeks while Nobile attempted to verify some basic facts. The reporter grew weary of the young man's manipulative tactics, and the investigation seemed to be going nowhere. He filed away his notes and lost touch with Melican, who apparently returned to New Orleans and resumed his drifter existence.[13]

Nobile revisited Melican's file following the public accusations by Kevin Lee Kite, however, and the reporter now discovered some interesting correlations between both stories. In fact, the *Village Voice* reporter claimed that the accounts constituted a "perfect forensic fit" and that he had uncovered "a sexual profile from two independent people" that revealed a consistent pattern of activity. The article did raise some troublesome questions for Covenant House. Both Kite and Melican described very similar sexual activities and behavior. Further, since Melican's accusations dated from 1986, it became impossible to dismiss them as mere "copycat" charges. And Nobile himself attempted to present a balanced view of the agency at times, softening the accusatory tone of his story. He asserted that "the word about Covenant House in Times Square—like the word in corporate board rooms and the oval office—is good." He also acknowledged that "no New Yorker has done as much for the least of our children" as Ritter and noted that the founder continued to live modestly. "If Father Ritter were a greedy schemer like Jim Bakker or a flaming hypocrite like Jimmy Swaggart, there would be more joy and less tragedy in his ordeal," the reporter observed.

But the *Voice* article appeared vulnerable on many grounds. Nobile engaged in broadly speculative analyses of Ritter's fund-raising newsletters, claiming that "the homoeroticism of some passages leap off the page and have become legend among gays." He used the article as an opportunity to criticize Covenant House's policy concerning condom distribution and safe-sex counseling, thus lending some credence to Ritter's suggestion that he had been victimized by a gay conspiracy. The "perfect forensic fit" between the Kite and Melican stories could be interpreted as little more than formulaic stylistic similarities that represented the words of two fundamentally unreliable and publicity-seeking young men. Covenant House questioned Nobile's journalistic integrity and objectivity, focusing on his *Penthouse* past and noting his hostility toward the Meese Commission members and their findings. Dennis Duggan, a *New York Newsday* reporter who staunchly defended Ritter during this phase of the crisis, responded to the *Village Voice* revelations by succinctly observing that "sex will sell a lot more papers. . . . We are not talking about Woodward and Bernstein here, we are talking fan-magazine stuff that more properly belongs in the National Enquirer."[14]

Despite these doubts concerning the story, and the fact that Melican's own whereabouts remained unknown, the *Village Voice* successfully reinvigorated the seemingly dormant scandal. Nightly news reports now broadcast the paper's unflattering cover photograph of the founder, who appeared distraught and grim, with furrowed brow, holding his head in his hand. Kevin Kite emerged from his stay at the Payne-Whitney psychiatric clinic, confidently chatting with television reporters and granting an interview to *Outweek*, New York City's lesbian and gay newspaper. Covenant House once again found its credibility under siege, precisely at the moment when it appeared to be recovering from the damaging December revelations. Senior staff members, however, felt that they had one more important card to play. The agency had cultivated good relations with the *New York Times* throughout the crisis, and that paper's editorial board had grown increasingly disturbed with the tabloid journalism that defined so much urban reporting in the metropolis. The *Times*, which had taken a cautious approach to the story, now agreed to assign an investigative team to examine the allegations. Covenant House administrators exhibited tremendous optimism concerning this development, assuming that the agency would be vindicated by a universally respected media outlet, thereby restoring public confidence. When the *Times* issued its front-page findings on 6 February, however, the results appeared devastating, and unprecedented turmoil engulfed the agency. The newspaper's sensational revelations effectively ended the second phase of the crisis.[15]

The *Times* discovered that a third man, Darryl J. Bassile, had contacted both the newspaper and Franciscan authorities with a story that roughly paralleled the other accusations. Bassile described a childhood marred by sexual abuse from his stepfather, a horrifying stay at the Mount Loretto orphanage on Staten Island during which time he had been beaten and gang raped by other residents, and an early adolescence spent sleeping on rooftops and under railroad trestles in Flushing, Queens. He found his way to Covenant House in 1973, at the age of fourteen, and claimed that Bruce Ritter soon established a sexual relationship with him that lasted until the young man ran away from the shelter in 1975. Bassile's allegations proved especially damaging for several reasons. He had revealed the details to a psychotherapist in April 1989, thus undermining any claim that he might constitute a "copycat." He originally contacted Franciscan officials privately in early January and only approached the *Times* when he feared that the order would not conduct a thorough investigation. This essentially invalidated the suspicion that he sought only publicity or money. Bassile generally spoke highly of Covenant House and Ritter, observing that he had received considerable help from "caring counselors" and asserting that he merely wanted "the man to get help with his problems." The affair, if true, clearly involved illegal sexual activity with a minor. Though the statute of limitations had expired, thus precluding any possible criminal indictment, the Franciscans now needed to conduct their own investigation, and Ritter's future would hang in the balance.[16]

As the Bassile story broke in the *New York Times*, additional information surfaced in the *New York Post* concerning Kevin Lee Kite. Charles Sennott, the journalist who broke the story in December, now reported on the mechanism by which Covenant House had procured the name of Timothy Warner for Kite. Early in 1989, Ritter instructed his staff to contact a priest in upstate New York, who agreed to secure a baptismal certificate for their use. Such a certificate would allow the organization to obtain a social security card, passport, and other forms of documentation for Kite. The cooperating priest searched through parish records and came upon a boy named Timothy Warner, who had been born in 1970, baptized that same year at Saint John's Church in Jamestown, New York, and died of leukemia in 1980. Since Kite claimed to be nineteen years old in 1989, Warner seemed to be a perfect match in terms of age. The upstate priest created and predated a new baptismal certificate bearing Warner's name and familial information, and this document formed the basis of Kite's new identity. The late Timothy Warner's parents still lived in Jamestown, however, and when they learned from reporters that Covenant House had appropriated their son's name in order to protect a former male prostitute they expressed shock and outrage. Television newscasters arrived in Jamestown, visiting the Warners' modest middle-class dwelling and highlighting a lovingly constructed photograph display called "Memories of Tim, 1970–1980" that the couple maintained in their living room. Betty Warner appeared hurt and confused, telling reporters, "It's got me baffled. They're dragging my poor son's name in the gutter. And he was a good kid, he really was. . . . Covenant House, it's not a very nice house, as I understand it." The organization's formal apology and efforts at damage control could no longer compete with a growing public perception that the agency had engaged in poor judgment, bizarre intrigue, and questionable ethical activities that served mainly to cover up its founder's misdeeds. Radical change appeared inevitable.[17]

Bruce Ritter seemed to recognize the implications on 6 February, the day that the *Times* story appeared. He announced his intention to "take several weeks off to rest and recuperate and to deal with the personal stress" caused by the controversy. In fact, however, the Franciscans issued their own statement the same day that cast the founder's leave of absence in a somewhat different light. The Rev. Connall McHugh, the minister provincial, stated that the order had directed Ritter "to begin a period of rest and recuperation without responsibility for Covenant House" until the Franciscans completed their own internal investigations. McHugh's statement signaled that the friars had some reason to believe that sexual abuse had occurred in the Bassile case and that Ritter needed to be removed from his responsibilities at least temporarily. The Franciscans' statement devastated the founder. According to the *New York Post*, he spent his last night in New York City in civilian clothes, wandering aimlessly around the Port Authority Bus Terminal and moving "slowly past the scores of street kids that peddle drugs and prostitution inside the seedy" transit facility. Covenant House as an institution, however, needed to focus immediately and move rapidly if it hoped to survive the new revelations. The directors scheduled an emergency meeting for the night of 6 February as the crisis entered its third phase.[18]

The board decided to elect one of its own members, Frank Macchiarola, to serve as acting president and chief executive officer. Macchiarola, who held a professorship at the Columbia University Graduate School of Business and had served as New York City's schools chancellor, appeared a shrewd choice at first glance. He enjoyed an impeccable reputation with the media, felt comfortable in the public eye, drew upon the resources of his own talented team of public relations and policy consultants, and managed numerous controversies during his distinguished career. Macchiarola immediately placed himself front and center, holding press conferences, working the media at every opportunity, and taking a hands-on approach to his administrative responsibilities. His aggressive style soon alienated fellow board members and senior staff, many of whom believed that he spent too much time polishing his own reputation and searching for convenient scapegoats within the agency. Macchiarola, on the other hand, insisted that his problems stemmed from an institutional culture of secrecy that stymied his efforts, claiming that "I was the guy with the light and they said 'You know what? It's too bright in here.'" He also blamed administrators at the agency who remained loyal to Bruce Ritter for resisting necessary changes. In any case, it soon became clear that the former schools chancellor would not provide the orderly transition and stable interim leadership that the board craved.[19]

Macchiarola's stormy three-week tenure as acting president ended during an emotionally charged board meeting held on 27 February. Ritter attended and addressed the directors for ten minutes, announcing his intention to resign as president and chief operating officer, in accordance with the wishes of his Franciscan superiors. The founder then left Covenant House for the final time, issuing a brief resignation statement that urged the public "to continue to support those good kids because the work of Covenant House is truly the work of the church and of God." Ritter's resignation, however, did not completely sever his ties with the agency. He also needed to resign his position as sole member of the corporation, and discussions over this matter continued for the next several weeks. Ritter resigned as sole member only after the board incorporated four more conditions into its bylaws. First, the board agreed that Covenant House would continue its commitment to the policy of open intake. Second, the bylaws stipulated that the president and chief executive officer should always be a Roman Catholic priest, brother, or member of a women's religious community. Third, the organization underscored its obligation to remain faithful to its Catholic origins and act in conformity with official Church traditions and philosophies at all times. Fourth, the Provincial of the Immaculate Conception Province of the Order Minor Conventuals remained entitled to a permanent seat on the board. The directors further agreed that any modification of these core principles would require a unanimous vote.[20]

Macchiarola also attended the 27 February board meeting. He fully anticipated his own installation as president and chief executive officer and presented a series of recommendations to his fellow directors. Macchiarola called for numerous procedural reforms, internal investigations, and reviews by outside experts that would address the rumors swirling around the organization and begin to rebuild its credibility. Board members found the program palatable but considered the former schools chancellor too controversial and bombastic to spearhead the agency during this critical period. "We accepted the plan and rejected the man," quipped board member Mark Stroock, as the directors voted 15-1 to remove Macchiarola and install Jim Harnett as interim president and chief executive officer. Macchiarola promptly resigned from the board, and the meeting abruptly ended.

The Ritter and Macchiarola resignations inaugurated a fourth and final phase of the crisis. Some issues appeared resolved. Less than twenty-four hours following Ritter's departure, District Attorney Morgenthau announced that he decided against filing any criminal charges in connection with the Kite allegations. Morgenthau noted the existence of "questionable financial transactions," but he found "insufficient evidence" to produce an indictment. Most observers assumed that Ritter's resignation prompted Morgenthau to close his investigation for the good of the agency, though all parties denied that any deal had been brokered. With the threat of legal action seemingly behind them, the board moved rapidly on several fronts in order to restore confidence. The directors immediately inaugurated a search for a permanent president and chief executive officer. During March, they also engaged several prominent consultants and experts to review all allegations and independently assess various agency operations. Kroll Associates, an investigative firm headed by former New York City police commissioner Robert McGuire, bore the primary responsibility for examining any sexual misconduct, financial improprieties, or other scandalous charges leveled against the organization. Ernst & Young, an independent accounting firm not previously connected with Covenant House, reviewed the agency's internal financial procedures. Richard Shinn, executive vice president of the New York Stock Exchange and former president of the Metropolitan Life Insurance Company, agreed to assess compensation packages in light of allegations concerning excessive administrative salaries. The Child Welfare League of America accepted the task of analyzing Covenant House's social service programs. The directors established an independent oversight committee, consisting of several prominent and nationally respected individuals not affiliated with the agency, in order to monitor institutional cooperation with the investigators, receive all reports, and evaluate the consultants' recommendations.[21]

Of course, it would take several months to complete these investigations, and Covenant House needed to take more immediate steps. Harnett sought to stabilize internal operations and repair sagging morale. On 5 March, he issued a memo acknowledging that "there have been examples of behavior at Covenant House which were serious errors" and pledged "to govern and manage Covenant House according to the highest of professional standards during this interim period." Harnett plainly observed that "it is wrong for anyone, including the Acting President of Covenant House, to fraternize with a resident outside our Centers." He terminated the safe house program, emphasizing that residents should neither receive unsupervised apartments for personal use nor work as staff within the agency. He reaffirmed Covenant House's commitment to open intake and client confidentiality, though he defended the decision to reveal Kevin Kite's identity as one "made with the best interests of Covenant House and our kids in mind." Harnett also announced a new policy for reporting allegations of misconduct to appropriate administrators and directors so that proper investigations might occur fairly and expeditiously. Finally, he noted the need to consolidate operations and cease new initiatives until the financial situation became clearer. Covenant House decided temporarily to shelve plans for new shelters in New Jersey and Washington, D.C., limiting those programs to outreach services only. The organization also abandoned a proposed scheme by Ritter to expand into Asia. Harnett's memo set a new tone for the agency. It implicitly offered the promise of more open communication with staff, greater managerial accountability, uniform professional standards, procedural reform, and clear administrative direction. It marked the end of the Ritter era. Unfortunately, events continued to move in unexpected directions, and issues arose that sabotaged any efforts at orderly reform.[22]

On 6 March, the day after Harnett issued his memo, Covenant House found itself on the front page of the *New York Times* once again. The newspaper devoted its major local headline to sensational revelations that a "$1 million fund" within the organization had been "tapped by Ritter to make 4 loans" to board members and relatives. These new financial allegations placed the ministry under fresh public scrutiny at the moment that the founder's resignation had offered the promise of a temporary respite. This complex controversy stemmed from the manner in which Ritter obtained payment for his services from Covenant House. Religious orders typically receive salary compensation directly from institutions that employ priests, brothers, and sisters. The community thereupon usually provides the individual with a stipend for living expenses and retains the rest of the reimbursement. Ritter's case, not surprisingly, varied somewhat from the norm. The Franciscans allowed him full discretionary authority over his salary, and he maintained his own checking account. Through a series of shrewd investments in Greif Brothers stock during the early 1980s, this account grew to several hundred thousand dollars. Ritter decided in 1983 to remove the money from his checking account and establish a nonprofit entity called the Franciscan Charitable Trust as a holding mechanism for the accumulated cash. The trust would allow him to obtain certain tax advantages, increase his flexibility concerning disbursements, and ensure that Covenant House, rather than the Franciscans, would benefit from his investment policies. Ritter documented the trust's purpose in his filing with the Internal Revenue Service as supporting his various ministries and especially providing confidential financial assistance to children in his safe house program.[23]

Covenant House's involvement with the Franciscan Charitable Trust increased during the mid-1980s. After Ritter had been appointed to the Meese Commission on Pornography in 1985, he became concerned that his $98,000 salary from the organization might subject him to public criticism. He thereupon asked Covenant House to decrease his official salary to $38,000 and to earmark the remaining $60,000 as an annual contribution to the trust. Robert Cardany, Covenant House's treasurer, refused to approve these transactions if Ritter remained as the trustee of the Franciscan Charitable Trust. The founder thereupon decided to remove himself from that position and to designate Ed Burns, Covenant House's attorney, as the trustee instead. Cardany now considered the donations appropriately legal, began making contributions to the account, and deposited $300,000 in the Franciscan Charitable Trust between 1986 and 1989. As the trust's assets increased to nearly $1 million over the course of the late 1980s, several aspects of the arrangement became controversial. Ritter had never informed the full board of the trust's existence or its transactions, even as some individual members remained aware of the situation. No evidence existed that the money had been used for ministerial purposes during the 1980s, though the founder insisted that he planned eventually to liquidate the assets and transfer the money to Covenant House. Ritter did use the trust funds, however, to loan money and engage in real estate transactions with two board members as well as loan money to his sister and a former Covenant House resident during the late 1980s. Though the loans bore market interest rates and the individuals proved to be reliable risks who reimbursed the trust in a timely manner, the transactions created at least the appearance of impropriety. Revelations concerning these financial machinations further undermined public confidence during a critical juncture. To the casual observer, Ritter seemed to be mixing personal and institutional finances in questionable ways. The directors projected an image of confusion, and outsiders detected a crisis of stewardship. Ralph Pfeiffer, the board chairman, perhaps inadvertently fostered this public perception when he observed in a newspaper interview that "what we don't know is monumental." Ed Burns, who had served as the ministry's attorney since 1972, described the organization as being in a "meltdown" following the new financial revelations. New York State attorney general Robert Abrams now stepped up his own investigation concerning the charity's finances. The National Charities Information Bureau soon withdrew its approval of the ministry, concluding that Covenant House did not meet its standards for proper board governance. Additional confirmation that Ritter himself and two senior staff members had received substantial salary advances and housing loans from Covenant House, again without the knowledge or authorization of the board, further exacerbated the crisis atmosphere.[24]

New allegations damaged the ministry throughout March as the situation worsened. Macchiarola's departure clearly stimulated journalists to probe more deeply into institutional affairs. The former schools chancellor continued to enjoy excellent rapport with the media, and his displeasure concerning his treatment by the board exacted a significant public relations price. He granted several interviews during which he accused the agency of operating according to "a fortress mentality" and living "in a bunker." Asserting that Covenant House now needed "more sunlight" and that they had installed "a figurehead" at the helm instead, he claimed that he personally could have carried the "casually run charity into the modern world" through his administrative expertise. Macchiarola provided the media with information concerning executive salaries, alleging that waste and profligate spending existed at the highest levels. He also furnished reporters with leads and documents concerning other allegations and potentially damaging stories. One especially bizarre example involved the charge that Covenant House officials had hindered a 1989 murder investigation involving a former gay client who had been stabbed to death by a transvestite in the hallway of a midtown apartment building. Published reports, which relied heavily on information supplied by Macchiarola and his staff, suggested that the deceased youth had been involved in a homosexual relationship with at least one "closeted official" at the agency and that a prostitution ring may have operated out of the Under 21 facility itself. Covenant House's Kroll Associates investigation ultimately found no evidence to support any claims connected with the case, but in the crisis atmosphere of March 1990, anything seemed possible and publishable.[25]

The media frenzy continued unabated as disgruntled employees, former community members, and anyone who held a personal or professional grudge against the organization now found a ready audience. The scope and variety of the published reports appears staggering in retrospect. One reporter claimed to uncover information that Covenant House conspired with officials at a Massachusetts college to operate a sophisticated call boy ring throughout the northeastern United States. Another television newscaster suggested that Casa Alianza constituted a front for money-laundering and gun-running operations that supported the contra rebels in Nicaragua. A third story alleged that Rights of Passage counselors routinely ignored alcohol binges, crack cocaine use, violent brawls, and crime sprees among resident youths. The *New York Post*, feeling especially vindicated by Ritter's resignation and contemptuous of current management, even ran a story in its "Page Six" entertainment column headlined "Shocker at Covenant House Party." The *Post*'s gossip columnist excoriated agency employees for inviting a transvestite dressed as the entertainer Madonna to lip-synch popular lyrics at a staff farewell party, where the performer sat "on a nun's lap in front of 150 people," thus bringing further "embarrassment" to the "scandal-scarred institution." No story concerning Covenant House appeared too trivial or too outlandish to appear in the public press.[26]

More substantive critics also emerged during the crisis to lodge their own philosophical complaints against the organization and its practices. William Treanor, the executive director of the American Youth Work Center and a longtime skeptic concerning the Covenant House philosophy, wrote several opinion pieces suggesting that the organization's shelters constituted

little more than "convenient flophouses" that should be shut down. In Treanor's view, Ritter "ran a one-man show" and "flouted the rules of sound
social-work practice" by ignoring federal regulations and housing children
in "vice-ridden downtown areas." John MacNeil, who had served as executive director of the Covenant House program in Toronto during the early
1980s and left the agency in bitterness, now granted several interviews and
emerged as an especially vocal critic. He referred to the shelter as "a revolv-
ing door, McDonald's style, eat and run" and claimed that "the Covenant
House approach doesn't do any good—it just guarantees that they will be
customers there the next day." Even Edward I. Koch, the former mayor who
now served as a television commentator on the CBS affiliate in New York,
used the opportunity to needle Father Ritter. Characterizing his former
nemesis as "an old friend of mine," Koch informed viewers that the Franciscan "has done a disservice to the very institution he loves" by lobbying
board members to replace Frank Macchiarola and that the founder's "inability to let go" turned his resignation into little more than "a charade."
Covenant House's critics had found it difficult to gain an audience during
the 1980s when virtually all publicity concerning the ministry appeared positive and upbeat and Ritter seemed unassailable. Now they boldly entered
the fray, interpreting the organization's current problems as a parable for
everything that they perceived to be wrong with the agency. Issues became
confused and distorted, snap judgments played out daily in the news media,
and Covenant House, it seemed, could do nothing right. Commentators lost
track of the facts surrounding the scandal and failed to address the specific
problems and errors that fueled the crisis. They highlighted the most sensational allegations, demonized the administrative staff, and demanded a
complete institutional overhaul. Under the circumstances, it remained difficult for those within the agency to maintain composure and perspective.[27]

Covenant House also needed to walk a very fine line, since not all critics spoke with one voice. Many supporters and staff members felt that the
organization had treated Ritter and his loyal followers shabbily. Anne Donahue, for example, the former faith community member who now served as
executive director of Covenant House's program in California, submitted
her letter of resignation on 9 March 1990. She charged that the organization
had "sold out to media pressure from the very beginning of this crisis, and
failed to defend the renegade, anti-institutional philosophy that gave it its
spirit, its vision, and its soul." From Donahue's perspective, such decisions
as the abolition of the safe house program meant that the agency had bowed
to "public opinion" and the "so-called professional standards of the social

work industry." She indicted senior management for not remaining faithful to Ritter's alternative philosophy and fatally compromising his standards in the interest of bureaucratic survival: "As one who still believes in Bruce's vision, I have no interest in being a part of this new institution." Donahue's comments reflected her own disillusionment, but they also voiced the sentiments of several committed administrators and volunteers who feared that the resignation of the founder would lead to a complete dismantling of his program.[28]

Donor reactions also varied wildly, making it difficult to craft an appropriate institutional response. The organization distributed comment cards to contributors during the early spring of 1990, and responses revealed strong support for Ritter. One donor condemned "the railroading of Rev. Ritter" and instructed the agency to "remove my name from your mailing list since it will be a waste of postage to continue it." Another informed the board that "the devil works in insidious ways. . . . Fr. Ritter should not have been forced to resign at all and the 'liar' should be severely punished and Father reinstated. That is when I'll continue my contribution to Covenant House." A third insisted that "Fr. Ritter has been given a very raw deal. . . . 'Let him who is without sin cast the first stone.'" And one Long Island contributor noted that "this Kite character may be mentally sick but frankly I would like to see someone knock him on his ass. Pardon my French. My anger at Kevin Kite comes from being an Irishman who in his youth never took any crap from anyone & I must admit shamefully loved a good fair scrap." Nearly half of the nineteen thousand comment card responses expressed support for both Covenant House and Ritter, but a significant constituency also demanded full disclosure, exhibited dismay over high executive salaries and loans to directors, questioned the board's competence, and vehemently disagreed with the founder's resignation. It became impossible for most observers to disentangle the complicated strands of the crisis, and the cumulative effect of four months of bad publicity simply created a culture of disbelief and disillusionment that defied a coherent solution. Board members recognized during the dark days of March that they needed to take yet another bold and immediate step in order to restore confidence until the internal investigations ran their course.[29]

The directors, prompted by their public relations consultants, finally decided to seek their salvation with the Archdiocese of New York. Pfeiffer and several colleagues met with Cardinal O'Connor early in March to iron out a cooperative arrangement. The cardinal had characterized Covenant House as "a mess" during one of his press conferences, and he publicly insisted that the archdiocese had no plans to assume control over the agency. Privately, however, he hoped to work closely with the board and explore the possibility of a more formal affiliation. As the cardinal informed Pfeiffer, "the entire organization is in a life-death situation," and Covenant House now needed to sacrifice some institutional autonomy in the interest of survival. Cardinal O'Connor agreed to provide an acting president for the organization, thereby allowing Harnett to return to his former post as chief operating officer. This step would effectively bury persistent press accusations that the agency remained in control of "Ritter's right hand man." The cardinal insisted that Covenant House's philosophical underpinnings must remain consistent with archdiocesan policies and principles, and that clear roles and responsibilities must differentiate the acting president's functions from those of the chief operating officer. The board essentially agreed with his conditions, and the archdiocese acknowledged that the agency needed to retain such unique practices as open intake. On 23 March, Cardinal O'Connor appointed Msgr. William J. Toohy, the associate director of Catholic Charities, and Msgr. Timothy A. McDonnell, the episcopal vicar of West Manhattan and pastor of Holy Trinity Church on West Eighty-second Street, as a team responsible for directing Covenant House.[30]

Msgrs. Toohy and McDonnell exerted a stabilizing and calming influence on Covenant House over the next several months. Their archdiocesan affiliation, professional stature, and long experience with charitable institutions enhanced public credibility. Newspaper coverage receded as Harnett, who constituted a lightning rod for tabloid critics throughout early March, remained behind the scenes and resumed his more purely administrative responsibilities. The monsignors retained cordial relations with the media, but they ended the practice of responding immediately to all stories and allegations, preferring to let the internal investigations continue at their own pace. Tensions still remained high within the organization, of course, during this period of uncertainty and turmoil. Many highly placed administrators left the agency during the spring and summer of 1990, owing to their close association with Ritter, their role in various controversial transactions, or their sense that the organization would not recover and that they needed to move on. The committed stalwarts, who remained loyal to the organization and its work, including Jim Harnett, Robert Cardany, Patricia Connors, and Patrick Kennedy, operated within an atmosphere characterized by high stress levels, mental exhaustion, and overwork. As Harnett recalled, "one thing that's not good is, it's not wise to put in fifteen to eighteen hours a day, six or seven days a week, and think that you're really functioning at the top of your game."[31]

Even as media pressures lessened, difficult administrative decisions loomed large. Donations declined, forcing the agency to face dramatic cutbacks. The board voted to slice $10 million from the 1991 fiscal year budget, prompting a series of drastic measures in April of 1990. Executives assumed a 5 percent salary reduction, and all managerial employees found their wages frozen. Corporate contributions to the subsidiaries decreased by amounts ranging from 33 percent to 50 percent. Significant layoffs occurred, as Covenant House eliminated eighteen of sixty positions in the Nineline program and forty-four of the remaining 150 salaried corporate jobs. The agency initiated hiring freezes, deferred capital expenditures, slashed travel budgets, completely closed the Washington, D.C., office, and consolidated the Under 21 and Rights of Passage programs in order to increase operating efficiencies. Fund-raising and direct mail solicitations remained sluggish through the summer, with July contributions exhibiting a 32 percent decrease from 1989 levels. The organization's relatively meager endowment and significant long-term mortgage obligations exacerbated the problems. Staff morale plummeted, and the fact that such a drastic contraction occurred in the wake of the extraordinary expansion of the late 1980s added to the general depression. Further nervousness concerning the outcome and potential impact of the Kroll investigation, as well as the uncertainties involving the search for a permanent chief executive officer, meant that the general atmosphere would remain tense throughout the spring and summer months despite the best efforts and considerable administrative skills of Msgrs. Toohy and McDonnell.[32]

Even as the financial crisis deepened, Covenant House's senior staff began to assess the harsh lessons that they had learned from the scandal. At the most basic level, crisis management procedures appeared inadequate. Inexperienced board members and administrators had felt an intense pressure to issue immediate statements and respond to all allegations. This sometimes muddied the message for media members and supporters, who heard conflicting stories from various sources. Covenant House needed one credible designated spokesperson who could deal with accusations consistently and concisely. Further, the organization now recognized the importance of providing a complete and accurate accounting at the outset. Individual facts and informational nuggets had trickled out over the course of nearly three months, prolonging the scandal and keeping the organization in the news. Covenant House often appeared reactive and confused. More accurate and complete initial statements might have defused the controversy, or at least shortened its duration. One agency attorney observed,

"To the press, the first allegations may simply put your organization 'in play.' They now want more. If you try to hide something, they're likely to find it. And continued press coverage can cause the organization to bleed to death."[33]

The crisis also illustrated a need for internal administrative reform. Bruce Ritter had struggled throughout his ministerial career with the problem of balancing his charismatic leadership style against the rules, regulations, and routine procedures that typically governed complex institutions. The scandal suggested that charisma still reigned supreme at Covenant House in 1990, at great cost to the ministry. Authority remained concentrated in the founder, no clear line separated individual and institutional interests, and personal loyalty too often trumped good stewardship. When allegations of sexual misconduct surfaced against the founder, no mechanism or will existed to conduct a serious inquiry. It appeared unseemly to question, let alone to investigate, the president's motivations or ethical behavior. This reaction reflected a managerial style common to many faith-based ministries. The historian Joel Carpenter has observed that nonprofit institutions tend to operate "via personal referrals and networks of friendly trust in matters of personal and charitable finances."[34] Covenant House certainly fit that pattern, and its religious character added still another dimension. Calls for greater bureaucratic control could be, and often were, perceived as efforts to dilute the agency's charisma and vision, leading it down the slippery slope toward dull routine and excessive professionalization. Faith remained an essential component that knit together the diverse elements within the organization. Faith in the founder, however, if unchecked by internal controls, could justify erratic behavior, arbitrary decisions, and imperious rule. The tension between charisma and bureaucracy remains endemic to faith-based ministries. It would fall to Ritter's successor to redefine the appropriate balance for Covenant House.

On another level, the crisis reflected the emergence of a new tabloid moment in American religious history. Church scandals and spectacles long constituted excellent media copy, but the climate changed significantly in the late 1980s. When Oral Roberts barricaded himself inside his Tulsa, Oklahoma, prayer tower in March of 1987, declaring that God had ordered him to either raise $8 million for his ministry in two weeks or go "home" to heaven, he kicked off an extraordinary series of telescandals that rocked American evangelicalism for the next two years. Jim and Tammy Faye Bakker, Jimmy Swaggart, Jessica Hahn, and Jerry Falwell became household names over the course of 1987 and 1988. Secular media outlets gleefully moved from one tacky melodrama to another, focusing on the extravagant lifestyles, financial excesses, drunkenness, womanizing, deceit, and sexual kinkiness that seemed to pervade televangelical culture. From Tammy Faye Bakker's air-conditioned and plushly carpeted doghouse to Jessica Hahn's *Playboy* pictorial, the juicy scandals contained a series of convenient symbols that reporters found easy to exploit. Journalists recycled old myths concerning fundamentalist hypocrisy and successfully repackaged them for a media-obsessed and celebrity-driven popular audience. The televangelists themselves, who built their reputations and financial empires through the creative use of contemporary media, played out their psychodramas and disagreements largely on television talk shows. Ted Koppel's *Nightline* devoted sixteen separate programs to the scandals, including a riveting hour-long primetime special, "The Billion Dollar Pie," that generated the highest ratings in the show's history.[35]

Covenant House's troubles obviously bore little resemblance to the wide-ranging televangelist controversies. Yet, incredibly, people drew connections. *Commonweal*, the influential and respected liberal Catholic review, editorialized in May of 1990 that "for Catholics, the tragedy engulfing Ritter seems to have a parallel in the hypocrisies of evangelists Jimmy Swaggart and Jim Bakker." One donor informed Covenant House that "when the Bakker and Swaggart scams were going on, I felt good about donating to your group because I thought you were on the level. . . . You're no better than Jim Bakker, and probably should end up where he is. When I was young my mother used to tell me that a liar is worse than a thief. Well you people are both." Another Brooklynite observed, "I am very angry, sad, unhappy & disappointed about this whole matter. I have lost a lot of faith in people and charities. Papers are full of incidents where ministers, etc., are doing the same thing. I now have to think very carefully about giving my meager donations." A New Jerseyan vowed to withhold all contributions until "Father Ritter comes clean just like Jimmy Swaggart."[36] Unfortunately for Covenant House, the crisis occurred during a time of extraordinary public cynicism and media suspicion concerning high-profile ministerial leaders. The shadow of the televangelist scandals loomed large over Covenant House, and it became easy to highlight superficial similarities. Casual observers might cavalierly dismiss Ritter as yet another hypocritical preacher, building a multimillion dollar organization and engaging in questionable sexual activities. Press outlets could fit the founder's story into the well-worn and successful template that they had developed when covering the earlier scandals. Fact blurred with fiction, emphases became distorted, and simplistic caricatures replaced complex realities. Ritter, in common with the televangelists, always had possessed an excellent intuitive sense of how to take advantage of modern media in order to communicate his message. He understood that donors identified with people more than institutions and that the most effective way to win support for his cause was to personalize the ministry. Now, that very personal identification appeared as a significant corporate liability. Covenant House faced the formidable challenge of crafting an appropriate public relations strategy to promote the organization in an altered and increasingly confrontational media climate.

Finally, the crisis played itself out within a larger context that contained enormous implications for American Catholicism. The historian Philip Jenkins has argued that clergy sexual abuse offered "a model example of a social problem that undergoes mushroom growth, receiving virtually no attention from media or policy makers before about 1984–1985, yet becoming a major focus of public concern within a few years."[37] The case of Gilbert Gauthe, a Roman Catholic priest in Louisiana who was indicted and convicted on molestation charges in 1985, proved pivotal in shaping public opinion. The journalist Jason Berry, as well as correspondents and editors at the *National Catholic Reporter,* carefully chronicled Gauthe's misdeeds for a national audience and also raised disturbing questions concerning the Catholic Church's institutional response. Investigative reporting revealed that dioceses and religious orders lacked uniform procedures for dealing with priests who had sexually abused children and parishioners. Bishops sometimes quietly transferred suspected pedophiles and ephebophiles to new parishes where they continued their ministry among children and adolescents. Clergymen who underwent counseling that supposedly cured their affliction often reverted to their former behavior patterns. Some dioceses apparently placed a higher premium on avoiding publicity than on reaching a fair and just accommodation with victims. The *Gauthe* case pointed toward a culture of clericalism within church circles that seemed designed to protect those within the ranks and insulate institutional practices from lay scrutiny.[38]

During the late 1980s, clergy sexual abuse became a common rallying point for participants in the culture wars that polarized American Catholics. Liberals claimed that the scandals stemmed from the Church's hierarchical governance structure, illustrated the dangers of clerical celibacy, reflected a hypocritical institutional attitude toward sexuality, and pointed toward the need to reconsider the issue of women's ordination. Conservatives decried the existence of homosexuals within clerical ranks, complained about the

proliferation of "lavender seminaries," and called for increased traditional-
ism and church discipline as a means of resolving the crisis. These debates
largely defined the issue in Catholic terms, despite statistical evidence indicating that priests appeared no more likely to abuse children than other
adults who worked with young people. As additional real and imagined victims came forth with their stories in the late 1980s, popular consciousness
concerning the problem increased. New therapeutic practices that accepted
the notion of "recovered memory," high-profile lawsuits against individual
dioceses, and additional media exposés kept the sexual abuse issue in the
public eye. In November of 1989, as Kevin Kite carried his allegations to
the *New York Post,* conservative protestors demonstrated at the National
Conference of Catholic Bishops' meeting in Baltimore, charging that the
ecclesiastical hierarchy refused to investigate pedophilia scandals and systematically engaged in cover-up campaigns.[39]

The Covenant House crisis occurred against this backdrop of heightened lay anxiety concerning priests' sexual behavior. Public revelations during the late 1980s created an atmosphere that cast suspicion on Catholic
clergymen and assured that the charges against Ritter would immediately
reach a receptive audience. The founder's risky behavior with Kevin Kite
during 1989 appears even more inexplicable considering this broader social
context. The widespread belief that diocesan officials and religious agencies
routinely covered up sexual abuse cases also placed Covenant House administrators in a defensive and vulnerable position. The Melican and Bassile
allegations concerned incidents that supposedly occurred during the early and
mid-1970s when the organization operated in an even more informal and
freewheeling fashion. Covenant House's mere inability to locate files and to
document policies from this loosely structured period in its institutional
history lent credence to the suspicion that the organization had something
to hide. It remained easy to construct a circumstantial case that pointed
toward a broad-based conspiracy as new allegations surfaced over the
course of several months. Few observers had the time or interest to dissect
each individual charge and assess its validity. Rather, they simply received a
general impression that something seemed terribly amiss.

Considering all of these factors, it appeared quite possible during the
spring and summer of 1990 to conclude that Covenant House would soon
collapse under the cumulative weight of the allegations and innuendos.
Most public officials and social work professionals, even some who remained skeptical of institutional practices and methods, believed that this
would constitute an unmitigated disaster. As the *New York Times* observed,

Covenant House's $88 million budget accounted for three times the amount of money that the federal government spent on youth shelters. Joyce Hunter, who frequently had criticized Under 21's approach to gays and lesbians in her capacity as social services director for the Hetrick-Martin Institute, stressed that "we don't want to see it fold. We need that place and there are a lot of good people working there." Even Charles Sennott, the *New York Post* reporter, ultimately concluded that "what remains clear is that Covenant House is a desperately needed provider of services to an often forgotten segment of the population." The crisis severely jeopardized those services. Covenant House's future depended heavily on finding new and effective leadership to carry out its mission. The search for a new president and chief executive officer took on enormous importance.[40]

Figure 10. Sr. Mary Rose McGeady, D.C., and New York governor Mario Cuomo, sharing a laugh. The board of directors enacted a series of internal reforms and turned to a sixty-two-year-old Daughter of Charity with extensive experience in the social work world in an effort to save the organization from possible dissolution in 1990. Photograph courtesy of the Covenant House Archives.

Chapter 8
Rebirth

We confidently predict that not many years from now we will all look back at the moment of Covenant House's greatest pain and see that it was also a moment of birth of a new, stronger, even more effective instrument of goodness under a superb new leader, Sister Mary Rose McGeady.

—*New York governor Mario Cuomo*

Being president of Covenant House is, for me, the opportunity of a lifetime—the opportunity for me to recommit myself to what has been the great preoccupation of my life: service to our youth and their care.

—*Sr. Mary Rose McGeady, D.C.*[1]

Board members moved rapidly to find a new president. By late March of 1990, they had engaged the executive search firm of Russell Reynolds Associates to locate and interview suitable candidates. The process, however, appeared daunting. Covenant House's well-publicized crisis, shaky financial situation, and tarnished reputation had transformed the agency into a very risky venture. The bylaw stipulation that mandated the selection of a Catholic priest, brother, or member of a women's religious community as president further limited the potential applicant pool. The position itself required extensive administrative experience, demonstrated fund-raising ability, a strong commitment to serving troubled youth, and superior communications skills. Perhaps most important of all, the organization desperately needed a new symbol. Covenant House required a leader who could inspire trust, restore credibility, project stability, and regain the confidence of a diverse constituency of supporters. The new president would necessarily walk a fine line. It remained critical to respect the very real accomplishments of the past yet equally important to alter the institutional culture so that the agency could survive the demise of its founder and transcend his personal vision. Board members hoped to locate a suitable individual who exhibited exceptional maturity, deeply ingrained humility, and an unflagging commitment to service. They believed that they found that person in July of 1990, when a sixty-two-year-old Daughter of Charity accepted the challenge to rebuild the organization.[2]

Sr. Mary Rose McGeady, D.C., brought unique credentials and strengths to the presidency. Her background and personal profile perfectly coincided with Covenant House's needs at this important moment in its institutional history. The new president had spent a lifetime working with children, possessed appropriate academic degrees in psychology and sociology, and operated from a professional social work perspective. She favored a more holistic approach toward troubled youths, which promised to bring fresh programmatic ideas to the agency. She also had no previous experience with Covenant House, minimal contact with the founder, and a cursory knowledge of internal institutional issues, observing that "the only thing I knew about Covenant House in that period was whatever was in the paper." This outsider status proved advantageous in light of the recent crisis, allowing her to assume a neutral posture with a deeply divided staff. Gender and religious commitment played important roles in her selection. The nature of the sexual abuse scandal prompted the board to search for a woman, and one with an impeccable personal history, in order to remove any taint or suspicion from the organization. The directors recognized that the new leader needed to have a solid reputation and a high profile visibility within Catholic circles in order to mend fences with the institutional church. It appeared a tall order, but a detailed examination of the new president's life and career illustrates the ways in which her personal story made her an appropriate choice for this formidable position.[3]

Mary Rose was born on 28 June 1928, in Hazleton, Pennsylvania, near the center of the state's coal-mining industry.[4] She fondly recalls "a very happy home life," growing up in a stable, caring, working-class family with loving parents and two siblings. Both parents had graduated from high school, and her father had supplemented his secondary education by learning the new technology of air conditioning. This skill resulted in a job offer from the U.S. Department of the Interior, and the McGeadys moved to Washington, D.C., in 1934. They weathered the Depression reasonably well, purchasing a new row house in a rapidly developing area of the city, remaining steadily employed, and participating fully in the area's vibrant Catholic subculture.[5] The children all attended local parish schools, and Mary Rose earned a competitive scholarship to the Immaculate Conception Academy in Washington, a well-respected high school administered by the Daughters of Charity of Saint Vincent de Paul. The McGeady family exemplified the striving, respectable, hard-working urban Catholics who persevered through the troubled times of the 1930s and early 1940s, achieving some limited economic mobility and building a solid ethical and financial foundation for their children. As Sister Mary Rose recalled years later, "until the war, we had a very predictable life. We got up in the morning, we went to school, we came home, we played in the street." Structure, routine, order, and regularity played an important role in her upbringing.

The decision to enter religious life apparently came easily, provoking little conflict or anxiety. Sister Mary Rose remembered that "when I was in the fifth grade . . . there was a story in our reader about a sister taking care of a sick child. . . . I remember the book, I can remember the picture, the sister. . . . I was so impressed with that story and that sister that somewhere in my ego the decision was kind of born there, if you will . . . kind of like that's what I want to do when I grow up." She continued to cultivate her spiritual life and interests throughout adolescence, finding several role models and mentors among the Daughters of Charity of Saint Vincent de Paul who taught at Immaculate Conception Academy. Indeed, the Vincentian tradition, with its emphasis on living simply, caring for the poor, maintaining a rich devotional life, and dedicating oneself to service exerted a strong attraction for her. The Daughters of Charity administered numerous schools, hospitals, orphanages, and child care institutions throughout the United States, thus offering sisters rich opportunities for diverse good works.[6] Sister Mary Rose volunteered at Saint Ann's Infant Home in Washington during high school, working with the Daughters who staffed that institution as teachers, nurses, and social workers. Child care seemed to be her special calling, and the possibility of pursuing that ministry made the Daughters of Charity an appropriate match for her interests. She continued to believe throughout her life that the impulse to serve children emanated from divine origins: "I guess it's just a gift in your heart. . . . It's just a gift from God, you know." Mary Rose McGeady elected to follow her heart and cultivate her gift after graduating from Immaculate Conception Academy, entering the sister formation program with the Daughters of Charity of Saint Vincent de Paul in Emmitsburg, Maryland, in 1946.

She studied at Emmitsburg until 1948, when the Daughters sent their new recruit to teach at the Home for Catholic Children in Boston, a large-scale orphanage that housed approximately 150 children, most of whom were between the ages of three and twelve.[7] Sister Mary Rose worked with orphaned, homeless, and disturbed children at this facility for nine years while also earning her B.A. in sociology and psychology from Emmanuel College. Her experiences in Boston reaffirmed her commitment to working with troubled children and introduced the young daughter to the overwhelming problems that accompanied familial separation and parental neglect. Most children at the home had either been committed by the judicial system or sent to the institution owing to some domestic trauma or tragedy. Sister Mary Rose retained "a lot of sad memories of that place." She learned the importance of establishing close personal relationships with children, of understanding the experiences that produced destructive behavior, and of keeping families together whenever possible. She also apparently impressed the administration of her religious order with her ability, commitment, and approach. The Daughters of Charity assigned her in 1957 to serve at the Astor Home for Children in Rhinebeck, New York, where she assumed the position of executive director in 1961.

Astor Home existed as an experimental facility, established by the State of New York in 1952 and administered by the Daughters of Charity under the auspices of Catholic Charities of the Archdiocese of New York. The program attempted to deal with seriously disturbed children whose behavior appeared too problematic and aggressively destructive for other institutions. A 1959 report described typical Astor Home residents as "children the schools could not contain, for whom the courts had no solution, whose own parents were desperate, and for whom foster homes at the point of placement were contra-indicated." The institution sought to reach these children by establishing a residential treatment center that would be staffed by a full complement of child psychiatrists, psychologists, social workers, psychiatric nurses, and educators. The program concentrated on small numbers of children, with the residential population never exceeding thirty-five at any one time during the 1950s. Each child remained under the care of a team that carefully monitored individual progress and developed a coordinated program designed to meet the resident's unique needs. Group living, remedial education, structured leisure activities, and individual therapy constituted the four basic elements of each treatment plan. Social workers especially emphasized aftercare, ultimately seeking to reintegrate children into families and communities. Research also played an important role in Astor Home. Administrators forged strong connections with New York City's academic and professional communities in order to generate innovative treatment approaches and to study behavioral patterns among the residents.[8]

Sister Mary Rose thrived in the dynamic intellectual atmosphere at Astor Home. She earned her M.A. in clinical psychology from Fordham University in 1961, conducted her own research projects, and applied her theoretical classroom training to the practical reality of administering a residential facility. She also achieved a more sophisticated understanding of the ways in which relational therapy, psychotherapy, and pharmacology could work together when developing treatment plans for individual children. As the executive director, she shaped the program in several ways. During her tenure, Astor Home expanded its physical facilities, began admitting girls, opened its first group homes in the Bronx, and inaugurated the Dutchess County Child Guidance Clinic in Rhinebeck. Many of these innovations illustrated her growing conviction that smaller programs, intensive aftercare efforts, and careful endeavors to reintegrate children into broader community networks appeared necessary. Sister Mary Rose had begun to establish her reputation as a leading expert on child care issues, and her religious community took careful note. In 1966, the Daughters of Charity returned her to Boston and placed her in charge of the Nazareth Child Care Center. She rapidly transformed Nazareth into a facility capable of treating seriously disturbed children, who composed a large percentage of that institution's clientele. Sister Mary Rose imported several successful elements of the residential treatment program from Astor Home to Nazareth. She increased the clinical staff, provided new therapeutic programs for children, and initiated a nongraded school that would move individuals along at their own pace. By the time she left Nazareth in 1971, the institution resembled a much more modern child care operation.[9]

Sister Mary Rose's next assignment placed her in a very different institutional and cultural milieu. The Vincentian priests who administered Saint John the Baptist Church in the Bedford-Stuyvesant neighborhood of Brooklyn had contacted the Daughters in 1970 about the possibility of establishing a foundation connected with their inner city parish. This invitation especially attracted the order. It provided the sisters with an opportunity to cooperate with priests who shared their Vincentian tradition. It also reaffirmed the community's own mandate to concentrate on works that brought them in close contact with the poor. Bedford-Stuyvesant was a heavily African American, poverty-stricken, densely populated, crime-ridden, drug-infested, and politically neglected urban neighborhood, dominated by five high-rise public housing projects. Approximately fifteen thousand Catholics lived within Saint John's parish boundaries. Puerto Ricans accounted for three-quarters of the Catholic population, with African Americans composing the remainder of the parishioners. The neighborhood desperately needed a wide range of social services. At Saint John's, the daughters sensed a perfect chance to initiate precisely the types of community-based experimental ministries that many religious orders began to emphasize during the late 1960s and early 1970s. The order accepted the challenge, assigning Sister Mary Rose and four additional daughters to establish the foundation in 1971.[10]

Sister Mary Rose's arrival in Brooklyn marked an important milestone in her career. She would reside in Bedford-Stuyvesant almost without interruption for the next three decades.[11] She became energized by inner city work and increasingly convinced that "as Daughters of Charity that's where we belong. . . . If you're going to pretend to be in the service of the poor, it's ridiculous to think 'Well, I'm in service to the poor, but I don't live there.'" The sisters opened a dialogue with neighborhood leaders, shaping their ministry in response to needs that the residents themselves articulated. They established numerous social programs at Saint John the Baptist Church, including adult education offerings, catechetical classes, a soup kitchen, a thrift shop, counseling services, support groups, and job training initiatives. Sister Mary Rose, however, also assumed a somewhat unique role within her community. Shortly following her move to Bedford-Stuyvesant, she met with the Rev. Joseph M. Sullivan, the executive director of Catholic Charities for the Diocese of Brooklyn.[12] She requested a position with Catholic Charities, which would allow her to earn much-needed income for the community at Saint John's while simultaneously maintaining her professional involvement in social work circles. Father Sullivan appointed her as executive director of the Learning Center for Exceptional Children, thereby inaugurating a long-term partnership between Sister Mary Rose and the diocese of Brooklyn. For the next eight years, she occupied a series of major administrative posts with Catholic Charities, earning considerable attention within church and state as an advocate for the needs of both children and mentally ill adults.[13]

Sister Mary Rose's responsibilities at Catholic Charities placed her at the center of several volatile and tumultuous controversies concerning mental health. During the 1970s, deinstitutionalization proceeded on an unprecedented scale in New York as state hospitals discharged large numbers of mental patients onto city streets. Many remained homeless. Others found their way into poorly managed and largely unregulated adult homes, where they failed to receive proper medical care and psychiatric treatment. The problems appeared especially intense in Queens. Mental patients who had been discharged from the massive Creedmore Psychiatric Center in the Middle Village section of the borough dramatically altered the character of such nearby neighborhoods as the Rockaways. Under Sister Mary Rose's direction, Catholic Charities soon became the most significant provider of outpatient services in Queens. She completely revamped the agency's neighborhood clinics, expanding the Catholic Charities budget for mental health services in local communities from $300,000 to well over $6 million. Some of her more significant innovations included daycare services for discharged patients, new mental health clinics for children and adults, and an apartment program for adult home residents who could function with minimal counseling and supervision. Sister Mary Rose proved politically adept as well, vigorously and tirelessly lobbying city and state officials in order to secure better funding for mental health programs and to increase governmental regulation over group home profiteers. She even received state funding for a model single-room residential building on the grounds of Creedmore that housed nearly 170 mentally ill and homeless adults. This pioneer facility eventually was dedicated as Rose House as a way of honoring her long-standing contributions and advocacy efforts.[14]

In 1979, Sister Mary Rose accepted a position with Catholic Charities of the Archdiocese of New York to administer the Kennedy Child Study Center in Manhattan. This center offered a day treatment program for slowly developing and retarded children under the age of ten. It especially emphasized infant services and provided parents with strategies intended to maximize their children's progress. Sister Mary Rose's affiliation with the Kennedy Center proved relatively brief. In 1981, the Daughters of Charity elected her as visitatrix, a position comparable to that of provincial superior in other religious communities. She moved to DePaul Provincial House in Albany, where her new responsibilities included oversight for eight hospitals and seventeen schools as well as various social welfare and child care agencies that were scattered over eleven states. As visitatrix, Sister Mary Rose especially emphasized ministries and programs that served the poorest clients in all of the order's works. Her term of office expired in 1987, whereupon she returned from Albany to Catholic Charities in the diocese of Brooklyn, spending the next three years as associate executive director with responsibility for all programs in Queens County.

Sister Mary Rose thus had earned widespread respect and recognition within religious and social work circles by the time Covenant House's search committee began its deliberations in 1990. She had worked with emotionally disturbed children and mentally ill adults for over forty years, supplementing her real-world experience with relevant academic training in psychology and sociology. Her position at Catholic Charities provided an intense administrative experience in an exceedingly complex environment: by 1990, her portfolio included forty programs in Queens that employed over eight hundred people and accounted for approximately $40 million in annual expenditures. City and state officials acknowledged her abilities by appointing her to numerous mental health advisory councils, and she had developed a successful track record of securing public funding for her programs. Perhaps most significantly, she never lost touch with the day-to-day problems and realities that defined life for the urban poor. Her residence in Bedford-Stuyvesant, her regular visits to clinics throughout Queens, and her immersion in the Vincentian tradition of serving the least fortunate suggested that she remained close to the streets and completely driven by her mission. Sister Mary Rose's comments upon the dedication of Rose House bear repeating in this context: "So this is a very happy day for me, but I also want to say that I look forward to an even happier day—the day that we can close this place. . . . It will be a great day to rejoice, it will be a day that truly dedicates to the Lord, when everybody in this town has decent housing and proper care."[15]

Covenant House's board clearly recognized that Sister Mary Rose would bring instant credibility, stature, and prestige to the troubled organization. The trustees began aggressively recruiting her during the spring of 1990, but she declined their overtures on several occasions. She remained reluctant to leave Catholic Charities and wondered whether she possessed the stamina and wherewithal to save Covenant House. Several colleagues in Brooklyn urged her to consider the offer. Peter Della Monica, a friend and fellow associate director at Catholic Charities, articulated the views of many during one private conversation: "It's almost like your life has been a preparation for Covenant House. You spent all these years taking care of crazy kids, upset kids, and then you've been in administration. . . . You know, maybe this is really a call for you." Still, Sister Mary Rose needed to undertake a period of discernment and spiritual reflection before making any commitment. At a particularly critical juncture "I went away and made a retreat. And I really prayed, I really asked God to help me to know what He wanted. And I got to the point that I really felt like the hand of God was on me." After receiving that revelation, the final decision appeared clear. She accepted the board's offer in July, with the proviso that she could begin work in September.[16]

Press coverage and public reaction proved uniformly enthusiastic. John Cardinal O'Connor perhaps best summarized the prevailing popular response in his *Catholic New York* column, emphasizing themes that would appear repeatedly in both religious and secular media outlets. The cardinal described the new president's demeanor as "about as no-nonsense looking as they come," thus presenting her as a stern but fair taskmaster who would tolerate no misconduct and would restore order to the troubled institution. He also took note of the fact that "she calls herself *Sister* Mary Rose and doesn't invite anybody to call her anything less," thereby serving notice that Covenant House's new leader considered her vocation and her spiritual commitments very serious matters. Other newspapers used remarkably similar language in describing the presidential transition. The *New York Post* headline, for example, proclaimed, "Nun Will Lay Down Covenant House Law," leading its story with the observation that "a no-nonsense nun will take over as president of scandal-wracked Covenant House." Press accounts carefully noted that the institution's new leader received visitors "in her powder-blue habit," thus implicitly contrasting her appearance to Bruce Ritter's often informal and secular dress.

Reporters also portrayed Sister Mary Rose as a savvy pragmatist, claiming that her practical bent made her "as comfortable in a board room as she is on the street." An article in the youth-oriented *Spin* magazine best illustrated the dual image of traditional piety and street-smart hipness that quickly attached itself to the new president. The publication caricatured Sister Mary Rose as "a woman who looks the part of Old World convent life with her rubbery walking shoes, blue veil, doughy face ornamented with oversize glasses, and a wave of steely hair." *Spin* reporters also promised readers, however, that they would "get the straight dope from the good sistuh" as "the language of the streets falls trippingly from this nun's tongue." Perhaps the "no-nonsense" label proved most enduring, eventually prompting the pantyhose corporation of the same name to proclaim Sister Mary Rose as its "No Nonsense American Woman of the Month" in August 1994. The new president well understood the power of such perceptions, observing that "I am very aware that I am a symbol. And I use that as much as I can. . . . I also think that the fact that I was a woman and a nun in a habit helped to restore the image of Covenant House."[17]

Sister Mary Rose's stature and image clearly provided the first important step in restoring institutional credibility. Agency leaders well understood, however, that other issues still required resolution. Covenant House's oversight committee planned to release the results of its Kroll investigative report during the summer. Board members and senior administrators anticipated this event with great trepidation. The directors had authorized the investigation in March, hoping that an objective and thorough outside review would provide a broader perspective on the scandal and offer a satisfactory accounting to critics. Between March and August, however, Covenant House continued to hemorrhage money and lose support. Many administrators believed that the lengthy investigation merely prolonged the prevailing crisis atmosphere. They felt that the organization would benefit most from a more rapid resolution. Kroll, however, proceeded at its own pace, placing a higher premium on thoroughness than on speed. An eight-member investigative team, consisting of former FBI agents, ex–New York City police detectives, forensic accountants, and research assistants spearheaded the project. The firm eventually interviewed over 150 board members, administrators, staff, present and former residents, and Faith Community members in compiling the report. Covenant House's board remained wary of the final product, carefully selecting a Friday in August to share the document with the media in order to minimize news coverage. Two directors even voted against accepting the report and opposed its public dissemination.[18]

Kroll Associates did not shy away from forthrightly assigning responsibility for the institution's troubles. The report voiced considerable criticism concerning the directors' past failures to monitor institutional affairs. It also carefully reviewed the inappropriate transactions between the Franciscan Charitable Trust and some board members, documented the questionable and illegal loans to corporate officials, and raised some conflict of interest issues involving competitive bids. The most sensational revelations, however, clearly concerned Bruce Ritter. The report documented fifteen allegations of sexual misconduct against the founder, ranging in time between 1970 and 1989. Kroll concluded that "the cumulative evidence . . . that Father Ritter engaged in sexual activities with certain residents and made sexual advances toward certain members of the Faith Community is extensive." Investigators acknowledged that no individual allegation could be proved beyond question but unambiguously asserted that "it is our opinion that, if Father Ritter had not resigned, the termination of the relationship between him and Covenant House would have been required. . . . Father Ritter exercised unacceptably poor judgment in his relations with certain residents." Many loyal supporters found this conclusion an especially bitter pill to swallow and wondered whether its publication would further damage the ministry.[19]

Generally, however, the report placed the agency in a positive light. The investigators concluded that "there is far more right with Covenant House than there was wrong with it." By the time that the oversight committee issued its report, after all, the organization had already anticipated and implemented many of its recommendations. The board had reorganized its operations in a manner designed to achieve more effective administrative oversight. The directors eliminated the sole member structure of the corporation, established an audit committee, and reinvigorated their finance committee. The board diversified its own membership in terms of race, gender, and ethnicity, adding directors with substantial experience in the nonprofit sector as well.[20] New policies had been established concerning grievance procedures, disciplinary proceedings, conflicts of interest, loans to officers, competitive bidding, organizational contributions to other charities, presidential compensation practices, and the employment of relatives. Several problematic programs within the agency, including the Institute for Youth Advocacy, the Safe House Program, and Dove Messenger Services, had been eliminated. Evidence that some payroll fraud occurred in the Under 21 Security Department, as well as documentation involving some irregularities within petty cash disbursements, all received prompt attention and a thorough response. The board's proactive efforts to increase internal accountability and modify its administrative structure resolved several other nagging problems. New York State attorney general Robert Abrams agreed in February of 1991 to conclude his civil investigation of the charity, expressing satisfaction with the structural overhaul. The Council of Better Business Bureaus and the National Charities Information Bureau also restored Covenant House to their approved lists early in 1992, based largely on these board reforms.[21]

Other investigations that occurred under the aegis of the oversight committee proved fairly benign. Ernst & Young suggested some relatively minor accounting modifications but found no evidence of widespread problems. Richard Shinn's compensation report concluded that virtually all managerial salaries "fall at or below the mid-point of the individual evaluations" and that managerial practices appeared "professional" and reflected "fair compensation." The Child Welfare League's investigation characterized Under 21 as a "generally well-conceived [and] appropriately structured . . . response to the needs of homeless youth." The league did urge Covenant House to consider more carefully the ways in which emergency shelter, crisis intervention, transitional care, and therapeutic treatment might fit together within a coherent overall program. It also observed that the organization needed to work more effectively with similar service providers and regulatory bodies, toning down its confrontational rhetoric concerning these groups and modifying its own claims to uniqueness. It further exhorted the agency to acknowledge that open intake, despite its centrality to the program, remained realistically limited by client behavior, shelter capacity, and any organization's inherent inability to respond to all resident needs. By and large, however, the league concluded that Covenant House "constituted an irreplaceable resource to the City of New York and is a sound model for delivering critically needed services to a population that is seriously underserved."[22]

These investigations effectively muted any popular or journalistic out-cry that might have resulted from the release of the Kroll report. Ritter's complete estrangement from the agency and his rapid disappearance from public life further removed the scandal from the media glare. The founder left New York City following his resignation and remained largely in seclu-sion for the remainder of his life. He consistently denied all allegations and elected not to cooperate with the Kroll investigation. He also refused to enter a counseling program prescribed by the Franciscans, viewing such a step as an admission of guilt. Though he severed his ties with the order, Rit-ter arranged to remain in the priesthood by receiving an ecclesiastical trans-fer to a diocese in India during the spring of 1991. Throughout the 1990s, the founder pursued a quiet and relatively isolated existence at a farmhouse in rural Otsego County, New York, using his birth name of John. He de-clined requests for interviews, remained in contact with only a small circle of close associates and family members, and rarely responded to overtures from former colleagues at Covenant House. Neighbors and acquaintances reported that he lived a simple spiritual life, celebrating mass daily at a pri-vate chapel that he had added to his Decatur farm. The founder's health deteriorated in the late 1990s, and he died of cancer on 7 October 1999. Only a few close friends attended his private memorial service, and Ritter's asso-ciates informed Covenant House that he expressly wished no public institu-tional acknowledgment of his death. His ashes were buried beneath a statue of Saint Francis, near the stone walls behind his farmhouse. His quiet and peaceful final years contrasted dramatically with his previously flamboyant public career. A few obituaries recalled his meteoric rise to prominence and the subsequent scandal, but the media had long since moved on. Even by the time that Sr. Mary Rose McGeady assumed charge of the organization in September 1990, Bruce Ritter seemed like old news.[23]

Still, the scandal's lingering impact reverberated throughout the orga-nization during the early 1990s. Sister Mary Rose recognized that rebuilding public credibility would remain her top priority during her first few years in office, and she moved immediately on several fronts in order to accomplish that goal. First, she stabilized her top-level administrative staff. Remarkably, no purges or firings followed her assumption of the presidency. Jim Harnett and Robert Cardany remained in place as chief operating officer and trea-surer respectively. Patricia Connors received a promotion to a senior vice presidential position. Denise Scelzo, who had administered the very suc-cessful direct mail program during the late 1980s, became the senior vice president for fund-raising and development. These decisions signaled the new president's desire to build upon the substantial programs that had grown during the late 1980s, and they alleviated some fear and uncertainty among employees. Sister Mary Rose's even-handed approach won her considerable respect and good will throughout the organization. Her refusal to sacrifice senior staff or to target convenient scapegoats proved to be an excellent internal strategy, though it puzzled media observers and failed to satisfy some vocal critics. The administrators who labored long and hard to keep the organization afloat during the troubled winter and spring of 1990 found their efforts rewarded. Sister Mary Rose judiciously supplemented her existing staff with some new additions. She hired Tom Kennedy, for example, an experienced social service administrator who had served as assistant to the commissioner in the New York State Office of Mental Health, as senior vice president for program development in the fall of 1990.[24] Richard Hirsch joined the organization as senior vice president for public relations in 1993. This core administrative team remained in place for the remainder of her thirteen-year tenure as president, and the continuity proved critical in rebuilding the organization. Covenant House's top-level staff retained an invaluable historical perspective and knowledge base concerning the ministry. Their shared experience in surviving the crisis also proved an important unifying bond. It enhanced their strong corporate commitment, cemented their enduring personal and professional relationships, and heightened their investment in the agency's well-being.

Sister Mary Rose confidently delegated administrative decisions and details to her senior staff, which contrasted notably with previous institutional practice. This allowed her more freedom to pursue another important component of her rebuilding strategy: spending considerable time with financial contributors. The new president maintained a rigorous travel schedule, visiting Covenant House sites, attending donor receptions, and meeting people. She believed that, in terms of fund-raising, "the most important thing I did as president was make the Sister Mary Rose name on a letter a real, live lady." Her style differed from that of the founder. Ritter excelled before large audiences, often inspiring listeners with his eloquent rhetoric and carefully crafted sermons. Sister Mary Rose especially enjoyed speaking with people one-on-one in smaller settings: "First of all, I'd give a talk for about thirty minutes, answer their questions, and then stand around and just be with them so that they thought they got to know this lady who's signing the letter. I met thousands and thousands of people that way. And I think it made a difference." Executive directors at subsidiary sites typically scheduled multiple receptions throughout their states to coincide with her annual presidential visits. Such influential and well-connected board members as Nancy Dickerson Whitehead arranged small weekday evening or Sunday afternoon cocktail parties in New York City, where Sister Mary Rose could mingle with donors in more informal gatherings for a few hours. The new president proved intentional and diligent in seeking out opportunities to promote the Covenant House cause to contributors. She carried a fundamentally new message to these gatherings, however, and her vision altered public perceptions concerning the agency's work.[25]

Sister Mary Rose's social critique proved more far-reaching and systemic than that of her predecessor. She rarely mentioned juvenile prostitution, male hustlers, or predatory chicken hawks when discussing institutional programs. She toned down this sensationalist rhetoric in favor of presenting a more complex and comprehensive portrait of the young people who sought shelter at Covenant House. A lifetime of working with children had convinced the new president that factors other than the sex industry had produced the "American tragedy" that necessitated Covenant House programs throughout the United States. Most often, she focused on the theme of "disconnected kids," emphasizing the sad stories of the children who found shelter at Covenant House. Sister Mary Rose worried that adolescents in many homes suffered "the discomfort of feeling totally alone, suspended in space, without roots, without a base to cling to" owing largely to unstable familial structures. These children lacked "human connectedness," and their inability to develop enduring social relationships resulted in a "disorganized life style lacking any consistent pattern of values and goals." Single-parent households, teen pregnancies, poor urban educational systems, substance abuse, and inadequate institutional support networks contributed to the problem. Sister Mary Rose, drawing upon her experience at such places as Astor Home and Nazareth, believed that Covenant House's program worked best when it both satisfied immediate material needs and helped to reintegrate individual children into larger social and familial networks. She hoped to use her platform as president to continue her advocacy efforts, working to improve public policy approaches to housing, family counseling, adolescent pregnancy services, child placement, drug prevention, and welfare. She spoke frequently about the "deterioration of the family," firmly believing that this constituted the overriding social issue facing Americans. Sister Mary Rose viewed Covenant House as one vital effort in providing a "continuum of care" for young people, but always recognized that both the problems and the solutions far exceeded the capacity of any individual agency. Increased cooperation with other service providers, rather than competition, would define her tenure as president.[26]

Sister Mary Rose's efforts to stabilize the administrative staff, cultivate the donor base, and alter the institutional message produced substantial long-term dividends. In the short run, however, fallout from the crisis continued to handicap the program. Even a cursory glance at the institutional balance sheet reveals the problem. Public contributions had exceeded $88 million for the 1989–90 fiscal year. They declined by over $22 million during the following year and did not approach the 1990 level again until 1998. Further, Covenant House's debt exceeded $38 million as Sister Mary Rose began her tenure, with the prospect of a large balloon payment looming in January of 1993. Severe cost-cutting measures continued through the early 1990s as contributions remained flat and revenues fluctuated at between 76 percent and 83 percent of their 1990 peak.[27] In late 1991, for example, the organization announced another round of layoffs, eliminating thirty-five corporate positions and slashing $3 million from the local program in New York. Subsidiaries received smaller contributions from the national office, thereby affecting programs everywhere. In California, Covenant House canceled its option to purchase the Hotel Hollywood on Sunset Boulevard in Los Angeles, scaling back the program to a more modest level. In New Jersey, the organization abandoned plans to open a crisis center in Trenton and continued to confine its Newark and Atlantic City operations to street outreach. Even Houston, which retained a strong local donor base and enjoyed more autonomy than many other sites, faced major cutbacks. Still, only one program closed its doors completely during these lean years. The board decided to terminate its Panama initiative in 1992, owing primarily to the fact that youth homelessness appeared inconsequential in that country, where the existing Covenant House functioned largely as a daycare center. Despite the commitment to keeping the shelters in operation, cutbacks and retrenchment remained in effect throughout the organization during the early 1990s.[28]

Administrators recognized that they needed to accomplish more than merely cut the budget if the agency hoped to recover and move forward. They therefore implemented more aggressive financial maneuvers designed to place the nonprofit on a sound footing. Senior staff spent considerable time and effort between 1990 and 1994 attempting to retire Covenant House's substantial debt. They worked especially hard to refinance a $21.4 million obligation to the Resolution Trust Corporation (RTC).[29] By June of

1992, Covenant House had secured a five-year loan of $12.5 million from Chemical Bank to cover part of this refinancing, and the RTC agreed to forgive an additional $4.4 million. Interestingly, the Franciscan Charitable Trust, which Ritter had agreed to liquidate and transfer to the organization as part of his resignation arrangement, played an important role in the negotiations with Chemical Bank. The financial institution insisted that Covenant House deposit the $1 million proceeds from the Franciscan fund in its reserves as a condition of the loan, a stipulation that the organization honored upon receiving this money in September 1993. The agency also began selling off large quantities of unused and underutilized real estate in the early 1990s as part of an effort to build its cash reserves. The board authorized the divestiture of its two remaining Manhattan group homes on West Fifteenth Street and West Forty-seventh Street in 1990 as well as several farms and additional smaller properties that had been received as donations. After numerous false starts, the directors also finally concluded agreements to sell both the Times Square Hotel in 1991 and the assemblage of buildings on Eighth Avenue and Forty-fourth Street in 1994. Cumulatively, these measures proved effective, and Covenant House's financial situation eventually improved. By April of 1994, the corporation boasted over $26 million in cash reserves, and the directors voted to pay down their entire debt. This step proved critical in improving the organization's credibility with major donors and financial institutions, and the worst of the crisis appeared to be over.[30]

The indebtedness and revenue shortfalls also stimulated Covenant House to reconsider some past decisions and chart some new fiscal goals. The National Maritime Union complex on Seventeenth Street, for example, had long proven controversial with some administrators who questioned the building's size and utility. The Rights of Passage (ROP) program never occupied more than a small portion of the massive facility, which also drained agency resources by requiring considerable maintenance and up-keep expenses. Some institutional officials felt that the property mainly satisfied the founder's obsessive real estate acquisitiveness and served little programmatic purpose. In 1995, the board sold the portion of the complex known as the Plaza Building, which fronted on Ninth Avenue, to the Chinese Service Center for Scholarly Exchange for over $4 million. Though Covenant House retained the remainder of the facility for administrative offices and ROP purposes, the agency no longer exhibited an inordinate institutional interest in speculative real estate ventures.[31]

Similarly, the board resolved to diversify its fund-raising strategies and to make better use of its cash reserves. Direct marketing still generated approximately 80 percent of all donations throughout the 1990s, but the organization experimented with new approaches and techniques. Throughout the crisis, Covenant House shared more substantive information with its supporters, offering updates concerning administrative changes and internal investigations along with its traditional appeal letters. The development department also inaugurated an annual fund program in an effort to regularize contributions. One professional fund-raising journal noted that Covenant House had modified its rhetoric and pursued a noticeably "more PG, more family-oriented, and more overtly religious" direct mail strategy in the early 1990s. These shifts illustrated the new emphasis on institutional accountability, long-term financial stability, and realistic rhetoric that permeated the agency throughout the decade.

Corporate executives also spent more time developing income-generating programs in order to augment direct mail revenues. The board's finance committee carefully considered appropriate investment strategies for $11 million in cash reserves that remained after eliminating the debt in 1995, with the directors eventually settling on a balanced combination of equities, mutual funds, and treasury bonds. Covenant House initiated a gift annuity program for donors, which many other charities historically had used to great advantage in generating long-range financial resources. The New York office nurtured stronger and more independent boards among the subsidiaries, delegating them with greater responsibility to oversee local fund-raising efforts. At the urging of Sister Mary Rose, the executive directors and development staff more aggressively pursued public funding. Covenant House and its affiliates received several major grants during the early 1990s from such agencies as the U.S. Department of Health and Human Services and the U.S. Department of Housing and Urban Development, for example, in order to support its programs for homeless pregnant teenagers, young mothers, and substance abusers. The crisis clearly had altered many aspects of institutional life, sometimes moving Covenant House in healthy new directions.[32]

Eventually, these strategies began to bear fruit. By 1995, the agency finally had begun to recover from its financial crisis. As the debt dissipated and fund-raising stabilized, administrators once again found it possible to turn their attention to programmatic considerations. Several themes dominated the period between 1995 and 2003. Territorial expansion resumed in earnest. Covenant House established new programs in Washington, D.C. (1995), Orlando (1996), Vancouver (1997), Detroit (1997), Oakland (1998),

St. Louis (1998), Nicaragua (1998), Philadelphia (1999), and Atlanta (2000).³³ Older operations also experienced revitalization. New crisis centers finally opened, for example, in Atlantic City (1997) and Newark (2000). Sister Mary Rose especially emphasized programs that promised early intervention, vocational training, and aftercare services. She supported such initiatives as community resource centers and day treatment centers that served mentally ill adolescents who lacked the stability and skills to seek employment. Sister Mary Rose summarized her programmatic innovations in 2002 by observing that "we're certainly not just a shelter agency anymore. We're a rehabilitation center."³⁴ The late 1990s also witnessed important changes in institutional style and culture. Covenant House projected a very different public image in 2003 from that projected in 1989, as a humbler and more cautious agency emerged from the crisis.

Washington, D.C., which constituted the first new site to open since 1989, reflected the way in which institutional emphases had changed. The agency spent considerable time preparing needs assessment surveys and cultivating local support before opening its new facility in the troubled and poverty-stricken Anacostia neighborhood, located in the southeastern quadrant of the district. Covenant House administrators met with archdiocesan officials and social service providers throughout 1993 and 1994 before making any programmatic commitments.³⁵ They selected an executive director, Vincent Gray, who boasted extensive political connections, strong community roots, and impeccable Catholic credentials on his résumé.³⁶ Nancy Dickerson Whitehead, a socially prominent Covenant House board member with wide-ranging Capitol Hill contacts, organized a kickoff event that featured both James Cardinal Hickey as a special guest and First Lady Hilary Clinton as the keynote speaker. The project drew support from ideologically diverse church officials and politicians representing both major parties. It exhibited a collaborative, conciliatory, and nuanced approach that placed a high premium on consensus and avoided controversy whenever possible.³⁷

Washington proved typical in that the organization carefully covered all ecclesiastical and secular bases wherever it decided to open a new facility in the 1990s. Shortly after assuming office, Sister Mary Rose visited bishops and Catholic Charities offices in all dioceses where Covenant House maintained a presence. She stressed cooperation, seeking to build trust "wherever strained relationships, or no relationships existed in the past." When local communities or service providers resisted the agency's plans to establish programs in specific cities, as happened in Chicago and Minneapolis during the 1990s, Covenant House quietly withdrew from the field. The president actively served on the boards of such organizations as the National Campaign to Prevent Teen Pregnancy, the International Catholic Child Bureau, and the Menninger Foundation, thus nurturing contacts within the social work profession. The agency now exhibited a greater willingness to work with other social service agencies and to subject its programs to broader professional scrutiny. It largely abandoned the maverick stance that had formed such an important feature of its high institutional profile during the 1980s.[38]

The Washington program also demonstrated the fact that temporary shelters no longer appeared synonymous with Covenant House. A storefront community center and a mobile outreach van anchored the Anacostia program when the agency first opened its doors in May of 1995. The center, which sought to provide "a one-stop approach to addressing the needs of youth and their families," reflected a new commitment to offer a broader range of social services in inner city neighborhoods. Covenant House opened its first community service centers in the Bronx in 1992 and Brooklyn in 1993. Before long, these facilities found themselves counseling nearly two hundred clients per month. Sister Mary Rose increasingly recognized that Covenant House crisis centers reached only a small fraction of the urban children who needed services, so she proposed more aggressive early intervention programs at all sites. In Washington, administrators freely admitted that "most children and youth in Anacostia do not fit the traditional image of the Covenant House kids because they have not run away from home or become homeless—yet." The center stressed preventive measures for children who still possessed some familial or social infrastructure, offering such services as tutoring, medical referrals, and legal advice. Covenant House quietly had shifted its primary focus away from emergency shelter and toward more comprehensive counseling and educational programs. A crisis center eventually opened in Anacostia in 1997, but the shelter remained modest in size and scope compared with the older facilities, containing a total of only twenty-two beds for homeless youths and their children. Washington's community service center, however, attracted greater levels of funding and larger numbers of youths, reflecting an altered focus throughout the organization.[39]

Employment programs played a prominent role in Washington, indicating another significant programmatic thrust. The site concluded an agreement in 2000 with the Alexandria Seaport Foundation and the Washington Navy Yard, which enabled youngsters to secure paid apprenticeships building boats and learning construction techniques. A $325,000 grant from the D.C. Children and Youth Investment Trust Corporation allowed the Washington subsidiary to establish a woodworking program in 2001 known as Anacostia Artisans, which introduced local youths to carpentry, cabinet-making, drafting, and design. Adolescents and young adults served internships with master craftsmen and simultaneously completed coursework that exposed them to elementary business concepts. Job training, of course, did not constitute a radical new departure for Covenant House. The Rights of Passage program, which began in 1985, had institutionalized the concept within the agency. Programs in the 1990s expanded and diversified existing efforts, building upon the entrepreneurial spirit, corporate partnerships, and governmental support that fueled earlier endeavors. All sites received a directive to develop and upgrade such programs. In New York, for example, Covenant House renovated its regional job training center on the third floor of the National Maritime Union Building in 1997, incorporating high technology equipment and new computer courses into the curriculum. Similarly, the Culinary Arts Program in New York received an infusion of energy when the organization established Ezekiel's Café in 1997. This small storefront eatery in New York's Greenwich Village neighborhood provided Covenant House trainees with experience in food preparation and presentation, customer relations, restaurant management, and sanitation techniques. Such programs often proved costly and administratively challenging to operate, but they exemplified the commitment to move beyond immediate care. Covenant House still viewed temporary shelter as its most important program, but it now also acknowledged a broader institutional mission that continued to evolve during the 1990s.[40]

Advocacy activities remained central to this evolving mission, and Covenant House's approach to political issues in the 1990s most clearly illustrated the cultural shift that had occurred within the agency. Sensational press conferences, controversial claims, and vocal attacks on particular politicians appeared a thing of the past. Sister Mary Rose instead encouraged staff members and executive directors to prepare position papers, meet with legislators, and testify at governmental hearings. She continued to speak out concerning the needs of children, but her message most often focused on the complex and multifaceted social factors that affected urban youths. The organization's 1996 strategic plan concerning advocacy issues, for example, identified three principal priorities: assessing the impact of welfare reform, promoting the need for job training programs, and encouraging the restoration of federal funding to social agencies. Covenant House explicitly stated that "we see ourselves as partners with community agencies and associations in efforts to improve the lives of families and children." This rhetorical retreat from the confrontational language of the 1980s reflected a significant change. Public relations efforts tended toward such inclusive events as the organization's annual Candlelight Vigil, which first took place in New York City on Thanksgiving eve in 1991. Several thousand supporters gathered that night in Times Square to light candles, pray, and listen to homeless youths describe their struggles. Covenant House tried to use such noncontroversial tactics as a way to focus attention both on its own programs and on the ongoing reality of homelessness among adolescents.[41]

Elements of a more confrontational advocacy culture persisted within the organization, however, even as conciliatory styles became institutionalized. Casa Alianza offers an excellent example. The Central American program proved particularly volatile during the 1990s. Human rights abuses continued to occur routinely in Guatemala, where police and other security agents frequently targeted street children for intimidation. Amnesty International estimated in 1992 that approximately five thousand poverty-stricken and homeless children roamed the back alleys of Guatemala City, sleeping in parks, stealing sunglasses and neck chains to sell in local flea markets, and inhaling carpenters' glue from plastic bags in order to get high and numb their senses. Authorities blamed youth gangs for escalating crime and violence in the Guatemalan capital, and security forces carried out a campaign of brutal repression against homeless children in the early 1990s. Beatings, tortures, and executions appeared common. Sources estimated that authorities murdered over forty street children in 1990 alone, often mutilating their bodies by slicing off ears, burning out eyes, and cutting out tongues as a warning to potential witnesses. Covenant House during the 1980s had remained silent concerning the human rights situation in Guatemala, nurturing friendships with governmental authorities who supported its various programs. That situation changed dramatically after 1989 when Casa Alianza received new leadership in the person of Bruce Harris.[42]

Harris had been born in Dorset, England, in 1955, but received his academic training in the United States. He earned a bachelor's degree in international studies from the School for International Training in Brattleboro, Vermont, and a master's degree in international management from the American Graduate School of International Management in Glendale, Arizona. The British native decided as a young man that he wished to labor among poverty-stricken people in economically depressed countries, and he approached his work with a missionary zeal. Between 1978 and 1980, he traveled the world with the Up With People international singing group, coordinating tours and arranging publicity for the organization's musical spectaculars. In 1983, he began a six-year tenure with the Save the Children Federation, administering the agency's programs in Mexico and Bolivia. By the time he joined Covenant House in 1989, Harris had garnered valuable administrative experience in the nonprofit sector and considerable familiarity with political life in Central and South America. Still, he found the situation for street children in Guatemala shocking and horrifying. Violence, disease, poverty, and addiction appeared synonymous with urban street life among the young children in his care. The Casa Alianza director concluded that charitable organizations needed to move beyond their individual rehabilitative programs to confront public officials and demand substantive political change if they hoped to have a meaningful social impact. One particular incident proved pivotal in crystallizing Harris's vision.[43]

During the early morning hours of 4 March 1990, a thirteen-year-old homeless boy named Nahaman Carmona Lopez sat in front of a Guatemala City shopping center, inhaling glue with several friends between the ages of six and fourteen. The troubled young Salvadoran had arrived in Guatemala a few years earlier, spent most of his short life on the streets, and periodically sought help at Casa Alianza. A group of local policemen approached the boys on 4 March, seized their glue, and began pouring it over their heads. When Nahaman resisted, the security squad savagely beat him, kicking him into unconsciousness, breaking six ribs, slashing his back, immersing his head in glue, and lacerating his liver. He died ten days later of multiple injuries, having suffered severe internal hermorrhaging and liver failure. Bruce Harris became deeply moved and affected by Nahaman's fate, and he began an aggressive campaign to keep the boy's memory alive and to bring his murderers to trial. Harris buried the boy on Casa Alianza's grounds, creating a cemetery for street children and inscribing the words "I only wanted to be a child and they wouldn't let me" on his tombstone. He filed over forty judicial cases in 1990 against security agents who had been suspected of beating, torturing, and murdering homeless youths, eventually winning unprecedented convictions against the four Guatemalan National Police officers who kicked Nahaman to death.[44]

Harris built upon his success in the Nahaman case in order to develop a more comprehensive public relations and legal strategy for promoting social justice. He narrated a 1991 BBC special, "They Shoot Children, Don't They?," which offered powerful testimony concerning the murder and torture of Guatemalan street children and received several positive profiles on

British and American television programs thereafter. He continued the frustrating process of prosecuting police officers and security guards in the Guatemalan courts and broadened his advocacy efforts into other areas. Harris charged that political authorities colluded with kidnappers in supplying babies for illegal adoptions to wealthy foreigners. The Casa Alianza director claimed that local black market entrepreneurs even extracted healthy organs from Guatemalan babies for sale abroad. Harris also confronted corporate interests over a variety of issues. He especially chastised H. B. Fuller, a Minneapolis glue manufacturer, demanding that the corporation place controls over the sale of its product in Guatemala, given the substance's role in fostering street-level addiction among young children. Harris developed Casa Alianza's legal aid department into a strong advocacy

Figure 11. Nahaman Gefte Carmona Lopez: "Solo quise ser un niño y no me dejaron." Bruce Harris, the executive director of Covenant House–Latin America, emerged in the 1990s as an outspoken international advocate for children's rights and proved willing to confront political and corporate interests when necessary, as this cemetery for murdered street children on the Casa Alianza grounds in Guatemala eloquently testifies. Photograph courtesy of the Covenant House Archives.

operation, cultivating alliances with such organizations as Amnesty International and emerging as a prominent spokesperson for human rights.

Harris also aggressively challenged authorities in other Latin American nations where Covenant House maintained a presence. He spoke out against the detention of Honduran children in prison cells with hardened adult criminals, raised issues concerning the sexual exploitation of children in Costa Rica and Mexico, and participated in international campaigns to curtail child labor practices. Harris's confrontational tactics brought unprecedented visibility and acclaim from human rights activists to Casa Alianza during the 1990s. Amnesty International honored him in 1991 as a "human rights hero." Sweden bestowed its 1996 Olof Palme Prize on him for promoting international understanding and contributing to global security. In 2000, Casa Alianza received the Conrad N. Hilton Humanitarian Award, which carried a monetary prize of $1 million, to recognize its "extraordinary contribution toward alleviating human suffering." Harris's leadership proved instrumental in transforming Casa Alianza from a relatively modest philanthropic endeavor with close ties to governmental officials into a highly visible and internationally respected institution that took a prophetically critical stance toward Latin American political authorities.[45]

Harris's approach to advocacy did exact significant personal and institutional costs. Guatemalan security forces responded to his efforts with a systematic campaign of intimidation and occasional violence. Casa Alianza employees reported numerous suspicious phone calls and death threats throughout 1990 and 1991. Some staff members were victimized by abduction attempts, and other social workers received severe beatings from unknown assailants. Harris himself became particularly unnerved when gunmen sprayed one of his group homes with bullets and when a funeral wreath with a threatening message arrived at his residence. He began regularly wearing a bulletproof vest and eventually relocated his family to Mexico in 1991. Tensions persisted throughout the 1990s, even though direct physical threats eventually subsided. Indeed, Harris's activism periodically posed a dilemma for Covenant House officials. Sister Mary Rose preferred to work through existing diplomatic channels and to maintain open lines of communication with authority structures. Harris, who remained profoundly disturbed by injustice and corruption, courted open confrontation and press coverage. Both approaches contained validity, but they sometimes constituted an uncomfortable fit within the same institution. Harris's outspoken posture undeniably provided Covenant House with an edge that its Latin American programs often lacked during the 1980s. Casa Alianza could now count many prominent international rights advocates among its supporters. Political leaders in the Central American countries where the organization operated often kept the ministry at arm's length, but Harris's visibility remained high throughout the world.[46]

Attention proved more difficult to attract within the United States as memories of the Ritter scandal faded from the public consciousness. Covenant House rarely appeared on the front pages of the metropolitan dailies or as the lead story on local news broadcasts as the 1990s wore on. The organization had recovered from the crisis financially and programmatically, but its public profile appeared much lower within secular circles. Several factors accounted for this diminished domestic visibility. As its programs continued to diversify, Covenant House's message grew too diffuse for easy popular consumption. The agency refused to fall back on broad caricatures, titillating tales, and bombastic claims to describe its work. Midwestern runaways, "Minnesota Strip" prostitutes, and pretty call boys largely disappeared from the institutional literature. The issue of youth homelessness itself appeared frustratingly endemic to contemporary urban life, resisting quick fixes, easy categorizations, and simple solutions. Covenant House now acknowledged the intractability of the problem, but by embracing complexity the organization paid a real public relations price. As Ritter instinctively understood, and as the agency painfully learned in 1990, boldly sketched morality tales played most effectively over the airwaves and in print. Novelty, controversy, and shocking pronouncements generated excitement and buzz. Steady stewardship, conciliatory behavior, and measured statements received minimal attention. Covenant House recovered from its crisis in part by embracing responsibility and by adopting a more prudent institutional persona. Its reemergence as an exceedingly reliable ministry in the 1990s earned it widespread support and attracted nearly universal praise. Respectability rescued the institution from possible ruin. Caution, however, sometimes muted its public voice and lessened its willingness to strike a prophetic pose.

Covenant House had elected to modify its style significantly and place its internal operations more in conformity with professional norms throughout the nonprofit world. All such choices involve costs and benefits, but institutional survival necessitated change in this instance. As she prepared to retire in the fall of 2003, Sister Mary Rose might have taken considerable comfort in the institutional choices that occurred over the previous thirteen years. Covenant House teetered on the verge of dissolution when she began her presidency, but it appeared remarkably healthy upon her departure. The budget had grown to nearly $120 million in 2002, nine new sites had been developed since 1990, and all local programs now incorporated substantial training and aftercare components. The agency enjoyed generally good relations with colleagues throughout the social work world, carefully cooperated with Catholic charitable causes, and largely repaired its reputation with donors. Covenant House continued to do good work and to make a difference in many individual lives. A study conducted by the Menninger Foundation in 2000 revealed that nearly 90 percent of former shelter clients believed that the agency had satisfied their immediate needs and provided them with a safe place to live. Six months following their discharge, over 70 percent of the clients had achieved some form of favorable housing, and approximately half of those who had enrolled in one of the agency's job training programs remained employed. All signs pointed toward a revitalized and healthy organization. The transition to new leadership in 2003 seemed comparatively smooth and effortless. Sr. Patricia A. Cruise, S.C., who most recently served as executive vice president of the Red Cloud Indian School in Pine Ridge, South Dakota, assumed the presidency in September and found a stable situation in place upon her arrival.[47]

This apparent stability, however, obscured a very colorful and contentious institutional history. Covenant House began as an unstructured and vaguely conceived "ministry of availability" in a small New York City neighborhood in 1968. It drew its initial inspiration from countercultural movements within American Catholicism, East Village street culture, and the personal life histories of its founders and volunteers. Within two decades, the organization had blossomed into a complex and highly successful international charity with a clear focus on serving homeless youths. This whirlwind institutional transformation forced Covenant House's leaders to confront a series of theoretical, practical, and personal issues. They grappled with especially perplexing philosophical problems. Board members, senior administrators, and staff agonized over the proper place of charisma, bureaucracy, prophetic social criticism, advocacy, corporate alliances, and religious commitment within the ministry. The organization could not move forward without engaging these broader theoretical concerns.

Practical considerations also played an important role in defining Covenant House. Pragmatic choices by powerful individuals often altered institutional directions at key moments. Bruce Ritter's relentless determination to focus on homeless youths, incorporate the agency, open a series of group homes in Manhattan, and eschew a broader social ministry defined the early years. Sr. Mary Rose McGeady's commitment to develop multifaceted programs that operated according to professional social work standards significantly shaped the more recent history. Other seemingly straightforward programmatic shifts, such as the decisions to open a crisis center in Times Square, expand beyond New York City, and develop vocational programs, generated far-reaching and unanticipated consequences. These departures from past practice dramatically changed the ministry, though their full significance appeared obvious only in retrospect.

But theoretical concerns and practical considerations did not drive all decision making. Less rational and more personal factors also affected institutional life. Human frailty played an important part in determining the agency's history. This element emerged most obviously as the controversies involving Bruce Ritter unfolded throughout 1990. During the heat of the moment, it became easy for critics to dissect the personal flaws, errors in judgment, and administrative missteps that contributed to the immediate scandal. Over the longer term, history taught a more important lesson. Covenant House survived its potential demise by openly confronting the sexual abuse scandal. The agency appropriately modified its internal structure, revamped its administrative policies, and renewed its commitment to its core mission. Covenant House reformed itself, constructively built upon its complex past, and transcended its most severe crisis. A stronger and more credible institution emerged.

Appendix 1
Covenant House Timeline, 1968–2003

1968
Fr. Bruce Ritter leaves his teaching post at Manhattan College and moves with Fr. James Fitzgibbon to 274 East Seventh Street, near Avenue D, on the Lower East Side, to begin a "ministry of availability" to the poor in the neighborhood. Both Franciscans are formally assigned to Saint Brigid's Church in New York City.

1970
Fr. James Fitzgibbon moves out of 274 East Seventh Street apartment in order to devote more time to drug counseling and other community ministries.
Bruce Ritter, Adrian Gately, Patricia Kennedy, and Paul Frazier create the Covenant I Community.

1972
Covenant House receives a grant from New York City Addiction Services Agency.
Covenant House formally incorporates and establishes a board of directors.
The intake center and corporate office are established at 504 LaGuardia Place, New York.
Bruce Ritter writes his first direct mail appeal letter to donors.

1973
A girls' group home is established at 40 West Eleventh Street, New York, staffed largely by the Franciscan Sisters of Syracuse.
A boys' group home is established at 207 Wheeler Avenue, Staten Island, New York.
A boys' group home is established at 746 East Sixth Street, New York.
A girls' group home is established at 218 West Fifteenth Street, New York.
Corporate office space is acquired at 40 West Twelfth Street, New York, and offices are transferred from 504 LaGuardia Place.
Bruce Ritter incorporates Testamentum as a real estate holding company that would lease property to Covenant House.

1974
A boys' group home is established at 267 East Seventh Street.
The boys' group home closes at 274 East Seventh Street.

1975

Bruce Ritter announces his intention to resign as executive director.

A girls' group home is established at 264 East Tenth Street.

Covenant House amends its constitution to establish the organization as a "corporation sole," with Bruce Ritter as the sole member.

1976

Bruce Ritter announces plans to open a "multi-service center" near the Port Authority Bus Terminal.

Covenant House acquires an assemblage of buildings on Eighth Avenue and Forty-fourth Street.

Covenant House relocates administrative offices from 40 West Twelfth Street to 260 West Forty-fourth Street.

A girls' group home is established on West Forty-seventh Street.

1977

Under 21 is opened on Eighth Avenue near Forty-fourth Street.

Faith Community volunteer program is established.

1978

A girls' group home is established on Staten Island.

1979

Covenant House begins leasing the former Manhattan Rehabilitation Center on Forty-first Street and Tenth Avenue from State of New York for the nominal rate of one dollar per year and relocates most Under 21 operations to this site, expanding medical and social services.

The Eighth Avenue and Forty-fourth Street assemblage remains open as a crisis center.

1980

Bruce Ritter meets with Knights of Malta in Rome and announces plans to expand outside of New York City.

Covenant House phases out its group home program and closes all group homes, excepting the facilities on West Forty-seventh Street and West Fifteenth Street.

1981

Covenant House restructures operations into a parent board and subsidiary boards, with Bruce Ritter assuming the title of president of the parent corporation. Under 21 (the New York program) is created as a subsidiary corporation, and Under 21 subsidiaries are proposed in other cities.

Faith Community members travel to Guatemala to establish Casa Alianza program (as Covenant House is called in Spanish).

1982

Casa Alianza program officially opens in Antigua, Guatemala.

Covenant House Toronto program is established.
Institute for Youth Advocacy is established at Covenant House to litigate, lobby, and research issues relating to youth homelessness and child pornography.

1983
Covenant House Texas program is established in Houston.

1984
President Ronald Reagan praises Bruce Ritter in his State of the Union Address.
Covenant House purchases the Times Square Motor Hotel on Eighth Avenue and Forty-third Street.
James Harnett is named chief operating officer of Covenant House.

1985
Covenant House Florida is established in Fort Lauderdale.
Bruce Ritter is named as a member of Attorney General Edwin Meese's Commission on Pornography.

1986
Rights of Passage program is established in New York as a transitional living program for shelter residents.
Off the Streets outreach program is established in New York City, with overnight vans seeking to offer food and counseling to homeless youths.
Casa Alianza expands programs to Guatemala City.

1987
Covenant House New Orleans is established.
Casa Alianza program is established in Tegucigalpa, Honduras.
Nineline runaway hotline program is established.
Rights of Passage program for women is established in New York.
Bruce Ritter publishes book, *Covenant House: Lifeline to the Street.*
Covenant House purchases the National Maritime Union Building at Ninth Avenue and Seventeenth Street in New York.

1988
Casa Alianza program is established in Mexico City.
National Maritime Union Building is officially dedicated as Rights of Passage facility.
Casa Alianza program is established in Panama City.
Covenant House California program is established in Los Angeles.
Covenant House Alaska program is established in Anchorage.

1989
AIDS education program is initiated at New York Crisis Center.

Covenant House New Jersey is established, with street outreach programs in Atlantic City, Newark, and Trenton.

Bruce Ritter is accused of sexual misconduct and financial impropriety in December, and Manhattan district attorney announces an investigation.

New York Post spearheads journalistic investigation of Covenant House.

1990

Bruce Ritter steps aside on 6 February and resigns as president on 27 February, after continuing stream of allegations.

Manhattan district attorney ends investigation following 27 February resignation.

Frank Macchiarola is installed as acting president and chief executive officer on 6 February but is removed from the position and resigns from board of directors on 27 February.

James Harnett is installed as acting president and chief executive officer on 27 February, but is removed from the position and returns to his former position as chief operating officer on 23 March.

Board reaches agreement with John Cardinal O'Connor, whereby Msgr. William J. Toohy and Msgr. Timothy A. McDonnell are appointed as team responsible for directing Covenant House, effective 23 March.

Sr. Mary Rose McGeady, D.C., is appointed president of Covenant House in July and assumes responsibilities in September.

Board initiates extensive procedural and administrative reforms.

Kroll investigative report, commissioned by the board and monitored by an oversight committee, is released in August.

Covenant House suffers severe budget cutbacks, layoffs, and a $22 million drop in private contributions.

Covenant House New Jersey programs in Atlantic City, Newark, and Trenton begin operating in storefront locations.

1991

New York attorney general concludes civil investigation of Covenant House, expressing satisfaction with the board's structural overhaul.

A second round of layoffs and budget cutbacks is initiated.

Covenant House concludes agreement to sell Times Square Motor Hotel.

First Candlelight Vigil is held on Thanksgiving eve in Times Square.

1992

Charles Sennott, the *New York Post* reporter instrumental in investigating Bruce Ritter, publishes his book, *Broken Covenant.*

Panama program is closed.

Covenant House New Jersey closes its program in Trenton.

Council of Better Business Bureaus and National Charities Information Bureau restore Covenant House to approved lists.

First community center is established in Bronx, New York.

1994
Covenant House sells assemblage of buildings on Eighth Avenue and Forty-fourth Street.

1995
Covenant House program is established in Washington, D.C.
Covenant House sells portion of the National Maritime Union Building known as the Plaza.

1996
Casa Alianza receives Olof Palme Prize to honor its leadership as well as the work of its executive director, Bruce Harris, in promoting human rights causes.
Covenant House New Jersey opens first crisis center in Newark.
Covenant House Florida establishes program in Orlando.

1997
Covenant House program is established in Vancouver.
Covenant House Michigan program is established in Detroit.
Covenant House New York opens regional job training center.
Ezekiel's Café, a culinary arts training program, opens for business in Greenwich Village, New York.

1998
Covenant House Missouri program is established in St. Louis.
Casa Alianza program is established in Nicaragua.
Covenant House California establishes program in Oakland.
Covenant House fund-raising program returns to pre-1990 levels.

1999
Covenant House Pennsylvania program is established in Philadelphia.
Bruce Ritter dies at his home in upstate New York on 7 October.

2000
Covenant House Georgia program is established in Atlanta.

2002
Covenant House public support and revenues exceed $120 million.

2003
Sr. Mary Rose McGeady, D.C., retires as president of Covenant House.
Sr. Patricia A. Cruise, S.C., is appointed president of Covenant House and assumes office in September.

Appendix 2

Total Public Support and Revenue, 1974–2003

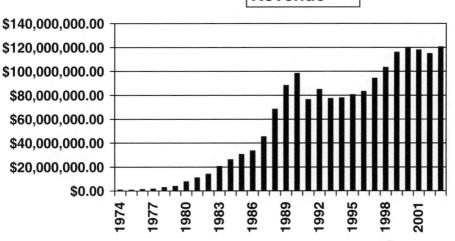

"Total public support and revenue" includes contributions to the ministry as well as grants, contracts, donated services, investment income, and revenue from special events. In 1989–90, for example, contributions slightly exceeded $88 million, but "total public support and revenue" actually approached $100 million. Source: Treasurer's Office, Covenant House, New York.

Sites and Executive Directors, 1972–2004

Covenant House–New York
Father Bruce Ritter, 1972–80
Sr. Gretchen Gilroy, 1981
Ronald Williams, 1982–88
Joe Borgo, 1989
Bruce Henry, 1990–2004

Covenant House Latin America–Casa Alianza (1981)[1]
John Boyle, 1981–83
Patrick Atkinson, 1984–88
Bruce Harris, 1989–2004

Covenant House Toronto (1982)
John MacNeil, 1982–83
Mary A. McConville, 1984–88
Ruth daCosta, 1989–2004

Covenant House Texas–Houston (1983)
Gregory L. Bublitz, 1983
C. Lynne Halbert (Acting Administrative Director), 1984
Larry Norton (Acting Executive Director), 1985
Malcolm Host, 1986–89
Carolyn Larsen, 1990–97
Ronda Robinson, 1998–2004

Covenant House Florida–Ft. Lauderdale (1985)[2]
Nancy Matthews, 1985–96
David Spellman, 1997–2002
James M. Gress, 2003–4

Covenant House New Orleans (1987)
James R. Kelly, 1987–88
Phil Boudreau, 1989–92
Maudelle Cade, 1993–2000
Stacy Horn Koch, 2001–4

Covenant House Alaska–Anchorage (1988)
    Fred Ali, 1988–89
    Elaine Christian, 1990–94
    Deirdre Phayer, 1995–2004

Covenant House California–Los Angeles (1988)[3]
    Anne Donahue, 1988–89
    Fred Ali, 1990–98
    George R. Lozano, 1999–2004

Covenant House–New Jersey (1990)[4]
    Ronald Williams, 1990–92
    James White, 1993–2004

Covenant House–Washington, D.C. (1995)
    Vincent Gray, 1995–2004

Covenant House Michigan–Detroit (1997)
    Sam Joseph, 1997–2004

Covenant House Vancouver (1997)
    Sandy Cooke, 1998–2004

Covenant House Missouri–St. Louis (1998)
    Marian Wolaver, 1998–99
    Christina Fagan, 2000–04

Covenant House Pennsylvania–Philadelphia (1999)
    Jerome Kilbane, 1999–2004

Covenant House Georgia–Atlanta (2000)
    Andre Eaton, 2000–2004

Notes

Introduction

1. A reasonably representative spectrum of opinion concerning the Bush proposal can be found in "Bush's Faith Initiative Draws Reactions," *National Catholic Reporter,* 9 February 2001, p. 6. Peter Dobkin Hall, "Diminished Authority: Church, State, and Accountability," *Non Profit Times,* 1 March 2001, provides an interesting perspective on the Bush proposals.

2. One scholar who has spent considerable time studying religious philanthropies is Peter Dobkin Hall. See especially Peter Dobkin Hall, *Inventing the Nonprofit Sector and Other Essays on Philanthropy, Voluntarism, and Nonprofit Organizations* (Baltimore: Johns Hopkins University Press, 1992). Hall and his colleagues at the Program on Non-Profit Organizations at Yale University, such as Paul J. Dimaggio and Walter W. Powell, have produced an important body of scholarship concerning these organizations.

3. An extensive scholarly literature concerning nineteenth-century religious voluntary associations exists, but historians have not paid nearly as much attention to twentieth-century faith-based organizations. A few noteworthy recent exceptions include Dorothy M. Brown and Elizabeth McKeown, *The Poor Belong to Us: Catholic Charities and American Welfare* (Cambridge: Harvard University Press, 1997); Joel A. Carpenter, *Revive Us Again: The Reawakening of American Fundamentalism* (New York: Oxford University Press, 1997); and Judith Weisenfeld, *African American Women and Christian Activism: New York's Black YWCA, 1905–1945* (Cambridge: Harvard University Press, 1998).

4. The classic statement concerning charismatic and institutional authority can be found in Max Weber, *On Charisma and Institution Building,* ed. S. N. Eisenstadt (Chicago: University of Chicago Press, 1968).

5. H. Richard Niebuhr, *Christ and Culture* (New York: Harper & Row, 1951), still constitutes the classic statement of the issues that religious institutions face concerning their relationship to the larger culture.

6. Jason Berry, *Lead Us Not into Temptation: Catholic Priests and the Sexual Abuse of Children* (New York: Doubleday, 1994), remains the most comprehensive treatment of the Lafayette, Louisiana, scandals.

7. Philip Jenkins, *Pedophiles and Priests: Anatomy of a Contemporary Crisis* (New York: Oxford University Press, 1996), pp. 38–41, discusses the significance of the Ritter scandal in this context.

8. Bruce Ritter, *Covenant House: Lifeline to the Street* (New York: Doubleday, 1987).

9. Charles M. Sennott, *Broken Covenant: The Story of Father Bruce Ritter's Fall from Grace—How Power, Politics, and Sex Rocked the Foundation of the Sprawling Covenant House Charity* (New York: Simon & Schuster, 1992).

Chapter 1

1. Bruce Ritter, *Covenant House: Lifeline to the Street* (New York: Doubleday, 1987), pp. 3–4.

2. Charles M. Sennott, *Broken Covenant* (New York: Simon and Schuster, 1992), pp. 65–67.

3. "Man of the Year," *Time*, 6 January 1967, pp. 1, 18–23.

4. Information concerning Louis C. Ritter and his family in this and succeeding paragraphs has been gleaned from the following sources: "Ritter, 39, Veteran Dead from Illness," *Trenton Evening Times*, 11 May 1931, p. 14:7; "Reminiscences of FBR's Family," n.d., Covenant House Archives; and U.S. Manuscript Census, 1920, Microfilm Box 2718, Reel 40, Rutgers University Libraries. The sources disagree concerning Louis's actual birth date: the 1920 Census states that he was born in 1888, but the newspaper obituary lists him as being 39 years old in 1931. The best general history of Trenton's industrial development during this period is John T. Cumbler, *A Social History of Economic Decline: Business, Politics, and Work in Trenton* (New Brunswick: Rutgers University Press, 1989).

5. In addition to sources cited in the previous note, see Helen Almy West, *A History of Hamilton Township* (Trenton: Trenton Printing Company, 1954), pp. 117–18. Bruce, incidentally, was baptized under the name John Ritter. He took the name Bruce upon professing his vows as a Franciscan, but he is referred to throughout the text as Bruce for simplicity's sake.

6. "Reminiscences of FBR's Family"; "Bruce Ritter," *Current Biography*, 1983, pp. 325–28; "Ritter, 39, Veteran Dead from Illness."

7. "Reminiscences of FBR's Family."

8. Sennott, *Broken Covenant*, pp. 45–46; *Current Biography*, 1983, p. 325; Oral History Interview with Juniper Alwell by Peter Wosh, 17 November 1998, Covenant House Archives. The Order of Friars Minor Conventual is one of the three independent religious communities, along with the Friars Minor and the Friars Minor Capuchin, that constitute the Franciscan Order. All three communities trace their lineage to 1209, when Pope Innocent III gave verbal approbation to St. Francis of Assisi's promulgation of poverty, preaching, and penance as the rules for his followers. Various reform movements and interpretations of Francis's life within the order eventually produced the three independent communities. The first Conventual foundation within the United States was established in St. Louis in 1879, though Franciscans had labored in the Americas for over two centuries.

9. Mark Massa, *Catholics and American Culture: Fulton Sheen, Dorothy Day, and the Notre Dame Football Team* (New York: Crossroad Publishing, 1999), p. 91.

10. Jay Dolan, *In Search of American Catholicism: A History of Religion and Culture in Tension* (New York: Oxford University Press, 2002), p. 182. Will Herberg,

Protestant-Catholic-Jew: An Essay in Religious Sociology (Garden City, N.Y.: Doubleday, 1955). Charles R. Morris, *American Catholic: The Saints and Sinners Who Built America's Most Powerful Church* (New York: Random House, 1997), pp. 196–99, discusses Catholic-oriented movies.

11. The literature concerning immigrant Catholicism and Americanism is massive. A few good and readable overviews include John T. McGreevy, *Parish Boundaries* (Chicago: University of Chicago Press, 1996), pp. 7–28; Morris, *American Catholic*, esp. pp. 141–195; Massa, *Catholics and American Culture*; and Dolan, *In Search of American Catholicism*.

12. Many of these themes are discussed in Massa, *Catholics and American Culture*, as well as in Morris, *American Catholic*.

13. Oral History Interview with Shawn Nolan by Peter Wosh, 17 November 1998; Oral History Interview with Juniper Alwell by Wosh, 17 November 1998; Oral History Interview with James Fitzgibbon by Peter Wosh, 22 June 1999, Covenant House Archives. For general histories of the Franciscans in America, see Jeremiah J. Smith, *History of the Conventual Franciscans in the United States, 1852–1906* (Union City: Order of Friars Minor Conventuals, 1988); *A Century of Franciscan Apostolate by the Order of Friars Minor Conventual in the Americas, 1852–1952* (Syracuse: Artcraft Press, 1952); *Silver Jubilee of St. Anthony-on-Hudson, Rensselaer, New York, 1912–1937* (Albany: Boyd Printing, 1937).

14. Thomas Merton, *The Seven Storey Mountain* (New York: Harcourt Brace and Company, 1988).

15. Massa, *Catholics and American Culture*, pp. 37–56; and James T. Fisher, *The Catholic Counterculture in America,1933–1962* (Chapel Hill: University of North Carolina Press, 1989) both demonstrate Merton's significance for lay Catholics.

16. Merton, *The Seven Storey Mountain*, esp. pp. 147–48.

17. Oral History Interview with Juniper Alwell by Wosh, 17 November 1998; Oral History Interview with Shawn Nolan by Wosh, 17 November 1998; Oral History Interview with James Fitzgibbon by Wosh, 22 June 1999, Covenant House Archives.

18. Oral History Interview with Juniper Alwell by Wosh, 17 November 1998; Oral History Interview with Shawn Nolan by Wosh, 17 November 1998; Oral History Interview with James Fitzgibbon by Wosh, 22 June 1999, Covenant House Archives.

19. Oral History Interview with James Fitzgibbon by Wosh, 22 June 1999; Oral History Interview with Juniper Alwell by Wosh, 17 November 1998.

20. Brother C. Luke to Very Rev. William D'Arcy, 19 March 1963; William M. D'Arcy to Brother C. Luke, 21 March 1963; Brother C. Luke to Very Rev. William D'Arcy, 27 March 1963; Brother C. Luke to Bruce Ritter, 27 March 1963; Fr. Bruce M. Ritter to Brother C. Luke, 30 March 1963; Owen Bennett to Rev. Brother C. Luke, 10 April 1963; Bruce Ritter, "Application for a Teaching Position in the Department of Theology," all in Bruce Ritter File, Theology Department Records, Manhattan College Archives.

21. Oral History Interview with Luke Salm by Peter Wosh, 18 August 1999, Covenant House Archives.

22. Oral History Interview with Luke Salm by Wosh, 18 August 1999; Oral History Interview with David Cullen by Amy Surak, 15 February 2001, Covenant House Archives.

23. The Second Vatican Council has been studied from a variety of perspectives. Two useful books that illustrate the ideological divides characteristic of this period are Mary Jo Weaver, *What's Left? Liberal American Catholics* (Bloomington: Indiana University Press, 1999); and Mary Jo Weaver and R. Scott Appleby, *Being Right: Conservative Catholics in America* (Bloomington: Indiana University Press, 1995).

24. Gabriel Costello, *The Arches of the Years* (Riverdale: Manhattan College, 1980), pp. 235–36; *Manhattanite*, 1966, p. 142, *Manhattanite*, 1965, p. 225, Manhattan College Archives.

25. Costello, *The Arches of the Years*, pp. 199–248. Oral History Interview with Adrian Gately by Peter Wosh, 21 July 2000; Oral History Interview with Gil Ortiz by Amy Surak and Peter Wosh, 11 August 1999; Oral History Interview with Luke Salm by Wosh, 18 August 1999, Covenant House Archives. Impressionistic information concerning collegiate culture was also acquired by reviewing the weekly issues of the student newspaper, the *Manhattan Quadrangle*, from 1962 to 1969, Manhattan College Archives.

26. Oral History Interview with Adrian Gately by Wosh, 21 July 2000; Oral History Interview with Paul Frazier by Peter Wosh, 29 September 2000; Oral History Interview with Dave Cullen by Surak, 15 February 2001, Covenant House Archives.

27. *Manhattan Quadrangle*, 27 October 1965 and 8 November 1965, Manhattan College Archives.

28. *Manhattan Quadrangle*, 16 November 1966 and 16 January 1967, Manhattan College Archives; Oral History Interview with Patricia Kennedy by Peter Wosh, 21 July 2000; Oral History Interview with Adrian Gately by Wosh, 21 July 2000; Oral History Interview with Luke Salm by Wosh, 18 August 1999, Covenant House Archives.

29. Minutes of the Organizational Meeting of the Theology Department, 1967 and 15 December 1967; Brother B. Edward O'Neill, "A Report of the Committee on Student Services of the Board of Trustees of Manhattan College," 25 September 1969, Manhattan College Archives.

30. *Manhattanite*, 1968, p. 36; *Manhattan Quadrangle*, 6 October 1967, Manhattan College Archives. Costello, *Arches of the Years*, p. 298.

31. Oral History interview with Paul Frazier by Wosh, 29 September 2000; Oral History Interview with Patricia Kennedy by Wosh, 21 July 2000; Oral History Interview with David Gregorio by Amy Surak, 29 November 1999; Oral History Interview with Dave Cullen by Surak, 15 February 2001, Covenant House Archives. Cullen recalled that Ritter once gave a speech justifying American intervention in Vietnam as a "just war" in the Augustinian sense. Frazier also felt that antiwar activists on the Catholic left never truly trusted Ritter on this issue and remained suspicious concerning his supposed FBI links. Sennott, *Broken Covenant*, pp. 67, 89; *Manhattan Quadrangle*, 19 December 1969.

32. Mary Cole, *Summer in the City* (New York: P. J. Kennedy and Sons, 1968), is an excellent treatment of Fox's program. See also Ana Maria Diaz-Stevens, *Oxcart Catholicism on Fifth Avenue: The Impact of Puerto Rican Migration on the Archdiocese of New York* (Notre Dame: University of Notre Dame Press, 1993), esp. pp. 147–74.

33. Oral History Interview with Patricia Kennedy by Wosh, 21 July 2000; Oral

History Interview with Gil Ortiz by Surak and Wosh, 11 August 1999, Covenant House Archives. "Hot Town–Summer in the City," *Manhattan Quadrangle*, 22 September 1967; *Manhattanite*, 1968.

34. Bruce M. Ritter, "The Growing Separation Between Church and Student: A Study in Ambivalence," *Manhattan College Alumnus* (Winter 1968), pp. 1–8; John Leo, "Young Catholics Altering Values," *New York Times*, 13 February 1968, p. 88; "Poll Probes Student Morality," *Jasper Journal*, 29 September 1967; "Jasper Religion as Shown by the CLCensus," *Jasper Journal*, 10 November 1967.

The survey itself nicely illustrates the way in which Manhattan College's experience proved instrumental in the formation of Covenant House and the way in which networks that had been formed at Manhattan College made Covenant House possible. Ritter relied on two students, James Kennedy and Paul Bukovec of the class of 1968, to help him devise the questions. James Kennedy was the brother of Patricia Kennedy. After completing medical school, he became director of the medical services program at Covenant House as well as an influential board member and Ritter's personal physician. Paul Bukovec had been a friend of Patricia Kennedy since the two attended a Christian Brothers grammar school in West New York, New Jersey. The point remains that personal connections and relationships forged at Manhattan College played an enormous role in the early history of Covenant House. Oral History Interview with Adrian Gately by Wosh, 21 July 2000; Oral History Interview with Patricia Kennedy by Wosh, 21 July 2000, Covenant House Archives.

35. Costello, *The Arches of the Years*, p. 297.

36. Ritter, "The Growing Separation Between Church and Student," p. 5; Oral History Interview with Luke Salm by Wosh, 18 August 1999, Covenant House Archives.

37. Bruce Ritter to Luke Salm, 25 January 1965, Bruce Ritter File, Theology Department Records, Manhattan College Archives.

38. David M. Schulze to John J. Maguire, 22 January 1968; Joseph P. O'Brien to David Schulze, 26 January 1968; John J. Maguire to David Schulze, 6 March 1968, Vicar Provincial's Correspondence, Immaculate Conception Province, Conventual Franciscan Archives, Rensselaer, N.Y.

Chapter 2

1. Bruce Ritter, *Covenant House: Lifeline to the Street* (New York: Doubleday, 1987), pp. 5–7.

2. A discussion of the significance of this 1969 snowstorm can be found in Vincent J. Cannato, *The Ungovernable City: John Lindsay and His Struggle to Save New York* (New York: Basic Books, 2001), pp. 395–97. Charles M. Sennott, *Broken Covenant* (New York: Simon and Schuster, 1992), pp. 70–77, claims that this initial group of children actually arrived at Ritter's doorstep in 1970 and that they subsequently harbored considerable resentment against Ritter. Sennott also suggests that Ritter sexually approached one of the boys, though no other evidence exists to corroborate the claim.

3. Ritter, *Covenant House: Lifeline to the Street*, pp. 4–6.

4. A good brief overview of East Village history can be found in Graham Hodges, "East Village," in Kenneth Jackson, ed., *The Encyclopedia of New York City* (New Haven: Yale University Press, 1995), p. 358. See also Janet Abu-Lughod, et al, *From Urban Village to East Village: The Battle for New York's Lower East Side* (Cambridge: Blackwell, 1994). The terms *East Village* and *Lower East Side* contain a variety of historical meanings and associations. Ritter often described his ministry as being located on the Lower East Side. Most New Yorkers would label his immediate environs, which constituted the northern portion of that district, as the East Village or Alphabet City. I use *Lower East Side* and *East Village* synonomously throughout the text, reflecting Ritter's own designations. For a fascinating study of the area, see the documentary film *Seventh Street* (2003), written and directed by former neighborhood resident Josh Pais and distributed by Paradise Acres Productions.

5. J. Anthony Lukas, "The Two Worlds of Linda Fitzpatrick," *New York Times*, 16 October 1967, p. 1.

6. Lukas, "The Two Worlds of Linda Fitzpatrick," p. 1; John Kifner, "The East Village: A Changing Scene for Hippies," *New York Times*, 11 October 1967, p. 32; "Girl, Youth Found Slain in 'Village' Cellar," *New York Times*, 9 October 1967, p. 1; "Police Inquiry in Hippie Slayings Leaves Family of Girl 'Puzzled,'" *New York Times*, 17 October 1967, p. 1; Leticia Kent, "High on Life and Deader Than Dead," *Village Voice*, 12 October 1967, p. 1; Paul Williams, "The Hippies Are Gone, Where Did They Go?," *Village Voice*, 26 October 1967; Albin Krebs, "Friends Call Linda Fitzpatrick the Girl Who Had Everything," *New York Times*, 10 October 1967. More sensational coverage, complete with extensive and graphic crime-scene photos, can be found in the *New York Daily News* during this period.

7. Richard Goldstein, "Love: A Groovy Idea While He Lasted," *Village Voice*, 19 October 1967, p. 1.

8. John Kifner, "The East Village: A Changing Scene for Hippies," *New York Times*, 11 October 1967, p. 32.

9. Don McNeill, "Home Is Bittersweet on Lower East Side," *Village Voice*, 19 January 1967, pp. 9, 13.

10. "Why an East Village Newspaper?," *East Village Other*, October 1965, p. 2; *East Village Other*, 17 September 1969; Vincent J. Cannato, *The Ungovernable City*, pp. 218–25.

11. Joan Cook, "The Runaway: 'It Can't Happen to Me,' Parents Say, But It Does," *New York Times*, 18 August 1967; *Time*, 7 July 1967; *Time*, 18 August 1967.

12. *Time*, 7 July 1967; *Time*, 15 September 1967; Robert S. Ellwood, *The Sixties Spiritual Awakening: American Religion Moving from Modern to Postmodern* (New Brunswick: Rutgers University Press, 1994), pp. 177–89; Claudia Dreifus, "Guerilla Medicine Comes to the Lower East Side," *East Village Other*, 5 November 1969; Claudia Dreyfus, "St. Mark's Free Clinic," *East Village Other*, 21 January 1970. A brief history of Huckleberry House is available on the organization's website at Huckleberry Youth Programs, *Our History*, <http://www.huckleberryyouth.org/history.html> (6 January 2004).

13. *Jolly Friar*, August 1968, p. 1, Immaculate Conception Province, Conventual Franciscan Archives, Rensselaer, N.Y. Oral History Interview with James Fitzgibbon

by Peter Wosh, 22 June 1999; Oral History Interview with Shawn Nolan by Peter Wosh, 17 November 1998, Covenant House Archives. Ritter, *Covenant House: Lifeline to the Street*, p. 5.

14. Shawn Nolan, "Province Chapter Report," 1969, Ordinary Province Chapter, 6–9 October 1969; *Program, Organization, and Management Study, Immaculate Conception Province Order of Friars Minor Conventual*, Booz, Allen & Hamilton, Inc., 23 March 1971, Immaculate Conception Province, Conventual Franciscan Archives, Rensselaer, N.Y. Interestingly, David Schulze, the provincial who initially authorized Ritter's inner city apostolate, himself left the order and eventually married, much to the surprise and consternation of several of his colleagues.

15. Oral History Interview with Steven Torkelson by Peter Wosh, 17 August 2000, Covenant House Archives.

16. Oral History Interview with Steven Torkelson by Wosh, 17 August, 2000; Oral History Interview with James Fitzgibbon by Wosh, 22 June 1999; Oral History Interview with Shawn Nolan by Wosh, 17 November 1998, Oral History Interview with Juniper Alwell by Peter Wosh, 17 November 1998, Covenant House Archives. "Prefectae Caritatis," in Austin Flannery, ed., *The Basic Sixteen Documents. Vatican Council II. Constitutions, Decrees, Declarations* (Northport, N.Y.: Costello Publishing, 1996), pp. 385–401. David M. Schulze to John J. Maguire, 22 January 1968, Vicar Provincial's Correspondence, Immaculate Conception Province, Conventual Franciscan Archives, Rensselaer, N.Y.

17. "'Teams of Priests' to Direct Parishes," *New York Times*, 16 September 1967, p. 20; John Leo, "Bridge Between 2 Eras," *New York Times*, 3 December 1967, p. 81; *History of St. Brigid's Parish, 1848–1948* (n.d.), copy located in St. Brigid's Church, New York, N.Y. Wayne Ashley, "The Stations of the Cross: Christ, Politics, and Processions on New York City's Lower East Side," in Robert A. Orsi, ed., *Gods of the City* (Bloomington: Indiana University Press, 1999), pp. 541–66.

18. Eleanor Blau, "Church's Slum Experiment Ends in Dissent," *New York Times*, 11 April 1972; Edward B. Fiske, "Parishioners Protest Suspension of a Priest Here," *New York Times*, 2 March 1972; Ashley, "The Stations of the Cross," pp. 346–47.

19. Blau, "Church's Slum Experiment Ends in Dissent"; Edward B. Fiske, "Parishioners Protest Suspension of a Priest Here," *New York Times*, 2 March 1972; Ashley, "The Stations of the Cross"; "Notes from Conversation with Matthew Thompson," 7 July 1999, St. Brigid's File; Oral History Interview with Gil Ortiz by Amy Surak and Peter Wosh, 11 August 1999, Covenant House Archives. "Chronology of Events in Experiment," December 1969 to November 1971; Minutes of Meetings of Steering Committee, 1970–71, St. Brigid's Church, New York, N.Y.

20. "Notes from Conversation with Matthew Thompson," 7 July 1999, St. Brigid's File; Oral History Interview with Marguerite Colonnese by Peter Wosh, 22 June 1999, Covenant House Archives. Minutes of Meetings of the Parish Council, 1970–71; "Chronology of Events in Experiment," December 1969 to November 1971, St. Brigid's Church, New York, N.Y.

21. Mary Cole, *Summer in the City* (New York: P. J. Kennedy & Sons, 1968), pp. 147–67, 188–91. Oral History Interview with Marguerite Colonnese by Wosh, 22 June 1999, Covenant House Archives.

22. Ritter, *Covenant House: Lifeline to the Street*, pp. 4–5; Oral History Interview with James Fitzgibbon by Wosh, 22 June 1999, Covenant House Archives.

23. Ritter, *Covenant House: Lifeline to the Street*, p. 5. Oral History Interview with James Fitzgibbon by Wosh, 22 June 1999; Oral History Interview with Paul Frazier by Peter Wosh, 29 September 2000; Oral History Interview with Juniper Alwell by Wosh, 17 November 1998, Covenant House Archives.

24. Oral History Interview with James Fitzgibbon by Wosh, 22 June 1999; Oral History Interview with Gil Ortiz by Surak and Wosh, 11 August 1999, Covenant House Archives.

25. Ritter, *Covenant House: Lifeline to the Street*, pp. 8–9; Oral History Interview with James Fitzgibbon by Wosh, 22 June 1999; Oral History Interview with Juniper Alwell by Wosh, 17 November 1998; Oral History Interview with Shawn Nolan by Wosh, 17 November 1998; Oral History Interview with David Gregorio by Amy Surak, 29 November 1999, Covenant House Archives.

26. Oral History Interview with Adrian Gately by Peter Wosh, 21 July 2000; Oral History Interview with Patricia Kennedy by Peter Wosh, 21 July 2000, Covenant House Archives.

27. Oral History Interview with Paul Frazier by Wosh, 29 September 2000, Covenant House Archives.

28. Oral History Interview with James Fitzgibbon by Wosh, 22 June 1999; Oral History with Juniper Alwell by Wosh, 17 November 1998, Covenant House Archives.

29. Oral History Interview with Patricia Kennedy by Wosh, 21 July 2000; Oral History Interview with Paul Frazier by Wosh, 29 September 2000, Covenant House Archives.

30. "Covenant I: East Seventh Street Cooperative," Provincial Chapter Reports, 7 February 1970, Immaculate Conception Province, Conventual Franciscan Archives, Rensselaer, N.Y.

31. All quotations are from "Covenant I: East Seventh Street Cooperative," Provincial Chapter Reports, 7 February 1970, Immaculate Conception Province, Conventual Franciscan Archives, Rensselaer, N.Y. Other discussions concerning Covenant I can be found in Oral History Interview with Patricia Kennedy by Wosh, 21 July 2000; Oral History Interview with Adrian Gately by Wosh, 21 July 2000; Oral History Interview with Paul Frazier by Wosh, 29 September 2000, Covenant House Archives.

32. These criticisms can be gleaned from handwritten comments on the document "Covenant I: East Seventh Street Cooperative," Provincial Chapter Reports, 7 February 1970, Immaculate Conception Province, Conventual Franciscan Archives, Rensselaer, N.Y. The decision itself, along with a summary of the discussion, can be found in Minutes of Meeting of the Definitory, 7 February 1970, Conventual Franciscan Archives, Immaculate Conception Province, Rensselaer, N.Y. The consulting firm was Booz, Allen and Hamilton.

33. Oral History Interview with David Gregorio by Surak, 29 November 1999; Oral History Interview with Paul Frazier by Wosh, 29 September 2000; Oral History Interview with Steven Torkelson by Wosh, 17 August 2000, Covenant House Archives. Letter from "Eric" to Ann Landers, 18 April 2001, document in possession of author.

34. Oral History Interview with Paul Frazier by Wosh, 29 September 2000, Covenant House Archives.

Chapter 3

1. Bruce Ritter, *Covenant House: Lifeline to the Street* (New York: Doubleday, 1989), pp. 51–52.

2. Ritter, *Covenant House: Lifeline to the Street*, p. 52.

3. "Instrument of Directors In Lieu of Organization Meeting of Covenant House," 7 November 1972; Minutes of Meetings of the Board of Directors, 7 December 1972, 14 March 1973, 11 April 1973, 13 June 1973, Covenant House Archives.

4. Minutes of Meetings of the Board of Directors, 7 December 1972, 14 February 1973, 11 April 1973, 13 March 1974, Covenant House Archives.

5. The quotation concerning the Staten Island facility can be found in Covenant House Annual Report, 1973, RG 5, Series IX, Box 13, Folder 19, p. 5. Ritter reported to the board that the Middleburgh experiment failed owing to "conflicting philosophies and lifestyles" among the resident staff as well as an inability to secure strong on-site leadership. The extraordinary expenses necessary to renovate the facility in order to meet the New York Department of Social Service's standards as well as conflicts with the local community and school board, also played a role. Covenant House vacated the facility by March of 1973, though the organization retained use of the facility until the fall, when it reverted back to the Franciscans. Minutes of Meetings of the Board of Directors, 7 December 1972, 10 January 1973, 14 February 1973, 14 March 1973, 9 May 1973, 10 October 1973, Covenant House Archives.

6. Covenant House Annual Report, 1973, RG 5, Series IX, Box 13, Folder 9, pp. 1, 9, Covenant House Archives. Charles M. Sennott, *Broken Covenant*, p. 89.

7. Minutes of Meetings of the Board of Directors, 27 June 1973, 10 October 1973, 12 December 1973, Covenant House Archives.

8. Minutes of Meetings of the Board of Directors, 14 February 1973, 13 March 1974, Covenant House Archives. Sennott, *Broken Covenant*, pp. 67, 89.

9. Covenant House Annual Report, 1973, RG 5, Series IX, Box 13, Folder 9, pp. 3, 7–8

10. Covenant House Annual Report, 1973, RG 5, Series IX, Box 13, Folder 9, pp. 6, 9; Oral History Interview with Dave Cullen by Amy Surak, 15 February 2001, Covenant House Archives.

11. Minutes of Meeting of the Board of Directors, 14 February 1973; Oral History Interview with Adrian Gately by Peter Wosh, 21 July 2000; Oral History Interview with Patricia Kennedy by Peter Wosh, 21 July 2000, Covenant House Archives.

12. Oral History Interview with Patricia Kennedy by Wosh, 21 July 2000; Oral History Interview with Adrian Gately by Wosh, 21 July 2000, Covenant House Archives.

13. Covenant House Annual Report, 1973, RG 5, Series IX, Box 13, Folder 9, p. 8; Oral History Interview with Patricia Kennedy by Wosh, 21 July 2000; Oral History

Interview with Paul Frazier by Peter Wosh, 29 September 2000; Oral History Interview with Shawn Nolan by Peter Wosh, 17 November 1998, Covenant House Archives. Secretary of the Definitory to Rev. Bruce Ritter, 10 October 1971; Aubert J. Clark to Bruce Ritter, 20 April 1972; Shawn Nolan to Mother M. Viola, 1 November 1972, Vicar Provincial's Correspondence, Conventual Franciscan Archives, Rensselaer, N.Y.

14. Oral History Interview with Dave Cullen by Surak, 15 February 2001, Covenant House Archives.

15. Oral History Interview with Shawn Nolan by Wosh, 17 November 1998; Oral History Interview with Juniper Alwell by Peter Wosh, 17 November 1998; Oral History Interview with Steven Torkelson by Peter Wosh, 17 August 2000, Covenant House Archives.

16. Oral History Interview with Dave Cullen by Surak, 15 February 2001; Oral History with Steven Torkelson by Wosh, 17 August 2000, Covenant House Archives. Kathy Wallace illustrates the close connections between family, community, and institution that defined the early Covenant House group. Ritter convinced his niece to move to East Seventh Street in 1972, where she met and soon married Dave Cullen. After they subsequently divorced, she married David Gregorio, an ex-Vincentian priest and a Covenant House administrator as well.

17. Covenant House Annual Report, 1973, RG 5, Series IX, Box 13, Folder 9, Covenant House Archives, provides the 1973–74 financial projections as well as the 1972–73 income statements.

18. Ritter, *Covenant House: Lifeline to the Street*, p. 10. Direct mail, of course, did not constitute a new fund-raising or marketing strategy, and has a long American history. For a useful overview, see Richard Kielbowicz, "Origins of the Junk-Mail Controversy: A Media Battle over Advertising and Postal Policy," *Journal of Policy History* 5, no. 2 (1993), pp. 248–72. Religious historians have tended to focus on televangelism during the 1970s and 1980s, neglecting the other ways in which ministries raised funds and often redefined their mission in the process. For a glance at another prominent ministry that offers a good comparison to Covenant House, see Ken Waters, "How World Vision Rose from Obscurity to Prominence: Television Fundraising, 1972–1982," *American Journalism* (fall 1998), pp. 69–93. A good historical overview of late twentieth-century fund-raising issues in religious organizations can be found in Barry Gardner, "Technological Changes and Monetary Advantages: The Growth of Evangelical Funding, 1945 to the Present," in Larry Eskridge and Mark A. Noll, eds., *More Money, More Ministry: Money and Evangelicals in Recent North American History* (Grand Rapids: William B. Eerdmans, 2000), pp. 298–310.

19. Ritter, *Covenant House: Lifeline to the Street*, pp. 17, 22, 25.

20. Ritter, *Covenant House: Lifeline to the Street*, pp. 26, 38–41.

21. Ritter, *Covenant House: Lifeline to the Street*, pp. 18–19, tells the story of Dave. The incident involving a youth who leaped from the fifth floor tenement window was also discussed in several oral history interviews. See, for example, Oral History Interview with Dave Cullen by Surak, 15 February 2001, Covenant House Archives.

22. Ritter, *Covenant House: Lifeline to the Street*, pp. 22, 25, 38.

23. Covenant House's total revenues for the 1972–73 fiscal year stood at $421,591, and its expenditures totaled $447,204, thus resulting in a $15,613 deficit.

Covenant House Annual Report, 1973, RG 5, Series IX, Box 13, Folder 9, Covenant House Archives.

24. Minutes of Meeting of the Board of Directors, 14 November 1973; Oral History Interview with Steven Torkelson by Wosh, 17 August 2000, Covenant House Archives. Polier (1903–87), daughter of Rabbi Stephen Wise, had been a social reformer and child welfare activist since the 1920s. A friend and ally of Eleanor Roosevelt, she had been appointed as New York's first woman judge in 1935 and presided over family court until her retirement in 1973. *Guide to the Justine Wise Polier Papers*, unpublished finding aid, Schlesinger Library, Radcliffe Institute, Harvard University.

25. Oral History Interview with David Gregorio by Amy Surak, 12 April 2000; Minutes of Meetings of the Board of Directors, 9 January 1974, 13 February 1974, 13 March 1974, 12 June 1974, Covenant House Archives. Some projects initiated by Chase, such as the proposed major capital campaign, never materialized. Mary Mahoney remained a long-time friend and financial supporter of Covenant House. Her husband, James Maguire, a prominent New York attorney, served on Covenant House's board of directors from 1976 until 1990.

26. "Young & Rubicam, 1973–1975," RG 5, Series IX, Box 14, Folder 19; Minutes of Meetings of the Board of Directors, 10 October 1973, 12 December 1973, 12 June 1974, 13 July 1978, Covenant House Archives. Mark Stroock, a senior vice president at Young and Rubicam, served on the Covenant House board from 1978 through 1990.

27. Covenant House Annual Report, 1973, RG 5, Series IX, Box 13, Folder 9, pp. 3–4, Covenant House Archives.

28. "Addiction Services Agency: A Study of Mismanagement," City of New York Office of the Comptroller, Research and Liaison Unit, 10 August 1973, John V. Lindsay Papers, Box 3, Folder 35, Department of Records and Information Services of the City of New York. Covenant House Annual Report, 1973, RG 5, Series IX, Box 13, Folder 9; Minutes of Meeting of the Board of Directors, 7 December 1972, Covenant House Archives.

29. Minutes of Meeting of the Board of Directors, 7 December 1972, Covenant House Archives. The first group of board members included three official representatives: Msgr. Robert Arpie of Catholic Charities of the Archdiocese of New York; Mother Viola Kiernan, the superior general of the Franciscan Sisters of Syracuse; and Rev. Shawn Nolan, the provincial superior of the Conventual Franciscans. The remainder of the board consisted of the following friends and acquaintances of the founder, many of whom have been discussed in the text: Edmund J. Burns, Adrian Gately, Mary Hanrahan, E. Patrick Healy, Patricia Kennedy, Patrick Leonard, Edward Loughran, David Z. Orlow, and Selwyn I. (Si) Taubman.

30. Covenant House Annual Report, 1973, RG 5, Series IX, Box 13, Folder 9, Covenant House Archives.

31. Oral History Interview with David Gregorio by Surak, 29 November 1999, Covenant House Archives.

32. Minutes of Meetings of the Board of Directors, 7 December 1972, 10 January 1973, 14 February 1973, 10 October 1973, 18 September 1974, Covenant House Archives.

33. Oral History Interview with Patricia Kennedy by Wosh, 21 July 2001; Oral History Interview with Patricia Larkin by Peter Wosh, 4 August 1999; Oral History Interview with Kathryn Rush by Peter Wosh, 4 August 1999; Oral History Interview

with Steven Torkelson by Wosh, 17 August 2000, Covenant House Archives. The board of directors minutes from 1973 to 1976 contain regular reports on individual group homes, focusing on their unique situations. Staffing patterns are discussed in Minutes of Meeting of the Board of Directors, 11 December 1974, Covenant House Archives.

34. Oral History Interview with Patricia Kennedy by Wosh, 21 July 2001; Oral History Interview with Mother Viola Kiernan by Peter Wosh, 4 August 1999, Covenant House Archives.

35. David O'Brien, *Faith and Friendship: Catholicism in the Diocese of Syracuse, 1886–1986* (Syracuse: Catholic Diocese of Syracuse, 1987, pp. 416–19, contains an account of the struggles within the Franciscan Sisters of Syracuse during Mother Viola's administration. *Rejoice and Renew, 1860–1985* (Syracuse: Sisters of the Third Franciscan Order, 1985), details the various ministries of the order and offers a good historical overview.

36. Mother M. Viola to Rev. Bruce Ritter, 25 October 1972, Archives of the Franciscan Sisters of Syracuse, Syracuse, N.Y.

37. "History of Franciscan Sisters at Covenant House," ca. 1976, unpublished manuscript in the Archives of the Franciscan Sisters of Syracuse, Syracuse, N.Y.

38. "History of Franciscan Sisters at Covenant House," ca. 1976, unpublished manuscript at Franciscan Sisters of Syracuse Archives, Syracuse, N.Y.; *Rejoice and Renew, 1860–1985*, pp. 55–56; Minutes of Meeting of the Board of Directors, 14 November 1973, Covenant House Archives.

39. Minutes of Meeting of the Board of Directors, 7 December 1972; Oral History Interview with Patricia Kennedy by Wosh, 21 July 2000; Oral History Interview with David Gregorio by Surak, 29 November 1999; Oral History Interview with Patricia Larkin by Wosh, 4 August 1999, Covenant House Archives.

40. Oral History Interview with Kathryn Rush by Wosh, 4 August 1999, Covenant House Archives. The Minutes of Meetings of the Board of Directors for the entire 1973 through 1974 period in the Covenant House Archives contain numerous accounts of incidents and community conflicts at the residential facilities.

41. Minutes of Meetings of the Board of Directors, 13 June 1973, 27 June 1973, 8 May 1974, 12 June 1974, 1 July 1974, Covenant House Archives. Jerome Hornblass to Bruce Ritter, 25 July 1974, Chron Files, Addiction Services Agency Collection, New York Department of Records and Information Services, New York, N.Y.

42. Oral History Interview with David Gregorio by Surak, 29 November 1999, Covenant House Archives.

Chapter 4

1. Bill Reel, "A Times Square Parable. On a street of sin, there dwelt a pimp and a priest . . ," *New York Daily News*, 20 May 1977.

2. "Covenant House and Affiliates (Historical Information) Combined Statement of Financial Position & Statement of Activities, Fiscal Years 1973 to Date," 2000, Covenant House Archives.

3. An extensive literature exists concerning New York City's financial crisis during the mid-1970s. See, for example, Ken Auletta, *The Streets Were Paved with Gold* (New York: Random House, 1979); Roger E. Alcaly and David Mermelstein, eds., *The Fiscal Crisis of American Cities: Essays on the Political Economy of Urban America with Special Reference to New York* (New York: Vintage Books, 1976); Charles R. Morris, *The Cost of Good Intentions: New York City and the Liberal Experiment, 1960–1975* (New York: W. W. Norton, 1980); and Martin Shefter, *Political Crisis, Fiscal Crisis: The Collapse and Renewal of New York City* (New York: Basic Books, 1985).

4. This story has been pieced together from a variety of newspaper and magazine accounts. Some of the most helpful include "Texan Said to Admit Role in 25 Killings," *New York Times*, 10 August 1973, p. 1; James P. Sterba, "Texas Police Find Four More Bodies; The Total Is Now 23," *New York Times*, 11 August 1973, p. 1; James P. Sterba, "Murder Charges Are Filed Against Two Teen-age Boys in Houston Case," *New York Times*, 12 August 1973, p. 37; James P. Sterba, "Texas Toll of Boys Rises to 27 In Nation's Biggest Slaying Case," *New York Times*, 14 August 1973, p. 1; James P. Sterba, "Father Recalls Vain Search for Son, Feared to Be Among 27 Slaying Victims in Houston," *New York Times*, 17 August 1973, p. 18; Paul L. Montgomery, "Houston Finds Murder Ring Random, Enigmatic Intrusion," *New York Times*, 21 July 1974, p. 41; "The Houston Horrors," *Time*, 20 August 1973, 102:24; "The Nicest Person," *Newsweek*, 20 August 1973, p. 32.

5. Bayh's bill is discussed in Minutes of Meeting of Board of Directors, 1 July 1974, Covenant House Archives. Covenant House never applied for funding, owing to the small nature of the appropriation and the fact that the organization sought money elsewhere.

6. The public response to the Houston murders can be discerned in the following articles: Celeste MacLeod, "Street Girls of the '70s," *Nation*, 20 April 1974, pp. 486–88; "Runaways: Rising U.S. Worry," *U.S. News & World Report*, 3 September 1973, p. 34; *New York Times*, 3 July 1974, 12:2, *New York Times*, 10 July 1974, 28:3. The Mayhew quote can be found in Paul L. Montgomery, "Houston Finds Murder Ring Random, Enigmatic Intrusion," *New York Times*, 21 July 1974, 102:24.

7. "More Kids on the Road—Now It's the Throwaways," *U.S. News & World Report*, 12 May 1975, 78:49–50; Celeste MacLeod, "Street Girls of the '70s," *Nation*, 20 April 1974, pp. 486–88; "Why Children Are Running Away in Record Numbers," *U.S. News & World Report*, 17 January 1977, 82:62; Nathaniel Sheppard Jr., "With 20,000 Runaways in City, Police Are Confident That Chances for a Mass Tragedy Are Slight," *New York Times*, 16 August 1973, pp. 16–17. A representative study from this period that echoes many of these themes can be found in Christine Chapman, *America's Runaways* (New York: Morrow, 1976). The claim here is not that these observations really reflect historical reality but rather that contemporaries in the 1970s viewed the problem as historically distinct and without precedent.

8. "The Houston Horrors," *Time*, 20 August 1973, 102:24; "Runaways: Rising U.S. Worry," *U.S. News & World Report*, 3 September 1974, p. 34; Celeste MacLeod, "Street Girls of the '70s," *Nation*, 12 April 1974, pp. 486–88; Nathaniel Sheppard Jr., "With 20,000 Runaways in City, Police Are Confident That Chances for a Mass Tragedy Are Slight," *New York Times*, 16 August 1973, pp. 16–17; "Why Children Are

Running Away in Record Numbers," *U.S. News & World Report*, 17 January 1977, 82:62; "Youth for Sale on the Streets," *Time*, 28 November 1977, 110:23.

9. Bruce Ritter, *Covenant House: Lifeline to the Street* (New York: Doubleday, 1987), pp. 25–26.

10. The best general history of Times Square consists of the series of essays in William R. Taylor, ed., *Inventing Times Square: Commerce and Culture at the Cross-roads of the World, 1880–1939* (New York: Russell Sage Foundation, 1991). Josh Alan Friedman, *Tales of Times Square* (Portland: Feral House, 1993), is an interesting and idiosyncratic history of the sex industry in the area, written by a former reporter for *Screw* magazine. Robert P. McNamara, ed., *Sex, Scams, and Street Life: The Sociology of New York City's Times Square* (Westport: Praeger, 1995), is very good on redevelopment efforts. The *New York Times* quotes can be found in "Times Square Zoning," *New York Times*, 11 October 1975, 30:2. See also "New Times Square . . . ," *New York Times*, 16 April 1974, 38:2.

11. William H. Daly, "Law Enforcement in Times Square, 1970s–1990s," in McNamara, *Sex, Scams, and Street Life*, pp. 97–106. Extensive newspaper coverage and periodic exposes of the sex industry permeated the New York media during the early and mid-1970s. Some important articles include Gail Sheehy, "Cleaning Up Hell's Bedroom," *New York*, 13 November 1972; Gail Sheehy, "The Landlord's of Hell's Bedroom," *New York*, 20 November 1972; Ted Morgan, "Little Ladies of the Night," *New York Times*, 16 November 1975, pp. 34–50; Nathaniel Sheppard Jr., "Bars Offering Nudity and More Survive Despite the Authorities," *New York Times*, 14 May 1977; Howard Blum, "Investigation of the Sex Industry Begun by New York State and City," *New York Times*, 13 May 1977, p. B2; Selwyn Raab, "Refusal by Police to Raid Hotel Stirs Controversy Among Agencies," *New York Times*, 26 October 1977; Murray Schumach, "New Police Policy Frees Prostitutes of Round-Up Fears," *New York Times*, 4 April 1976, 1:1; Charles Kaiser, "New Zoning to Curb Pornography Places Submitted by Beame," *New York Times*, 12 November 1976; "Mayor Beame Leads Pornography Raids," *New York Times*, 25 March 1977, p. D12:1; Selwyn Raab and Nathaniel Sheppard Jr., "Mobsters Skim New York City Sex Industry Profits," *New York Times*, 27 July 1977, 1:2.

12. Ted Morgan, "Little Ladies of the Night," *New York Times*, 16 November 1975, p. 34.

13. "'Chicken-Hawk' Trade Found Attracting More Young Boys to Times Square," *New York Times*, 1977; Selwyn Raab, "Pimps Establish Recruiting Link to the Midwest," *New York Times*, 30 October 1977, 1:6; Selwyn Raab, "Prostitutes from Midwest Vanish From 8th Avenue During Hunt by Visiting Police," *New York Times*, 10 November 1977, B2; Nathaniel Sheppard Jr., "Teen-Age Runaways Turn to Prostitution as Rebellion," *New York Times*, 13 November 1977, 20:1; Nathaniel Sheppard, "Money, Not New York, Lures Minnesota Prostitutes," *New York Times*, 25 November 1977. For a more complex treatment of the phenomenon that features an interview with Sr. Lorraine Reilly, who ran four shelters for youths in the Bronx, see George Vecsey, "For Young Urban Nomads, Home Is the Streets," *New York Times*, 1 June 1976, 37:5.

14. Barbara Campbell, "Help Sought for Children Used in Pornography," *New York Times*, 14 January 1977, II 3:1; Peter Bridge, "What Parents Should Know and Do

About Kiddie Porn," *Parents' Magazine*, January 1978, 53:42–43; "Child Pornography: Outrage Starts to Stir Action," *U.S. News & World Report*, 13 June 1977, 82:66; "Child's Garden of Perversity," *Time*, 4 April 1977, 109:55–56; William Reel, "The Kids These Days! (and those days)," *New York Daily News*, 19 August 1977, p. 30.

15. T. J. English, *The Westies: Inside the Hell's Kitchen Irish Mob* (New York: G. P. Putnam's Sons, 1990), contains a good description of the neighborhood. See esp. pp. 50–52.

16. John L. Hess, "Hell's Kitchen Is Caught in the Clash of Urban Renewal and Urban Removal," *New York Times*, 19 April 1974, 39:2; "The Clinton Community," *New York Times*, 24 September 1974, 40:2; Joseph P. Fried, "Plan for Convention Center Here Jeopardized By City's Fiscal Ills," *New York Times*, 5 August 1975, 1:5; Joyce Maynard, "Cruising 'Johns' Are Targets of Drive on Vehicular Prostitution," *New York Times*, 8 May 1976, 27:3; "Midtown People Call Car Lots Outdoor 'Bordellos,'" *New York Times*, 1 December 1976, II, 3:3; Judy Klemesrud, "Cardinal Urges Assault on Smut and Prostitution," *New York Times*, 6 April 1977, II:2; Friedman, *Tales of Times Square*, pp. 127–32; English, *The Westies*, pp. 114, 130–31.

17. Conversation with Rev. John P. Duffell by Peter Wosh, 15 November 2002, Covenant House Archives.

18. Conversation with Fr. John Duffell by Wosh, 15 November 2002, Covenant House Archives; Minutes of Meetings of the Board of Directors, 10 May 1976, 17 June 1976, 8 September 1976, and 5 January 1977, Covenant House Archives.

19. Conversation with Fr. John Duffell by Wosh, 15 November 2002; Minutes of Meeting of the Covenant House Board of Directors, 2 June 1976, Covenant House Archives. Duffell had been serving as a member of the executive committee of the Priests' Senate and was scheduled to meet with Cooke in this capacity.

20. Minutes of Meetings of the Board of Directors, 2 June 1976, 17 June 1976, 8 September 1976, Covenant House Archives.

21. Minutes of Meetings of the Covenant House Board of Directors, 2 June 1976, 8 September 1976, Covenant House Archives.

22. Minutes of Meetings of the Board of Directors, 17 June 1976, 8 September 1976, 5 January 1977, 23 March 1977, Covenant House Archives. "Grant Report– Covenant House," Charles E. Culpeper Foundation Archives, Rockefeller Archive Center, Tarrytown, N.Y.

23. Barbara Campbell, "Help Sought for Children Used in Pornography," *New York Times*, 14 January 1977, II, 3:1; Francis X. Clines, "A Haven for the Sexually Exploited," *New York Times*, 18 January 1977, 28:1; E. J. Dionne Jr., "An Oasis for Runaway Teen-Agers Appears in a Pornographic Desert," *New York Times*, 2 April 1977, 33:5; Bill Reel, "The Pain and Reporting the Pain," address delivered at the 44th Annual Meeting of the National Catholic Council on Alcoholism and Related Drug Problems, 11–14 January 1993, San Pedro, Calif., Covenant House Archives. Oral History Interview with Robert Cardany by Amy Surak, 23 September 1999, Covenant House Archives.

24. Minutes of Meetings of the Board of Directors, 12 February 1975, 12 March 1975, 13 April 1975, 25 June 1975, Covenant House Archives. Oral History Interview with Shawn Nolan by Peter Wosh, 17 November 1998, Covenant House Archives. Ritter's subsequent explanation of his mindset during this period can be found in

Bruce Ritter, *Covenant House: Lifeline to the Street*, pp. 52–56. Charles M. Sennott, *Broken Covenant* (New York: Simon & Shuster, 1992), pp. 98–101, interprets the board change as an example of Ritter's "new-found autocracy" and "a brilliant, almost Napoleonic ploy by a master manipulator." Essentially the board change transformed Covenant House into a membership corporation, with Ritter appointed as the sole member of the corporation. He would then elect members of the board of directors, who would manage the organization. This arrangement is the one used by dioceses throughout the United States, where individual bishops function as the "corporation sole." When the Covenant House board approved this arrangement in June 1975, members clearly perceived it as a temporary arrangement that would precede either formal affiliation with the Franciscans or the appointment of additional members of the corporation by the Franciscan Order. This never occurred, and Ritter remained the sole member.

25. These administrative changes can be traced in Minutes of Meetings of the Board of Directors, 19 October 1977, 25 May 1978, 13 July 1978, 18 October 1978, 6 December 1978, Covenant House Archives. A key moment in this drive toward institutional reorganization occurred during a two-day planning conference, held at the Millbrook, New York, farm of Robert Macauley on 3 and 4 November 1978, and attended by "key members of the Covenant House staff." Macauley, who would soon emerge as a powerful board member and major advisor to Ritter, offered his bucolic Dutchess County property for the purpose, and the results of the meeting are summarized in the 6 December 1978 board of director's minutes.

26. Ritter's discussion concerning formal affiliation with the Franciscans can be found in the Minutes of Meetings of the Board of Directors, 12 February 1975, 12 March 1975, and 25 June 1975. See also "Reports Presented to the Ordinary Provincial Chapter," Immaculate Conception Province U.S.A., St. Anthony-on-Hudson, Rensselaer, N.Y., 3–7 May 1976, 1.31; Provincial Chapter Meeting, Immaculate Conception Province, 16–19 July 1979, St. Anthony-on-Hudson, Rensselaer, N.Y., p. 25; Aubert J. Clark to Very Reverend Joseph C. Towle, 27 December 1977; Joseph C. Towle to Bruce Ritter, 12 October 1977, Vicar Provincial's Correspondence, Immaculate Conception Province, Conventual Franciscan Archives, Rensselaer, N.Y.; Minutes of Meeting of the Board of Directors, 5 January 1977, Covenant House Archives.

27. Ritter, *Covenant House: Lifeline to the Street*, p. 59; "The Religious Dimension of the Under 21 Project," *Manual for the Under 21 Multi-Service Center*, 1977, p. 10, RG 1, Series VIII, Box 32, Folder 26, Covenant House Archives; *A Report from Father Bruce for 1979/1980*, Annual Reports, Covenant House Archives.

28. Minutes of Meetings of the Board of Directors, 25 June 1975, 12 November 1975, Covenant House Archives. William L. Juska to Edmund J. Burns, Correspondence Files, 1974–80, Box 13, Folder 5, Edmund J. Burns Papers, Covenant House Archives. Oral History Interview with Shawn Nolan by Wosh, 17 November 1998, Covenant House Archives. Mary Hanrahan's official letter of resignation has not been located. The Kennedy and Gately resignations also were prompted by Ritter's decision to lay off some staff members and slash salaries for social workers, again reflecting a new commitment to managerial efficiency. Oral History Interview with Patricia Kennedy by Peter Wosh, 21 July 2000, Covenant House Archives.

29. Bruce Ritter, *Covenant House: Lifeline to the Street*, pp. 45–47, 60–62, 93–95.

30. *60 Minutes*, March 1979, videotape copy available in Covenant House Archives. Amy Surak, "Rev. Bruce Ritter: Anti-Porn Crusader and Working-Class Priest," unpublished M.A. thesis, New York University 1999, copy in possession of author, provides a good discussion of the changing image of the ministry and the importance of the *60 Minutes* program.

31. *60 Minutes*, March 1979, videotape copy in Covenant House Archives.

32. Minutes of Meetings of the Board of Directors, 19 October 1977, 16 November 1977, 7 December 1977, 25 May 1978, 13 July 1978, Covenant House Archives, all illustrate Ritter's growing concern with institutional advocacy. A representative sampling of Ritter's ongoing feud with municipal officials during this period can be found in Stephen Thorkelson, "'Sin Street' Priest Rescues Boy, Girl Prostitutes from New York Pimps," *National Catholic Reporter*, 26 January 1979, p. 4; "Furor Follows 'Recreational Sex' Ruling," *Yonkers Herald-Statesman*, 26 January 1978; William Reel, "Times Square: Haven and Hell," *New York Daily News*, 18 January 1978; Martin King, "The Best Times Sq. Stop for Runaways," *New York Daily News*, 23 December 1977, p. 8; Steve Dunleavy, "Money Can't Hush Him," *New York Post* (n.d.); Selwyn Raab, "Police Manpower Tripled in the Times Square Area," *New York Times*, 13 June 1978, 3:1; Barbara Campbell, "Help Sought for Children Used in Pornography," *New York Times*, 14 January 1977. Covenant II was never actually incorporated, but the organization did eventually establish an Institute for Youth Advocacy within its own corporate structure.

33. "Manual for the Under 21 Multi-Service Center," RG 1, Series VIII, Box 32, Folder 26, Covenant House Archives; Marlene Cimons, "A Crisis Center for Kids," *Los Angeles Times*, 5 February 1978, p. 17; Ritter, *Covenant House: Lifeline to the Street*, pp. 87–88.

34. Minutes of Meetings of the Board of Directors, 7 December 1977, 13 July 1978, 18 October 1978, 6 December 1978, Covenant House Archives.

35. "A Times Sq. Youth Shelter Seeks Evictions to Expand," *New York Times*, 28 January 1979, p. 45.

36. "A Times Sq. Youth Shelter Seeks Evictions to Expand," *New York Times*, 28 January 1979, p. 45; Minutes of Meetings of the Board of Directors, 18 October 1978, 6 December 1978, 4 April 1979, Covenant House Archives. Ritter's perspective on the controversy can be found in *Covenant House: Lifeline to the Street*, pp. 87–92.

37. "State Help Solves Dispute on Times Square Youth Center," *New York Times*, 16 September 1979; "Franciscan Strikes Blow Against Children Exploiters," *Syracuse Catholic Sun*, 26 December 1979; Robert J. Mogado to Father Ritter, 28 March 1979, Bruce Ritter File, "Governor's Name Files, 1975–1982," Microfilm Reel 129, Hugh Carey Papers, New York State Archives and Records Administration, Albany, N.Y.; Minutes of Meetings of the Board of Directors, 4 April 1979, 28 June 1979, Covenant House Archives. Covenant House's connection with Cahill at the time is a bit unclear. Ritter claims that Msgr. James Murray, the director of Archdiocesan Catholic Charities, constituted the principal go-between (Ritter, *Covenant House: Lifeline to the Streets*, p. 88). Charles M. Sennott credits Peter Grace with playing an influential role in the negotiations (*Broken Covenant*, p. 123). Hugh O'Neill, who at this point was serving as a member of the Carey administration in Albany,

apparently had no direct role in the negotiations between Ritter and Carey, though he participated in drafting the lease arrangement with Ed Burns, Covenant House's attorney. Oral History Interview with Hugh O'Neill by Peter Wosh, 15 January 1999, Covenant House Archives.

38. "State Help Solves Dispute on Times Square Youth Center," *New York Times*, 16 September 1979; "New Shelter for Homeless Youth Dedicated in Times Square Area," Press Release, Religious News Service, 14 December 1979; "Runaways Gain a New Refuge," *New York Times*, 13 December 1979; "Covenant House Tour," 12 December 1979, Covenant House Archives.

39. Oral History Interview with Robert Cardany by Amy Surak, 23 September 1999, Covenant House Archives. "Memorandum to File Re: Under 21," 8 May 1978, Ritter Correspondence, Box 43, Folder 524, Justine Wise Polier Papers, Arthur and Elizabeth Schlesinger Library on the History of Women in America, Cambridge, Mass. For an interesting account of Polier's career, and especially her work in the 1970s to end racial and religious discrimination in the foster care system, see Nina Bernstein, *The Lost Children of Wilder: The Epic Struggle to Change Foster Care* (New York: Pantheon, 2001).

Chapter 5

1. J. Peter Grace to Bruce Ritter, 28 December 1981, "Grace, Peter," RG 1, Box 29, Folder 4, Covenant House Archives.

2. Covenant House Annual Report, 1980–81, pp. 12–13; Covenant House Annual Report, 1984, pp. 4–5; Covenant House Annual Report, 1985, p. 3; Annual Report on Corporate and Foundation Funding, 1985, Covenant House Archives.

3. "Covenant House Group Program: A Proposal to Discontinue Service," Minutes of Meeting of the Board of Directors, 27 March 1980, Covenant House Archives.

4. "Covenant House Financial History," in "Special Report to Peter Grace, 1982," RG 8, Box 1, Folder 26, Covenant House Archives. See Appendix 2.

5. "Covenant House Group Home Program: A Proposal to Discontinue Service," Minutes of Meeting of the Board of Directors, 27 March 1980, 17 April 1980, Covenant House Archives.

6. "Covenant House Financial History," in "Special Report to Peter Grace, 1982," RG 8, Box 1, Folder 26, Covenant House Archives; Minutes of Meetings of the Board of Directors, 27 March 1980, 17 April 1980, 29 May 1980, Covenant House Archives.

7. *A Report from Father Bruce for 1979/1980*, Annual Report, Covenant House Archives; Minutes of Meetings of the Board of Directors, 17 April 1980, 29 May 1980, Covenant House Archives. One issue that concerned several board members involved educational facilities. In June 1975, the New York City Board of Education agreed to start a special school for Covenant House's group home residents. Board and staff feared that the closure of the group homes would stimulate the city to close the school. Ultimately, however, these fears proved groundless. The board agreed to

continue providing teachers, and the school continued to be used by the Under 21 residents.

8. Oral History Interview with Sr. Patricia Larkin by Peter Wosh, 4 August 1999, Covenant House Archives.

9. "Special Report to Peter Grace, 1982," RG 8, Box 1, Folder 26, Covenant House Archives, contains a good chronological history of the agency as well as information concerning the number of full-time staff. Bureaucratic changes, corporate restructuring, and key staffing changes can be traced through the board of directors minutes. See especially Minutes of Meetings of the Board of Directors, 24 January 1980, 27 March 1980, 20 November 1980, 29 January 1981, Covenant House Archives.

10. Ritter's date book appears to confirm Macauley's account. The first recorded meeting between the founder and Macauley occurred on May 14, 1977, shortly after the appearance of the Reel column. Bruce Ritter, Appointment Book, 1977, RG 1, Series VI, Box 27, Folder 8, Covenant House Archives. Versions of the Macauley story can be found in Charles M. Sennott, *Broken Covenant* (New York: Simon & Schuster, 1992), p. 111; "How Covenant House's Board Chairman Talked Father Ritter into Writing Those Letters," *Chronicle of Philanthropy*, 3 October 1989, p. 8. Steve Kemper, "The Miracle Worker," *Pursuits*, Spring 1988, pp. 28–35; Robert Macauley to Bruce Ritter, 5 December 1984, RG 1, Series VI, Box 29, Folder 8, Covenant House Archives.

11. Basic biographical information concerning Macauley can be found in Ann Marsh, "AmeriCares' Success Hailed, Criticized," *Hartford Courant*, 11 August 1991, p. 1; Russ W. Baker, "A Thousand Points of Blight: AmeriCares, George Bush's Favorite Charity, Dispenses Bitter Medicine Around the World," *Village Voice*, 6 January 1991, pp. 22–29; Donna Greene, "Solo Effort That Led to Worldwide Relief," *New York Times*, 27 April 1997.

12. Some of these themes can be found in the following correspondence from Robert Macauley to Bruce Ritter: 7 July 1981, 14 July 1981, 27 August 1982, 13 December 1982, 3 February 1983, 3 June 1983, 28 June 1983, 1 June 1984, 21 June 1984, 19 November 1984, 26 November 1984, 18 August 1984, RG 1, Series VI, Box 29, Folder 8, Covenant House Archives. See also: Oral History Interview with Jim Harnett by Amy Surak, 6 September 2001, Oral History Interview with Robert Cardany by Amy Surak, 23 September 1999, Covenant House Archives.

One of Macauley's wealthy business associates was John C. Dempsey, who headed the Greif Brothers Corporation, which owned and operated a series of containerboard and industrial packaging businesses throughout the United States. Dempsey personally contributed significant sums to Covenant House, and the organization's investments in Greif Brothers stock netted a handsome return. Greif eventually purchased Virginia Fibre in the 1990s. Macauley, interestingly, constituted one of the few non-Catholics on the Covenant House board, though he retained a lifelong interest in Catholicism. His wife, Leila, remained a committed evangelical and the family also maintained a relationship with Rev. Pat Robertson of the Christian Broadcast Network, who both supported and publicized Macauley's philanthropies.

13. Robert Macauley to Bruce Ritter, 15 September 1984, RG 1, Series VI, Box 29, Folder 8, Covenant House Archives. Discussions concerning the need to expand, diversify, and restructure the board can be found in Minutes of Meetings of the

Board of Directors, 24 January 1980, 1 October 1981, 19 November 1981, 27 January 1983, 30 June 1983, 6 October 1983, 31 January 1984, 28 June 1984, and 20 September 1984. Macauley formally assumed chairmanship of the board in 1985, replacing Si Taubman in that capacity and thereby institutionalizing the real power relationships on the board. The twelve board members active in September 1984 included no minority members and only three women: Margaret Crawford, a member of the Faith Community who began volunteering with Covenant House in 1977; Donna Santarsiero, the executive director of the Brooklyn Bureau of Community Service, who first met Ritter when she was working as a program evaluator for the New York State Board of Social Welfare in 1971; and Sr. M. Aileen Griffin, superior general of the Sisters of St. Francis. Other board members, in addition to Macauley, included Dr. James Kennedy, a former student of Ritter's at Manhattan College and the brother of Patricia Kennedy, who also served as director of medical services for Covenant House and was Ritter's personal physician; James J. Maguire, an attorney and husband of Mary B. Mahoney, an early Ritter supporter and financial contributor; Richard Schmeelk, an executive at Salomon Brothers; Mark Stroock, an executive at Young & Rubicam; Si Taubman, a member of the original board and executive at Ziff-Davis; Anthony Terracciano, an executive at Chase Manhattan Bank who took a very limited role at Covenant House; James Makrianes, who operated his own executive recruiting and business consulting firm, known as Haley Associates; and the Rev. Briant Cullinane, Minister Provincial of the Franciscan Friars. Most board members were either acquaintances of Ritter from the early 1970s or executives at institutions that had a long history of supporting the ministry.

14. The most systematic critique of Americares can be found in Russ W. Baker, "A Thousand Points of Blight," *Village Voice*, 8 January 1991, pp. 22–28. See also Penny Lernoux, *People of God: The Struggle for World Catholicism* (New York: Viking, 1989), p. 295; Sennott, *Broken Covenant*, pp. 175–77; and the information compiled by Group Watch, which is available on The Public Eye website. The Public Eye, *Group Watch: Americares Foundation,* June 1991, http://www.publiceye.org/Group_Watch/Entries-08.html#TopofPage (6 January 2004).

15. On J. Peter Grace, see *Current Biography* (1960), pp. 162–64; Elizabeth Lesley, "Fall from Grace," *Business Week*, 29 May 1995, pp. 60–70; Lernoux, *People of God*, pp. 291–97; George Getschow, "Cardinal's Friend: J. Peter Grace Shows How Big Names Raise Big Money for Charity," *Wall Street Journal*, 8 May 1987; F. Lise Beebe, "J. Peter Grace: A Dynasty's Driving Force," *American Way*, 1 December 1986, pp. 36–43; and Kenneth N. Gilpin, "J. Peter Grace, Ex-Company Chief, Dies at 81," *New York Times*, 21 April 1985, p. B6.

16. Grace's contributions to the Covenant House program are detailed in Minutes of Meetings of the Board of Directors, 29 May 1980 and 18 March 1982. See also Peter Grace File, RG 1, Box 29, Folder 4, Covenant House Archives.

17. Ritter's associates all agreed that he maintained a simple lifestyle despite his increasing association with wealthy and powerful individuals. David Gregorio, for example, who rejoined the Covenant House staff in the late 1980s, observed that "he lived in a shelter. He dressed very down. He drove a Honda Accord or something. He wasn't driving like a really fancy car. . . . His lifestyle was never anything

but very simple and bordering on poor at times." Oral History Interview with David Gregorio by Amy Surak, 12 April 2000, Covenant House Archives.

18. On Ritter's rhetoric during the early 1980s, consult Bruce Ritter, *Covenant House: Lifeline to the Street* (New York: Doubleday, 1989), esp. pp. 108–11, 131–33, 161–64, 197–200, 219–21.

19. On the president's commission, see "Amazing Grace," *New York*, 18 February 1985, pp. 43–47. Grace's "oratorical mistake" was covered in the following articles: "Business Aide to Reagan Criticizes Food Stamps," *New York Times*, 28 May 1982, p. A12:6; Joseph B. Treaster, "Head of Reagan Panel Apologizes to Puerto Ricans," *New York Times*, 29 May 1982, p. 7:1; "150 Protest Against U.S. Aide," *New York Times*, 2 June 1982, p. B4:6. Bruce Ritter to J. Peter Grace, 8 June 1982, Peter Grace File, RG 1, Series VI, Box 29, Folder 4, Covenant House Archives.

20. Minutes of Meetings of the Board of Directors, 29 May 1980 and 20 November 1980, Covenant House Archives. "Special Report to J. Peter Grace," RG 8, Box 1, Folder 26, Section I, Covenant House Archives. A good source on the history of philosophy of the Faith Community can be found in several training and orientation videos: "Covenant House History" with John Boyle, 13 October 1980, 40 minutes; "The Covenant Process As Environment" with Steven Torkelson, ca. 1980, 50 minutes; "Covenant Community: History" with Bruce Ritter, May 1984, all produced by Covenant House's Audio/Visual Media Services, Covenant House Archives.

21. Marvin Liebman, *Coming out Conservative* (San Francisco: Chronicle Books, 1992), passim.

22. Liebman, *Coming out Conservative*, pp. 226–31. On the results of Liebman's direct mail operations at Covenant House, see Minutes of Meetings of the Board of Directors, 27 March 1980, Covenant House Archives.

23. The demographic survey is appended to the Minutes of Meetings of the Board of Directors, 26 April 1984; see also Minutes of Meetings of the Board of Directors, 20 November 1980, Covenant House Archives.

24. Sennott, *Broken Covenant*, pp. 118–22, 149–50, 167–70, 179. See also Robert Macauley to Bruce Ritter, 3 February 1983, RG 1, Series VI, Box 29, Folder 8, Covenant House Archives; Patrick Atkinson to Bruce Ritter, 29 January 1982 and Patrick Atkinson to Robert Macauley, 4 April 1983, RG 1, Series VI, Box 27, Folder 11, Covenant House Archives; Oral History Interview with James Harnett by Surak, 6 September 2001; Oral History Interview with David Gregorio by Surak, 12 April 2000, Covenant House Archives.

Few women occupied important administrative positions during this period, and Ritter's informal network often blunted their influence. Sr. Gretchen Gilroy, who had been serving as executive director of the Under 21 program, resigned from Covenant House in 1985. Her departure left only two women in key administrative posts: Patricia Connors, the senior vice president for human resources, and Sandra Hagan, the senior vice president for program development. Men occupied eight important positions within Ritter's administrative team: chief operating officer, senior vice president and treasurer, general counsel, senior vice president for financial support, senior vice president, vice president and secretary, executive director of the Institute for Youth Advocacy, and executive director of Under 21. Anne Donahue, a 1982 graduate of Georgetown Law School, was one of the only women volunteers who eventually occupied a full-time administrative post within Covenant House. She worked at the Institute for Youth Advocacy and eventually became the executive director of Covenant House's program in Los Angeles. The fact that so few women moved into major administrative positions within the agency seems especially jolting considering their numerical predominance among the volunteers.

25. "Regarding Rome" memo, undated, RG 1, Series VI, Box 29, Folder 37, Covenant House Archives.

26. Lernoux, *People of God*, pp. 283–301, contains information concerning the Knights of Malta and their Latin American initiatives.

27. The letter from Macauley to Grace is quoted in a letter from Peter Grace to William Simon, 19 January 1982, "Special Report to J. Peter Grace," RG 1, Box 1, Folder 26, Covenant House Archives.

28. Bruce Ritter, "Dictating Machine Transcript," 2 May 1980, RG1, Series VI, Box 29, Folder 37, Covenant House Archives.

29. Ritter, "Dictating Machine Transcript," 2 May 1980; Ritter to Most Rev. Donald Kos, 6 May 1980; Ritter to Most Rev. Basil Heiser, 6 May 1980, RG 1, Series VI, Box 29, Folder 37, Covenant House Archives. Ritter did not abandon his Rome project easily. It constituted a major topic of discussion during his private audience and conversation with Pope John Paul II in 1981. See Minutes of Meetings of the Board of Directors, 1 October 1981, Covenant House Archives.

30. Bruce Ritter, "Dictating Machine Transcript," 2 May 1980; Bruce Ritter to Baroness Vittinghoff-Schell, 6 May 1980, RG 1, Series VI, Box 29, Folder 37, Covenant House Archives.

31. Bruce Ritter to J. Peter Grace, 6 May 1980, RG 1, Series VI, Box 29, Folder 37; Robert Macauley to Bruce Ritter, 14 July 1981, RG 1, Series VI, Box 29, Folder 8, Covenant House Archives..

32. Stephanie Russell, "'Family Plan' Meeting's Guatemala Site Blasted," *National Catholic Reporter*, 6 June 1980, p. 1.

33. Amnesty International, *Guatemala: A Government Program of Political Murder* (London: Amnesty International Publications, 1981).

34. Alan Riding, "Guatemala: State of Siege," *New York Times*, 24 August 1980, VI: 16–29, 66–67; Warren Hoge, "Repression Increases in Guatemala as U.S. Is Seeking to Improve Ties," *New York Times*, 3 May 1981, 1:2. Penny Lernoux, *Cry of the People: The Struggle for Human Rights in Latin America—The Catholic Church in Conflict with U.S. Policy* (New York: Penguin, 1991) remains the best general treatment of the growth of liberation theology and the changing nature of church-state relations in Latin America. The assassination of Archbishop Oscar Romero by Salvadoran right-wing terrorists as he celebrated Mass at a hospital chapel in March of 1980, along with the brutal murder of four U.S. women missionary workers in El Salvador in December of that year, further ratcheted up tensions throughout the region.

35. June Carolyn Frick, "Guatemalan Priest: We Don't Have Pope's Ear," *National Catholic Reporter*, 7 March 1980, p. 5; Warren Hoge, "Guatemalan Clerics Targets of Violence," *New York Times*, 5 May 1981, p. 5; June Carolyn Frick, "Guatemalan Bishops Rap Violence as 'Insanity'," *National Catholic Reporter*, 20 June 1980, p. 4; Stephanie Russell, "Guatemalans Report Massacres," *National Catholic Reporter*,

14 November 1980, p. 3; June Carolyn Frick, "Papal Critique of Guatemala: 'No Comment,'" *National Catholic Reporter*, 5 December 1980, p. 16; Stephanie Russell, "'Family Plan' Meeting's Guatemala Site Blasted," *National Catholic Reporter*, 6 June 1980, p. 1.

36. The Billings method had been invented in 1972 by two Australian physicians who had been connected with the Catholic Family Planning Centre in Melbourne, Australia. See Katharine Betts, "The Billings Method of Family Planning: An Assessment," *Studies in Family Planning: An Assessment*, 15:6, November–December 1984, pp. 253–66. Wilson's unwieldy organizational name appeared designed primarily so that supporters might use the clever acronym WOOMB. Some information concerning the history of WOOMB-USA can be found in Patricia Donovan, "The Adolescent Family Life Act and the Promotion of Religious Doctrine," *Family Planning Perspectives*, 16:5, September–October 1984, pp. 222–28. The organization subsequently changed its name to the Family of the Americas Foundation, its current designation. See the organization's website: Family of the Americas, < http://www.familyplanning.net> (6 January 2004).

37. Alvaro Arzu, who was thirty-three years old at the time he met Ritter, was described by one reporter as a "blond-haired, blue-eyed scion of a wealthy family." He subsequently served as mayor of Guatemala City (1985–90), minister of foreign affairs (1991), and president of Guatemala (1996–2000). Larry Rohter, "Guatemalan Who Pledges to 'Avoid Excesses' Is Narrowly Elected," *New York Times*, 9 January 1996, I 5:2.

38. "Latin America: Guatemala," RG 1, Series III, Subseries IV, Box 18, Folders 4 and 20; Minutes of Meeting of the Board of Directors, 27 September 1980, Covenant House Archives.

39. Minutes of Meetings of the Board of Directors, 27 September 1980, 20 November 1980, Covenant House Archives. RG 1, Series III, Subseries IV, Box 18, Folders 1, 4 and 20; RG 1, Series IV, Box 27, Folders 11 and 16, Covenant House Archives. The executive directors at Casa Alianza during this period were John Boyle (1981–83) and Patrick Atkinson (1983–89).

40. Gregory Loken to Ed Burns, 19 February 1981; Gregory Loken to Bruce Ritter, 19 February 1981; Gregory Loken to Bruce Ritter, Ed Burns, and Sandy Hagan, 16 June 1981, RG 1, Series III, Subseries IV, Box 18, Folder 20, Covenant House Archives.

41. Minutes of Meeting of the Board of Directors, 29 January 1981; "Guatemala," description of program, 1982, Covenant House Archives; Sennott, *Broken Covenant*, pp. 133–34.

42. "Guatemala," description of program, 1982, Covenant House Archives.

43. "A Model for Establishing Youth Services in Other Countries and Cities," 1981, Covenant House Archives. See Appendix 3.

Chapter 6

1. Ronald Reagan Presidential Library website, "Transcript of Message by President on the State of the Union," http://www.reagan.utexas.edu/resource/speaks/1984/12584e.htm (8 January 2004).

2. "Special Report to J. Peter Grace," 1982, RG 8, Box 1, Folder 26, Section V, pp. 1–5, Covenant House Archives.

3. The Institute for Youth Advocacy was established in 1983, with Gregory Loken as the first director. See Minutes of Meeting of the Board of Directors, 30 June 1983, Covenant House Archives.

4. "Transcript of Message by President on the State of the Union," *New York Times,* 26 January 1984, p. B8; *Final Report of the Attorney General's Commission on Pornography* (Nashville: Rutledge Hill, 1986); Bernard Weintraub, "Bush Calls for New Volunteer Effort," *New York Times,* 23 June 1989, p. A6:4. Complete financial statements can be found in Covenant House's published annual reports during the 1980s. See Appendix 2.

5. Significant additions to the board of directors during the middle and late 1980s included Richard Schmeelk, managing director of Salomon Brothers (1984); William E. Simon, former U.S. secretary of the treasury and chairman/CEO of the Wesray Corporation (1985); Frank Macchiarola, former New York City schools chancellor and director of The Academy of Political Science (1986); Denis P. Coleman, managing director of Bear, Stearns & Company (1986); Ralph Pfeiffer, retired chairman of the board of IBM World Trade (1986); Ellen Levine, vice president and editor-in-chief of *Woman's Day* magazine (1986); Raymond Peterson, executive vice president of Hearst Magazines (1986); Clarence Wood, vice president of external affairs for The Urban League (1986); and Edward Shaw, executive vice president and general counsel for Chase Manhattan Bank (1988). Pfeiffer eventually replaced Macauley as chairman of the board in 1989.

6. Minutes of Meeting of the Board of Directors, 31 January 1984; Oral History Interview with James Harnett by Amy Surak, 6 September 2001, Covenant House Archives, provides much of the information contained in the next two paragraphs.

7. Harnett had been born in the Bronx, but his family joined the massive Catholic exodus to southern Long Island in the mid-1950s. The Diocese of Rockville Centre, which was created in 1957 to encompass Long Island, soon grew into one of the largest dioceses in the nation. Harnett recalled serving as an altar boy at his parish, progressing through Catholic elementary and secondary education, and participating in Catholic Youth Organization athletic activities. For many middle-class suburban Catholic families who migrated from urban areas during this period, social life remained centered around the parish. Joan de Lourdes Leonard, *Richly Blessed: The Diocese of Rockville Centre, 1957–1990* (Long Island: Diocese of Rockville Centre, 1991), contains excellent information on the growth of Catholicism on Long Island.

8. Thomas DeStefano, quoted in Robert E. Murphy, *History of Catholic Charities, Diocese of Brooklyn, 1899–1999* (Brooklyn: Catholic Charities, Diocese of Brooklyn, 2002), pp. 140–41.

9. Bishop Joseph Sullivan, who served as vicar for human resources in the Diocese of Brooklyn and had worked with Harnett in Catholic Charities, apparently proved instrumental in bringing him to Ritter's attention. Harnett's initial reluctance stemmed mainly from his indecision about whether he wished to return to a church-related agency.

10. Oral History Interview with James Harnett by Surak, Covenant House Archives, 6 September 2001.

11. Douglas Martin, "Reduced 'Take' on Oil Curbs Alaska's Plans," *New York Times,* 27 March 1983, IV, 5:1; "Alaska Turning from Oil Boom to Reality," *New York Times,* 13 March 1986, p. A14; Wallace Turner, "Alaska Shaken by Oil-Revenue Drop," *New York Times,* 26 August 1986, p. A10:3; Paul A. Witteman, "In Alaska: Boom Times Yield to a Bitter Bust," *Time,* 30 March 1987, 129:18; Jean Lamming, "Covenant House Shelter Helps Teens in Crises," *Anchorage Daily Times,* 30 October 1988, p. B1.

12. The Diocese of Anchorage stretched for nearly 140,000 miles across south central Alaska but contained less than thirty thousand Catholics. Molly Brown, "Hurley, Successor, Team Up Temporarily," *Anchorage Daily News,* 20 January 2000, p. B1; Lamming, "Covenant House Shelter Helps Teens in Crises," *Anchorage Daily Times,* 30 October 1988, p. B1; Francis T. Hurley to Bruce Ritter, 6 April 1987, RG 1, Series II, Subseries I, Box 7, Folder 23, Covenant House Archives. Some background on the history and development of these shelters can be found at the following website: Archdiocese of Anchorage, Catholic Social Services, *Programs,* http://cssalaska.org/programs.html#emergency (9 January 2004).

13. Memo from Jim Harnett to Mary Rose McGeady, 18 October 1993, RG 1, Series II, Subseries II, Box 7, Folder 31, Covenant House Archives. Minutes of Meetings of the Board of Directors, 23 April 1987 and 16 July 1987, Covenant House Archives; Fred Ali to Bruce Ritter, 7 October 1988, RG 1, Series I, Box 7, Folder 25, Covenant House Archives; Oral History Interview with James Harnett by Surak, 6 September 2001, Covenant House Archives.

14. Fred Ali to Bruce Ritter, 16 August 1988; Covenant House Alaska Board Report, January–March 1989, RG 1, Series II, Subseries I, Box 7, Folder 21, Covenant House Archives; Fred Ali to Trevor Libscombe, 1 September 1989, RG 1, Series II, Subseries I, Box 7, Folder 33, Covenant House Archives; Covenant House Alaska Annual Report, 1989, RG 1, Series II, Subseries I, Box 7, Folder 32, Covenant House Archives; Covenant House *Annual Report,* 1989, Covenant House Archives. For the 1986–87 fiscal year, Covenant House's New York shelter reported that 86 percent of its children were African American or Hispanic, while the figure for Houston stood at 51 percent. Fort Lauderdale constituted another notable exception: seventy-seven percent of the children using that facility identified themselves as white. Covenant House, *Annual Report,* 1987, Covenant House Archives.

15. Fred Ali to Brenda Moscarella, 31 January 1988, RG 1, Series II, Subseries I, Box 7, Folder 20; Executive Director Report Minutes Book, 1988–97, RG 1, Series I, Box 7, Folder 25; Board of Directors, 1988–95, RG 1, Series II, Subseries I, Box 7, Folder 21; Legal 1988–89, RG 1, Series II, Subseries I, Box 7, Folder 28; Jim Caldarola to Bruce Ritter, 14 February 1989, RG 1, Series II, Subseries I, Box 7, Folder 23, Covenant House Archives. Charles Wohlforth, "She Left the Street and Found a Family," *Anchorage Daily News,* 23 December 1990, p. A1; Katya Simpson, "House Aids 300 Youths Each Month," *Tundra Times,* 31 July 1989.

16. Bruce Ritter to Sandy Hagan, 25 February 1982, RG 1, Series II, Subseries VI, Box 47, Folder 8, Covenant House Archives. This document contains an excellent summary of the early negotiations concerning Fort Lauderdale, and the entire file provides a good reconstruction of the early development.

17. Paul S. George, "Where the Boys Were," *South Florida History Magazine*, 1991:1, pp. 5–8; "Permanent Vacation," *Playboy*, 30:8, August 1983, pp. 74–79.

18. Estella May Moriarty to Bruce Ritter, 14 October 1982, RG 1, Series II, Subseries VI, Box 47, Folder 9, Covenant House Archives; "Fort Lauderdale Needs Assessment," 1982, RG 1, Series II, Subseries VI, Box 47, Folder 9, Covenant House Archives.

19. Bruce Ritter, *Covenant House: Lifeline to the Street* (New York: Doubleday, 1987), pp. 170–73.

20. "FBR Visit to Fort Lauderdale, 5–12/13–83," and Joseph Donnelly to Bruce Ritter, James Kelly, and Sandra Hagan, 20 June 1983, RG 1, Series II, Subseries VI, Box 47, Folder 10, Covenant House Archives; Robert O. Cox to Bruce Ritter, 23 February 1984, RG 1, Series II, Subseries VI, Box 47, Folder 11, Covenant House Archives; Paul Shannon, "Teen Shelter Opens with Little Fanfare," *Miami Herald*, 29 September 1985. Other problems also surfaced in Fort Lauderdale concerning the purchase of the Sand Castle Motel when the owner died and his son proved less cooperative with Covenant House. Eventually, these issues were negotiated and successfully resolved.

21. Kathy Saunders, "Covenant House Florida Changes Executive Directors: Nancy Matthews Was First Head of Fort Lauderdale Program," *Florida Catholic*, 12 June 1997; Margo Harakas, "Amen, Covenant," *Fort Lauderdale Sun Sentinel*, 29 May 1997, p. 1E; "Neighborhood Covenant," *Miami Herald*, 27 September 1985; Covenant House, *Annual Report* 1989, p. 26.

22. Minutes of Meetings of the Board of Directors, 18 March 1982, 15 October 1982, and 30 June 1983, Covenant House Archives; "Why Under 21-Boston?," n.d., RG 1, Series II, Subseries II, Covenant House Archives; Jean Dietz, "Major Youth Shelter Planned for Boston," *Boston Globe*, 16 January 1983, p. 21. Ritter had hoped to open an Under 21 facility in Los Angeles as early as 1980, but Timothy Cardinal Manning and Roger Cardinal Mahoney opposed his efforts both on philosophical grounds and owing to potential conflicts with existing Catholic Charities operations. Covenant House began operating in Los Angeles only after independently securing a $5 million grant from the Burton G. Bettingen Foundation for this purpose in 1988. RG 1, Series II, Subseries III, Box 8, Folders 6, 27, and 28, Covenant House Archives.

23. Jean Dietz, "Boston Businessmen Upset over Plan for Youth Shelter," *Boston Globe*, 6 February 1983, p. 21.

24. Joseph Nese, "Memorandum for Board of Directors, Under 21–Boston," 24 February 1983, RG 1, Series II, Subseries II, Box 7, Folder 36, Covenant House Archives.

25. Thomas J. Reese, *Archbishop: Inside the Power Structure of the American Catholic Church* (New York: Harper & Row, 1989), p. 73; Charles M. Sennott, *Broken Covenant* (New York: Simon and Shuster, 1992), pp. 138–44; Jean Dietz, "Major Youth Shelter Planned for Boston," *Boston Globe*, 16 January 1983, p. 21; Thomas J. Martorelli, Letter to the Editor, "Cardinal Medeiros Ignored Pleas from Bridge," *Boston Globe*, 13 February 1983; Celine Gallo to James R. Kelly, "Memo Concerning Negative Publicity in Boston," 24 February 1983, RG 1, Series II, Subseries II, Box 7, Folder 36, Covenant House Archives.

26. Jean Dietz, "Major Youth Shelter Planned for Boston," *Boston Globe*, 16 January 1983, p. 21; "Why Under 21–Boston," RG 1, Series II, Subseries II, Box 7, Folder 40, Covenant House Archives.

27. Sennott, *Broken Covenant*, pp. 140–41; Minutes of Meetings of the Board of Directors of Under 21 Boston, Inc., 28 February 1983 and 13 July 1983; Draft Statement of Understanding Between Bruce Ritter and Bernard Law, 30 August 1984; Bruce Ritter to Paul Hellmuth, 12 October 1984, RG 1, Series II, Subseries II, Box 7, Folder 36, Covenant House Archives; Minutes of Meeting of the Board of Directors, 17 April 1985, Covenant House Archives.

28. Bruce J. Henry, Memo Re: Recidivism, 5 November 1985; "An In-Depth Study of Three Recidivists," RG 1, Series VIII, Box 31, Folder 24, Covenant House Archives. When Covenant House staff discharged residents for inappropriate actions, they provided them with cards indicating the amount of time that they were required to stay away from the facility. The duration varied according to the offense ranging, for example, from thirty days for failing to follow one's plan, to sixty days for being away without leave, to permanent for initiating violence or using forbidden substances. In Tim's case, he once received a permanent card, banning him from the facility, for carrying a knife on the premises. He successfully appealed this discharge to Covenant House's ombudsperson, however, and returned to the shelter four months later.

29. Gerry Stuhlman to Sr. Alicia Damien, "Special Report," 1 August 1986, RG 1, Series VIII, Box 30, Folder 19, Covenant House Archives.

30. Oral History Interview with David Gregorio by Amy Surak, 12 April 2000, Covenant House Archives.

31. "Rights of Passage Program Narrative," December 1985, Subject Files; "Rights of Passage: Myth, Rituals, and Symbols," May 1988, RG 1, Series VIII, Box 32, Folder 11; Patrick Kennedy to Richard Schmeelk, 2 March 1987, RG 8, Box 1, Folder 28, Covenant House Archives.

32. Minutes of Meetings of the Board of Directors, 26 April 1984, 28 June 1984, Covenant House Archives; Minutes of Meetings of the Advisory Committee of the Rights of Passage Program, 19 August 1985, 6 November 1985, RG 1, Series VIII, Box 32, Folder 3, Covenant House Archives; "Rights of Passage Fifteen Month Report, 3/26/86–7/15/87," RG 1, Series VIII, Box 32, Folder 11, Covenant House Archives; "After Graduating from the Streets, Homeless Youths Find Better School," *New York Times*, 9 August 1987; "Helping Dropouts Drop In," *Newsweek*, 3 August 1987.

33. Oral History Interview with Bruce Henry by Amy Surak, 6 November 2000, Covenant House Archives.

34. Oral History Interview with David Gregorio by Surak, 12 April 2000, Covenant House Archives.

35. "Rights of Passage Fifteenth Month Report, 3/26–86–7/15/87," RG 1, Series VIII, Box 32, Folder 11, Covenant House Archives; "Report to the Board of Directors," March 1987, RG 1, Series I, Box 7, Folder 11, Covenant House Archives.

36. "Off the Streets Program Expansion Proposal," 1986, RG 8, Box 1, Folder 19, Covenant House Archives; Minutes of Meetings of the Board of Directors, 25 September 1986, 20 January 1987, and 14 September 1989, Covenant House Archives; Bob Drogin, "Teams in Van Cruise N.Y. to Aid Runaways," *Los Angeles Times*, 26 December 1986, p. 1; Catherine Hazard, "Helping Kids off the Streets," *US*, 23 February 1987, p. 71; Bob Herbert, "Hell on Wheels in Downtown Parking Lot," *New York Daily News*, 17 May 1988, p. 12; "Nobody Cared About Them . . ." unidentified

newspaper clipping, ca. August 1987, "Outreach Van" subject file, Covenant House Archives.

37. Minutes of Meetings of the Board of Directors, 20 January 1987, 16 July 1987, 21 January 1988, 29 September 1988, Covenant House Archives; "Politicians Join Ad Council in Launch of Nineline Ads," *Adweek*, 4 September 1989, p. 8; "Lives on the Line," *ROLM Customer*, January 1991; Nick Jesdanun, "Nineline Walks the Fine Line with Kids," *Newsday*, 18 August 1989; Patricia Connors, with Dorianne Perrucci, *Runaways: Coping at Home and on the Street* (New York: Rosen, 1989), contains a series of stories drawn from Nineline telephone calls and compiled by the director of the program. Only one of the six Public Service Announcements from 1989, "Lost Girl # 2," featured a nonwhite character. Covenant House's annual reports from the late 1980s also invariably featured blonde-haired boys on the cover.

38. Richard Meislin, "Sexual Portrayals Using Children Legal Unless Obscene, Court Rules," *New York Times*, 13 May 1981, p. 1.

39. An interesting sketch of Harold Fahringer appears in the State University of New York, University of Buffalo, *UB Today: University of Buffalo's Online Alumni Magazine*, Winter 1997, http://www.buffalo.edu/UBT/UBT-archives/05_ubtw97/profile3.html (9 January 2004).

40. Bruce Ritter, *Covenant House: Lifeline to the Street*, pp. 119–21, 148–52; Linda Greenhouse, "Justices Uphold Barring Children in Pornography," *New York Times*, 3 July 1982, p. 1; David Marglick, "Pornography Ruling: Court's Decision Sparks Little Outcry: Other Laws Cover Proscribed Activity," *New York Times*, 3 July 1982, p. 36.

41. Gregory A. Loken, "Institute for Youth Advocacy: A Proposal," 11 June 1982, RG 1, Series V, Box 24, Folder 21, Covenant House Archives; Minutes of Meetings of the Board of Directors, 30 June 1983, 17 April 1985, and 30 June 1988, Covenant House Archives; "Annual Report on Outreach," Covenant House *Annual Report*, 1983, pp. 20–21, Covenant House Archives; Charles M. Sennott, *Broken Covenant* (New York: Simon & Schuster, 1992), pp. 195–96.

42. Peter Steinfels, "Cardinal O'Connor, 80, Dies: Forceful Voice for Vatican," *New York Times*, 4 May 2000, p. 1, presents a useful summary of the cardinal's tenure in New York City.

43. Archdiocese of New York, "Fact Sheet on Executive Order 50 and the Church-City Controversy on Sexual Orientation," 1985, RG 1, Series VIII, Box 30, Folder 20, Covenant House Archives; Joyce Purnick, "O'Connor Says He Might Reject City's Financing," *New York Times*, 14 December 1984, p. 1:5. The cardinal and the mayor outlined their perspectives on the issue in: John Cardinal O'Connor and Mayor Edward I. Koch, *His Eminence and Hizzoner: A Candid Exchange* (New York: William Morrow, 1989), pp. 93–130. The *New York Daily News*'s banner front-page headline on 17 June 1984 proclaimed in all capital letters: "O'CONNOR NIXES GAY RIGHTS ORDER," thus setting the tone for much subsequent tabloid coverage. In fact, O'Connor and his colitigants had reached an agreement with the city to resolve their disagreement concerning the executive order by appealing to the courts.

44. Merrick T. Rossein to Ronald L. Williams, 15 April 1985, and Russell Bryant to Ed Burns, 9 May 1985, RG 8, Box 1, Folder 9, Covenant House Archives; Joyce Purnick, "New York Studying the Hiring Practices of Catholic Agencies," *New York Times*, 1 June 1985, p. 1.

45. Bruce Ritter, "Confidential Memo: Prepared in Connection with Litigation," 24 June 1985, and Lawrence Cusack to Bruce Ritter, 25 June 1985, RG 1, Series VIII, Box 30, Folder 20, Covenant House Archives; Joyce Purnick, "Court Overrules Order by Koch on Sexual Bias," *New York Times*, 29 June 1985.

46. Minutes of Meetings of the Board of Directors, 15 November 1984 and 30 January 1985, Covenant House Archives; Toby Axelrod, "Wary Eye Cast at Covenant's New House," *Chelsea Clinton News*, 20–26 September 1984, p. 3; Owen Moritz, "Swap of the Homeless?," *New York Daily News*, 11 October 1984, p. 12; "Plan to Buy Times Square Hotel Prompts Debate," *New York Times*, 14 October 1984, p. 41; Edward I. Koch to Bruce Ritter, 16 October 1984, and Bruce Ritter to Edward I. Koch, 13 November 1984, RG 1, Series VI, Box 29, Folder 9, Covenant House Archives.

47. Minutes of Meetings of the Board of Directors, 24 June 1986, 20 January 1987, and 23 April 1987, Covenant House Archives; George W. Goodman, "City Limiting S.R.O. Conversions," *New York Times*, 23 December 1984, Sec. VIII, p. 2:1; Alan Finder, "S.R.O. Tenants Lose Homes Despite Ban on Conversions," *New York Times*, 22 January 1987, p. 1:1; Alan Finder, "Council Passes Bill on S.R.O. Hotel Conversions," *New York Times*, 23 January 1987, Sect. II, p. 5:6. The initial eighteen-month moratorium was subsequently extended for six months, through January 1987. At that point, the city council passed a new five-year moratorium on SRO conversions, which did allow property holders to convert their units if they paid a fee of $45,000 per unit to the city. In 1989, however, the New York State Court of Appeals declared the moratorium unconstitutional, declaring that the law infringed on owners' rights to determine the use of their property. The United States Supreme Court subsequently refused to hear the city's argument, and the state court of appeals decision proved final.

48. Minutes of Meetings of the Board of Directors, 24 June 1986, 20 January 1987, 23 April 1987, 21 January 1988, 30 June 1988, and 19 January 1989, Covenant House Archives; Beverly Cheuvront, "Heartbreak Hotel," *City Limits* October 1987, pp. 12–15; "Motel Sale to Fund Covenant House Program," *Catholic New York*, 7 January 1988; Winston Williams, "Investment Sours for a Times Sq. Shelter," *New York Times*, 17 March 1987, p. B1; Michael Powell, "New Life for Times Square Hotel," *Newsday*, 28 January 1991; "The Times Square Test: Promising Experiment in an Old Hotel," *New York Times*, 15 November 1992. Additional negative publicity stemmed from the fact that financing for the venture had been arranged by Charles H. Keating Jr., the Phoenix financier who was both a friend of Ritter and a substantial supporter of Covenant House. Keating's Lincoln Savings and Loan Association remained at the center of a financial scandal that engulfed the savings industry during the late 1980s, and he himself became a visible symbol for speculative irresponsibility and congressional influence-peddling by 1989. The Times Square Hotel developed in interesting ways after Covenant House finally divested itself of the property. Since 1991, the hotel has been owned by a nonprofit corporation, Common Ground Community Development, that has renovated the building and transformed it into a large SRO with 650 efficiency units. Residents include a mixed population that consists of the working poor, former mental patients, and people with special medical needs. Oral History Interview with Robert Cardany by Amy Surak, 8 November 1999, Covenant House Archives.

49. Bruce Ritter to John Cardinal O'Connor, 30 September 1987, RG 1, Series VIII, Box 31, Folder 10, Covenant House Archives; Barbara Lippman, "It Wasn't in Architect's Original Design," *New York Daily News*, 16 September 1987; "On West 17th, A Little Bit More of West 17th," *New York Times*, 11 August 1996.

50. Mary Sgammato to Ron Williams, 24 August 1987, in "Special Meeting of Covenant House Board of Directors" packet, 28 August 1987, RG 1, Series VIII, Box 31, Folder 9, Covenant House Archives; Barbara Lippman, "How Fight Began," *New York Daily News*, 4 October 1987; Al Amateau, "Chelsea Shelter Opposition Grows," *Chelsea Clinton News*, 23–29 July 1987, p. 1; Jere Hester, "Dinkins Criticizes Plan for Shelter in Chelsea," *Chelsea Clinton News*, 13–19 August 1987, p. 1; Al Amateau, "Unusual Alliance Forms in Chelsea over Shelter Plan," *Chelsea Clinton News*, 20–26 August 1987, p. 1.

51. Special Meeting of Covenant House Board of Directors, 28 August 1987, RG 1, Series VIII, Box 31, Folder 9, Covenant House Archives.

52. Elizabeth Kolbert, "City, Seeking Space for Prisoners, Will Condemn Chelsea Building," *New York Times*, 16 September 1987; Marcia Kramer and Larry Sutton, "City Vows to Throw Away the Key," *New York Daily News*, 16 September 1987; Patricia Hurtado, "Koch, Priest in 'Maritime' Battle," *New York Newsday*, 16 September 1987; Jane McCarthy, "City Raids Priest's Hotel," *New York Post*, 18 September 1987; Sam Howe Verhovek, "Koch and Priest Trade Barbs in Battle for a Chelsea Building," *New York Times*, 23 September 1987; Robert Carroll, "Ritter Will Fight On: Ed's No Pushover, Either," *New York Daily News*, 23 September 1987, p. 21; "Holy War! Times Square Priest Rips Koch," *New York Post*, 23 September 1987, p. 1; Bob Herbert, "The Mayor Steps on a Helping Hand," *New York Daily News*, 24 September 1987, p. 12; Alan Bautzer, "Koch, Priest Battle for NMU Center," *West Side Spirit*, 28 September 1987.

53. "N.M.U. Editorial," *Westsider*, 17–23 September 1987, p. 4; Tracey Regan, "Taking a Look at Covenant," *Chelsea Clinton News*, 1–7 October 1987, p. 1; William Murphy, "Koch Surrenders in Battle over Chelsea Building," *New York Newsday*, 27 October 1987, p. 7; Owen Fitzgerald and Don Gentile, "Mayor Gives In to Ritter," *New York Daily News*, 27 October 1987; Todd S. Purdum, "Koch and Victorious Priest Declare Peace," *New York Times*, 14 October 1988; Mary Cantwell, "These Kids Aren't Going To Be Addicts," *New York Times*, 19 November 1988. Covenant House News Release, 13 October 1988, and Bruce Ritter to Edward I. Koch, 14 October 1988, RG 1, Series VI, Box 29, Folder 9, Covenant House Archives. Koch also reached into his pocket and contributed an additional ten dollars to Covenant House at the dedication ceremony, much to the delight of the assembled press corps.

54. Oral History Interview with James Harnett by Surak, 6 September 2001; Oral History Interview with Bruce Henry by Surak, 6 November 2000; Oral History Interview with Robert Cardany by Surak, 23 September 1999. Ralph Pfeiffer, the retired chairman of the IBM World Trade Corporation, became chair of the board in 1989 and attempted to inaugurate a formal long-range planning process. His plan relied on IBM consultants and required broad participation across the organization. Much board activity in 1989 involved developing a strategic plan. Minutes of Meetings of the Board of Directors, 25 September 1986, 30 June 1988, 25 April 1989, 14 September 1989, 21 November 1989, Covenant House Archives.

Chapter 7

1. Rev. Bruce Ritter Press Conference, Videotape, 14 December 1989, RG 2, Series IV, Box 12, Item 9; "Statement from Fr. Bruce Ritter, OFM Conventual," 6 February 1990, RG 1, Series IX, Box 34, Folder 14; Bruce Ritter, "Resignation," 27 February 1990, RG 1, Series IX, Box 33, Folder 12, Covenant House Archives.

2. Charles M. Sennott, "DA Probing Rev. Ritter," *New York Post*, 12 December 1989, p. 7. The story in the following pages has been reconstructed from a variety of sources, including extensive press coverage. The most useful documents included Charles M. Sennott, *Broken Covenant* (New York: Simon & Schuster, 1992), pp. 215–25; Gabriel Rotello, "Cover Up House? Kevin Kite Talks about His Relationship with Father Bruce Ritter and Covenant House," *Outweek*, 21 January 1990; Minutes of Special Meeting of the Covenant House Board of Directors, 11 December 1989, Covenant House Archives; Philip Boudreau to Greg Loken, 8 December 1989, and Kerry Jacobsen, "Memo Regarding Greg Hutcherson," 8 December 1989, RG 1, Series IX, Box 34, Folder 2, Covenant House Archives. Each Covenant House facility contained an ombudsman who could serve as an advocate for youths who wanted to appeal dismissals from the facility or felt that they needed some form of intervention with administrators, counselors, and social workers.

3. Warner had identified himself as "Greg Hutcherson, of Gainesville, Texas" when he arrived at the crisis center in New Orleans. Ritter felt that Hutcherson needed a new identity in order to protect him from organized crime elements. He initially introduced the young man to staff members in New York as his nephew, "Tim Wallace." When Ritter's niece discovered this and objected, the founder instructed his staff to procure another new identity for the young man, and they eventually settled on the name Tim Warner. For convenience sake, he is referred to as Tim Warner throughout the text.

4. Minutes of Meeting of the Board of Directors, 11 December 1989, Covenant House Archives. Covenant House retained Stanley S. Arkin as special counsel to represent Ritter in possible criminal matters; named Thomas Barr of Cravath, Swaine, and Moore as special counsel for the organization; and instructed its auditors, Deloitte and Touche, to review all relevant accounts. Oral History Interview with James Harnett by Amy Surak, 6 September 2001, Covenant House Archives.

5. Minutes of Meeting of the Board of Directors, 11 December 1989, Covenant House Archives; Ralph Blumenthal, "Image of Covenant House Eroded by Sex Charges," *New York Times*, 6 February 1990, p. 1. Local evening news reports on 13 December heavily covered the Peter Max auction, stationing reporters in the studio and obtaining interviews with Peter Max, such celebrity participants as Jerry Stiller, corporate executives and Covenant House board members, and staff. Ritter's absence from the event appeared newsworthy to the local broadcasters. See the videotape newscasts in RG 2, Series IV, Box 13, Item 1, Covenant House Archives.

6. Edwin Diamond, "Breaking a Covenant?: The Post's Ritter Probe," *New York*, 8 January 1990, pp. 16–17; Charles M. Sennott, "DA Probing Rev. Ritter," *New York Post*, 12 December 1989, p. 7; Mike Pearl and Charles M. Sennott, "Second Youth Linked to Free Ride at Covenant," *New York Post*, 13 December 1989, p. 2; Charles M. Sennott and Mike Pearl, "Ritter 'Witness' Tells the Post About Taping," *New York*

Post, 14 December 1989, p. 5; Charles M. Sennott, "Experts Question Ritter's Secret Program," *New York Post*, 15 December 1989.

7. Bill Reel, "Father Bruce, I'm Still in Your Corner," *New York Daily News*, 14 December 1989; Ronald Sullivan, "Covenant House Under Scrutiny," *New York Times*, 14 December 1989, p. B5; Patrick Clark and Don Singleton, "Ritter 'Cooperating' but DA Says Probe in 'Earliest Stages'," *New York Daily News*, 14 December 1989, p. 5; Don Singleton, "It Just Isn't So, Ritter Says of Sex Allegations," *New York Daily News*, 15 December 1989, p. 3; Ronald Sullivan, "Ritter Denies Sex Allegations on Covenant House," *New York Times*, 15 December 1989. Harnett's comments, along with Morgenthau's statement, can be found on various local newscasts. See RG 2, Series IV, Box 13, Item 1, Covenant House Archives.

8. Rev. Bruce Ritter Press Conference, Videotape, 14 December 1989, RG 2, Series IV, Box 12, Item 9; "Vatican AIDS Meeting Hears O'Connor Assail Condom Use," *New York Times*, 14 November 1989, p. A10:3; "Pope Asks Global AIDS Effort," *New York Times*, 16 November 1989, p. 10:3; Jason DeParle, "111 Held in St. Patrick's AIDS Protest," *New York Times*, 11 December 1989, p. B3; Todd S. Purdum, "Cardinal Says He Won't Yield to Protests," *New York Times*, 12 December 1989, p. B3:1.

9. Rev. Bruce Ritter Press Conference, Videotape, 14 December 1989, RG 2, Series IV, Box 12, Item 9. For reaction to the press conference, see Don Singleton, "It Just Isn't So, Ritter Says of Sex Allegations," *New York Daily News*, 15 December 1989, p. 3; Ronald Sullivan, "Ritter Denies Sex Allegations on Covenant House," *New York Times*, 15 December 1989; Charles Sennott, Bill Hoffmann, Mike Pearl, and Esther Pessin, "I Made Mistake in Judgment–Ritter," *New York Post*, 15 December 1989, p. 4. Local news broadcasts also proved positive: New York's CBS affiliate, in a typical account, informed viewers that Ritter "broke the silence" on 15 December, as "the priest came armed with proof to back [his account] up," facing the cameras and "handling himself in a confident manner." Covenant House officials felt so pleased with the outcome of the press conference that they provided free video copies to donors upon request. Videotape newscasts are available in RG 2, Series IV, Box 13, Item 1, Covenant House Archives. Robert Cardany, the Covenant House treasurer, combed the agency's accounts and certified that the money spent on Warner actually totaled $9,793.33, an amount that implied certitude and exactitude.

10. Charles Sennott, *Broken Covenant*, pp. 288–89; Don Singleton, "My Son Lies, Says Father in Ritter Case," *New York Daily News*, 21 December 1989; M. A. Farber, "Priest's Accuser Is Called Liar by His Father," *New York Times*, 21 December 1989. The Ritter quotation, as well as the Alton Kite interview and newscasters' judgments, can be found in RG 2, Series IV, Box 13, Item 1, Covenant House Archives.

11. Donna Santarsiero to Ralph Pfeiffer, 5 March 1990, RG 1, Series IX, Box 33, Folder 21; Bruce Ritter Letter to Donors, 21 December 1989, RG 1, Series IX, Box 33, Folder 21; Bruce Ritter's interviews are contained in RG 2, Series IV, Box 13, Item 1, Covenant House Archives.

12. James Harnett, quoted in Minutes of Meeting of the Board of Directors, 14 February 1990, Covenant House Archives. *New York Times*, 9 January 1990; A. M. Rosenthal, "Passage from Ezekiel," *New York Times*, 11 January 1990, p. A23. Television newscasts can be found in RG 2, Series IV, Box 13, Item 1, Covenant House Archives.

13. Philip Nobile, "The Secret Life of Father Ritter," *Village Voice*, 30 January 1990, pp. 25–32. Nobile's account of the Meese Commission, which contains extensive material concerning Ritter's participation, was published as Philip Nobile and Eric Nadler, *United States of America vs. Sex: How the Meese Commission Lied About Pornography* (New York: Minotaur, 1986).

14. Nobile, "The Secret Life of Father Ritter"; Dennis Duggan, "New Ritter Allegations Old Trash," *New York Newsday*, 24 January 1990, p. 4. Philip Nobile, appearing on "Jack Cafferty's Newsline," FOX TV program videotape, RG 2, Series IV, Box 13, Item 1, Covenant House Archives. Nobile and Duggan appeared on several local television news shows, debating each other concerning the Ritter controversy and carrying on their war of words in print during this period. Nobile's article included a sidebar written by Allan Solomon titled "Censoring Safe Sex?" that focused on Covenant House's relationship with gay activists and claiming that the agency exhibited some hostility to openly gay residents. The "forensic fit" described by Nobile focused on the nature of the sexual activity: according to Kite and Melican, it typically began with a dinner invitation, followed by hugging, mutual masturbation, occasional oral intercourse, and silence afterward.

15. The videotape newscasts are contained in RG 2, Series IV, Box 13, Item 1, Covenant House Archives. The *Village Voice's* cover photo became an iconic representation of the crisis and also appeared on the book jacket of Charles Sennott's *Broken Covenant*. Gabriel Rotello, "Cover Up House? Kevin Kite Talks About His Relationship with Father Bruce Ritter and Covenant House," *Outweek*, 21 January 1990, pp. 39–45. Oral History Interview with James Harnett by Surak, 6 September 2001, Covenant House Archives, discusses the agency's efforts to cultivate the *New York Times*. The *Times* article appeared as Ralph Blumenthal et al., "Image of Covenant House Is Eroded by Sex Charges," *New York Times*, 6 February 1990, p. 1.

16. Ralph Blumenthal et al., "Image of Covenant House Is Eroded by Sex Charges," *New York Times*, 6 February 1990, p. 1. Newscasters now descended on Bassile's home in Ithaca, New York, where he worked at a center for the disabled. He appeared serious, soft spoken, and low key during the telecasts, projecting an image of someone who had been hurt and damaged by his past, in sharp contrast to the confident self-assurance of Kevin Lee Kite. See the newscasts RG 2, Series IV, Box 13, Item 1, Covenant House Archives.

17. Charles M. Sennott, "Ritter Youth Was Given Dead Boy's ID," *New York Post*, 5 February 1990, p. 7; Charles M. Sennott, "Covenant: We Gave Ex-Hooker Dead Boy's ID," *New York Post*, 6 February 1990, p. 6; Betty Warner's comments were contained in newscasts available in RG 2, Series IV, Box 13, Item 1, Covenant House Archives. Gregory A. Loken to Frank Macchiarola, 14 February 1990, RG 1, Series IX, Box 34, Folder 5, Covenant House Archives. Loken, who headed the Institute for Youth Advocacy, had played the principal role, under Ritter's direction, in obtaining the baptismal certificate for Kite.

18. "Statement from Fr. Bruce Ritter, OFM Conventual," 6 February 1990, RG 1, Series IX, Box 34, Folder 14, Covenant House Archives; Charles M. Sennott, "Ritter Ousted," *New York Post*, 7 February 1990; Minutes of Meeting of the Board of Directors, 6 February 1990, Covenant House Archives. A fourth sexual allegation, by a thirty-three-year-old former Covenant House resident named Paul Johnson, also

surfaced in the *New York Post* on 7 February. Johnson claimed to have participated in a six-year affair with Bruce Ritter that began in 1975, and he also related some fantastic stories concerning money laundering, but the young man's own criminal background, which included credit card fraud, corporate malfeasance, and parole violations, damaged his credibility. See Charles M. Sennott, "Fourth Sex Charge in Priest's Scandal," *New York Post*, 7 February 1990, p. 5.

19. Minutes of Meetings of the Board of Directors, 6 February 1990 and 14 February 1990, Covenant House Archives. Charles M. Sennott, *Broken Covenant*, pp. 303–13, discusses reactions to Macchiarola's administration. The quote is from Murray Weiss and Joe Nicholson, "New Covenant House Scandal," *New York Post*, 1 March 1990.

20. No minutes exist for this pivotal board meeting. The sequence of events has been reconstructed from the following: Minutes of Meetings of the Board of Directors, 7 March 1990, 14 March 1990, 24 March 1990; James Barron, "Ritter and Successor Quit Covenant House Posts," *New York Times*, 28 February 1990, p. 1; "Text of Statement by Father Ritter," *New York Times*, 28 February 1990, p. 22; Kevin McCoy, "Ritter Exits in Sorrow; Macchiarola Quits In Uproar," *New York Daily News*, 28 February 1990, p. 3; Michael Powell, "Aftermath Salvos Fly," *New York Newsday*, 1 March 1990, p. 5; Murray Kempton, "House Must Mend Some Errant Ways," *New York Newsday*, 1 March 1990, p. 5; Dennis Duggan, "Founder Casts Giant Shadow over Shelter," *New York Newsday*, 1 March 1990, p. 5; Andy Court, "Frank, Incensed: Why Frank Macchiarola Got Tossed out of Covenant House," Scandal subject file, Covenant House Archives.

21. Joe Nicholson and Esther Pessin, "Morgenthau Clears Father Bruce," *New York Post*, 1 March 1990, p. 5; Timothy Clifford and Paul Moses, "DA Concludes Ritter Probe: No Charges Against Priest," *New York Newsday*, p. 5; Minutes of Meetings of the Board of Directors, 7 March 1990, 14 March 1990, 24 March 1990, 26 March 1990, Covenant House Archives; "Statement of the Oversight Committee of Covenant House," A Report to the Board of Directors and the Oversight Committee of Covenant House," 3 August 1990, Covenant House Archives. The Oversight Committee was chaired by William Ellinghaus, the former president of American Telephone and Telegraph, and also consisted of Rabbi Marc Tanenbaum, Rev. Theodore M. Hesburgh, Cyrus Vance, and Paul Volcker. The Kroll Associates investigation operated under the direction of Cravath, Swaine, and Moore, the prominent New York City law firm.

22. Memorandum from Jim Harnett to All Staff, 5 March 1990, RG 1, Series IX, Box 33, Folder 21, Covenant House Archives. The board ratified the termination of the safe house program and the policy concerning allegations of misconduct at its 7 March meeting. Other new policy reforms at the board level concerned conflict of interest statements, competitive bidding practices, prohibitions on employing relatives, approving expenditures above a certain threshold, and new financial controls. See RG 1, Series IX, Box 33, Folder 12, Covenant House Archives; and Minutes of Meetings of the Board of Directors, 7 March 1990, 14 March 1990, 24 March 1990, and 26 March 1990, Covenant House Archives.

23. Ralph Blumenthal with M. A. Farber, "A $1 Million Fund Tapped by Ritter to Make 4 Loans," *New York Times*, 6 March 1990, p. 1. The most coherent description

of the Franciscan Charitable Trust is contained in "A Report to the Board of Directors and the Oversight Committee of Covenant House," 3 August 1990, pp. 19–24, Covenant House Archives. The arrangement between the Franciscans and Ritter, it should be noted, was not unique, though uncommon.

24. "A Report to the Board of Directors and the Oversight Committee of Covenant House," 3 August 1990, pp. 21–24, 25–26. Pfeiffer's quote can be found in M. A. Farber, "O'Connor Is Moving to Clear Up 'Mess' at Covenant House," *New York Times*, 10 March 1990, p. 1. Burns's quote can be found in Ralph Blumenthal with M. A. Farber, "A $1 Million Fund Tapped by Ritter to Make 4 Loans," *New York Times*, 6 March 1990, p. 1. Minutes of Meeting of the Board of Directors, 14 March 1990 and 24 March 1990, Covenant House Archives. Oral History Interview with Robert Cardany by Amy Surak, 8 November 1999, Covenant House Archives. As a result of the revelations concerning the fact that they had received loans from the trust, James T. Kennedy and James Maguire both resigned from the board of directors. The issue concerning loans to staff members also appears complex. Not-for-profit corporations are not permitted to make loans to officers or directors, though such educational not-for-profit corporations as colleges and universities may do so. Ritter received a $25,000 salary advance in July 1989 that, as interpreted under section 716 of the New York Not-for-Profit Law, would constitute an illegal loan. Covenant House also provided a $100,000 housing loan to one senior administrator and a $60,000 relocation loan to another. Neither administrator was an officer of Covenant House, and the loans thus appeared not to violate the state statute. Still, the loans had not been brought to the attention of the board and once again at least presented an appearance of impropriety. Edmund Burns resigned his position as the corporate counsel in 1990 as a result of all of these issues involving loans and the manner in which the trust functioned. Covenant House engaged Cravath, Swaine, and Moore, one of the largest and most powerful firms in New York City, to serve as its attorneys on a pro bono basis thereafter.

25. Michael Powell, "Aftermath Salvos Fly," *New York Newsday*, 1 March 1990, p. 5; Rose Marie Arce and Michael Powell, "Covenant House Covered Up Links to Murdered Client," *New York Newsday*, 13 March 1990, p. 3; Gabriel Rotello, "The Broken Covenant," *Outweek*, 28 March 1990, pp. 42–47, 53. The fact that the murdered youth had appeared in a publicity photograph in Covenant House's 1989 annual report appeared to add credibility to the story initially.

26. James Harnett to Robert Maguire, Memo Re: Accusations and Allegations Concerning Covenant House Officials, 5 March 1990, RG 1, Series IX, Box 33, Folder 21, Covenant House Archives, conveniently summarizes the allegations. See also "A Report to the Board of Directors and the Oversight Committee of Covenant House," 3 August 1990, pp. 31–33, which dismissed all of the allegations concerning the transvestite murder and cover-up, the call-boy ring, and the contra support as lacking any evidentiary basis. For representative news articles, see Kevin McCoy, "Cov House 'Violent,' 'Haphazard': Study Tells of Crack Fights," *New York Daily News*, 9 March 1990, p. 7; Rose Marie Arce and Michael Powell, "Covenant House Program Rife with Drugs, Violence," *New York Newsday*, 14 March 1990, p. 2; Russell W. Baker, "The McDonald's of Youth Services," *Village Voice*, 20 March 1990, pp. 27–31; Richard

Johnson, "Shocker at Covenant House Party," *New York Post*, 12 June 1990, p. 6. The Contra allegations first appeared on CBS-TV's "Hard Copy," 14 and 15 February 1990. See the videotape collection in RG 2, Series IV, Box 13, Item 11, as well as the media coverage in Box 14, Item 5, Covenant House Archives.

27. William Treanor, "Rebuild, Don't Fix, Covenant House," *New York Times*, 10 March 1990, p. 25; William Treanor, "Covenant House's Misguided Approach to Youth Work," *Christian Science Monitor*, 28 March 1990. Russell W. Baker, "The McDonald's of Youth Services," *Village Voice*, 20 March 1990, pp. 30–31, relies heavily on MacNeil. Koch's comments can be found on videotape in RG 2, Series IV, Box 14, Item 10; Rosanne Haggerty Redmond and Mark Redmond, "The Paradoxes of Covenant House: Mythmaking & Livesaving," *Commonweal*, 18 May 1990, pp. 311–16, provides an interesting perspective on the organization from two former community members who grew disillusioned with the founder and the work over the course of their tenure.

28. Anne Donahue to Hugh Dickson Druary and Ralph Pfeiffer, 9 March 1990, RG 1, Series II, Subseries III, Box 8, Folder 17, Covenant House Archives.

29. Emilyn DuHamel Brower to Ralph Pfeiffer, 25 April 1990, "Memorandum Re: Comment Card Response to Date," RG 1, Series IX, Box 34, Folder 9, Covenant House Archives; Walter Kelly to James Harnett, 16 January 1990, RG 1, Series IX, Box 33, Folder 21, Covenant House Archives.

30. M. A. Farber, "O'Connor Is Moving to Clear Up 'Mess' at Covenant House," *New York Times*, 10 March 1990, p. 1; Joe Nicholson and Linda Stevens, "O'Connor Taps 2 Priests to Head Covenant," *New York Post*, 24 March 1990, p. 3; Linda Stevens, "O'Connor: Covenant Chiefs Their Own Men," *New York Post*, 26 March 1990; John Cardinal O'Connor to Ralph Pfeiffer, 12 March 1990, RG 1, Series IX, Box 33, Folder 21; Minutes of Meetings of the Board of Directors, 24 March 1990, Covenant House Archives.

31. Major administrators who left the agency included John Kells, Gregory Loken, John Joseph Spanier, Christopher Walton, and Patrick Atkinson. Several board members also resigned in March for various reasons, including, in addition to Frank Macchiarola, Si Taubman, James Kennedy, James Maguire, Donna Santarsiero, Theodore Forstman, and James Makrianes. Mark Stroock, who had been a very visible member of the board and worked extraordinary hours during the crisis, stepped down for personal health reasons. Robert Macauley remained on the board during the crisis period but made it known following Ritter's resignation that he intended to leave his directorship when a new president arrived. "Resignations of March 7, 1990 and Other Resignations, March 14, 1990," RG 1, Series IX, Box 33, Folder 12; Robert Macauley to James Harnett, 28 February 1990, RG 1, Series 1, Box 4, Folder 6; Oral History Interview with James Harnett by Surak, 6 September 2001, Covenant House Archives.

32. Minutes of Meetings of the Board of Directors, 25 April 1990 and 18 May 1990, 13 June 1990, 10 July 1990, 30 July 1990, Covenant House Archives. James Harnett to Covenant House Board of Directors, "Memo Re: Budget, Fiscal Year 1991," 25 April 1990, RG 1, Series IX, Box 33, Folder 13, Covenant House Archives; Josh Barbanel, "Reeling from Its Own Crisis, Covenant House Scales Back," *New York Times*, 28 April 1990, p. 1; R. Christopher Walton, "Surviving the Ultimate Crisis," *Fund*

Raising Management, June 1991, pp. 24–28; Timothy Massad, "Advising Non-Profits in Crisis Situations: Our Experience with Covenant House," August 1994, Covenant House Archives.

33. Timothy Massad, "Advising Non-Profits in Crisis Situations: Our Experience with Covenant House," August 1994, Covenant House Archives.

34. Joel A. Carpenter, "Contemporary Evangelicalism and Mammon: Some Thoughts," in Larry Eskridge and Mark A. Noll, *More Money, More Ministry: Money and Evangelicals in Recent North American History* (Grand Rapids: William B. Eerdmans Publishing), p. 401.

35. Susan Friend Harding, *The Book of Jerry Falwell: Fundamentalist Language and Politics* (Princeton: Princeton University Press, 2000), pp. 247–69. A standard account of the Bakker scandals by the journalists who had been most involved in breaking the story is Larry Martz with Ginny Carroll, *Ministry of Greed: The Inside Story of the Televangelists & Their Holy Wars* (New York: Weidenfeld & Nicholson, 1988).

36. "Renewing the Covenant," *Commonweal*, 18 May 1990, p. 307; Emily Du-Hamel Brower to Ralph Pfeiffer, Memo Re: Comment Card Response to Date," 25 April 1990, RG 1, Series IX, Box 34, Folder 9, Covenant House Archives.

37. Philip Jenkins, *Priests and Pedophiles: Anatomy of a Contemporary Crisis* (New York: Oxford University Press, 1996), p. 3.

38. Jason Berry, *Lead Us Not into Temptation: Catholic Priests and the Sexual Abuse of Children* (New York: Doubleday, 1992), chronicles the unfolding of the Gauthe crisis. Other influential books concerning the sexual abuse scandals within the Church include: Frank Bruni and Elinor Burkett, *A Gospel of Shame: Children, Sexual Abuse, and the Catholic Church* (New York: Perennial, 2002), and The Investigative Staff of The Boston Globe, *Betrayal: The Crisis in the Catholic Church* (New York: Little, Brown and Company, 2002).

39. Jenkins, *Pedophiles and Priests*, esp. pp. 34–41, 95–112, 140–48; Pat Windsor and Joe Feuerherd, "U.S. Bishops Battle Issues at Bicentennial Meeting," *National Catholic Reporter*, 17 November 1989, p. 7. See also Robert A. Orsi, "A Crisis About the Theology of Children," *Harvard Divinity Bulletin*, spring 2002, pp. 27–29, who suggestively argues that the pedophilia crisis had been interpreted in political terms but that the debate should really include a theological dimension that focuses on the "presence/absence" of children in Catholic theology.

40. Josh Barbanel, "Reeling from Its Own Crisis, Covenant House Scales Back," *New York Times*, 28 April 1990, p. 1; Joyce Hunter, quoted in Ralph Blumenthal, Suzanne Daley and M. A. Farber, "Image of Covenant House Is Eroded by Sex Charges," *New York Times*, 6 February 1990, p. 1; Charles Sennott, *Broken Covenant*, p. 342. See also Paul Solotaroff, "Dead Boys: Fast Sex and Slow Suicide on the West Side Docks," *Village Voice*, 30 January 1990, pp. 33–37.

Chapter 8

1. The remarks by Mario Cuomo and Sr. Mary Rose McGeady were from Sister. Mary Rose's inauguration as president of Covenant House in February 1991. A

complete videotape of the ceremony can be found in RG 2, Series V, Box 18, Tape 23, Covenant House Archives.

2. Minutes of Meetings of the Board of Directors, 26 March 1990 and 10 July 1990, Covenant House Archives. Sr. Mary Rose McGeady was named president in July of 1990, but she actually assumed office in September since she had been serving as associate executive director for Catholic Charities of the Diocese of Brooklyn and required time to effect the transition.

3. Oral History Interview with Sr. Mary Rose McGeady by Peter Wosh, 27 February 2002, Covenant House Archives.

4. Most of these biographical details and quotations, unless otherwise noted, have been taken from a series of oral history interviews with Sr. Mary Rose McGeady by Wosh, 11 January 2002 through 1 May 2002, ten tapes, Covenant House Archives.

5. Sister Mary Rose's mother was employed as a bookkeeper during this period. Sister Mary Rose describes the family as "respectable working-class," bordering on "middle-class."

6. The Daughters of Charity trace their American foundation to 1809, when Mother Elizabeth Ann Seton established the Sisters of Charity of St. Joseph in Emmitsburg, Md. In 1810, the Emmitsburg community began observing the rules of the French Daughters of Charity, which had been founded by Saint Vincent de Paul and Saint Louise de Marillac in 1633. The Emmitsburg foundation formally united with the French Daughters of Charity in 1850. The Daughters' apostolates concentrated especially on education, health care, and child care. They remained especially active in many large urban dioceses throughout the nineteenth and twentieth centuries. Humility, simplicity, and charity remain the fundamental cornerstones of the community. Each house, for example, is governed by a "sister servant" rather than a "superior," owing to Saint Vincent de Paul's desire that those in charge of sisters look upon themselves as servants.

7. The institution had been founded in 1864 as the Home for Destitute Catholic Children, and the Daughters of Charity began administering the facility in 1866. In 1953, the name was changed to Nazareth Child Care Center, and the institution moved from its urban location on Harrison Avenue to a more suburban and spacious physical plant in Jamaica Plain. *Home for Catholic Children*, Booklet, 1949, Archives of the Archdiocese of Boston; *Nazareth Child Care Center*, Booklet, n.d., Archives of the Archdiocese of Boston.

8. "The Astor Home: A Psychiatric Treatment Center for Children," 1959, Archives of the Daughters of Charity of Saint Vincent de Paul, Albany, N.Y.

9. "Astor Home for Children," History and Personnel Report, 1975, Archives of the Daughters of Charity of Saint Vincent de Paul, Albany, N.Y.; *Nazareth Child Care Center*, Booklet, n.d., Archives of the Archdiocese of Boston.

10. "St. John's Parish Center, Brooklyn," Historical Sketch, 1995; Memo from Sr. Eileen to Sr. Mary Basil, 10 June 1972, Saint John's Parish Church in Brooklyn, Folder 2; Sr. Mary Rose McGeady, "St. John's Parish Center, Brooklyn, N.Y., Account of Opening and Works," St. John's Parish Church in Brooklyn, Folder 2; "Beginnings in Brooklyn," 17 October 1971, Archives of the Daughters of Charity of Saint Vincent de Paul, Albany, N.Y.; *100th Anniversary of the Church of St. John the Baptist, 1888–1988*

(Brooklyn: St. John the Baptist Parish Center, 1988), Archives of the Diocese of Brooklyn. It should be noted that, owing largely to problems in securing suitable living arrangements, the Daughters of Charity did not actually move into residence at the Bedford-Stuyvesant church until June of 1972. Sister Mary Rose had been designated as sister servant of the community in Brooklyn.

11. Sister Mary Rose did relocate to Albany from 1981 through 1987, when she served a term as visitatrix for the Northeast Province of the Daughters of Charity.

12. Father Sullivan was ordained a bishop in 1980.

13. Sister Mary Rose served Catholic Charities of the Diocese of Brooklyn as executive director of the Learning Center for Exceptional Children (1971–72); manager of the Bushwick Human Service Center (1972–73); and director of Mental Health Services (1973–79), also with responsibility for Vicariate C, comprising most of central Queens (1973–76) and Vicariate D, comprising northern Brooklyn and northwestern Queens (1976–79).

14. Robert E. Murphy, *History of Catholic Charities, Diocese of Brooklyn, 1899–1999* (Brooklyn: Diocese of Brooklyn, Catholic Charities, 2002), pp. 149–50. The facility at Creedmore actually opened in 1985 as the result of a grant secured through the state's Residential Care Center for Adults legislation but was dedicated as Rose House in 1989.

15. Sr. Mary Rose McGeady, "Dedication of Rose House," RG 2, Series VI, Box 18 Videotape 2, Covenant House Archives.

16. Oral History Interview with Sr. Mary Rose McGeady by Wosh, 28 February 2002, Covenant House Archives.

17. Cardinal John J. O'Connor, "A Lot of Trust," *Catholic New York*, 27 September 1990, p. 5; Joe Nicholson, "Nun Will Lay Down Covenant House Law," *New York Post*, 12 July 1990; Charles M. Sennott, "Brooklyn Nun to Run Covenant House," *New York Daily News*, 12 July 1990; Jessie Mangaliman, "Covenant Kids Get a Sister," *New York Newsday*, 12 July 1990, p. 6; "Covenant House's New Broom," *New York Times*, 16 July 1990; Tracy Early, "Brooklyn Nun Takes Over at Covenant House," *Brooklyn Tablet*, 21 July 1990, p. 3; Claudia McDonnell, "'She Never Gives Up': Nun Who'll Head Covenant House Is Articulate Advocate for Kids," *Catholic New York*, 19 July 1990, p. 3; Patrice Adcroft, "Interview: Sister Mary Rose McGeady," *Spin*, June 1993, pp. 67–70, 95; Oral History Interview with Sr. Mary Rose McGeady by Wosh, 13 March 2002, Covenant House Archives.

18. Robert Macauley and William J. Flynn dissented, and both resigned from the board shortly thereafter. Minutes of Meeting of the Board of Directors, 30 July 1990, Covenant House Archives. Covenant House's public relations team reasoned that, by releasing the report on a Friday, it would appear in the Saturday sections of most newspapers, when weekly readership appeared at its lowest ebb. Further, the organization timed release of the report to occur on 3 August, when many New Yorkers vacationed or at least spent weekends out of the city. The release date proved unexpectedly fortuitous in another way, since it coincided with the beginning of the first Gulf War. The *New York Times* banner headline on 4 August read "IRAQIS MASS ON SAUDI FRONTIER; ARABS AGREE TO MEET ON CRISIS; BUSH IS READY TO HELP IF ASKED." Covenant House's story appeared somewhat innocuously on page 25, in the metropolitan section. Gulf War coverage dominated the

news throughout the remainder of the month. Ralph Blumenthal, "Ritter Inquiry Cites Reports from the 70's," *New York Times*, 4 August 1990, p. 25.

19. *Statement of the Oversight Committee of Covenant House: A Report to the Board of Directors and the Oversight Committee of Covenant House*, 3 August 1990, p. ii, Covenant House Archives. This statement is also known as the Kroll Report, and is referred to as the Kroll Report throughout the text.

20. *Statement of the Oversight Committee of Covenant House. A Report to the Board of Directors and the Oversight Committee of Covenant House*, 3 August 1990, p. i, Covenant House Archives. The eight new directors included William Aramony, president of the United Way of America; Fr. Timothy S. Healy, S.J., president of the New York Public Library; Dr. Everlena M. Holmes, dean of the School of Health Sciences at Hunter College, City University of New York; Thomas Huhn, president and CEO of Alexander Proudfoot PLC; Dr. Ralph I. Lopez, associate professor of pediatrics at New York Hospital–Cornell Medical Center; William W. K. Rich, vice president at IBM; Sr. Margaret Sweeney, former president and CEO of St. Vincent's Hospital and Medical Center in New York; and Nancy Dickerson Whitehead, president of the Television Corporation of America as well as a noted television commentator.

21. Minutes of Meetings of the Board of Directors, 19 March 1991 and 29 January 1992; "Covenant House Agrees to Overhaul Corporate Structure and Finances," News Release from Attorney General Robert Abrams, 27 February 1991, Covenant House Archives.

22. *Statement of the Oversight Committee of Covenant House. A Report to the Board of Directors and the Oversight Committee of Covenant House*, 3 August 1990, pp. 35–38, 44, 47–50. The Kroll Report contained executive summaries from the Ernst & Young, Shinn, and Bureau of Child Welfare studies.

23. The farmhouse had been provided to Ritter by a former Covenant House board member. Charles M. Sennott, *Broken Covenant* (New York: Simon & Schuster, 1992), pp. 334–37; Tina Kelley, "In Quiet Fields, Father Ritter Found His Exile," *New York Times*, 22 October 1999, p. B1; Anthony Ramirez, "Rev. Bruce Ritter, 72, the Founder of Covenant House for Runaway Children," *New York Times*, 13 October 1999; Sr. Mary Rose McGeady to Covenant House Board of Directors, Memorandum Re: Death of Father Ritter, 13 October 1999; "Covenant House Statement on Fr. Bruce Ritter," 13 October 1999, Bruce Ritter Biographical File, Covenant House Archives.

24. Minutes of Meeting of the Board of Directors, 19 November 1990, Covenant House Archives.

25. Oral History Interview with Sr. Mary Rose McGeady by Wosh, 13 March 2002, Covenant House Archives.

26. Sister Mary Rose articulated these sentiments in the John Courtney Murray Forum Lecture, which she delivered at Fordham University Law School on 9 May 1991. Her remarks were reprinted as "Disconnected Kids: An American Tragedy," *America*, 15 June 1991, pp. 639–45.

27. See Appendix 2.

28. Financial statements appear in the Covenant House Annual Reports. Public contributions progressed as follows: $88.7 million in 1990, $66.8 million in 1991, $65.4 million in 1992, $68.6 million in 1993, $66.7 million in 1994, $65.8 million in

1995, $67.0 million in 1996, $75.7 million in 1997, and $83.6 million in 1998. See Minutes of Meetings of the Board of Directors, 25 April 1990, 30 July 1990, 31 October 1990, 19 March 1991, 13 June 1991, 26 September 1991, 13 November 1991, 25 March 1992, 29 January 1992.

29. The Resolution Trust Corporation (RTC) had been established by Congress under the Financial Institutions Reform, Recovery, and Enforcement Act of 1989 to replace the Federal Savings and Loan Association, following the failure of over seven hundred savings and loan banks in the United States. The RTC remained responsible for selling the assets of failed savings and loans, as well as paying insured depositors. Since several of Covenant House's mortgages, including most notably the Times Square Motor Hotel, had been financed by Charles Keating's failed Lincoln Savings and Loan Corporation, the RTC remained responsible for recovering the assets. The duties of the RTC itself were transferred to the newly created Savings Association Insurance Fund in 1995.

30. Minutes of Meetings of the Board of Directors, 25 April 1990, 10 July 1990, 25 March 1992, 17 June 1992, 23 June 1993, 22 September 1993, 10 November 1993, 13 April 1994, 29 June 1994, 21 September 1994, 16 November 1994, Covenant House Archives.

31. Minutes of Meetings of the Board of Directors, 13 April 1994, 29 June 1994, 1 March 1995, 13 September 1995, 11 June 1997, Covenant House Archives. The Plaza Building was subsequently sold by the Chinese Service Center for Scholarly Exchange to a group of hotel developers and investors for $19 million. The new owners carried out a $33 million renovation project that transformed the former Covenant House facility into a thematic Maritime Hotel, which included an expansive lobby, two restaurants, a ballroom, a ten-thousand-square-foot garden, and nautical-style rooms that "evoke a snug but stylish cruise ship cabin." The $250-per-night hotel and the fashionable nightclub, both of which opened for business in 2003, sought to attract a clientele that consisted of the "young, hip, and cool" in the words of one entrepreneur. This development reflected the transformation of Chelsea into a trendy New York City neighborhood, a far cry from the situation that existed when Ritter initially purchased the Maritime complex in 1987. "Onetime Home for Sailors Now for Landlubbers," *New York Times*, 27 April 2003, Section 11, p. 3; John Holusha, "From Grit to Chic to Tres Chic," *New York Times*, 23 November 2003, Section 11, p. 1.

32. Minutes of Meetings of the Board of Directors, 13 November 1991, 29 January 1992, 25 March 1992, 27 January 1993, 23 February 1993, Covenant House Archives. Laurie Peterson, "Rebuilding Covenant House," *Direct*, July 1994, pp. 31–36.

33. See Appendix 3.

34. Oral History Interview with Sr. Mary Rose McGeady by Wosh, 20 March 2002, Covenant House Archives.

35. Minutes of Meetings of the Board of Directors, 22 September 1993, 10 November 1993, and 13 April 1994, Covenant House Archives, indicate the careful steps taken to prepare for the Washington initiative. See also James Harnett to G. Richard Fowler, 16 June 1994; Sr. Mary Rose McGeady to James Cardinal Hickey, 22 June 1994; James Cardinal Hickey to Sr. Mary Rose McGeady, 24 June 1994; Sr. Mary McGeady to James Cardinal Hickey, 6 July 1994, RG 1, Series XII, Box 42, Folder 8, Covenant House Archives.

36. Vincent Gray had served as director of the District of Columbia Department of Human Services from 1991 to 1995 and had managed the Association for Retarded Citizens in the District between 1974 and 1990. "Covenant House Appoints Executive Director to Open New Youth Services Agency in Washington, D.C.," 3 January 1995, Press Release; Oral History Interview with Sr. Mary Rose McGeady by Wosh, 13 March 2002; Minutes of Meeting of the Board of Directors, 1 March 1995, Covenant House Archives.

37. Newt Gingrich to Sr. Mary Rose McGeady, 28 January 1995, Eunice Shriver to Covenant House–Washington, 1 June 1995, RG 1, Series XII, Box 42, Folder 7; "Covenant House Launches D.C.-Based Youth Services Program with Broad Support at Capitol Hill Event," Press Release, 19 April 1995, Covenant House Archives.

38. Sr. Mary Rose McGeady to His Eminence, Cardinal O'Connor, 12 June 1992, RG 1, Series XII, Box 39, Folder 22, Covenant House Archives. Covenant House Annual Reports, 2000 and 2001; Oral History Interview with Sr. Mary Rose McGeady by Wosh, 13 March 2002, Covenant House Archives.

39. "Vision for Residential Services," 1996, RG 1, Series XII, Box 42, Folder 7, Covenant House Archives; "Covenant House Comes to Washington," *Catholic Standard*, 11 May 1995, p. 1; "Covenant House New York, Summary Overview of Crisis Services," n.d., New York Subject File; Covenant House Annual Report, 1997; *Haven on Earth*, Annual Report of Covenant House Washington, 2001, Covenant House Archives. Washington's Covenant House program dedicated a new twenty-five-thousand-square-foot Community Service Center in 2003, in honor of Nancy Dickerson Whitehead, further reflecting the change in emphasis. Following the introduction of community centers in the Bronx and Brooklyn, new centers also opened in New Orleans (1994), Alaska (1995), Harlem (1996), Mexico City (1996), Tegucigalpa, Honduras (1996), and Guatemala City (1996). Community service centers at sites in the 1990s typically preceded the construction of shelters as, for example, in Orlando, Detroit, St. Louis, and Atlanta.

40. *Haven on Earth*, Annual Report of Covenant House Washington, 2001; Minutes of Meetings of Board of Directors, 18 September 1996, 18 September 1997, 18 March 1998, Covenant House Archives. Emily Gest, "Do Good by Eating Well at Ezekiel's," *New York Daily News*, 6 August 1997; Kathy Blake, "Ezekiel's Café Serves Community Good Food . . . and a Helping Hand," *Nation's Restaurant News*, 25 August 1997; Frederick Gabriel, "Good Service at Ezekiel's Café," *Crain's New York Business*, 6 October 1997.

41. Covenant House Annual Report, 1997, p. 12; Covenant House Annual Report, 1992, p. 7; Minutes of Meeting of the Board of Directors, 13 November 1991, Covenant House Archives.

42. Amnesty International, *Guatemala: Children in Fear*, May 1992; Lindsey Gruson, "Remembering a Tortured Child Who Lived the Streets of Guatemala City," *New York Times*, 14 October 1990, p. 3; Bruce Harris, "Street Children in Guatemala: Survival and Development Under the Threats of Death and Disappearance," Paper delivered at "Elimination and Terror" conference organized by Amnesty International, 4–6 September 1992, The Netherlands, Covenant House Archives.

43. For biographical information concerning Harris, see "Father to the Children with No One," *Dorset* (United Kingdom) *Evening Echo*, 28 February 1991, p. 11;

"Bruce's Helping Hand for Street Children," *London Observer*, 27 January 1991; Bruce Harris Biographical File, Covenant House Archives. His observations concerning the importance of advocacy are found in Bruce Harris, "Street Children in Guatemala: Survival and Development under the Threats of Death and Disappearance."

44. Amnesty International, *Guatemala: Extrajudicial Executions and Human Rights Violations Against Street Children*, July 1990, pp. 4–15; Amnesty International, *Guatemala: Criminal Proceedings: Human Rights Violations Against Street Children*, May 1991, pp. 1–3; Lindsey Gruson, "Remembering a Tortured Child Who Lived in the Streets of Guatemala City," *New York Times*, 14 October 1990, p. 3.

45. The most comprehensive description of Casa Alianza, along with a series of press releases describing Harris's advocacy efforts and awards, can be found on the institution's website. See Casa Alianza, Covenant House Latin America, http://www.casa-alianza.org/ES/index/phtm (12 January 2004). See also the Guatemala and Casa Alianza subject files in the Covenant House Archives.

46. Amnesty International, *Guatemala: Children in Fear*, May 1992, pp. 10–14, contains accounts of intimidation against Covenant House staff; Christine Toomey, "Briton in Bulletproof Vest Dodges Death in The Hole," *London Sunday Times*, 19 January 1992; Minutes of Meetings of the Board of Directors, 10 July 1990, 31 October 1990, 19 March 1991, 26 September 1991, Covenant House Archives; Oral History interview with Sr. Mary Rose McGeady by Wosh, 1 May 2002, Covenant House Archives.

47. The Menninger Clinic, *Project Connect and Assessment Project: Final Report*, August 2000, pp. 11–12, 16; "Covenant House Board of Directors Appoints a New President," Press Release, 2003, Covenant House Archives.

Appendix 3

1. Casa Alianza subsequently opened additional facilities in Guatemala City (1986), Honduras (1987), Mexico (1988), Panama (1988), and Nicaragua (1998). The Panama operation was closed in 1992.

2. Covenant House Florida opened a program in Orlando in 1996.

3. Covenant House California opened a program in Oakland in 1998.

4. Covenant House New Jersey actually began in 1989, with street outreach programs in Atlantic City and Newark, but the organization's storefront locations became operative in 1990.

Index

Acknowledgments

Sr. Mary Rose McGeady, D.C., the president of Covenant House from 1990 through 2003, initiated this project in 1997. She believed that the time had arrived to commission an honest agency history that met professional academic standards. Her generous support proved critical throughout the process. Sister Mary Rose authorized the creation of an institutional archives, granted access to all organizational records, agreed to a series of oral history interviews, and provided useful commentary on early drafts of the book. James Harnett, the chief operating officer at Covenant House, proved a pleasure to work with in every way. His wit and wisdom transformed the process of historical reconstruction into a fun and lively activity. Jim's forthright manner, remarkable eye for accuracy, practical sensibility, and good cheer kept things humming at all times.

The opinions and statements expressed in this book, of course, reflect my own beliefs and historical judgments. They do not represent the official views of Covenant House and should not be interpreted as such.

Amy Surak, currently the archivist at Manhattan College, deserves a special word of thanks for her hard work and outstanding contributions. She single-handedly created and organized the Covenant House Archives, extensively researched a variety of topics, conducted numerous oral history interviews, compiled the appendices, and insightfully critiqued the entire manuscript. Her ever-present intelligence, superior research skills, encyclopedic knowledge of Covenant House history, energetic enthusiasm, and lively sense of humor made her the perfect collaborator and a valued colleague.

I met many remarkable people during the course of my research and wish to especially thank the following individuals who agreed to be interviewed for the project: Rev. Juniper Alwell, Edmund J. Burns, Robert Cardany, Marguerite Colonnese, Rev. Canice Connors, Patricia Connors, David Cullen, Rev. John P. Duffell, James Fitzgibbon, Paul Frazier, Adrian Gately, Sr. Gretchen Gilroy, David Gregorio, Bruce Henry, Dick Hirsch, Patricia Kennedy, Sr. Eileen Kernan, Mother Viola Kiernan, Sr. Patricia Larkin, Rev. Shawn Nolan, Hugh O'Neill, Gil Ortiz, Sr. Kathryn Rush, Bro. Luke Salm,

Paul Saunders, Denise Scelzo, Matthew Thompson, and Steven Torkelson. Archives, archivists, and librarians proved critical to the research as well, and I wish to acknowledge the following: Leonora Gidlund at the New York City Department of Records and Information Services; Joseph Coen and Patrick MacNamara of the Archives of the Diocese of Brooklyn; Sr. Elaine Wheeler, Sr. Margaret Ahl, and John Diefenderfer of the Daughters of Charity Archives; Sr. Ann Michael of the Archives of the Franciscan Sisters of Syracuse; Fr. Stephen Merrigan of the Conventual Franciscan Archives; Robert Johnson-Lally of the Archives of the Archdiocese of Boston; Brenda Burk of the Indiana University–Purdue University Indianapolis Library; Anthony E. Lee of the Seton Hall University Library; Harry Welsh of the Manhattan College Library; and the staffs of the New York Municipal Library, New York State Archives, Rockefeller Archives Center, Schlesinger Library at Radcliffe, Bobst Library at New York University, and Saint Brigid's Church in New York City.

Finally, a few other friends and associates reviewed the manuscript and proved particularly supportive. Peter Agree at the University of Pennsylvania Press deserves tremendous credit for enthusiastically embracing the project from its earliest stages. Patrick Allitt of Emory University contributed valuable commentary at a crucial moment. Jodi L. Koste, an archival colleague at Virginia Commonwealth University, offered her special brand of southern hospitality combined with a sharply critical eye, as always. Paul H. Mattingly, a historian at New York University, provided his characteristically thorough and rigorous observations.

Patricia L. Schall has made me a much better writer, thinker, and person over the years. Thanks for everything.